MATTHEW HALL

Dark Psychology and Manipulation

Your Great Manual For The World of Manipulation Secrets, Body Language Psychology, NLP Techniques, and Dark Psychology To Become The Master Of Your Success

Copyright © 2020 Matthew Hall

All rights reserved.

© **Copyright 2020 - All rights reserved.**

The content contained within this book may not be reproduced, duplicated or transmitted without direct written permission from the author or the publisher.

Under no circumstances will any blame or legal responsibility be held against the publisher, or author, for any damages, reparation, or monetary loss due to the information contained within this book. Either directly or indirectly.

Legal Notice:

This book is copyright protected. This book is only for personal use. You cannot amend, distribute, sell, use, quote or paraphrase any part, or the content within this book, without the consent of the author or publisher.

Disclaimer Notice:

Please note the information contained within this document is for educational and entertainment purposes only. All effort has been executed to present accurate, up to date, and reliable, complete information. No warranties of any kind are declared or implied. Readers acknowledge that the author is not engaging in the rendering of legal, financial, medical or professional advice. The content within this book has been derived from various sources. Please consult a licensed professional before attempting any techniques outlined in this book.

By reading this document, the reader agrees that under no circumstances is the author responsible for any losses, direct or indirect, which are incurred as a result of the use of information contained within this document, including, but not limited to, — errors, omissions, or inaccuracies.

Table of Content

BODY LANGUAGE PSYCHOLOGY

Introduction 10
Chapter 1. How Non-Verbal Communication Works................... 18
Chapter 2. How to Understand People Through Body Language 28
Chapter 3. Manipulation Through Body Language 37
Chapter 4. Uses of Body Language... 43
Chapter 5. Guide to an Effective Body Language 50
Chapter 6. How to Persuade People 57
Chapter 7. How to Analyze People 64
Chapter 8. Dark Psychology Secrets 71
Chapter 9. How to Defend Ourselves of Dark Psychology 78
Chapter 10. The Power of Hands 86
Chapter 11. Body Language of a Child 91
Chapter 12. Reading People Through Their Mind...................... 97
Chapter 13. Myths About Body Language 105
Chapter 14. Who Is a Manipulator?.. 112
Chapter 15. Dark Psychology and Women 119
Chapter 16. Techniques of Dark Psychology............................ 126
Chapter 17. Practical Exercises For Mind Control Prevention.... 133
Chapter 18. Touch As a Form of Body Language 139
Chapter 19. Facial Expression As a Form of Body 144
Chapter 20. Manipulation In a Relationship 152
Chapter 21. How to Know if Someone Is Lying Through Body Language... 159

Chapter 22. How Body Language Improves Your Mindset.........166

Chapter 23. Proxemics 174

Chapter 24. Muscular Core, Posture, and Breathing...................177

Chapter 25. Hand Gestures and Arm Signals..............................182

Chapter 26. Different Types of People and How They Fit In the Social Circle 188

Chapter 27: Conclusion of Body Language.................................195

Chapter 28: Dark Psychology 197

Chapter 29. What Is Dark Psychology? 200

Chapter 30. Explication of Dark Psychology 206

Chapter 31. How To Use Dark Psychology.................................210

Chapter 32. Delving Into Dark Psychology................................216

Chapter 33. The History of Dark Psychology 222

Chapter 34. Advanced Techniques to Manipulate Human Psychology 229

Chapter 35. Mind Control... 235

Chapter 36. Mind Control Techniques.......................................241

Chapter 37. Influence People With Mind Control.................... 247

Chapter 38. Dark Persuasion 253

Chapter 39. Dark Persuasion To Lookout For 259

Chapter 40. Subliminal Persuasion... 265

Chapter 41. Psychological Manipulation................................... 270

Chapter 42. Psychological Manipulation Technique 275

Chapter 43. Covert Emotional Manipulation 282

Chapter 44. Covert Emotional Manipulation Tactics 289

Chapter 45. Brainwashing... 292

Chapter 46. Brainwashing Technique 296

Chapter 47. Hypnosis 301
Chapter 48. Hypnosis Techniques 308
Chapter 49. Mind Controls Hypnotism 315
Chapter 50. Dark NLP 322
Chapter 51. The Positive and Negative Aspects of Neuro Linguistic Programming 328
Chapter 52. Understanding Body Language 332
Chapter 53. Deception 340
Chapter 54. Dark Cognitive Behavioral Therapy 347
Chapter 55. The Art Of Using Your Mind to Succeed 353
Chapter 56. Dark Personalities 359
Chapter 57. The Dark Triad 367
Conclusion 374

HOW TO ANALIZE PEOPLE

Introduction 378
Chapter 1. Neuro-Linguistic Programming (NLP) 383
Chapter 2. How NLP Works, Importance of NLP, and is NLP Effective? 390
Chapter 3. Components of NLP and NLP Techniques 396
Chapter 4. The Swish Pattern 401
Chapter 5. Hypnosis 408
Chapter 6. Brainwashing 414
Chapter 7. How to Use NLP for in Sales 419
Chapter 8. How to Use NLP in Relationships 422
Chapter 9. NLP in Business 428

Chapter 10. Body Language and Behavior Imitation 436
Chapter 11. Using NLP to Manage People 442
Chapter 12. Protecting Yourself From NLP Mind Control 448
Chapter 13. Smart and Wise Goal-Setting Using Neuro-Linguistics 453
Chapter 14. Introduction of Persuasion 457
Chapter 15. History of Persuasion 461
Chapter 16. Six Principles of Persuasion 465
Chapter 17. Theories on Persuasion 470
Chapter 18. Persuasion Techniques 473
Chapter 19. Difference Between Persuasion and Manipulation .. 480
Chapter 20. Factors That Influence Persuasion 484
Chapter 21. Methods of Persuasion and Tricks Used By Mass Media And Advertising 489
Chapter 22. The Benefits of Learning About Persuasion 492
Chapter 23. Dark Persuasion 498
Chapter 24. Covert Persuasion 503
Chapter 25. Ethical Persuasion 507
Chapter 26. Difference Between Persuasion and Negotiation 513
Chapter 27. Deception 521
Chapter 28. The Dark Triad 527
Chapter 29. How To Analyze People 532
Chapter 30. Speed Reading to Understand People 540
Chapter 31. Advanced Tips and Tricks to Control People 548
Chapter 32. The Most Powerful Mind-Power Tool 554
Chapter 33. NLP Conclusion 560
Chapter 34. Covert Manipulation 565

Chapter 35. What is Manipulation? 571

Chapter 36. Examples of Manipulation? 578

Chapter 37. Introduction on Deception 584

Chapter 38. Techniques Used in Manipulation: Explication of Different Techniques 590

Chapter 39. How To Defend Yourself From Manipulation Techniques 596

Chapter 40. Qualities of a Manipulative Person 602

Chapter 41. Victim of Manipulation 609

Chapter 42. Strategies for Seduction, a Person with Manipulation 616

Chapter 43. Covert Emotional Manipulation: Introduction 621

Chapter 44. Covert Manipulation in a Love Relationship 628

Chapter 45. How the Mind Works When It Is Manipulated? 634

Chapter 46. Hypnosis 640

Chapter 47. Office Politics or Sociopathic Tricks? – The Workplace Manipulators 646

Chapter 48. Human Behavior and Manipulation 652

Chapter 49. Psychological Manipulation 658

Chapter 50. Turning the Tables 664

Chapter 51. Stages of a Relationship with a Covert Narcissist 670

Chapter 52. Covert Emotional Manipulation Methods 676

Chapter 53. Knowing Yourself 682

Chapter 54. Psychological Tricks to Examine Human Beings ... 688

Chapter 55. Basic Body Language Signals 694

Chapter 56. Strengthen or Change the Views of Others 700

Chapter 57. The Art of Persuasion 706

Chapter 58. Influence Without Manipulation 713
Chapter 59. Escape or Die 720
Conclusion 726

BODY LANGUAGE PSYCHOLOGY

Introduction

Body language involves using our physical behavior, expressions, and manners to reveal nonverbal information about ourselves, which is usually done unconsciously. Many people are not mindful of it, but you are continually giving out body cues and wordless signals that reinforce the interaction or contradict what you are trying to say in all your interactions.

Your entire nonverbal behavior transmits a loud and strong message that continues even after you stop talking. There are instances when what someone says might differ from what their body language is communicating. Hence, in this case, it will be easy for the person you are interacting with to pass you off as a liar. If someone asked for a favor and you gave a smile after giving a no, you have ended up confusing the person. With this kind of mixed-signal, the person might be confused about what to believe. However, if the person understands the concept of body language, they would probably just walk away since the body language is unconscious and gives someone away by revealing their real intention.

The Essence of Nonverbal Communication

The cues you are unconsciously giving out from your body are pretty essential and, as said earlier, give meaning to the interaction you are in. From your body cues, the person you are with will know whether you are interested in the relationship or not, whether you are hiding information or being explicit, and whether you are paying attention.

With nonverbal communication signals that complement what you say, you can build trust, rapport, and clarity. I am pretty sure you know what happens when your words and body language cues contrast!

In reading body language signals, you have to notice the body language people are giving out. It does not stop at that, and you have to be sensitive to yours as well. In understanding nonverbal communication, pay attention to the following roles it plays:

Repetition

In other words, it enforces the message you are trying to pass. You made a marriage proposal to your girlfriend, for instance. After popping the question and she accepted, you would generally expect her to smile, jump up and be excited. However, if she said yes with a straight face, I am pretty sure you know something is not right.

Contradiction

It can also refute the message you pass across, thus giving the signal that you might be lying. You came home from a two-week journey. Your wife greeted you and said she was excited to see you, but without a hug, a smile, or any facial expression to corroborate the statement. Something was off.

Substitution

Body cues often stand in place of verbal communication. In African culture, for instance, let us assume a guest visited a family. As this person was leaving, he offered the child some money. The mother gave the child "that kind of look," and the child took it as a cue to reject the offer.

Complementing

Body language cues might add more weight to the meaning of the message you are passing across verbally. Consider a man who tells his wife, "I love you" and drives off. Another man plants a kiss on the wife's forehead and says, "I love you" while looking into her eyes. Of these two, it is clear which one meant what he was saying.

Accenting

Your nonverbal cues can also emphasize the point you are trying to make. Saying no, alongside a shaking of the head, emphasizes the weight of the negation.

Without beating around the bush any more, let us examine how you can read various clues from body parts.

Reading Various Parts of the Body

Head Movement

Head movement is one of the meekest body languages to decode. However, for someone who has no clue what this nonverbal communication signal means, hardly will they make sense of it. To explain the head movement, I have here two scenarios:

As part of the exercise to get a job, a candidate must decide why he is the best candidate for the job. During the presentation, his audience, the hiring manager, nods quickly while the candidate desperately keeps trying to sell himself. He is unaware of the hiring manager's message, which clearly shows he is wasting his time.

Consider another candidate giving the same presentation. As he goes off trying to sell himself, the hiring manager leans back with his head tilted. Oblivious to the meaning of this body language, the candidate does not try to shed light on the point that triggered the manager's body reaction. He is ignorant of the body language; hence, he keeps on blabbing.

Reading the Face

There are many expressions we can reveal with our faces. Even babies and toddlers are smart enough to decode this body language cue. That a smile reveals happiness or satisfaction or a frown shows dissatisfaction or sadness. There are times when the facial expression could give insight into what is going on with a person. A person who says they're fine with a slight frown, for instance, could be lying.

It is a universal expression that conveys a wide range of emotions, such as sadness, fear, panic, anxiety, worry, disgust, distrust, happiness, and many others. The best part is that this expression does not change or vary with people.

Many people, in a bid to hide their real intention, desperately try to control the face. However, a careful study of the face can give you a clear glimpse into the message someone is trying to pass across. There are times when someone might hide primary body language, such as raised eyebrows, smiles, frowns, etc. Be sure to look out for the subsequent:

A warm and genuine smile does light up the whole face. It indicates happiness. It is also an unmistakable symbol that the other party is enjoying your company.

On the other hand, a phony smile is a polite way of showing approval, even if they do not enjoy the conversation or interaction. For you to detect a phony smile, take a look at the side of the eyes. The lack of crinkles is all you need to pass a smile off as fake.

The Eye Window

The eyes disclose a lot regarding a person. It explains why the eyes are referred to as the window to the soul. Besides, it is an essential and natural communication process for you to note all interactions' eyes.

In communicating with people, it is customary to note eye contact, whether someone is averting your gaze or not, the rate of blinking, and their pupils' size.

The following explains some nonverbal clues from the eyes:

Eye gaze

A person interested and paying attention to a conversation will look directly into your eyes while having a conversation. However, they might break eye contact once in a while because prolonged eye contact is rather uncomfortable. A distracted and uninterested person, on the other hand, will often break eye contact and look away. This person might be awkward or is trying to hide their true feelings.

Blinking

While blinking is an entirely natural process, the frequency matters. A person uncomfortable or in distress will blink more often. On the other hand, infrequent blinking means that a person is intentionally trying to control their eye movements.

Pupil Size

Pay attention to pupil size as it is very subtle and affected by the room's light level. However, emotions also affect pupil dilation, causing small changes in the pupil's size. It explains why someone with highly dilated eyes is either aroused or interested in a person.

Hand Movements

Some cues can easily be found from the hand's position and pattern of movement. We explain this in detail:

When someone has their hands in their pockets, they could be lacking confidence, hiding information, or just being defensive.

When a person unconsciously points to another person in a group or meeting while making a speech, there might be some common ground they share.

In communicating with someone, there is the presence of an obstacle. It is in the form of an object between you, and the person translates to the person trying to block you out. In this circumstance, your goal should be to build rapport and gain such a person's trust.

A person talking with the palms facing up is likely, to be honest. Such a person is not hiding the palm since they most likely have nothing to hide.

The Mouth

The expressions and movement of the mouth are pretty vital in decoding body language as well. It is why a worried, anxious, or insecure person will likely chew their lower lip. Some forms of nonverbal communication cues from the mouth will be examined below. A person, to be polite, might cover the mouth if the other party is yawning. Be watchful, as it can be done to cover up a frown as well.

Pursed lips

When a person tightens up their lip, it could signal objection, disapproval, or distaste.

Lip biting

It is common when a person is anxious, worried, or stressed.

Covering the Mouth

It could be done to hide emotional reactions like smiles or smirks.

A Slight Change in Direction

A person's feelings can be seen through the direction of the mouth. As a result, someone happy or in a good mood might have their mouth slightly turned up. A slightly turned-down mouth, on the other hand, could signal sadness or displeasure.

The Importance of Reading People

The world is made of people. Life is better enjoyed when you have people to relate with. However, your survival in the world also depends on your ability to decide when not cooperating with some people. So, your ability to read people is essential.

There are times you are unconsciously cooperating with others. The fact that you walk gently to your place of work without causing a scene or doing anything to warrant unnecessary attention is an act of cooperation with the rest of the society on some level. You don't just awaken up one day and choose to go on a killing spree. You are connected to the Internet and the rest of the world alike. All these things require some form of human cooperation.

For this to occur, people unconsciously have to come to an appropriate form of agreement and acceptable behavior on some level. All in all, cooperating with people is pretty important, and your decision whether to cooperate or not comes down to your ability to read people.

The best salesman knows how to coax you because they are good at analyzing people. They can get you into buying what they have to offer, even if you do not need what they are offering. The better you are at reading other people's motives, the better you can deal with such a person.

Chapter 1. How Non-Verbal Communication Works

Being able to connect well is extremely important when wanting to succeed in the personal and professional world, but it isn't the words you say that scream. It is your body language that does the screaming. Your gestures, posture, eye contact, facial expressions, and tone of voice are your best communication tools. These can confuse, undermine, offend, build trust, draw others in, or put someone at ease.

There are many times where what someone says and what their body language says is different. Non-verbal communication could do five things:

- Substitute—It could be used in place of a verbal message.

- Accent—It could underline or accent your verbal message.

- Complement—It could complement or add to what you are saying verbally.

- Repeat—It could strengthen and repeat your verbal message.

- Contradict—It could go against what you are trying to say verbally to make your listener think you are lying.

Many different forms of Non-verbal communication will be looked at, and we are going to cover:

- Gestures—These have been woven into our lives. You might speak animatedly; argue with your hands, point, wave, or beckon. Gestures do change according to cultures.

- Facial expressions—You will learn that the face is expressive and shows several emotions without speaking one word. Unlike what you say and other types of body language, facial expressions are usually universal.

- Eye contact—Because sight tends to be our strongest sense for most people, it is an essential part of Non-verbal communication. The way someone looks at you could tell you whether they are attracted to you, affectionate, hostile, or interested. It might also help the conversation flow.

- Body movement and posture—Take a moment to think about how you view people based on how they hold their heads, stand, walk around, and sit. The way a person carries gives you much information.

Lower Body

The arms share much information. The hands share a lot more, but legs give us the exclamation point and tell us precisely what someone is thinking. The legs could say to you if a person is open and comfortable. They could also imply dominance or where they want to go.

Upper Body

Upper body language can show signs of defensiveness since the arms could easily be used as a shield. Upper body language could involve the chest. Let's look at some upper body language.

Leaning

If someone leans forward, it will move them closer to another person. There are two possible meanings to this. First, it will tell you that they are interested in something, which could just be what you are talking about. But this movement could also show romantic interest. Second, leaning forward could invade a person's personal space; hence, leading to a threat. It is often an aggressive display. It is done unconsciously by influential people.

The Superman

Bodybuilders, models commonly use this, and it was made famous by Superman. It could have various meanings depending on how a person uses it. Within the animal world, animals will try to make themselves look bigger when they feel threatened. If you look at a house cat when they get spooked, they will stretch their legs, and their fur stands on end. Humans also have this, even if it isn't as noticeable. It is why we get goosebumps. Because we can't make ourselves look bigger, we have to develop arm gestures like putting our hands on our waist. It shows us that a person is getting ready to act assertively.

The Chest in Profile

If a person stands sideways or at a 45-degree angle, they are trying to accentuate their chest. They might also thrust out their chest, more on this in a minute. Women do this posture to show off their breasts, and men will show off their profile.

Outward Thrust Chest

If someone pushes their chest out, they try to draw attention to this part of their body. It could also be used as a dreamy display. Women understand that men have been programmed to be aroused by breasts. If you see a woman pushing her chest out, she might be inviting intimate relations. Men will thrust out their chests to show off their chest and possibly trying to hide their gut. The difference is that men will do this to women and other men.

Hands

Human hands have 27 bones, and they are a very expressive part of the body. It gives us much capability to handle our environment.

Reading palms isn't about just looking at the lines on the hands. After a person's face, the hands are the best source for body language. Hand gestures are different across cultures, and one hand gesture might be innocent in one country but very offensive in another.

Hand signals may be small, but they show what our subconscious is thinking. A gesture might be exaggerated and done using both hands to illustrate a point

Face

People's facial expressions could help us figure out if we trust or believe what they are saying. The most trustworthy expression will have a slight smile and a raised eyebrow. This expression will sow friendliness and confidence.

We make judgments about how intelligent somebody is by their facial expressions. People who have narrow faces with a prominent nose were thought to be extremely intelligent. People who smile and have joyous expressions could be thought of as being smart rather than someone who looks angry.

Mouth

Mouth movements and expressions are needed when trying to read body language. Chewing on their lower lip might indicate a person who is feeling fearful, insecure, or worrying.

If they cover their mouth, this might show that they are trying to be polite if they are yawning or coughing. It might be an effort to cover up disapproval. Smiling is the best signal, but smiles can be interpreted in many ways. Smiles can be genuine, or they might be used to show cynicism, sarcasm, or false happiness.

Negative Emotions

The silent signals that you show might harm your business without you even knowing it. We have over 250,000 facial signals and 700,000 body signals. Having poor body language could damage your relationships by sending other signs that you can't be trusted. They might turn off, alienate, or offend other people.

You have to keep your body language in check, and this takes much effort. Most of the time, you may not know that you are doing it, and you might be hurting your business and yourself.

Here are some emotions and how to spot them:

Fear, Anxiety, or Nervousness

Fear could happen when our basic needs get threatened. There are many different levels of fear. Suppose might be mild anxiety or full-blown blind terror. The various bodily changes that get created by fear can make this one easy to spot.

- Voice trembling.

- Errors in speech.

- Pulse rate extremely high.
- Vocal tone variations.
- Sweating.
- Lips trembling.
- Muscle tensions like their legs wrapped around something, clenched hands or arms, elbows are drawn in, jerky movements.
- Damp eyes.
- Holding their breath or gasping for breath.
- Not looking at one another.
- Fidgeting.
- Dry mouth indicated by licking their lips, rubbing their throat, or drinking water.
- Defensive body language.
- Face is pale.
- Fight or flight body language.
- Breaking out in a cold sweat.
- Any symptoms of stress.

Sadness

- Lips trembling.

- The flat tone of voice.
- Body drooping.
- Tears.

Anger

- Clenched fists.
- Invading body space.
- Leaning forward.
- Baring their teeth or snaring.
- Using aggressive body language.
- Neck or face is red and flushed.
- Displaying power body language.

Embarrassment

- Not making eye contact.
- Looking down and away.
- Neck or face is red and flushed.
- Changing the subject or trying to hide their embarrassment.
- Grimacing.
- Fake smiles.

Positive Emotions

When you have positive body language, it means that you are engaging, approachable, and open. It isn't saying that you need to use this kind of body language all the time or that it is the best signs that will show a person is friendly. It's just a good beginning point for reading positivity in others as well as yourself.

Non-verbal Signals Used Universally

Non-verbal communication is different for everybody and in different cultures. A person's cultural background will define their non-verbal communication since some communication types, like signs and signals, need to be learned.

Since there are different meanings in non-verbal communication, there could be miscommunication when people from different cultures try to communicate. People might offend others without really meaning to due to cultural differences. Facial expressions are very similar around the world.

Seven micro expressions are universal, and we will go more in-depth about these, but they are hate/contempt, anger, disgust, surprise, fear, happiness, and sadness. It might be different in the extent of how people show these feelings since, in specific cultures, people might readily show them where others won't.

Nods might also have different meanings, and this can cause problems, too. In some cultures, their people might not say "yes," but people from different cultures will interpret as "no." If you nod in Japan, they will solve it as you are listening to them.

Here are other non-verbal communications and how they differ in various cultures:

Eye Contact

Many Western cultures consider eye contact as a good gesture. It shows confidence, attentiveness, and honesty. Cultures such as Hispanic, Asian, Native American, and Middle Eastern don't think eye contact is a good gesture. They believe it is rude and offensive.

Unlike Western cultures that think it's respectful, others don't think this way. In Eastern countries, women absolutely can't make eye contact with men since it shows the power or sexual interest. Many cultures accept gazes as only showing an expression, but staring is thought of as rude in most.

Gestures

You need to be careful doing a "thumbs up" because it is very different in many cultures. Some view it as meaning "okay," but in Latin America, it is vulgar. Japan views it as meaning money.

Snapping your finger may be acceptable in some cultures, but it is disrespectful and offensive in others. In some Middle Eastern countries, showing your feet can be offensive. Pointing your finger is an insult in some cultures. People in Polynesia will stick their tongue out when they greet someone, but other cultures see it as a sign of mockery.

Touch

Touch is thought of as rude in most cultures. Some cultures look at shaking hands to be acceptable. Kissing and hugs, along with other touches, are looked at differently in different cultures. Asians are too conservative with these types of communications.

Patting someone's head or shoulder has different meanings in different cultures. Patting a child's head in Asia is extremely bad since their head is the sacred part of their body. Middle Eastern countries think people of opposite genders touching to be horrible character traits.

How and where a person gets touched could change the meaning of that touch. You need to be careful if you travel to various places.

Appearance

It is an acceptable form of non-verbal communication. Their appearance has always judged people. Differences in clothing and racial differences could tell a lot about anyone.

Making yourself look good is an important personality trait in many cultures. What is thought to be a good appearance will vary from country to country. How modest you get is measured by your appearance.

Chapter 2. How to Understand People Through Body Language

The Capital Importance of Body Language

Our bodies cannot show anything but what is in us. Our emotions use the sounding board. Therefore, we understand that our body's non-verbal part of communication always reflects our mental state, whatever the situation. Indeed, where does it come from, if not our psyche?

Body language is subject to physical law: energy does not vanish; it transforms. As electricity becomes light, heat, or movement, our psyche becomes body language.

Beware, the same gesture may have different meanings. For example, a person with arms crossed, a gesture generally interpreted as a negative signal. Indeed, arms crossed the pass to outsource refusal, withdrawal, skepticism, antipathy, etc. Sometimes this interpretation is accurate, but not always. What about a man struck, waiting for the bus? Is it expressly rejected? If so, to whom? Facing the bus? To other people like him at the bus stop? What if nobody exists? In this situation, arms crossed indicate nothing but being able to do nothing but wait. No reason to move, our man folds his arms.

To correctly decipher body language, you must first consider the action context. Also, as with verbal language, an "expression" that does not fit into a situation will have a high potential for misunderstanding.

Incorrect posture can reveal insecurity, fear, distrust, etc. On the other hand, the right posture gives the impression of strength, power, and confidence.

Understand more about using body signals to convey the desired impression.

Negative Body Language

Often, during a conversation, you can pass negative body language without realizing it.

Facial expressions and gestures end up showing several details.

Some negative postures that you should avoid in your client meetings:

- Hands-on-hips or pockets;
- Knees pointing to the exit door;
- Legs wide open;
- Crossed arms.

These attitudes are perceived, even if unconsciously, by the other person and can ruin a sale's progress.

Know other signs you should avoid avoiding transmitting the wrong body language.

Hand to Mouth

Experts analyze that when a person is not telling the truth, they usually cover their mouths.

Disparities of this posture habit are:

- Rub your lips;
- Dash the chin;
- Put stuff in front of the mouth.

Compressed Lips

Another negative body language is to compress your lips.

This act shows that the person is trying to avoid saying what he thinks.

That is, hiding your lips reveals that you don't want to answer any questions.

Defocused Look

Body language says a lot by looking.

A look without focus, or looking up and to the right, indicates confusion.

It is because, when looking away, the person is looking for a mental image.

Therefore, he shows a lack of clarity in his speech, as well as insecurity.

Forehead Contracted

In conversation, if the other person wrinkles his forehead, that's not a good sign.

These horizontal lines show a certain level of tension, doubt, or nervousness, which is a bad sign of body language.

Restricted Hand and Arm Movements

Keeping your hands behind your back or clinging to your body conveys the message of little confidence.

Another gesture to be avoided is to put your hands back or feet crossed behind the chair.

These are signs of discomfort.

Reading Body Language

Reading body language may help to assess the feeling behind or instead of the words spoken. The adult can quickly and instinctively understand that a child is frightened by thunder when they see the child screaming and covering their ears. However, there are misconceptions about body language, causing miscommunication unless the whole-body language is read.

The eyes have long been named the windows to the soul, and it may be this concept that created the greatest myth in reading bodies. It is widely assumed that if a person avoids eye contact or does not hold it, that person does not say the facts. It is a mistaken assumption though popularly known. Pathological liars may maintain sustained contact with the eyes because they realize most people assume that looking away from the eyes shows an untruth. People who say the truth do not keep eye contact because they clearly state evidence and feel no need to convince anyone of this.

When a person is depressed or uncomfortable, and avoidance of eye contact occurs. For example, a child being chastised by a parent would always look down on the ground instead of him looking in the parent's eyes. Painfully shy or nervous people, too, are having a tough time meeting another person's eyes in conversation. Someone with little actual knowledge of reading body language would find the people lying by the standard error in each of these instances. Instead, the child shows authority, the adult, contrite, and the shy person shows typical distress or uncomforted sign.

In addition to the eye movement, the overall body language used needs to be looked at. Fidgeting, drumming fingers, or playing with hair matched to a lack of eye contact shows that a person is dissatisfied with the situation or discussion topic. Still, eyes fixed on a distant point by a person with arms crossed, attentive to the conversation, shows, instead, serious attention and intense thinking on the topic of discussion.

The precise interpretation of body language may provide an insight into another person's thoughts, feelings, and emotions. However, to read correctly, it is essential to remember to look at the entire body's movements, or words, rather than treating part of the body as separate from the other parts.

Keys to Reading Body Language

Body language is the type of communication a person uses to respond to circumstances, including facial expressions. More than 54% of the way we communicate with each other consists of body language, 39% consists of how the voice is used, and just 7% consists of the words spoken. Developing one's ability to interpret and understand gestures and signs of body language would greatly benefit because it will help better understand and interact with other human beings.

Body language involves body expressions, gestures, eye contact, muscle tension, skin coloring, breathing rate, etc. Of course, you should remember that body language is different from people to people and various nationalities and cultures. Consequently, it is at all times good to check what is seen in a person. It can be achieved by answering similar questions and endeavoring to better-known individuals.

There is also a lot of myths about interpreting body language. Most deceptive books and internet guides don't teach people the right thing. There's the truth you need to learn about this, while popular reasoning can trick you into believing a person's ability to read body language is the real secret to finding lies. Some important body language secrets are:

Posture

In most situations, if you take the correct pose, you should build the right impression on people. Leaning a little towards a person can create an image of friendliness. It could also be that you have an interest in others. At the same time, seeing a level head establishes a sense of self-assurance and trust.

Legs

When a person is anxious, the legs are always moving around. It happens when the person tells lies and is bored too. It is safer to keep those legs crossed or even to give the opposite impression, to appear confident and polite to others.

Eye contact

If you keep healthy eye contact, you show concern and respect for others. And you still need to find a balance. When you hold too much eye contact, the other person would feel self-conscious. Sometimes, if you don't have enough eye contact, you can make the other person believe you're not involved in what's being addressed.

Arms

If you have primary arms crossed, you can make yourself look nervous or defensive. On the other hand, if you hold open arms, you will make yourself comfortable and embrace others.

Distance

If you hold a person close, you can make yourself look pushy or put yourself in his face. At the same time, keep a distance away may mean that you don't care about what's being addressed or don't care about it at all.

You can study a lot regarding other people through body language. Many people show all sorts of thoughts in the way they push the body. Here are examples of how to discover other people's opinions:

Confidence

A comfortable person will always stand tall, holding eye contact sold while smiling at you simultaneously. The person can go even further with the hands when making gestures.

Tips for Reading Body Language

Eye movement, gestures, posture, and facial expressions are characteristics of human body language. American human behavior expert Eric Barker explains that it is best to look at "unconscious behaviors that are not easily controlled and may contain a message." Can anyone decipher this language? Barker reveals eight tips.

Use Common Sense

For the expert, analyzing the context is essential. Crossing your arms can mean adopting a defensive posture or even trying to deceive you. However, if it is cold or if the person concerned is sitting in an armless chair, the meaning can be different (much more straightforward and harmless).

Observe the Mime

Imitating a gesture or verbal expression may mean that the person is in tune with you. The act of agreeing with someone or something is difficult to fake, so the expert believes that the best thing is to think in these cases.

Nerve Energy

The other's level of activity can reveal your interest and enthusiasm for what you are saying. Research from the University of Manchester in England states that women shake their feet when they are interested in a man. Men, on the other hand, are tending to do so when they are nervous.

Consistency

Someone who reveals a fluid and consistent speech, emphasizing certain words, demonstrates control and concentration. Showing determination as they speak, these people are difficult to influence (and seduce).

Don't Care About Individual Signs

It is not possible to distinguish what a person means by body language through a single action. It is best to look at the actions as a whole, as two or three signals can help identify what goes in the other person's head.

Create A Reference

Uneasiness and the habit of always talking do not necessarily reveal any problem. However, something may be wrong when these people suddenly become calm.

Consider Your Previous Considerations

A judgment about another person will be affected if you have an initial impression, whether positive or negative. The inclination is to give the benefit of the doubt to someone you think is similar to you.

The Most Significant Thing Is to Focus on The Whole Context

Eric Barker argues that the ability to understand body language will increase when "understanding that body language is part of a larger context. Then you will begin to pay attention to other facets of interaction: voice, appearance, clothing, etc."

Chapter 3. Manipulation Through Body Language

After leaving the University heading to the golden paved streets of London, a man saw a woman who was also a model for the entire newspaper—at this point in his life. He hadn't met anyone attractive in the real world. Every day he walked and tried to be friendly, even cool, and afterward, he knew that he had just made himself a fool!

Why did trump react to her in that way? How was it that she was so successful? Have you ever addressed people with a lack of trust? And what about those other people in his class-his friend knew almost nothing about them as adults, he had never really been told, but he wasn't shocked by their performance.

They all had a certain aura about them that all these people could have a hypnotic effect on the people around them without opening their mouths. He wants to talk about this hypnotic body language today because it can help you achieve more and perfection without really having to do so much other than subtly alter your non-verbal communication.

3 Non-verbal keys for Hypnotic communication:

True Smile and Real Laughter

He can remember when his parents invited friends for supper when he was a child when his mother always told him to make sure that he was smiling and to show his teeth when the guests were arriving (I was never cheeky enough to grow, although the man was tempted). His mother knew that smiles produced positive reactions from people on an intuitive level.

This man speaks here of a real, genuine smile—a smile from the center of your body, which reflects joy. A natural smile makes the eyes and face wrinkle; insincere people smile with their mouths alone. Genuine smiles are often from the subconscious mind; individuals can sense, see, and feel real. A genuine smile implies you smile all over your face-your muscles move, your cheeks rise, your eyes shrink, and your eyebrows slightly go down.

Smile more, then. However, smile happily, fun, and joyfully. Smile in the future.

The explanation of why a photographer uses 'cheese' is because it's a term that helps you relax your face muscles. It often gives a crooked smile. How many pictures did you see that the smiles are cheese-powered and not authentic?

Professor Ruth Campbell, University College London, says that in the brain there is a "mirror neuron" which triggers the neurology responsible for the acknowledgment of face expressions and causes an immediate, unconscious mirroring response. The world smiles at you once you smile. In other words, know it or not, very often the facial expressions we see are unintentionally expressed.

So, if you smile more often than not-people around you smile more sincerely-it means, they feel better about you. You build for yourself and others around you a better immediate environment. How would you feel if you walk down the street and seeing someone with such an unhappy or cross face? Science has exposed that the more you smile, the more positive reactions people give you.

Would you smile more if you watch a funny movie with friends? Robert Provine found that Laughter in people in social situations was more than 30 times more likely than alone. He discovered that Laughter has less to do with jokes and funny storytelling and more to do with relationship building. Laughter creates a connection.

If you smile (a real smile) at another man, they almost always return the smile with a genuine smile that gives both of you and you genuinely positive feelings because of cause and effect. It creates a cycle of comfort: you smile, and you feel the perfect smile, and feel good, etc.

Studies show that most meetings run smoother, last longer, have better results, and improve relationships dramatically if you make a point of regularly smiling and laughing until it becomes a custom. He guesses you already knew all this-yet you smile a lot. Does recent research show that we smile 400% more-how as a kid often? Do you smile at the world today?

Confidence

The person was missing when he was younger, embarrassingly answering the receptionist.

I remember watching a documentary about a schoolgirl murdered in Great Britain. The girl's parents gave a press conference calling for help in the apprehension of the killer. It was the fall of the murderers. The way the father behaved at this press conference prompted the police to suspect him and to show him that he killed his daughter at last.

Many criminals are caught not because they have clues but because they are responsible, conscious of themselves, and lack trust. These feelings are sufficiently communicated to create suspicions.

When we are emotionally congruent and trustworthy, our body language is positive and expresses it to the world.

Psychologists advise us that by modifying our physical actions, we can alter our attitudes. Thus, adopting the physiology of trust can help you appear and become more trustworthy. When you are confident and hold your body that way more often, cause and effect mean having your body feel secure.

I recall reading a book a little while ago, and it taught you three great ways to build confidence with your body alone: first, he suggested that you be a' front seater.' Wherever you go to movies, classrooms, meetings, and presentations, the back lines appear to fill up fastest, aren't they? Many people go back so that they aren't too visible. It often shows a lack of confidence in him. Start sitting up today, relaxed with other people's eyes, and build confidence.

Furthermore, making direct contact with the eyes tells you a lot about confidence. If someone avoids contact with the look, we might start wondering what's wrong with them or what they must hide. Lack of eye contact may indicate that you feel weak or that you are, in some way, afraid. Conquer this and let the person in the eye look–you don't have to stare hard! Just look in your eyes to tell them that you believe you are honest, open, confident, and comfortable.

Suppose you seem confident and think of yourself. In that case, the other person tends unconsciously to agree that there is something worth knowing about you-why should anybody else be if you aren't confident or feel good about yourself? It is implicitly conveyed beyond conscious minds, often with these sages' good feelings. David Schwartz gave the other great tip to walk 25%

faster. This man knows that his father always told him to slow down when he was taken to football to see his beloved Nottingham Forest as a boy because he was enthused and enthusiastic about their destination.

Psychologists link Slovenian stances and slowness to disagreeable attitudes towards oneself, work, and the people around us. But psychologists also tell us that by changing your posture and movement speed, you can change your attitudes. Body action is the result of mental action-and vice versa-as this man already said; cause and effect! The person with low morality is shuffling with little confidence and stumbles through life. Likewise, ordinary people are on average. You can see it, and you can hear it.

Confident people travel purposefully, they have to go somewhere important, and they will succeed when they get there. Open your chest, throw your shoulders back, lift your head, be proud of yourself, move a little faster, feel that your trust will grow. It doesn't have to be dramatic; just keep your body safe.

The Right-Hand Side of the Brain

Most people are right-handed, and as such, their thoughts and lives are processed on the right-hand side of their brain, and motor reactions and functional brain use reside on their brain's left-hand side.

Evolutionary psychologists debate it; most of them think we all have six raw emotions. All else is derived from these. Those six emotions are central: happiness. Surprise. Disgust. Fear. Rage. Anger. Sadness.

It's worth noting here that only two of them are good. If we are real, only one is guaranteed to be great to ourselves, isn't that?

Following April's foolish day, he is reminded how much he enjoys' his surprise!

The vast majority of our thoughts in our minds are somehow negative. It is accurate, and bad things tend to stand out much more than our minds' good things.

So, if you respond to anybody's right brain, you may unconsciously associate yourself in the right mind with all those emotions. You don't want to do it.

If you first meet someone to use this knowledge in life instead, put yourself, so they have to look slightly right to look at you. See your right eye when you shake your hands. He believes that this picture is so much on his website's right-hand side. That in his rooms, the man places his chair so that his customers need to look correct when we communicate.

There are three powerful things to remember when improving your success and performance without opening your mouth.

Note that if you smile and smile with enthusiasm, if you behave with faith and connect with the right brain pieces, you start resonating far more gradually with the whole world.

Chapter 4. Uses of Body Language

Body language and self-esteem go hand in hand. It allows for a beautiful mechanism to observe and monitor how people behave and feel. Awareness of our body language is essential for becoming effective and persuasive communicators. Hence, there are several applications for using, reading, and changing body language.

Therapeutic Applications

Body language plays a significant role in counseling, NLP, and hypnotherapy. For psychologists, body language allows them to read their clients' emotional state and gives them a way to build rapport. Observing the client's body language can help the psychologist read how the client responds to a specific discussion or questioning line.

Body language speaks when we can't. Health care professionals have known this for some time. Many studies have been conducted in it and psychology academic studies for professionals, including modalities on body language.

Common issues which can be examined and treated through the use of body language include:

Bipolarity

Individuals with this condition suffer a chemical imbalance that leads to severe depression and the inability to make decisions.

They often have low self-esteem that accompanies this disorder, and it is incredibly challenging to understand effectively or treat correctly. The person with bipolarity can be taught to manage their daily situations. Considering the link between body language and emotion, they can also enjoy relief by being trained to use positive body language. It is a means for them to use their body language to persuade their emotions to stabilize and improve. For their families, body language reading is also an effective way to monitor their loved one's state and intervene before incidents happen. Depression can often go unnoticed, and people will rarely speak out about it. They are not likely to say: "I'm feeling depressed."

Low Self-Esteem

Many of us have suffered the disturbing effects of low self-esteem in one way or another. The first victim is our ability to progress in life. A positive belief in yourself is needed to convince the rest of the world to believe in you. People can be trained in positive body language such as open positions, eye contact, and lifting the head. It's a case of falsifying it until you feel it. With enough repetitive use of persuasive body language, you can even convince yourself that you are stronger than you believe.

Trauma

Survivors of trauma suffer from a loss of power, feelings of inadequacy, and loss of confidence. They also have the burden of guilt, where they hold themselves responsible for what happened to them. Whether the trauma is due to a violent act, these individuals' emotional state is reflected in their body language. Body language may have been positive and inviting before the incident. The person may display negative body languages, such as crossed arms, slumping, excessive facial touching, and nervous ticks such as repetitive movement. With effective counseling, their progress to recovery can be tracked through counseling and monitoring their body language.

Abuse

Abuse can be physical, emotional, and sexual, but whichever of these it is, there is bound to be an overwhelming sense of a loss of power. The victim may need to be convinced that they can regain their strength and that it is okay to trust people. Body language is extremely efficient in this regard. Helping these survivors of abuse establish strong body language will increase their sense of their strength. Suffering abuse is also linked to a loss of trust in people and the world around them.

By helping the abuse victim understand others' body language, they can be aided in evaluating the world and those around them regarding what they see, not what they fear. It is already great empowerment to the abuse victim, as they can become a participant in life again and feel like they can make informed decisions.

Self-Development

Being an effective communicator is one of life's excellent skills that will open doors and lead to the self's emboldening. Self-development programs often include body language modalities where the participants are trained in positive body language and assertiveness.

Group Dynamics

People can be classed into two groups: introverts and extroverts. Introverts, as we know, are those people who tend to thrive in one-on-one communications and prefer to spend more time alone, while extroverts are the life of the party and go through life with a the-more-the-merrier attitude. Introverts often suffer a form of depression based on social settings. They do not do well in groups. As a result, their communication within a group dynamic tends to fizzle. Yet, communication is a learned skill. As we learn the words, sentence structures, and grammar of a new language, we can also learn how body language works.

Depression

People suffering from depression tend to convince themselves that they are not worthy, that they are to blame for some usually imaginary flaw, and that everyone around them judges them.

People with depression sometimes think that everyone else has it right, while they alone are suffering. In creating awareness of body language, they can see the world in a more realistic sense and realize that people everywhere go through trying times and are not alone.

By learning to focus on using positive body language, they can also begin to manage their condition, encouraging well-being.

OCD

This condition is known for the repetitive behavior that someone engages in to make themselves feel in control of their lives. At the root of this tragic condition lies the fear of losing power and a profound distrust in themselves and others. In extreme cases, this can even encompass excessive washing of hands to remove imaginary germs and avoid people because people have germs.

People with OCD tend to have a very negative view of the world, and their only safety comes from their repetitive behaviors. Using body language, they can be trained to notice positive feelings in others and incorporate them into themselves. As they learn to project a positive self-image, they will feel their stress levels diminish, which will lead to a reduction of their anxiety-driven obsessions. When they feel more balanced, they will begin to develop trust in themselves and those around them.

Destructive Body Imagery (Bulimia and Obesity)

Low body image is a tragic and very destructive condition to suffer from. It goes with low self-esteem, lack of trust, feelings of abandonment, and severe depression. Bulimia leads the sufferer to obsessively lose weight, while obesity is a condition where the sufferer wants to fill themselves due to their emotional disabilities.

Both these conditions are associated with a loss of reality. These people begin to see the world not as it is, but as they believe it to be, and their world view is almost always negative. They eat or refuse to eat, to hide from the world and themselves.

Body language is a way to find a connection back to the real world. In reading the body language being projected by those around us, we can see that many individuals are just like us. We are not alone. Using positive body language is a therapeutic way to recover a sense of self that is realistic and beneficial.

The Biological Feedback Mechanism of Body Language

Due to our loss of trust in other humans, we often turn to animals for comfort and assurance. We read into what people do, what they say, how they say it, and how they react. A salesperson will do this on a second-by-second basis to monitor the client's body language and adjust their body language to match. Techniques such as mirroring, open position, advancing or retreating, and touching can be used to have an effect on the other person and monitor how persuasive we are on them. If they have begun to trust us enough, they will start to do something we want; in which case, we will trust them since they've done something for us. This endless, nonverbal loop is known as a biological feedback mechanism.

Training and Exercises

Some numerous academies and colleges strive to train people in body language detection and application. They mention facts and case-studies, what to do and what not to do; however, not many of them detail precisely how to improve your body language in a step-by-step way. When considering the activities and desired results, we suggest the following steps be followed:

Observe

Look at the world around you. Notice the people in it and how they interact with each other. Identify people in similar situations to those that challenge you. It could be someone applying for a promotion at work, asking a girl on a date, and even haggling for a discount. Each situation will use the same skills but in different ways. It all boils down to body language.

Practice

It will require some bravery, which is perhaps why people do crazy things in foreign lands where no one knows them. Find some friends, set up a hidden camera if you have to, or undergo obedience training with your dog. The goal is to place yourself in a situation where you can practice some of the skills and how they can be used.

If you feel overwhelmed, you can practice at home with a mirror. You might even find some online help with an online counselor who can perhaps observe you over Skype.

Evaluate

Look at the recording you made of yourself, or talk to friends who are helping you. Don't look at your awkwardness; instead, focus on each body language technique, how you applied it, and what the response to it was.

You may even give yourself a score or write down what you need to focus on. Recall rejoicing the successes, no matter how small. Then it's time to repeat step two, practice.

It may seem like an incredibly arduous task to learn body language, but it certainly is worth it. These skills of using space, posture, facial expressions, eye contact, gesture, and touch are vital to leading a fulfilling life that has less conflict and misunderstanding in it.

Chapter 5. Guide to an Effective Body Language

Research has shown that, when you are aware of your own body's happenings, you can manipulate it by training yourself to have control and even mold it to have effective communication. Further research recommends that you take some breathing exercises before going into a meeting or presentation. It will help you calm and have the ability to take note of your posture and gestures while on presentation. As you have noted by now, mirroring is a good technique. Always try to be keen on what the next person is doing non-verbally and copy that. It will help you turn out to be more effective in your communication with them. They will understand you better because this tunes your mind to communicate more truthfully at a place of relaxation.

However, you should be careful while shaping your body language. It is to ensure that the body language that you portray matches with what you are trying to present. A mismatch may bring confusion and may not be relevant at the moment. The person you are in conversation with my mistake you for meaning something else contrary to what you intended. The secret to having control of your body language is taking your time to learn it and being aware of your non-verbal cues as you apply what you know.

The Body Language That Will Help You Take Charge of Your Space

Effective management involves individuals being able to encourage and have a positive influence. In planning for a necessary appointment, maybe with your employees, management team, or partners, you focus on what to say, memorizing critical points, and rehearsing your presentation to make you feel believable and persuasive. It is something you should be conscious of, of course.

Here is what you should know if you want to control your position, at work, in presentation, or as a leader.

Seven Seconds is What You Have to Make an Impression

First impressions are essential in market relationships. When somebody psychologically marks you as trustworthy, or skeptical, strong, or submissive, you will be seen through such a filter in any other dealings that you do or say. Your partners will look for the finest in you if they like you. They will suspect all of your deeds if they distrust you. While you can't stop people from having quick decisions, as a defense mechanism, the human mind is programmed in this way. You can learn how to make these choices useful to you. In much less than seven seconds, the initial perceptions are developed and strongly influenced by body language. Studies have found that nonverbal signals have more than four times the effect on the first impression you create than you speak. It is what you should know regarding making positive and lasting first impressions. Bear in mind several suggestions here:

- Start by changing your attitude. People immediately pick up your mood. Have you noticed that you immediately get turned off after finding a customer service representative with a negative attitude? You feel like leaving or request to be served by a different person. That will happen to you, too, if you have a bad mood, which is highly noticeable. Think of the situation and make a deliberate decision about the mindset you want to represent before you meet a client, or join the meeting room for a company meeting, or step on the scene to make an analysis.

- Smile. Smiling is a good sign that leaders are under using. A smile is a message, a gesture of recognition, and acceptance. "I'm friendly and accessible," it says. Having a smile on your face will change the mood of your audience. If they had another perception of you, a smile can change that and make them relax.

- Make contact with your eyes Looking at somebody's eyes conveys vitality and expresses interest and transparency. An excellent way to help you make eye contact is to practice observing the eye color of everybody you encounter to enhance your eye contact. Overcome being shy and practice this excellent body language.

- Lean in gently the body language that has you leaning forward, expresses that you are actively participating and interested in the discussion. But be careful about the space of the other individual. It means staying about two feet away in most professional situations.

- Shaking hands. This will be the best way to develop a relationship. It's the most successful as well. Research indicates that maintaining the very same degree of partnership you can get with a simple handshake takes a minimum of three hours of intense communication. You should ensure that you have palm-to-palm touch and also that your hold is firm but not bone-crushing.

- Look at your position. Studies have found that uniqueness of posture, presenting yourself in a way that exposes your openness and takes up space, generates a sense of control that creates changes in behavior in a subject independent of its specific rank or function in an organization. In fact, in three studies, it was repeatedly found that body position was more important than the hierarchical structure in making a person think, act, and be viewed more strongly.

Building your credibility is dependent on how you align your non-verbal communication

Trust is developed by a perfect agreement between what is being said and the accompanying expressions. If your actions do not entirely adhere to your spoken statement, people may consciously or unconsciously interpret dishonesty, confusion, or internal turmoil.

By the use of an electroencephalograph (EEG) device to calculate "event-related potentials"–brain waves that shape peaks and valleys to examine gesture effects prove that one of these valleys happens when movements that dispute what is spoken are shown to subjects. It is the same dip in the brainwave that occurs when people listen to a language that does not make sense. In a somewhat reasonable way, they simply do not make sense if leaders say one thing and their behaviors point to something else. Each time your facial expressions do not suit your words. For instance, losing eye contact or looking all over the room when trying to express sincerity, swaying back on the heels while thinking about the company's bright future, or locking arms around the chest when announcing transparency. All this causes the verbal message to disappear.

What Your Hands Mean When You Use Them

Have you at any point seen that when individuals are energetic about what they're stating, their signals naturally turned out to be increasingly energized? Their hands and arms continuously move, accentuating focus, and passing on eagerness.

You might not have known about this association before. However, you intuitively felt it. Research shows that an audience will, in general, view individuals who utilize a more prominent assortment of hand motions in a progressively ideal light. Studies likewise find that individuals who convey through dynamic motioning will, in general, be assessed as warm, pleasant, and vivacious. In contrast, the individuals who stay still or whose motions appear to be mechanical or "wooden" are viewed as legitimate, cold, and systematic.

That is one motivation behind why signals are so essential to a pioneer's viability and why getting them directly in an introduction associates so effectively with a group of people. You may have seen senior administrators commit little avoidable errors. When pioneers don't utilize motions accurately on the off chance, they let their hands hang flaccidly to the side or fasten their hands before their bodies in the exemplary "fig leaf" position. It recommends they have no passionate interest in the issues or are not persuaded about the fact of the matter they're attempting to make.

To utilize signals adequately, pioneers should know how those developments will be seen in all probability. Here are four basic hand motions and the messages behind them:

- Concealed hands—Shrouded hands to make you look less reliable. It is one of the nonverbal signs that is profoundly imbued in our subliminal. Our precursors settled on endurance choices dependent on bits of visual data they grabbed from each other. In ancient times, when somebody drew nearer with hands out of view, it was a sign of potential peril. Albeit today the risk of shrouded hands is more representative than genuine, our instilled mental inconvenience remains.

- Blame game—I've frequently observed officials utilize this signal in gatherings, arrangements, or meetings for accentuation or to show strength. The issue is that forceful blame dispensing can recommend that the pioneer lose control of the circumstance, and the signal bears a resemblance to parental reprimanding or play area harassing.

- Eager gestures—There is an intriguing condition of the hand and arm development with vitality. If you need to extend more excitement and drive, you can do such by expanded motioning. Over-motioning (mainly when hands are raised over the shoulders) can cause you to seem whimsical, less trustworthy, and less incredible.

- Laidback gestures—Arms held at midsection tallness, and motions inside that level plane, help you—and the group of spectators—feel focused and formed. Arms at the midsection and bowed to a 45-degree point (joined by a position about shoulder-width wide) will likewise assist you with keeping grounded, empowered, and centered.

In this quick-paced, techno-charged time of email, writings, video chats, and video visits, one generally accepted fact remain: Face-to-confront is the most liked, gainful, and impressive correspondence medium. The more business pioneers convey electronically, all the more squeezing turns into the requirement for individual communication.

Here's the reason:

In face to face gatherings, our brain processes the nonstop course of nonverbal signs that we use as the reason for building trust and expert closeness. Eye to eye collaboration is data-rich. We translate what individuals state to us just halfway from the words they use. We get a large portion of the message (and most passionate subtlety behind the words) from vocal tone, pacing, outward appearances, and other nonverbal signs. What's more, we depend on prompt input on others' quick reactions to assist us with checking how well our thoughts are being acknowledged.

Strong is the nonverbal connection between people. When we are in a certified affinity with somebody, we subliminally coordinate our body positions, developments, and even breathing rhythms with theirs. Most intriguing, in up close and personal experiences, the mind's "reflect neurons" impersonate practices, yet sensations and sentiments too. When we are denied these relational prompts and are compelled to depend on the printed or verbally expressed word alone, the cerebrum battles and genuine correspondence endures.

Innovation can be a great facilitator of factual data, but meeting in an individual is the key to positive relationships between employees and clients. Whatever industry you work in, we're always in the business of individuals. However, tech-savvy you could be, face-to-face gatherings are by far the most successful way of capturing attendees ' interest, engaging them in a discussion, and fostering fruitful teamwork. It is said that if it doesn't matter that much, send an email. If it is crucial for the task but not significant, make a phone call. If it is extremely important for the project's success, it is advised to see someone.

Chapter 6. How to Persuade People

Persuasion is a deliberate effort to change or alter a person's opinions, beliefs, or attitudes toward an issue, situation, object, or person. It is usually achieved by transmission of a message which could be verbal or symbolic.

While persuasion could be used in a manipulative sense, it is, in an actual purpose, different from manipulation. It is because, when persuading a person, he/she is usually aware of your efforts at changing their point of view and willingly or reluctantly allows you to try. In this instance, the person listens and concentrates on what you are saying and then tries to rationalize your ideas with reality before then putting whatever conclusions they come to comparison with what they believed.

Your role in the entire dynamic is to state your reasons for the change you are prescribing, give illustrations and evidence supporting your views and try to convince the target of your advances that your line of action or advice is their best bet. The main goal of this is getting them to switch to a state of reasoning. In this, persuasion resembles manipulation because your goal is still to push the target towards an outcome that they might ordinarily not have considered right.

The success attained in persuasion usually depends on the target's preconceptions and their strength, their perception of the person sharing the new message or idea, their perception of the message or idea, and finally, their perception of the conclusion on offer. Upon outlining these reasons, it should be clear to you that the subject of your effort would probably possess ideas that are at least dissimilar. If not contradictory to yours and as such, the entire process would either hinge on your persuasion being very convincing or the target's ability to meet a compromise between the conflicting ideas that would majorly mirror the changes you want.

Below are six major theories that explain how the human mind absorbs and reacts to information. Knowledge of these would greatly increase the odds of persuasion if you could pinpoint it in your target.

The Attribution Theory

It concludes that people would either attribute actions and characters to people and objects, respectively, either relative to the context they are being considered in or according to their emotional disposition.

When they attribute using context as a guide, they are likely to come to decisions that consider the environment of origin and situational factors. Such is seen when a person refrains from calling a product inferior or calling a person insensitive. Instead of arguing that the product has been made from the best possible items available to the manufacturer. The person is merely reacting as he has learned from his childhood environment.

However, when considering their emotional disposition, they tend to believe that whatever is convenient for them is the only right decision or approach for every other person. Consider this situation:

You meet a person at an event or gather and try to start a conversation with them, but instead of giving you a polite audience, the person appears preoccupied with their thoughts or acts aloof. Angered or annoyed, you walk away, and when asked for an opinion on the person, you characterize them as proud, arrogant, or self-important.

In this case, the characterization you have concluded is based solely on your emotional disposition and does not consider the situation or possible problems the other person might have. The idea is not to determine whether you are wrong or right but rather to analyze how you are likely to process information about people and things. You might be right about the person.

Another situation is when you have been accused of doing something wrong, and you claim that your accusers have failed to see things from your perspective and are only interested in their point of view.

It is a perfect example of considering things as regards context. In this case, probably because the things said are negative, you'd notice the emphasis placed on contextual understanding of actions. There is also a minor hint of the dispositional thinking coinciding.

The Conditioning Theory

In this case, the person is likely to do things. It is if they are conditioned to look like their own decisions instead of coercion. It is mostly utilized in the advertising industry where commercials, advertisements, and billboards convey information that would provoke positive feelings in the population of interest. They then connect such sentiments to their products, making you feel that the work would bring such a feeling into your life since you are more likely to purchase their product, thinking that your decision was an independent one.

It is usually possible because we generally perceive things based on our emotions and are more likely to buy things because they make us feel good.

The Cognitive Dissonance Theory

Based on this theory, it is assumed that people tend to aim for consistency in their thoughts, attitudes, and decisions. It is the cause why most individuals create principles that they strive to follow. Most people also seem intent on reconciling the contradictions as much as they can until they feel comfortable. I would give two examples of this.

Example 1

You have an extreme and deep-rooted need for canned food, either due to the laziness of having to cook meals or the frustrations at having to wait in queues for food. Then you are told that such canned meals could lead to cancer, and you don't want to have cancer. But you also don't want to stop eating canned food. So, instead of stopping with the habit, you comfort yourself that millions of people like you have the same habit and never have cancer.

The cancer theory might be untrue, but your eagerness to dispute the fact or at least make the consequences seem less severe is your own way of changing your mind or making the facts you have just learned seem less important or true. It is one of the ways of dealing with cognitive dissonance theory.

Example 2

Imagine a criminal with a conscience. It is probably hard to envision, but they do exist. Their criminal tendencies are clashing with their tender hearts and causing a bit of discomfort in such a situation. Such a person is very likely dealing with his/ her problems by giving in to the rationale that a criminal and wealthy life far outweighs the benefits of having a clean conscience or right heart.

Again, I am refraining from judging whether such a rationale is sound but am more focused on the fact that the person seems to give in to a motivation that overlaps with most people's general aim to deal with his discomfort.

The Judgment Theory

This one is straightforward to grasp. It merely proposes that when faced with a new piece of information or idea, a person's reaction is dependent on the way he/she currently feels on the topic. What this means is that we're likely to accept something that resonates with our current belief, reject something that doesn't fit in with our beliefs, or stay indifferent to something never considered before.

Therefore, when attempting to persuade a person, it is better first to determine their views on the topic to gauge whether you'd be successful and if your effort would eventually be worth it.

The Inoculation Theory

The inoculation theory supports the view that even if uninterested before in two points of view, once argued for, you are likely to pick the dominant point of view and stick with it. Here is an example:

You have never viewed a soccer game in your life, but one day you are relaxing on the beach and happen to find yourself stuck between two diehard soccer fans who support rival teams. An argument begins about whose team is better and more dominant, and they both turn to you, presenting their points like you are a seasoned fan and, after some time, ask you to judge who's better. You obviously would pick the person with the better argument to not betray your lack of knowledge on the subject. If another individual were to pose a question to you in the future, inquiring about which of those two teams is better, you'd probably find yourself arguing in favor of the choice you made then, maybe even with some of the same points that were used then.

It is the power of inoculations; the most powerful initial idea always takes root first.

Narrative Persuasion Theory

From experience, I think we would all accept that stories have a more enhanced effect on perception and opinions than abstract advice. People's attitudes and views towards objects and others tend to change when they are told compelling stories of such subjects.

The theory simply attempts to explain the heightened effect that can have on people if appropriately utilized. In this, the listener feels transported, which significantly affects their perception of events, making them more pronounced and vivid than they might have been if they had been expressed ordinarily and abstractly.

The Psychological Perspective

Ordinarily, persuading people would be difficult without the ability to organize and present an argument properly. But if inexperience in any or both of this is coupled with an inability to understand moods and stances. Your task would be made many times more likely to fail.

The ability to instantly sense and recognize a person's stance on an issue is difficult, not to talk of performing the same trick on an audience. Because of this difficulty, most speakers who are attempting to introduce people to a new point of view always tend to ask questions that would enable them to gauge the audience's stance before moving on with their presentation.

After asking such questions immediately, they usually watch out for visible reactions from the audience members, maybe a smile to indicate a knowledge of the topic, sitting up to indicate interest, turning away, or sighing to indicate disagreement, boredom, or even a person willing to answer. These simple markers give you an idea of how your message may be received and help you map out a strategy of approach. It is also a useful tool as people express themselves more sincerely when they do not feel particularly in the spotlight. If you are unsure, do not refrain from asking a few surface questions to test the waters or, more aptly, to feel out the crowd.

It should also be noted that numerous people might give an adverse reaction to one-on-one persuasion and would start arguments to further their points. The moment you realize that your attempt to persuade a person has deteriorated into an argument, it is sensible for you to stride away. Very few disputes occurring outside law courts ever get settled. Engaging in one would be fruitless and time-consuming. That time is better spent elsewhere.

Chapter 7. How to Analyze People

Logic alone cannot help you if you want to understand an individual. To know how to analyze the non-verbal initiative cues given off by people, you have to give in to the other vital forms of information. In order to do this, you have to give up any emotional baggage or preconceptions like ego clashes or old resentments that might be stopping you from clearly seeing someone—the clue to this to receive information neutrally without contorting it and staying objective.

Whether you are trying to read your kids, your partner, co-worker, or boss, in order to do so accurately, you have to bring down some walls and surrender to any biases. You have to willingly let go of old ideas that can be very limiting. Those who can analyze other people properly are trained to read and analyze the invisible. They have learned to look further than where people generally look by utilizing their "super senses" and can access life-changing intuitive insights.

Analyzing People Effectively

In order to recognize how your mannerisms and actions can affect other people, you have to be able to comprehend the alterations between how you communicate with different people and how you act around them.

You need to note how all these people's different behavior affects you and how your actions make you appear to them. A suitable method of practicing this is by thinking about how other people might behave around you based on how they consider you in their lives. Maybe they act in a different way around you than they do around other people.

People You Do Know vs. People You Don't

How you see and behave towards someone is greatly affected by how well you know them or how well you need to know them. Your closeness to someone or distance from someone in the aspect of your relationships will define the things you need to contemplate when you are analyzing both you're and the other person's behavior while you are interacting with them. In the end, this will also help you determine how you want to make use of these insights in order to analyze what they are trying to communicate with you correctly.

Here are four examples to better elaborate on this concept:

1. You have an unstable relationship with your mother. Your relationship is long-term and intensely involved. You aim to find out the origin of the complication and fix your relationship with her. To do this, you first need to consider a few things: how she fulfills her needs, her points of concentration, comprehensive information about her personal life, the way she communicates with you, her impulses, preferences, and her body language.

2. You are in a relationship with your significant other for about a year. As it's starting to get more serious, you consider asking him/her to move in with you. The relationship is intimate and medium-term. Your first objective should be to think whether moving in together would be a smart move. You want to figure out how they might respond when you ask them the question. The essential factors that you need to consider are their past experiences and personal life, how they communicate with

you, their impulses, preferences, and body language. Besides, you also need to consider how they go about fulfilling their requirements, their points of concentration, and their drive. You can also acquire more insight by consulting family and friends.

3. You are thinking about sharing innovation for a business idea with a co-worker. You have a relatively superficial relationship with this co-worker, and it is medium-term. You want to observe their behavior to determine whether the two of you are compatible to work together and whether he or she would be a suitable business partner before expressing your idea. You want to figure out how you should approach them to get the best response. You need to observe the following factors: how they verbally communicate with you, their impulses, preferences, and body language. In addition to that, defining their concentration and having some insight into their past experiences and personal life. It could also be beneficial in this case.

4. In the initial process of meeting someone, you might ask yourself whether they are attracted to you. You are attracted to them; however, before expressing your feelings to them, you want to get to know them better. At this time, your interpersonal relationship with this other person is superficial and relatively new. In addition to that, before expressing your feelings, you want to be sure that you are correctly interpreting their signals if the feelings are not mutual. You need to pay consideration to a few things with your first encounters with this person. Some of the influences you need to contemplate are their preferences, how they speak with you, their body language, and how they convey themselves around you. You can subtly acquire some details like their history with relationships in your first few conversations and use that information to determine how you will act.

Techniques by Which You Can Analyze People

- Sense emotional energy.

Our emotions well express the energy or "vibe" we give off. Our intuition helps us register these. Some people help improve our vitality and mood, and it feels good to be around them. However, others can be draining, and you just want to move away from them. Even though this subtle energy is invisible, it can be felt feet or inches from the body. It is known as chi in Chinese medicine. It's a vitality that is important to health.

Methods to Analyze Emotional Energy

1. Notice their laugh and tone of voice—A lot about our state of emotions can be conveyed via our voice's volume and tone. The frequencies of sounds create vibrations. Try to notice how the tone of someone's voice affects you while you are trying to analyze them. Ask yourself whether their style feels whiny, snippy, abrasive, or soothing.

2. Notice the feel of their touch, hug, and handshake—much like an electric current, emotional energy is also shared through physical contact. Ask yourself whether a hug or a handshake feels confident, comfortable, warm, or off-putting. Is the other person's hand limp, indicating that they are timid and non-committal? Or are they clammy, meaning anxiety?

3. Notice people's eyes—People's eyes send powerful energy. Studies have revealed that similar to the brain that sends electromagnetic signals beyond the body, and the eyes do this. Take time and try to watch people's eyes. Are they angry? Mean? Tranquil? Sexy? Caring? Also, try to understand whether someone seems to be hiding or guarding something

or are at home in their eyes, revealing their capacity for intimacy.

4. Since their presence, someone's company is like an emotional atmosphere surrounding us like the sun or a rain cloud. It's not essentially congruent with behavior or words but is the overall energy emitted by us. While you are trying to analyze people, try to notice: Are you feeling scared, making you want to back off? Or are you attracted by their social presence?

Listen to Your Intuition

Intuition is not what your head says. It's what your gut feels. It is the non-verbal information you can perceive beyond logic, words, and body language. What counts the most when you want to understand someone is who they are from within and not just their outer appearance. With the help of intuition, you can reveal a richer story by seeing further than the obvious.

Some intuitive cues you can look into:

1. Look out for intuitive empathy—You can experience an intense form of empathy when you can feel people's emotions and symptoms in your body. Therefore, when you analyze people, try to notice whether you are upset or depressed after an uneventful meeting or if your back hurts suddenly. Get some feedback to determine whether this is empathy or not.

2. Watch out for flashes of insight—You might get an "ah-ha" about people while you are conversing about them. It might come in a flash, so stay alert. If not, you might miss out on it. These critical insights might get lost as we tend to move onto the next thought very fast.

3. Feel the goosebumps—Goosebumps are amazing intuitive signals that tell us when we resonate with people who say

something that we connect with or when they inspire or move us. It can also take place when you feel a sense of déjà-vu. Déjà-vu is a feeling of recognition that you might have known someone before, although you haven't met.

4. Honor your gut feelings—During your first meetings, try to listen to your gut. Before you even have an opportunity to ponder about it, a visceral reaction already takes place. It conveys whether you are relaxed or not. Gut feelings take place very fast as a primal response. They act as your internal truth meter and convey to you whether you can trust someone or not.

Observe Body Language Cues

According to studies, words account for only seven percent of our method of communication. The remaining is represented by our voice (thirty percent) and body language (fifty-five percent). Stay fluid and relaxed while reading body language cues. Don't get overly analytical or intense. Simple sit back, be comfortable, and observe.

1. Interpret facial expression—Our feelings and emotions tend to get stamped on our faces. The deep frown lines convey Overthinking or worry. The smile lines of joy are depicted by the crow's feet. Pursed lips signal bitterness, contempt, or anger. Grinding teeth or clenched jaw are signs of tension.

2. Pay attention to posture—When you are trying to analyze someone's posture, ask yourself: Is their chest puffed out when they are walking, which is a sign of a big ego? Or do they cower while walking, which is a sign of low self-esteem? Or, is their head held high, confident?

3. Notice their appearance—When you are analyzing others, pay attention to their appearance. Are they wearing a t-shirt and jeans, indicating that they are dressed casually for comfort? A power suit with properly shined shoes that are indicating ambition and being dressed for success? Or a pendant like a Buddha or a cross displaying their spiritual values? Even a well-fitted top with cleavage, representing a seductive choice?

Learning how to analyze other people accurately takes time and practice, and obviously, every rule has some exceptions. However, you can improve your abilities to analyze others, communicate properly with them, and understand their thinking by keeping these points in mind while building your powers of observation.

Chapter 8. Dark Psychology Secrets

There is a concept in the world of psychology, which is called the dark triad. The obscure triad is a set of three personality traits, namely, Machiavellianism, narcissism, and psychopathy. This group of three is labeled dark, owing to the usual malignant habits correlated with certain characteristics. The dark triad's dramatic opposite is the lighter triad, which is a topic and debate for another book in itself. Although the three traits depicted on the dark triad in their studies are distinct, it is seen that they also overlap. It indicates that with blurred boundaries, a person who increases the success on the dark triad exam will likely have all these traits present. It might be hard to tell, for example, where narcissism stops and where psychopathy begins.

Discussions about the Dark Triad concept were initially begun in 1998. Three psychology experts do it. They asserted that Machiavellianism, narcissism, and psychopathology occurred overlappingly in normal samples. Two psychologists by the titles of Williams and Paulus would later invent a name for this group, in 2002: the dark triad.

There have often been discussions and debates about nature's part in seeking to comprehend the dark triad's personality traits. To put it simply, psychologists, behavioral scientists, and researchers were keen to know whether born or bred are Dark Triad persons. Are we born stupid and manipulative, or have we become so as a consequence of the things that we grow up to be exposed to? According to various research done, it has been noted that a dark triad has an important genetic basis to it. That is, some born with such susceptibility to the dark traits of the triad. However, in terms of heritability, narcissism, or psychopathy, rank greater than Machiavellianism. That is when contrasted to a parent that ranks high on the Machiavellian scale, a psychopathic mother or father is more willing to switch the characteristic to their offspring.

The dark triadic characteristics have also been seen to be underrepresented in top-level management in reports that might not be really friendly to someone working. When the dark triad elements are unpackaged in the segments below, it becomes evident why this recognition may be so.

Dark Triad: Narcissism

A narrative is revealed in the Greek myths of a young man named Narcissus. Narcissus was indeed a hunter renowned for his striking, good looks. Narcissus did not have a time of day for them, given the adoration he got from his admirers and even forced others to take their own lives to show their devotion. While there are several varieties of Narcissus's story, all of them refer to him being extremely self-absorbed, which eventually ended up in him going to die mortality that was retribution for his selfish ways. Thanks to the story of that young man, Sigmund Freud first coined the term narcissism. Freud, aptly titled On Narcissism in his famous 1914 essay.

In the simplest terms, narcissism is the increased and compulsive self-admiration which a person has towards himself and his personal features. A narcissist is always easy to recognize since they quickly offer away their behavior and values.

Asking yourself if you have a narcissist in their life? Here is what you should look for:

- Narcissists tend to feel good and always have the ability to be entitled.

- Type-A perfectionists are also narcissists.

- Narcissists have an unflagging thirst for control.

- Narcissists don't have a sense of limits.

How Do Narcissists Control People?

Now that you realize how well a narcissist looks, you're possibly curious about what the narcissist is doing to manipulate you in your life. How difficult can it be to remember, after all, that someone is attempting to manipulate you? The response is, it can be quite challenging, particularly when this person conceals their acts as only searching for you. Many narcissists are typically very clever and can fit in their daily life without drawing attention to them. They could also be very creative and talented, and the allure that tries to draw you to them will usually be that. When you're out there going to look for a narcissist-shaped monster, you might not be going to look for that skilled and super artistic friend who's always having a solution to everything. And still, she might be the only narcissist in the life who just thinks about competing or who gets injured along the way.

Narcissists are also quite keen liars, in addition to using their mentioned characteristics to the best of ability. Narcissists conduct routine the skill of deception in its various forms in a bid to be the celebrity of every show. Deception is the way the narcissist throws you off reality, so they stay in control. In either scenario, they always exist in an altered world where they are good, and everyone else is inferior to them. Hence, deceit is just a means for them to draw you through this repetitive story where they are the principal character.

Dark Triad: Machiavellianism

Niccolò Machiavelli, sometimes referred to as the founder of modern social science, was a Renaissance-era Italian who favored loads of hats. Machiavelli has been amongst others a historian, politician, poet, humanist, author, and diplomat. Machiavelli composed his most popular work, The Prince, in 1513. In this book, Machiavelli defined and advocated the usage of unscrupulous methods for obtaining and retaining political influence. The word Machiavellianism arose from this work and its endorsements, that was used to refer to the kind of politicians and tactics Machiavelli mentioned in his book. This word was later coined by psychology researchers to define a psychological characteristic marked by a lack of sympathy and a drive to succeed at the detriment of others, be it by deception, coercion, or the flouting of traditional dignity laws and morality. A person who displays Machiavellianism is, in the simplest form, willing to do almost anything if it meant playing. Machiavelli is the purpose of why the ending phrase justifies the means that exist.

Most work has been conducted since the introduction of the word Machiavellianism in philosophy to ascertain what determines the people who score highest on a Machiavellianism test, better known as high Mach's. High Mach's have been found to tend to value power, money, and competition above all else. High Mach's put a very cheap cost on things like building a community, family, and even love. Among those that score low above the Machiavellianism index, better known as low Mach's, the opposite is accurate.

Dark Triad: Psychopathy

Psychopathy is a feature of temperament marked mainly by a loss of empathy toward others. Psychopaths barely experience empathy for others and will rarely feel remorse even when other people have been hurt. There are various psychopathy views, but many of them always seem to agree on the three primary features that differentiate a psychopath from any normal individual. These three traits include fearlessness, lack of restraint, and meanness that any other person would consider uncomfortable.

Psychopaths are brave and aggressive and are not reluctant to step into new terrain even though they could be in danger. Although most individuals are usually overwhelmed by these conditions, psychopaths should be coping with such scenarios as if doing their everyday activities. Psychopaths often have a high degree of self-confidence as well as social boldness that allows them to interact with individuals without the shyness or anxiousness that others may have. Often, whenever a gruesome crime has been committed, you could perhaps hear about the nature of the investigation and shudder while going to think to yourself: how can a man live with himself for doing so? It's business as usual for a psychopath to kill someone and then grab a sunny face up at their local restaurant. It is not to say that all psychos have killed somebody. Some psychopaths instead rendered their lack of sympathy and susceptibility to other transgression and crimes.

Psychopaths show impaired regulation of the instinct, so they cannot regulate their impulses. When a regular human gets a desire of any kind, they can sometimes bring it under control and speak out of that state themselves. For instance, if you're having to deal with an irritating colleague who just won't be shutting up regarding their forthcoming bridal shower, you'll probably be able to combat the desire to slap them in their face. On the other hand, a psychopath will often be resolve by instinct and will react without giving it a second thought about the cost of everyone's decision. Psychopaths are susceptible to snapping in a simple way. Even one gets injured as they pop.

Common decency, when dealing with others, demands a certain level of decorum and kindness. It is not something of concern to psychopaths. While the majority of the people are worried about kindness and caring, the nicest person in the room will have no issue being a psychopath. Based on the situation in hand, they might be dramatic or execute about it.

The Dark Triad Practice

The dark triad test gauge how one score, as for the three practices of narcissism, Machiavellianism, or psychopathy, is concerned. The test is sometimes used in various settings, and by law courts and police in particular. The dark triad test is also used by corporations to gauge their employees. The primary reason the dark triad method is implemented is to assess an entity's personality characteristics and likely forecast their actions to prevent unsavory behaviors. It was noted that people who score high on the dark triad study are more likely to cause problems and social distress, whether in the work environment or even in their employment state. At the same time, these people will also likely have an easy time to attain leadership positions and gain sexual partners.

The dark triad test asks you to address a series of questions on a range of subjects like how you think about others and yourself, how you maintain track of details you could use to harm someone, and your general opinions on existence, death, and social experiences, among others. The dark triad test may be a nice way to gauge how you perform on the dark triad scale when self-administered. The dark triad test might not be very precise when administered by law courts and police as the respondent may purposely alter their answers to make them look better than it actually is. It is a primary drawback of the triad check in the night. If you're willing to take the dark triad exam, there are some online places where you'll be able to complete a study in minutes.

Be careful to take the test results too personally—sometimes, the justifications you give are based on the kind of day you are taking and not on the type of person you are being. In any event, if you recognize yourself as a respectable human being who always respectfully treats others and never harms others, then you shouldn't worry very much about what an experiment says about you.

Chapter 9. How to Defend Ourselves of Dark Psychology

First, Identifying Them

By now, we have examined the foundations of dark psychology, the psychological profiles that make up the Dark Triad, typical forms of manipulation in relationships, and how manipulation has manifested itself in society's institutions.

First, remember that simply because you are not currently in a personal or professional relationship that could be defined as manipulative does not mean that you are free of all danger and concern. Predators have had to learn the hard way to live and achieve success using cold and calculating psychology from which they truly do not ever get any rest.

Imagine being injured in a serious accident and losing the use of one or more of your limbs. Regardless of how much you would prefer to have the use of that limb back. You will be forced to find some way to adapt. Emotional predators do the same thing. But because their injuries are invisible, and because of the business world's competitive nature, they sometimes hold an advantage over us if we fail to maintain vigilance.

Emotional predators can blend into the normal landscape because it is easy for them to go through daily living motions.

They truly do not care if things don't work out because they have no value for their relationships or the things that society has established as having value.

Consider that the serial killer Ted Bundy worked on a crisis hotline while he stalked and murdered young women. He appeared successful, outgoing, handsome, and well-adjusted, but he was not. Or consider that the serial killer John Wayne Gacy, who murdered and buried in the crawl space beneath his home, almost 40 young men and boys, spent his days running a construction business, held fundraisers for local political leaders, and entertained sick children.

It may seem nauseating, especially with these extreme and dramatic examples. Still, for the emotional predator, society's important responsibilities are less a source of personal and professional satisfaction and fulfillment and more a perfect cover for their predatory addiction. As a result, you may find it helpful to develop some habits that will help you learn to classify some of the significant signs of emotionally predatory behavior.

Not everyone's life is perfectly organized or compartmentalized. Often environments and the people in them cross boundaries. Often in our daily lives, we wonder where things may have gone wrong. Quite often, the answer may be that we are trapped in a relationship with an emotional predator.

Regardless of the environment in which you meet people, you should always maintain a vigilant lookout for any of the following telltale signs of a predatory personality:

- Pathologically selfish people. They may go through friendship and love motions, but their emptiness is apparent when they fail to initiate social outings or when all encounters leave you feeling exhausted and drained.

- Emotional predators may offer lots of charm and flattery, but if there is a lack of substance to your interactions with them, you can be sure the compliments are probably false, too.

- Predators will exaggerate their accomplishments and even lie. If you call them on it, they will refuse to take responsibility or admit that they are wrong.

- A date or outing with an emotional predator may always be a high-stakes adventure. If you never seem able to engage with them simply over a cup of coffee and have a happy and fulfilling encounter, you may be dealing with a predator.

- Predators are bullies by nature and use anger as their primary means of communication. Avoid people who demonstrate a tendency to humiliate people or challenge anyone who seems to have more power or success than they do. Predators also use insults and putdowns to build themselves up. You may notice this kind of conduct directed at other people when you are out with a predator. For example, if you are at a café or restaurant, a predator may try to impress you by insulting or humiliating the staff.

- Predators are manipulative, which they often show by making promises and then not keeping them.

- Because predators lack a conscience and do not understand that their abusive behavior should make them feel bad, a telltale sign, maybe anyone who boasts about committing abusive actions or crimes

- Predators may also display parasitic behavior. If you are tangled with someone who is excessively lazy and uses you, you should find a way to end the relationship.

Guidelines

Of course, identifying the signs of predatory behavior is only half the battle. The other half is discovering a way to resolve the conflicts and repair the damage that inevitably follows in the wake of an encounter with an emotional predator.

The following are some general guidelines. Some of the tips are meant as suggestions that you should implement on a daily basis. They should become new habits that will now be part of your daily routine. It is important not to regard these tips as chores or burdensome or a diversion or interruption of your normal life. Think of these suggestions as your own personal investment in your daily professional development.

Suppose a virtuoso musician who plays violin for a symphony wants to stay at the top of his profession. In that case, no matter what else he does, one thing must remain constant: daily practice and a constant effort to stretch his repertoire by seeking out more challenging pieces, finding new forms of expression, and adding new skills to his resume. Consider a university professor in any department—being hired into a tenured position is the only beginning. The "publish or perish" mentality will soon take hold. He will find that continually refreshing his professional assessment of his area of expertise is as much a part of his daily professional routine as the more mundane tasks involved in classroom lectures.

So, it is with life in the modern world. To maintain a position of success and happiness and fulfillment, we must think like any gifted performer or professional. Constant vigilance and the continual addition of new weapons to your arsenal to fight the war against the growing threat of epidemic levels of emotional predation will keep your calendar full.

Buy a notebook, start a new spreadsheet, create a new folder in your favorite browser's bookmarks tab, and clear off a shelf on the bookcase in your office. This effort in your life can be just as much a passion and an investment in your success and happiness as the money you spent earning your college degree or the time and effort you spent building your professional network.

Most importantly, as we move down the list of tips for dealing with predators, remember that it is not unusual to find that recovery from such encounters, in some cases, may take years. Though the first step of dealing with a predator is ensuring, they are no longer physically present in your life. This step is not always easy to accomplish. And once you achieve this goal, actually repairing the damage they have caused may keep you very busy for some time to come. But relax—though the damage inflicted by emotional predators can grow increasingly worse over time, so the benefits of successfully dealing with these incursions can have increasingly beneficial returns over time.

Here are some suggestions:

Conduct A Self-Inventory

From time to time, read the details in the types of character traits that make people more susceptible to emotional predation. Look within and be truthful with yourself about your weaknesses. Don't do this as an exercise in self-abuse, though.

Consider that an emotional predator approaches you with only one goal in mind—to destroy you. You may not be entirely willing to examine yourself in an unflattering light, but an emotional predator who has made you a target may not have time for anything else.

Be Cautious

Whenever you are meeting new people, whether romantically or professionally, guard your personal information

Resist Projection and Gaslighting

When you encounter these environments, remind yourself that the goal is to defeat all genuine efforts to establish accountability.

Keep A Journal

You don't have to be eerie about it, but respect yourself enough to seriously take your personal and professional aspirations. Write down your thoughts and concerns at the end of the day, even if you can only manage a few sentences. The blank page will never pose the kind of threat to you that an emotional predator may.

By getting your complicated thoughts out of your head and on paper, you have unburdened yourself in a means that is most useful to you. A predator knows you have this need, and their willingness to listen may be designed as a trap.

Go "No Contact"

If you are in a professional or private relationship, and notice any of the signs of emotional predation, take steps immediately to end the relationship. Sometimes that may mean not replying to text messages, voice mail messages, or email messages. The predator may not like it and may react angrily, but if you try to enter into a negotiation or debate, you will be playing into their hands. Just say that you have decided not to respond any further, then stick to your plan.

Going "no contact," and in the modern world with all its digital communication, is a valid and acceptable tactic. If the predator continues to harass you, keep notes, and document their abuse. You may need to use it later if law enforcement becomes involved. Screenshots, text messages, email messages, and voice mail messages should all be saved and kept in a folder.

Get Help

Recognizing that you are in a relationship with a predator is the first step to escaping the relationship. Rescuing yourself must become your first priority. Remember that you will require professional help to solve this problem. If you are unsure how to proceed, take ten minutes out of your day, find a quiet place, and make a phone call. Don't worry about being perfect or feeling awkward. Professionals expect you to be at a loss and will know how to help.

Find A Support Network

You may need to seek the support of the law enforcement authorities. If you believe things are that bad, you are probably right. Don't let yourself be bullied or intimidated. As with a psychologist or helpline call, making the first call is the most important step. Even if things don't go exactly the way you think they should, by informing the local authorities, you will have placed yourself in a better position

Reinvent Yourself

Remember that as a victim of emotional predation, you will no longer be the person you once were and will have to restructure your thoughts and approaches to life.

Cheer Up

You have taken the first step toward defeating the predatory influences that have brought the dark cloud over your life. It is the first day of the rest of your life, not the last day of the life you used to live.

As you move forward with your new awareness of your surroundings' nature, the world may become a less intimidating place, and you will once again find the joy and happiness that seems to have been lost for so long.

Chapter 10. The Power of Hands

The hands have a power that we do not know at all, and we ignore it. They send a huge number of messages that most people can't get.

Hands have always been used in conversation, and their meaning has changed countless times over the years. An example is a handshake.

The act of shaking hands finds its roots in the past. When the ancient tribes met, they used to show their palms to show that they were not hiding anything.

The Roman Empire instead used to tighten the forearm, so both people were sure that the other did not hide anything under his sleeve. It was done because, in those days, it was normal going around with a knife under the sleeve and being safe. They adopted this habit.

But like all the customs that have passed from generation to generation, the one used by the Romans has turned into our handshake.

This gesture for us is used in a myriad of different situations. They were ranging from the classic greeting with friends to a handshake to establish a working agreement between two large multinationals.

Even in Japan, where the classic greeting has always been the bow, the handshake is widely used today.

The fact that it is now a widespread gesture does not mean that it is simple to do. Behind the handshake, there is a real-world of domination and submission.

Still, in ancient Rome, two people greeted each other with an arm-wrestling handshake, I define it.

In other words, it was not common to shake hands as we do today, but one person took the hand of the other from bottom to top and created the shape of a sandwich, so to speak. The most powerful person dominated the other.

Nowadays, this practice is not used, but the person you win always exists while handshaking. There are three different types of endings for a handshake, which are:

- Dominance
- Submission
- Equality

These attitudes are perceived at the unconscious level, and our body processes them in a particular way, and each of these can decide in which direction the conversation will go.

An example I can give you is that of a study done on some company managers.

Male or female makes no difference.

It has shown that 89% of them use the dominant handshake and always hold out their hand first so that they can control the handshake accurately.

The exact opposite is a submissive handshake. In this case, the person puts his hand palm up, granting the other person dominance. A bit like dogs do when they lie down and put their bellies to the sky.

You can use this handshake if you want your interlocutor to feel in control of the situation. You can use this squeeze when you go to make excuses, for example.

On the other hand, when the two people are in a position in which both want to turn the other's hand to dominate, a "bite" is created. It causes the people to be equal, and neither of them, in the end, gets the better.

So, if you want to create an equal relationship with the person in front of you, avoid him turning your hand, but most importantly, use the same amount of force that he uses.

Now let's use hypothetical numbers. If he applies a force of 9 out of 10 to the handshake and you apply one of 7 out of 10, you will have to increase the strength, or you will be dominated. The same thing you will have to do in reverse if you don't want to dominate.

In short, if he applies a force of 5 and you of 7, if you do not want to be seen dominant, you will have to lower the power of your grip forcefully.

But now I'll tell you a trick to never let yourself be dominated. Not even if you were to meet the president of the united states.

Indeed, with this technique, you will always and I repeat, always dominate the other. Always if in that situation you want to do it.

The technique is called "disarming the doers."

The technique consists of putting the arm outstretched with the palm facing down to not leave any escape for your interlocutor, and he will have to turn his hand and put himself in submission forcefully.

From that moment on, you can do whatever you want. You decide whether to dominate or be equal, but it will be very difficult for him to bring the situation in his favor.

A bit like it happens in games when you are three points above your antagonist, and the game is about to finish, he has to do a miracle to win; indeed, the options for him are to draw or to lose.

If you occur to find yourself in the situation where a person holds out his hand as described above, there is something you can do to reverse the situation.

Step forward with your left foot and make sure to bring his hand vertically. This practice is not simple because we tend to advance with the right, but you will see that it will come more than natural to you with a little training.

If you really can't take this step, there is another way to save yourself from domination, and that is the double catch.

When the other brings you to palm up, you use the other hand, free to return the hold to a tie. So right now, you are using two hands while he is using just one.

Staying on The Left Is an Unfair Advantage

During a handshake, your position is crucial, and staying on the left helps a lot if you want to dominate.

It happens because, on the right, you have no control over the situation, while on the left, you can actually do it.

Kennedy liked this technique very much, even if at that time, nothing was known about body language; he already applied it by intuition.

If you go to see all the photos where he meets with leaders and famous people, you will always find him on the left with the double grip.

A striking example of how Kennedy was a phenomenon with body language is when he won the Nixon election.

At that time, it was renowned that the people who only heard the two politicians' speeches were convinced that Nixon had won while those who watched the scene agreed otherwise.

It led Kennedy to win the election. Pretty important this body language, isn't it?

However, going back to the speech above, if you are on the right of the photo to be able to have an equal situation, reach out to force him to shake your hand as you want.

To conclude, I give you a summary.

Few people know what an impression they can make on a stranger, even if they are conscious of how vital it is to yield a great starting point in a conversation.

Take some time to experiment with the various handshakes with perhaps friends, relatives, or work colleagues to get familiar with it. During important moments you will know how to behave correctly.

Chapter 11. Body Language of a Child

First of all, we must dialog about why it is different from reading a child's body language. The first reason is that they are young and have not yet learned to control their emotions. If a child is sad, they cry. If a child is happy, they smile. If they are angry, they yell and make mad faces, and if they are embarrassed, their cheeks turn red, and they hide their face. Some children might even decide to tell you about the emotions that they are feeling. Children are new to the world and have no reason to hide the things they are going through.

Because of this, children have body language that is extremely easy to read. They do not distinguish how to control their emotions, so they always show how they feel. If you read the emotions of a child, you are reading what they truly feel.

Another important thing to note about reading the body language of children is that since they do not yet know how to hide their emotions, they also are unaware of the body language signs that they portray. They are not capable of sending the opposite signal of how they feel like adults are.

Their lack of awareness of their own body language can also make it easy to spot when a child is lying. A child might try to hide the truth through their words, but they do not have the wherewithal to think to conceal it in their body language as well, often allowing tells to slip through that they are not telling the truth or are omitting part of the truth.

For example, my sister has a five-year-old daughter who likes to sneak chocolate chip cookies before dinner. My sister always checks the Chips Ahoy package right before she starts making dinner, so she knows when a cookie is missing. She will still ask her daughter in the hopes that her daughter will confess on her own. My niece will most of the time try to lie about it (my personal favorite being when she claimed her father ate the cookie). However, no matter how convincing she might think she sounds, she has one big tell that she is lying: a huge smile plastered on her face. Because she thinks she is getting away with something so mischievous, this smile appears on her face as she is so proud of her deceit. When it is clear that she will not get away with it, this smile is usually replaced by another tell, i.e., her hanging her head while looking at the floor because she is ashamed at having been caught.

Everyone has the physical tell that gives them away when they are lying. Fortunately for parents, guardians, and teachers, children are unable to hide their tells until they are older and have more experience both with lying and reading their own body language.

Today that we know how simple it is to read the body language of a child, let's look into how important it is to pay attention to the signals a child is conveying. Whether you are around children a lot or not, you need to be able to read a child's body language so that you can do your part in ensuring that our children are healthy and safe. Like reading an adult's body language can help us determine if they are in a dangerous situation, we can also use a child's body language to determine if they are in any danger. The unlucky truth is that we live in a world in which people will abuse, kidnap, and otherwise harm children. We want to help children out of such situations, but it can often be hard to tell when something suspicious is going on.

Reading a child's body language can help us determine if there is more to the state than meets the eye. Because young children do not know how to control their body language, any discomfort they feel around a specific adult will manifest in such ways as to how they hold themselves around this person. For instance, if a child exhibits such body language as standing stiffly, hunching their shoulders forward to make themselves smaller, or avoiding eye contact with everyone, including the adult they are with, it could mean that they are afraid of something. If they flinch whenever the adult that they are with reaches over to touch them, it could very well mean that this fear stems from someone hurting them on a regular basis, most likely this adult. Also, suppose they refuse to initiate physical contact with this adult while still never wandering any significant distance from them. In that case, it could mean that they are afraid to have any intimacy with this adult and of doing anything to anger them.

Mind you, none of this is a reason to call the police or Child Protective Services on someone. After all, there are multiple interpretations of any given body language. Standing stiffly, hunching their shoulders forward, or avoiding eye contact, for example, could just mean that the child is not comfortable in that particular environment or with strangers. Flinching and avoiding initiating physical contact with the adult could indicate, rather than fear, that the child has a problem with physical touch overall or that they are mad with that adult for some reason. Not wandering far from the adult, even though it is natural for a child to want to explore, could simply show that the child is well behaved or not particularly comfortable with checking out their surroundings on their own.

Like with all body language reading, what a child's body language means often depends on the context. If you know the child and adult personally, it can be easier to determine what the child's body language means. If they are complete strangers, it will be trickier. Nevertheless, spotting such body language in a child will help you to be on alert so that if suspicion arises that the child is being abused or has been kidnapped, you will be ready to take action.

Reading a child's body language will also help you to be there for them emotionally. If you have a child or take care of a child for large amounts of time, they will consider you their support system. They need you to help them learn about their lives and the world around them. It includes learning how to handle their emotions.

Sometimes, a child might have an emotion that they do not yet know how to explain. They may express this feeling through body language but still feel frustrated when they are unable to put their experience into words.

As an adult who distinguishes how to read body language, you can help in this situation. You can read the nonverbal cues that the child is portraying and use them to help the child express his or her feelings verbally. It will help the child learn about their feelings and more about who they are. It will also help the child grow up knowing that feelings are healthy and that it is okay to share your struggles with those close to you. If you can help your child in this way and teach these things to your child at a young age, they will have significantly fewer emotional struggles over the course of their life. This understanding is important to any adult who deals with children, such as doctors, teachers, and parents dealing with other kids, such as their children's friends.

Parents and caregivers need to teach their children how to express their own body language. Still, they need to teach the kids about simple body language reading techniques. You might not want to call it body language reading to them because they either will not understand or will think the topic is boring, but this skill must be taught to children in whatever creative way necessary.

You might wonder why I believe it is important for children to be able to read body language since it is a science-based topic that can be complicated at times. We will explain why this is important now.

First, if your children understand that nonverbal communication has just as much meaning as the words they speak, they will understand the people around them at a new level. Take their time on the playground, for example. If they ask a friend to play with them and the friend says no but is looking at the ground and has another child staring at them as if to tell them not to play with the child, they will know that there is more meaning behind this situation. They will either be able to speak up for their friend and encourage them to do what they want. Or they will be deprived of worrying about what other people think or be able to walk away without feeling offended because they know that there was more to the conversation than a simple denied request to play. It might even be a sign that the friend was bullied away from playing, and your child will be able to express to a trusted adult what they saw.

Also, think about if your child sees a classmate that is not saying much when they usually talk all day, every day. If your child is aware of the body language of the people around them, they might notice this difference in behavior and ask the child what is wrong. It could make a profound change in the said child's day.

You might even consider the friendships that the child already has. As an adult, you know that being able to read simple body language allows you to have better friendships. It makes sense, then, that the same is true with friendships among children.

Your child will also be able to avoid being a bully better if they are aware of their own body language. They will understand that actions like rolling the eyes or walking away from someone when they are talking to them hurt just as much as mean words. They will understand these actions and avoid them to be nice to the people around them when other children might accidentally hurt their friends with actions like these without knowing the consequences.

When a child knows body language, they are able to make sure that their friends are comfortable with them. If the child sits close to a friend, they will be able to tell if the friend is okay with close contact or not. If the friend is not tolerable and shows signs of being uncomfortable, the child will know that the right thing is to move away.

A lot of these types of body language are things that children learn through real-life experience. The only problem with this is that real feelings are getting hurt if they are learning in real life, and real friends are feeling uncomfortable. The sooner a child acquires these skills, the sooner they can use body language to their advantage.

Chapter 12. Reading People Through Their Mind

How often have you heard somebody instruct you to simply say something because they can't guess what you might be thinking?

Things being what they are, this is just half evident. The individual disclosing to you this may not know, yet they are positively equipped to guess what you might be thinking. They do what desires to be done in a more unpretentious way than they see.

A great many people can actually figure out how to guess thoughts with preparing, time, center, and a specific arrangement of abilities. It isn't something just mystics can do.

Even though clairvoyants do have the best possible ability, preparing, and "gift of perusing," it is surely something that can be figured out how to a degree.

Before I give you how everything people can figure out how to understand minds, it's essential to know some foundation data on mind perusing.

When you understand the science and the brain research behind psyche perusing, you will see that it is a reachable undertaking for anybody with the assurance to learn. And there are also a few deceives you can use to give the hallucination that you understand personalities.

Those stunts become considerably more helpful when you know the reality behind brain perusing.

Characteristic Mind Readers

The motivation behind why anybody can figure out how to guess thoughts is because we do it as of now.

Even though our suspicions are often off-base, it's not because the cycle of psyche perusing comes up short. We can reflect on the considerations and sentiments of people we cooperate with.

In any case, we often center our response around what we figure they will do rather than what they are revealing to us they will do. We often observe somebody's outward appearances and body language and effectively surmise that they are discouraged, debilitated, cheerful, irate, or content.

However, what happens when somebody has a decent poker face? Would we be able to at present guess thoughts without these visual signs to guide us?

Of course.

Required Skills

Truly is don't take those numerous aptitudes to understand minds. All you want is the drive to learn and the eagerness to incline toward your instinct when it mentions to you what somebody is likely reasoning or feeling right now.

You'll clearly require some training before your capacities easily fall into place for you. Be that as it might, you do not take to purchase a precious stone ball, an exceptional deck of cards, or an abnormal outfit to guess the thoughts of others.

You should have the option to free your brain from all interruptions before you endeavor to guess what someone might be thinking. For certain people, this will be the ability that sets aside the most effort to create.

Maybe you could take some yoga classes. Not exclusively will they assist you with centering your psyche and your energy. However, they will likewise give you some quality adaptability and exercise.

If you are searching for additional assets, these may help.

Tips for Beginners

If you need to figure out how to understand minds, you can follow some basic hints to kick you off. Widely acclaimed mystic Kiran Behara created these tips.

Behara's customers incorporate the absolute most extravagant and most well-known appearances in amusement and Broadway. You should begin by rehearsing these tips for your loved ones.

You should see snappy outcomes; however, it will take some time and practice to guess total outsiders' thoughts.

So here we go.

Open up Your Spirit

Notwithstanding freeing your brain from all contemplations and stresses, you should open up your energy to the people and potential outcomes around you. Try not to consider anything.

You simply need to be available at the time. Your psyche and soul should absorb the energy radiated by the people and things around you. Yoga is incredible at showing us how to do this.

However, you can learn it all alone at home in the quietness of your room.

Simply ensure people will disregard you while you start to center your musings and energy.

Seeing and Not Seeing

Free your thoughts.

Take a couple of seconds to perceive the individual sitting close to you genuinely. Make a psychological depiction of their facial structure, hair, eyes, stance, body language, and other subtleties.

However, you likewise should see everything else around that individual.

You must have a psychological segment that isolates the individual's characteristics and the other things that don't have a place with that individual. Separate the individual from the seat they are sitting in or the divider behind them. These things must be envisioned with a particular goal in mind so you can feel all the energy being created around you.

Zero in on the Person

Presently you need to restore your concentration to that individual's face. Look at them legitimately without flinching for around 15 seconds. Try not to gaze too long, or you may intrude on the energy by causing the individual to feel awkward. Following 15 seconds pass, you will need to turn away.

Make a psychological image of their face and their eyes. What does their energy feel like? Sit peacefully now as you let the considerations and sentiments of that individual fill your psyche and your spirit. You have now really begun the cycle of psyche perusing.

Start a Conversation

It is the place you will reveal the contemplations and sentiments of the individual. You can pick any topic you like for discussion. Get some information about their work or their home life. The considerations that come racing into your own brain might be the same musings crossing the other individual's thoughts. You could promptly mention to the individual what you accept they are thinking. If you have a clad memory, you can store these contemplations for later to summarize your whole impression of their considerations in these meetings.

The key is to invite any contemplations that enter your psyche now. Regardless of whether those considerations are dull and irksome, you need to give the individual a precise perusing of their contemplations. So as to do that, you should keep your brain open to each chance.

Possibly you didn't have any sign before that your brother is discouraged, and this disclosure harms you. However, your brother should realize that you're presently mindful of his battles. And now you may have the option to support him. The capacity to guess thoughts will give you a ton of intensity; however, it's a brilliant force if you use it shrewdly.

Other Tips

There is other advice you can use to increase these tips. When you increment your capacities to zero in on others' musings and sentiments, you can use more tips to give you an away from what goes on in other people's psyches.

These tips will build your odds of progress and knock the socks off of your companions, family, and outsiders you meet in the city.

Passionate Intelligence

If you realize the individual you're conversing with, you can inquire whether they feel similar feelings you're feeling. You'll show restraint toward this. Numerous people aren't truly adept at naming their feelings. They may feel furious when they're truly simply worried.

They could feel apprehensive when they're simply prepared to proceed onward to something different. If the individual you converse with concurs with the feelings, you sense, inquire whether they can sort out any reasons they may be feeling thusly.

Finally, you can start to offer recommendations on what they ought to do close to intensify or diminish these sentiments. They will be flabbergasted at your premonition and acknowledgment.

It may sound more like psychiatry than mystic brain perusing. However, it's one of the key approaches to build up your regular aptitudes.

Create Keen Listening Skills

What do all incredible communicators share practically speaking? They should be acceptable to audience members.

When somebody talks, be totally at the time with them. Try not to tune in for having the option to react. Tune in to the other individual with the goal that you can measure and understand all that they are stating. Yet, you should likewise tune in to what they're not saying too. If somebody isn't anticipating the remainder of their day, there must be a purpose behind that. Cautious listening will assist you in revealing those reasons and make them known to the individual. So as to succeed, you'll have to figure out how to listen more than you talk some of the time. Listening is the manner in which you find out about people and their feelings.

Try Not to Ignore Emotions

The explanation people need compassion today is because they decide to. Throughout each day, we are told to disregard our emotions to complete our work. Then put on a solid face for the world.

The more we overlook our emotions, the snappier they disappear. Rather than considering the new email from the chief or what you'll have for supper later, consider how you feel. As per proficient mystics, the more you can react to your own emotions, the more you will have the option to peruse and react to other people's sentiments and considerations in your life.

Guessing thoughts is something everybody can do and isn't only something for proficient mentalists and mystic peruses. You probably won't experience a lot of accomplishment from the outset, yet you can accomplish incredible advancement with training. Absolutely never utilize your new capacities to increase a bit of leeway over another person.

If you can peruse their feelings incredibly well, you may have the option to utilize that to get your direction. Utilize your capacities to help people. Brain peruses can be extraordinary companions and emotionally supportive networks for people who simply need to vent.

You have probably thought about how things would be if you could guess other people's thoughts. A few individuals utilize their instinct for this, yet if you are not all that discerning, there is just a single decision left: reckoning out how to peruse people's body language.

We get over 55% of data through nonverbal correspondence. Allan Pease, an Australian body language master, expounded on this. Emulates, motions and other body developments can expose an individual and mention to you what they truly think or feel.

Chapter 13. Myths About Body Language

We are going to deal with some commonly harbored myths about body language and bust them to paint for you the real picture.

Body Language is Mostly Communication

Imagine having to understand what your friends say by muting your ears and simply watching their body language. Of course, you will fail at it! And odds are you will hate it too! If the world were to go mute and deaf all of a sudden and the only available form of communication left was body language. The entire planet would collapse within a matter of a few hours.

You cannot rely solely on body language to understand a person's behavior. Body language is only one form of communication and not even a major one. It is assistance to words and not the main player in the game. You cannot trust body language to help you understand what a person is saying without listening to their words. However, you can get a good or bad impression of their approach. It is a combination of communication skills that allows you to make your own decision about the honesty or reliability of the person with whom you are communicating. If you do give a clear message that you are honest by keeping your shoulders straight and looking your fellow speaker in the eye, you give a better impression than those who look downward and appear not to be taking much notice of what is being said.

Liars Avoid Eye Contact

One of the oldest myths about body language is that criminals try to avoid eye contact. Imagine if our prison system was based on the mere theory that everyone who avoided eye contact was a criminal. More than half of us would be rotting behind bars if that were the case. It is a fundamental principle of criminology and body language combined that those who lie find it hard to establish eye contact. However, an entire cult of criminals is so hardened and brazen that they have understood the art of lying and have no shame from marinating in eye contact.

They could lie about what they ate in the morning and still look straight into your eyes. Not just that, some of the notorious ones could lie to the extent of misleading and manipulating you to overthink and stress yourself out. The myth that those who have done something wrong would avoid eye contact is a thing of the past.

You can tell from the eyes the level of nervousness of the person with whom you are talking. If their eyes are constantly on the move, this is a good indication that they are not relaxed.

People Who Talk Too Fast Are Liars

Again, another one of those judgmental myths. When people talk fast, it does not mean that they are telling you lies all the way. It is true that some individuals do really talk fast when they are lying—but it does not mean the same the other way around. It depends on the context. Sometimes people talk fast because they are excited about what they are chatting about. Sometimes, that is just the way that they talk.

Maybe they are in a hurry and are trying to drive an important point home. That will force them to speak at a rapid pace and try to convey a message as soon as possible. Not all people who talk too fast are liars. The other thing to bear in mind is that some people are naturally fast talkers. They may have learned that way and may not be that articulate at getting their message across. Often, I have asked people to slow down when they talk in this way, but you will always have people whose level of nervousness comes into their speech flow. It doesn't mean they are lying or trying to hide something. It does mean that they have an inbuilt nervousness about public speaking. Use another body language in conjunction with fast speech to get a more accurate picture of the person.

Crossed Arms Is A Negative Sign

Another very commonly held myth is that crossed arms signify negativity of some kind. Generally, it so happens that in a group discussion, it is considered hostile to cross your arms and not participate in the ongoing discourse. However, crossed arms could mean a lot of other things, each as possible as the next.

Those watching a theatre play and sitting in the front row usually cross their arms in order to establish a sort of barricade between the artists and themselves. In such a case, the front row people feel vulnerable being exposed to the play from such a close angle, and crossing their arms is a form of shielding themselves. If you are in a state where those you are talking to are in a similar situation, such as a lecture room, then crossed arms can simply be doing the same thing. In a situation where manual work is being done, crossed arms may just be the speaker's way of relaxing himself between jobs. However, it still shows defensiveness and a lack of openness to other opinions for a public speaker.

Smiling While Speaking Is an Indicator of Honesty

You must have seen a public speaker employing this method. They tend to smile more when they speak rather than in other situations. Smiling conveys a feeling of security and honesty. However, most of these public speakers are so seasoned that they have mastered the art of smiling to the extent where they naturally smile while addressing a crowd. It is not plastic, but it is not genuine either. The process of smiling while speaking to a crowd has become so ingrained in their system that they cannot help but sprout a smile every time they climb a podium. However, Smiling is not a sure indicator of honesty, as is evident from development-promising politicians who are all smiles right before an election starts.

You will start to identify the difference between a genuine smile and that which would be summed up as "smarm" in order to try and charm an audience into liking a speaker who is not particularly likable. Smarm is the kind of smile that is forced, and when you are talking to others, you can generally recognize one from the other.

Fumbling Is A Sign of Lying

Not necessarily! Some people fumble naturally and have been diagnosed with the medical condition of stuttering from the very beginning. If you remember well, you will recall that we talked about how a lot of factors go into deciding the correct inference about a person's body language behavior.

While we enlisted only five of them, body language myths go on running for three miles at a stretch. It is vital to comprehend that body language is not the ultimate tool for deciphering people's true intentions and emotions. Sometimes, the tool of body language fails miserably. It is not in all circumstances that you can employ body language to give you the most accurate results.

If you assume it to be the ultimate mind reading weapon for you, you are in for a great shock. As it has been mentioned before, consider all the factors possible before applying the tool of body language to decode a person's behavior.

Body language should not be read in a vacuum. There must always be context surrounding a particular body behavior. You are undertaking it all erroneous if you isolate one instance of behavior and decode it. That is a method that will lead you to definite failure. Instead of that, try to observe body language patterns in the surroundings they are created in. Before jumping to conclusions based on one instance, understand that there may be a lot of reasons a person behaves the way they behave. Often times, it is the ongoing situation that makes a person act in a certain way.

With a female, you have to take into account the mood swings the fairer sex is subjected to on account of monthly instances of losing a reasonable amount of blood (menstruation). There could be regional factors too. Most people have their moods on a roller coaster. Mood swings are as common as cupcakes, and you have to acknowledge that people are not constant. Change is the only constant. I may not be the same person today as who I was yesterday. It is, in fact, a good sign that people change for only change could lead to evolution, and without evolution, people would go stagnant, not just evolutionarily but also mentally. Therefore, while trying to decipher a person's true feelings and motives, try to take everything there is into account and then start decoding.

Perhaps the person that you are talking to is nervous in a situation where it would be normal to be nervous. In this case, body language can be forgiven because it's justified.

Any Nonverbal Sign Is A Message

It is one big myth that needs to be busted. Many people assume that any non-verbal sign is a basis of communication. In fact, they believe that 90% of people's communication will come from nonverbal signs. But this is not true. If you accept this to be correct, you might misinterpret things or over-rely on something that does not lead you anywhere. However, you have to practice your own skills of reading your own body language and the body language of people that you have known for a long time. Perhaps you haven't really paid much attention to this, but it's time that you did because it enables you to recognize body language that has a hidden message and that which does not.

Nose Touching Is Indicative of Lying

Nose touching is said to be a universal sign for lying. But this is not true! What if the person scratching the nose has an allergy or is on the verge of sneezing? Maybe the person is really not doing it on purpose. In fact, many people take offense when people touch their nose while speaking. If you think the other person is doing it on purpose, you can simply ask if they have a cold, which will alert them not to do it anymore.

Nose touching can mean various things. It is not a good thing to fix when you are talking to someone, although it is an area of the body that may be giving you problems. You would be better carrying a handkerchief and dealing with the problem, rather than trying to prevent it by touching your nose. Also, this area of the face may have dry skin around it, which may be the reason for the touching. You need to consider each individual case before you assume that someone is lying. In fact, this sign isn't really one of lying at all, and you would be better looking at eye movements and using them as your guide.

Chapter 14. Who Is a Manipulator?

Manipulative humans are the styles of folks that use intellectual and emotional abuse to 1-up you, normally to serve their dreams for energy or manipulate. Disdain the fact that it could be difficult to tell if a person is manipulative while you first meet them. There are numerous developments that manipulative human beings regularly show, which can assist tip you off early to this kind of behavior. It is crucial to appear out for manipulation in a relationship, friendship, or with a family member because you fall prey to a manipulator. It could become challenging to reduce yourself unfastened as soon as you have gotten exceptionally worried in their life. Even though manipulators are, in the end, egocentric, they use numerous schemes and methods to cowl this up. That is why it's so difficult to perceive a manipulative character earlier than it is too late. This list will give you an excellent knowledge of what to look out for in a manipulative man or woman. If you get one or further of these tendencies to your so-referred to as friends, you higher run for the hills. So, without ado, right here are ten bona fide developments of manipulative people you have to appear out for.

Manipulative Human Beings Play the Sufferer

Manipulative human beings are well-known for always playing the victim's function and making themselves out to be extra harmless than they may be. Frequently, they exaggerate or even make up non-public problems in order that others sense sorry for them and sympathize with them. In dating, this trait of a manipulative individual often comes out as dependency or co-dependency. The manipulator may also fake to be vulnerable or weak or want consistent assistance to pull the innocent victim profound into their existence. They do that to attract quality humans to them like a magnet, a good way to exploit later and use them to meet their own egocentric wishes and dreams. With the aid of playing the prey, the manipulator can are searching for out and damage the kindness, mortified conscience, or caring and fostering instinct of the goal. Have you ever had a pal or family member who continuously requested you to lend them money or requested you to buy matters for them, the complete time making you feel guilty for now not having completed so inside the first vicinity? You have probably been coping with a manipulative person. With a bit of luck, you determined your manner out of the entice without too much struggling.

Manipulative Humans Inform Distorted or Half-Truths

Another terrible persona trait that manipulative human beings have is mendacity or distorting reality, so they usually come outright. Fantastic instances of this behavior encompass excuse-making, suppression of important information, underestimations, exaggeration, or hypocrisy. Manipulative humans realize how to bend reality to their advantage. They'll often miss or cover facts to be able to divulge them as being a liar. Manipulators deal with all interactions as though they may ultimately visit trial, and everything they say can be held towards them. As a consequence, they frequently skirt from one place to another the problem or make unclear statements so that when faced, they are able to claim they "never stated that" or that it's miles "no longer precisely what they said."

Manipulative Humans are Passive-Competitive

A similarly demanding character trait of a manipulative man or woman is that they're more frequently than not passive-competitive. A manipulative man or woman might also use this type of behavior to get out of something or to get their manner. They may even do that to make you furious lacking outright deed of something offensive towards you. A family member or friend who frequently forgets something crucial you've got instructed them or overlooks to do something for you that you requested them to perform passive-competitive maybe to control you. It is able to seem innocent, but it's far, in fact, a form of anger, and it isn't healthful for their nicely-being or your sanity.

Manipulative Humans Will Strain You

Manipulative human beings, just like salespeople, will frequently position strain on any other individual in hopes of having you decide before you are truly prepared to. The manipulator believes that you will easily crack and deliver into their desires by using anxiety and managing them. Just like the one's actual-property schemes that stress you to behave fast with the promise of big profits that don't certainly exist, manipulative humans will do something to get you to buy into their sport or advantage a few types of aspect over you. So, be cautious of all and sundry who pressures you to offer a solution earlier than you are equipped, mainly if money is involved.

Manipulative Humans Will Guilt Trip You

A manipulative buddy or family member will often guilt journey you into doing something which you do not want to do, or vice versa, out of something which you do want to do. The underlying cause for this is there, in the long run, selfish personality. Guilt journeys encompass unreasonable blaming from the manipulator, together with concentrated on your soft spot and holding you responsible for their happiness, achievement, or disasters. The manipulator works to goal your vulnerabilities and emotional faintness to coerce you into doing what they want you to do. A manipulative person will frequently make a person they may be in close courting with feel guilty if that character isn't always available. They anticipate absolutely everyone else to assist them in coping with their issues but do nothing in return. Anyone who continually expects you to be the shoulder they cry on, however, who is in no way there for you while you want the same, is most likely a manipulative person.

Manipulative People Provide the Silent Remedy

Have you ever been given the silent remedy from a friend, boyfriend, lady friend, or family member? Probabilities are you had been managing a manipulative person. Manipulative people are bullies. One of the approaches they torment others is with the aid of alienation. Actions like disregarding one man or woman in a collection, now not permitting them to voice their evaluations, or leaving them out are immature strategies used by manipulative adults to claim their dominance. With the aid of showing these behaviors, the manipulative character believes they're coming off as self-confident and powerful. In reality, however, they've low vanity and are extraordinarily self-aware. The handiest way they understand a way to make themselves sense higher is with the aid of hurting others. The next time somebody gives you the silent remedy, don't feel horrific, approximately writing them off completely. It's miles a positive sign of a manipulator and has to be no longer taken lightly.

Manipulative People Do Not Do Anything to Remedy Troubles

Manipulators will, by no means, take the blame for anything. It additionally means that they may in no way make contributions to resolving a hassle in worry that one day they will be held accountable for their movements. A manipulator intends to skate through life while not having to step up and take duty for something. While confronted with something with the aid of a chum or family member, they will both flat out lie and say they by no means did something incorrectly or will make all varieties of justifications for his or her conduct that get them off the hook. You will frequently have many unsettled arguments with a dishonest man or woman, which isn't good. A key sign of this is that a manipulator will regularly quit a controversy or conversation that isn't going their way, without you even realizing it. It's far vital to recognize the way to address warfare well; however, the manipulator cannot do this because they're so centered on themselves and always being inside the proper. Any exact dating may be one in which each human surely needs to assist every other. In case you are coping with someone who can in no way paintings through trouble with you, there is a great hazard that they are now not the proper individual for you.

Manipulative People Choose to Play on Their Home Ground

As we have already set up, the character of a manipulative man or woman is very controlling. A manipulative character will generally insist on assembly or interacting with you in an area in which they feel extra powerful and in control of the situation. It could be their workplace, automobile, domestic, or any other residence where the manipulator senses awareness and ownership. The manipulator, in the long run, does this for two motives. One, they want to hold the upper hand with the aid of being in their consolation sector. And two, they want to weaken you via taking you out of yours. It ought not to be just bodily, both. A manipulator will attempt to take you from your comfort area emotionally and financially as well. Be cautious of everybody who's in no way willing to come out of their comfort zone for you or meet you midway. It's far never an amazing sign.

Manipulative People Rationalize Their Conduct

If ever approached about their manipulative phrases and deeds, a manipulator will make it appear as if it is not a great deal or will shift the responsibility onto someone else, someway making you sense horrific for them usually. However, it's miles, the manipulator who makes a big deal out of things. Until you say something to them approximately it, and then they fireplace every cannon they have got back at you to distract you from the principal subject matter at hand. Manipulators also don't have any empathy for the humans who've helped them and could even pass up to attack those humans, need to experience protecting, or want to cowl up one among their actions or deeds. The manipulative man or woman commonly knows that they have trouble but make it out to look like it's miles the world towards them, instead of the alternative way around. To the manipulative man or woman, not anything they do is ever wrong. Instead, it is always a person else's fault, and there's usually an excuse to rationalize why the manipulative individual said or did what they did.

Manipulative Human Beings Shake Your Confidence

Manipulators regularly cross overboard messing about with different people with the aid of the use of little blow jabs and abuses. Genuine friends ought to sense relaxed poking a laugh at each other harmlessly, but manipulative human beings continually take it a step too some distance. They try this, particularly in groups or social conditions, to undermine others and set up their dominance. Suppose you have a pal that continually leaves you feeling much less than brilliant approximately yourself. In that case, they will be a manipulator, and you ought to cease your friendship with them without delay.

Chapter 15. Dark Psychology and Women

Dark psychology is usually linked with the exploited behavior of people. These types of behavior are perceived very negatively. They often complete successfully for power and resources, and it usually highlights for men, but the samples of women with diversities can also not be neglected. The women's associative behavior that is very antisocial and the trade that hypnotizes and underestimates women's ability to receive and be evil is often taken in very fewer women exploit others. Yet, all of our population don't expect a woman to be threatening. They are often taken very positively, softly, and non-threatening. Even if the women harm, it is minimized, and women are very less responsible for the reactions. Also, they are very less held responsible for the actions, and because of the reason women even have done because the behavior is so unexpected.

It is the reason women think whatever they do, they can always gain sympathy in front of society, which is not necessary but somehow true.

Not everybody knows this dark psychology horror. It would benefit the women, or if they are aware of themselves' darker side, they are afraid of the headed monster. They often don't like to talk about this Complex topic where it is often said that women are the worst Enemies of other women and themselves.

It is very weird to listen to this and talk about it where it is. It is one of the highest growths in society nowadays. Women's empowerment is stronger than any other Era. People are more liberal and more vocal about women's empowerment.

They talk about it more openly. The topic of feminism is so wide and addressed and portrayed in such a beautiful way that everybody comes ahead to give their part and add; however, there is something inside every woman that reacts against their kind goes against their own will.

How it may not look wrong; however, the journey is not so easy, which is a lot of people say that it's a woman who breaks down another woman. Downgrading other Downgrading by Downgrading by life can be hard sometimes anywhere pulling Each Other back. We don't think of it often, and it is a very innocent reality that we are not aware of. It remains in their selves. Town selves' personality is negative, but it is demeaning and taken as negative because that is how we perceive. We know it is a fact that we experience space at every stage of life, but we don't discuss that. We should not discuss that women's empowerment is all about human behavior should be controlled. The women's darkest psychology should also be understood and taken in charge as it is taken in charge of the men. With men, women can also be harmful when it comes to this as compared to men.

Gossiping

There is no boundary set by dark psychology for the people. That's the same with the woman. The backbiting and the gossiping nature are the women's basic nature; it has no boundaries that are defined fun in doing so ever they don't care if anybody sentiments are being hurt.

In contrast, they are being hurt. Women tend to talk so disgustingly about other women they find entertaining; however, it is very shameful because they don't understand how much attention-seeking. It is often taken as a trait of women; however, they don't understand how attention-seeking and how embarrassing it gets, no matter if people are enjoying it, but it still looks really bad. Gossiping might look fine but can ruin another person's reputation because nobody is born a perfectionist, and nobody is born Evil. They are good on the inside; however, if a person is spreading rumors about someone, it can ruin the reputation and affect them similarly, it can of the people themselves.

It is right to be fully solved. They are being offended because if a person is gossiping, for example, if they are gossiping and confronted about their bad habit, they lose control. It does not mean that they stop doing it because it is not bound. They won't do it that openly but they would still do it is because they feel there is nothing wrong with it, and once they are pinpointed for it, they would start to pull away from people instead of abandoning this habit of themselves. They are not that trustworthy to give out secrets to them, and they can also forget someone. When women gossip, they don't know when to stop and what to say, and it can hurt someone genuinely. It gives out negative energy from them. One of the biggest things that women associated with dark psychology give out so many negative Vibes from them that are not our society is used to looking at the home. When they have them too, they always think that they would be that sweet child of people when they are not.

Bad Wording

Usually, females criticize others without giving it a thought, which doesn't take charge of everything. A woman is working to make another woman let down, and they don't feel sorry for it. Older women are bringing down the younger ones; younger ones do it to the old ones. It is an unhealthy practice overall. The funny thing is that whatever they say is so easily digestible to the people that they don't even ask them to shut up then and there. The most common practice of this is in every household between a mother in law and daughter in law relation and even the value educated people tend to do it and the thing that is the part of human nature. However, they don't understand that it can lead to something very aggressive, and still, they don't stop or refrain from doing so.

Glaring

Women are born with the most beautiful eyes, and so are men. The woman is praised for the eyes throughout their life, but it is one of the women's most typical characteristics. They glare others to their soul and give out dirty looks to everybody around them, and it is an incoming threat in general.

We often talk about bringing changes in women's empowerment forever. They can do anything that brings joy to them, and they would judge another woman by clearing at the measure; it would make them feel any better.

But they do it so the other person can feel very uncomfortable and they find betterment in doing so and they would laugh out loud, later on thinking about it. It is a very belittle characteristic of every woman; however, they don't want to help the darker side of the personality, so as a result, they don't stop doing it.

Insecure and Jealous

Women are extremely unconfident as compared to men. The same thing arises when they fear losing anyone they are attached to or something they want badly. They are very fragile, and in that situation, they suffer more emotional jealousy than any other, and it is found in any age of the women regardless of how old they are, and they can do anything to for it. They don't want to lose someone they love no matter what happens. Women react to certain situations, and insecurity and jealousy are quite common in them; however, insecurity becomes an extreme obsession if it is not taken care of.

Comparison and Competition

It sometimes happens that people are very competitive. These are the words in the personality that bring out the best outcome in people, especially women. It gets negative when they demoralize and destabilize and push Each Other down when there is a cold war among them. It just comes with a very competitive nature and then compares them with other women irrespective of any relationship and friendship. It happens quite frequently, which is why we live in a place where there is so much competition going on. Everything is going so digital the competition becomes natural; however, there are two types of competition.

There are one healthy competition and one unhealthy competition among competitions, and women are competing against Each Other. They don't look at the outcomes and what it will bring, which is why it brings out an unhealthy competition between them that brings out the worst in them. It is always necessary to hold the Horses of the hidden and powerful demons, working on the dark side. They are always competing, and they need to know that everything is temporary, and harming anybody while working to get something is not something great to do.

Belittling

The darker side of every human being gives them the feeling that they are superior to others, and they have nothing to do in their life. When that happens to them is that they start thinking that the world revolves around them. They try to belittle others because it is very easy to do so instead of showing gratitude to them, and they do anything to make others wrong. When they are criticized or shown the reality, they won't do anything to make it better. Instead, they always put other people down and want to preserve their superiority over others. They always want to have a high status in front of everybody, so what they think is necessary to do so to look better and everybody, whereas they are just making a fool of themselves, which is quite toxic.

Women cannot usually understand this behavior. People must admit and examine themselves, which is the above dark psychology because it can disturb women's life and people around them because not every woman is like this.

But there are certainly some women whose darker side is more powerful than the other side of their life. Every human being has a dark and light inside. It happens women's approach is how they see different things. Similarly, when feminism has become the town's talk, women should understand that there is a light side of feminism and a dark side of feminism. There is so much more related to the community, especially when their traditional ideas on the concept of femininity. It targets women in a particular way of living in a particular way of acting; however, some women do not agree with the feminism idea and its criteria. They never oppose their beliefs, which are that living like a nice girl is not enough. It may be a pleasant experience to see what it takes to take the whole of the darker side. Still, they need to understand that feminine energy is such a beautiful gift for women to experience by the substrates woman to be only the underside of themselves. They are unaware of how the direct energy works, but they keep falling into a pit hole.

Chapter 16. Techniques of Dark Psychology

Reverse Psychology

A first tactic that a dark persuader can use is reverse psychology. This technique consists of assuming a behavior opposite to the desired one. It is with the expectation that this "prohibition" will arouse curiosity and induce the person to do what is desired.

Some people are known to be like boomerangs. They refuse to go in the direction they are sent to but take the opposite route. It works better when someone else is educated and chooses instinctively rather than thinking about things. They can introduce the intention to do X thing when they suggest the 'do not do X.' When you claim that you will do it, you may wonder whether you will do so.

A dark persuader can use this type of behavior because it is a weakness that the victim has. Take an example of a friend who loves to eat junk food at any opportunity he gets. The dark persuader knows this and will suggest that they eat because it will be good for him, knowing that the friend will choose fast food, anyway.

Reverse Psychology can be used in sales techniques when dealing with a difficult customer.

In this case, the seller can say: "this is a product for rich people. I don't know if it can work for you because it costs a lot of money".

So, the seller is like saying: "I don't want to sell it to you. It's not the right product for you since you can't afford it," just because reverse psychology leads the person to want the product even more.

Masking True Intentions (Door in the Face)

Masking true intentions is another tactic a dark persuader will use to get what they want. A dark persuader will disguise their true intentions from their victims and can use different approaches depending on their victims and the surrounding circumstance. One approach a dark persuader can use is using two requests consecutively because people find it hard to refuse two requests in a row. Take this example; a manipulator wants $500 from their victim. The dark persuader will begin by explaining why they need $1000 while stating what will happen if they cannot come up with that amount. The victim may feel guilt or compassion but will kindly explain to the manipulator that they cannot lend the amount because, quite frankly, it's more than they can manage to give when the persuader lessens the amount to $500, which was what they wanted from the beginning. They will attach the amount with some emotional reason where the victim will be unable to refuse the second request. The dark persuader walks away with the original sum, and the victim is left confused about what took place.

The Blame Game

If the manipulator wants to make you do something against your will, he will have a better chance of getting that behavior by making you feel guilty. Blame is one of the most powerful manipulation techniques known to humankind. Guilt can be used to manipulate people by making them feel inferior to the help and support they have received, or it can also be used to make others feel inadequate for a "condition" they have. Think about all those times you hear people say, "things would be different if I weren't sick." It is one of the most rudimentary ways to make someone feel guilty, but it is very powerful. Besides, you might hear others say things like, "remember when you need my help? Now I need your help." It is a clear attempt to convince someone to follow the manipulator's intentions.

Putting the Other Person Down

Through this technique, we try to make the other person feel less capable than he is. For example, you find every pretext to point out to the victim when makes a mistake, and you do it repeatedly to throw off his self-esteem. A person with low self-esteem is manageable and controllable, therefore manipulable. This way, the manipulator will feel in control of the situation.

When a person tries to manipulate you with this technique, remember that they will attack your identity, telling you phrases like "you are incapable" instead. They will never tell you, "you are behaving like an incapable person." To react to this technique, you have to detach yourself from this psycho-trap. Instead, you need to think that the person is judging your behavior at that moment and not your identity.

Leading Questions

It involves the dark persuader questions that trigger some response from the victim. A persuader may ask a question like, "do you think that this person could be so mean?" This question implies that the person will be bad in one way or another. An example of a non-leading question is, "What do you think about that person?" When we use leading questions, dark persuaders ensure that they use it carefully. Dark persuaders know that when the victim feels like they are being led to trigger a certain response, they will become more resistant to being persuaded.

When the dark persuader feels that the victim has to be aware that he or she is being led, they will immediately change tactics and return to asking the leading questions only when the victim has come down.

Fatigue Inducement

The impact of mental fatigue on perceptual, emotional, and motivational factors are complex. In exhaustion, special effects can be assumed to rely on the operation's essence that causes fatigue. This study investigated the impact of exhaustion on different activities based on working memory demands on brain function and efficiency. The results showed that driving quality was not impaired by exhaustion. The effects of fatigue on novelty therapy depended on the mental requirements for the task that caused fatigue.

Creating an Illusion

Create exaggeratedly high or unrealizable expectations. But presenting and selling them in such a powerful, persuasive, and tempting way for you that you'll end up believing it.

With this technique, it is likely to make the victim see the most beautiful future so that she will be willing to do anything to make it happen, even spend a lot of money. The goal is to make people "daydream" to give them the hope of living their lives to the full.

Commitment and Congruity

Highly skilled and sophisticated manipulators know that building trust capital is essential, especially when building a long-term approach. Think about the most sophisticated conmen you can imagine. These are individuals who take time, often years, building up trust around them through congruent behavior so that others can tumble into their trap.

At first, no one suspects the least bit in this individual as they have earned everyone's trust. As they gain more and more trust, they can use that trust capital to deceive others. It gives them some leeway in case they slip up. Given their track record, they will always have the benefit of the doubt.

This tactic is not common in less-sophisticated manipulators as it requires a great deal of dedication. Impulsive individuals will never be able to pull this off as they focus more on short-term rather than long-term gain. Through this type of tactic, many manipulators can build a name for themselves in their chosen domain. However, they are often exposed. When this occurs, the world is shocked to learn that who they thought was a pillar of their community was actually a manipulator.

One good example of this is a cheating spouse. An individual may cheat on their spouse for years without them noticing what's going on. Then, one day, the manipulator makes a mistake, whatever it is, and they are exposed. The shock that comes to the victim is overwhelming.

The reason why this tactic always backfires is due to the fact that the manipulator doesn't know when to stop. The longer they go without getting caught, the more they think the con will last forever. History has taught us that everyone gets caught eventually.

Reciprocity

It is the classic "quid pro quo," in other words; you scratch my back, I'll scratch yours. However, the victim doesn't know the extent to which they are being manipulated.

A great example of this can be found with informants.

When a manipulator wishes to extract information from someone, they may offer tidbits of information of their own in the hopes of motivating the victim to furnish the information the manipulator is looking for. However, the key to making this tactic work is that the manipulator must give information of little or no value while extracting information that may be profitable.

Manipulators also use this tactic when doing favors. They build up capital and then "call-in" favors. While this may seem like it's perfectly reasonable, it is a manipulation tactic as the manipulator doesn't do favors out of the goodness of their heart. They do it so that they can have people they can rely on in times of need. Alternatively, they can resort to guilt or even blackmail if the other party refuses to cooperate.

Scarcity and Demand

Often, manipulators realize that they have something, or at least have access to something, that people really want. When this occurs, they can manipulate those around them by creating a false illusion of scarcity.

Earlier, we talked about how advertisers generally use phrases such as "limited quantities available" or "while supplies last." These phrases have become so cliché that no one really buys into them anymore.

Yet, manipulators can make this work by creating a sense that there really is a scarcity of a product or service. Some of the more outright, devious ways of pulling this off are by planting fake informants who spread lies. When these lies spread, people may begin to panic and flock to get the products and services in question.

Another way of pulling this off is by spreading rumors on social media. Some people fall for it, and some don't. In the end, the goal is to create enough confusion so that no one is able to tell the difference.

Lastly, manufacturers may go as far as hoarding supplies in order to create an artificial scarcity. It has worked well throughout history. In fact, it's worked so well that it is illegal in most countries. Still, manufacturers can pull this off by controlling the entire supply chain of their products. So, any disruption along that line will cause scarcity, thereby creating panic in people. The manufacturers themselves are not responsible for the scarcity as they are not the ones who technically caused the issue.

Consensus

This tactic consists of setting situations in such a manner that people will agree to them regardless of what it is. Governments do this all the time. For instance, they know that no one will ever agree to a tax hike. Yet, they frame the situation in such a manner that if people wish to continue receiving government benefits, they need to accept the tax hike as there is no other way to fund it. So, people reluctantly accept the tax hike out of fear of losing their benefits.

Chapter 17. Practical Exercises For Mind Control Prevention

The real question here is why, in the first place, would anyone want to control your mind? Some people may not want to check out some of these exercises because they feel like there would be no reason for a person to try to control their minds in the first place, but you must know that there are many reasons people may want to control your mind. Some of the reasons why people would want to control your mind include:

- They want you to get something for them: It may be money, documents, or any other thing. They have chosen you because they know you are the only one that can get it for them. As such, you become their mind control project. There are even stories of people that say that they were robbed one way or the other, but when they checked the security tapes, the people who called the police were the robbers. Sounds strange, right? A professional can get you to rob your own house and plant a bomb in there by yourself, even if you have no bomb training.

- They may want information: This is another reason why someone would want to hypnotize you. You do not necessarily need to have money for someone to need something from you. They may need access codes or maybe the names of people in a place. What they want to do with the information is a total mystery, but the thing is that you might have succeeded in telling them things that you would not normally tell them if you were not hypnotized in the first place.

Exercise 1: Do Not Keep Your Eyes in One Position

People who tend to control the minds of others can be very skilled at times. Some of them would want to use everything they can to get your attention to persuade you and control your mind at all times. When you notice that you are in the presence of someone that wants to control your mind, try as much as possible to keep your eyes in random motion. Do not let your eyes focus on one thing simultaneously, especially if that thing is something they are holding.

There are various ways a person can control your mind, and your eyes are a good gateway for that to happen. You do not want your gateway to be wide open and for you to be defenseless when someone is trying to get into your mind. When someone is trying to control your mind, and you notice, all you have to do is avoid any kind of eye contact with them.

Do not let them think that they can get to you with your eyes because when they do, they will use that technique against you almost every single time. When people like that find your weak point, they tend to exploit it no matter how many times you try to hide it. It is why you mustn't let them know what that is in the first place.

You should not do certain things when trying to avoid eye contact with the person trying to control your mind. These things are said to be very important and should not be taken for granted. Some of these things include:

- **Don't let them know:** You should never let the person that is trying to control your mind know that you know what he or she is doing and, most importantly. Do not let them know that you are aware of their technique because when they know that you are aware of their technique, they will tend to change it immediately, and they might still be able to get you one way or the other. If you want to be able to get out of that problem, all you have to do is act oblivious.

- Don't get distracted: Getting distracted around a person who is trying to control your mind is the last thing you want to do when it comes to avoiding them. When you want to avoid something like mind control, you need to make sure that you are alert at all times. When you are avoiding the eyes of the people who are trying to control you, you mustn't forget and mistakenly gaze at them again because that might be your downfall. Keep your mind and body alert at all times because the moment you let your guard down, they would not hesitate to take advantage of you.

If you can keep your eyes in constant random motion and at the same time avoid all these pointers, there is a good chance that no one would be able to get into your mind no matter how many times they try. You should know that some professionals would go out of their way to get to you, but if you stick to all that you need to do, you would be one of their biggest challenges. If you play your cards right, you may be able to confuse them to the point that they would have to leave you alone and go for much easier targets. How do you confuse them? When they try to get to you with your eyes, let them get to the point that they think they have almost gotten you and make them know that they are still a long way from penetrating your mind. Once they notice that the closer they are to getting to your mind, the harder it gets; they would get confused because you would become a harder nut to crack.

Exercise 2: Don't Let People Copy Your Body Language

It is probably something that you thought was far from important, but it is. If you are in the presence of a person trying to control your mind and find out the person is sitting in the way you are seated. Even the person is mirroring your movements in any way, keep it in mind that the person is somehow trying to get inside your mind. It is why it is important to mind your surroundings at all times because they could get to you just by mirroring your hand gestures.

You may not notice them doing this because they can be subtle as they possibly can. If you even come in contact with the professionals, there is a huge chance that you will not be able to find out what they are up to until it is too late to go back. It is important to know that you may figure the person out if they are new in the game.

The thing is that professionals are very clean in their game, so clean that you may not know what they are doing until they are done. Still, when it comes to a rookie, you can be able to spot what he or she is doing almost immediately because they are not as clean as the professionals. A professional would mirror your movements and gestures very quietly, meaning that you would never catch them doing it. Still, a rookie, on the other hand, may tend to change his or her gestures immediately. You change yours. That's right; there is a huge giveaway. When you notice something like that happening around you, know that the person you are dealing with is a big-time rookie, and all you have to do is to mess with them and have fun with it. You can change your gestures and movements as often as possible and watch them get confused and break down.

There are certain things that you do not want to be doing. Especially when a person is trying to mirror your movements in any way at all, these things include:

- Never sit in one place: This is probably the last thing you want to do, especially if the person trying to mirror you is right in front of you. When you are in the presence of someone like that, all you have to do is keep moving around. You do not need to move around like a mad person. If not, they would know that you have made them.

Just move around casually like you have no idea what is going on around you, and if you can be in as many places as possible and still make as many gestures as possible, there is a good chance that they are not going to be able to see where you are going. Some of them may get so frustrated. Even decide to get your attention by subtly standing in front of you. It is so that you forget what exactly you are doing. But when they do, you can always change your gestures over and over again. It is to mess with their heads.

- Mind your surroundings: This may be hard for some people because many people find it hard to mind their surroundings, no matter how long you try to teach them. They are more focused on the things happening right in front of them and fail to see the things happening around them.

If you are that kind of person, getting into your mind would be a piece of cake because if you want to notice someone trying to get you, you have to be aware of your surroundings with every chance you get. Do not see something strange on the road or in your house and just let it go like that. Try as much as possible to investigate even if you do not get there by yourself.

- The bottom line to all of this is that if you know what is going on around you, you would be able to tackle and address it before it becomes too late, and when you address it early enough, there is absolutely no way that a person can easily control your mind.

It is imperative to know that these tips would not work for everyone, and you must also know that you would not be able to get the best results out of this if you practice it repeatedly. You need to practice in this context because there are many skilled mind control specialists out there, and you need to be on your game at all times. You do not need to sit down thinking that no one can get into your mind just because you have succeeded in successfully spotting one or two of them coming your way. There is a good chance that you will meet a person that is more than a professional. These mind control specialists do not need to get close to you to know what you are doing and control your mind.

Some of these kinds of people can come to you, and the only thing they have to do is to say a word to you, and that word may be able to trigger some series of events, and before you know it, you are under the control of someone you just met.

Chapter 18. Touch As a Form of Body Language

We engage in touching routinely. We commonly shake hands as greetings or assign to signal shared understanding. Touch, as a form of communication, is called haptics. For children, touch is a crucial aspect of their development. Children that do not get adequate touch have developmental issues. Touch helps babies cope with stress. At infancy, touch is the first sense that an infant responds to.

Functional Touch

At the workplace, touch is among effective means of communication, but it is necessary to keep it professional or casual. For instance, handshakes are often exchanged within a professional environment and can convey a trusting relationship between two people. Pay attention to the nonverbal cues that you are sending next time you shake someone's hand. Overall, one should always convey confidence when shaking another person's hand, but you should avoid being overly-confident. A firm pat on the back communicates praise and encouragement. Remember, people have varied reactions to touch as nonverbal communication. For instance, an innocent touch can make another person feel uncomfortable or frightened.

Touch can become particularly complicated when touch is between a boss and a subordinate. Generally, those in power will utilize touch with subordinates to reinforce the hierarchy of the workplace. It is usually not acceptable for it to occur the other way around. For this reason, you should make sure to be careful even in the instance of using the most trivial of touches and resolve to enhance your communication techniques with your juniors. A standard measure is that it is better to fail but remain on the side of caution. Functional touch includes being physically examined by a doctor and being touch as a form of professional massage.

Social Touch

In the United States, a handshake is the most common way one engages in social touching. Handshakes vary from culture to culture, though. In some countries, kissing one or both cheeks are more common than a handshake. In the same interactions, men will allow a male stranger to touch them on their shoulders and arms, whereas women feel comfortable being touched by a female stranger only on the arms. Men are likely to enjoy a female stranger's touch while women tend to feel uncomfortable with any touch by a male stranger. Equally important, men and women process touch differently, which can create confusing and awkward situations. One should be respectful and cautious. For instance, while you stand close to a stranger on an elevator, it is not acceptable to stand so close to them that you contact him or her.

Friendship Touch

The types of touches allowed between friends vary depending on the context. For instance, women are more receptive to touching female friends compared to their male counterparts. Touch is different depending on the closeness of the family and the sex of the family member. Displays of affection between friends are almost always appreciated and necessary, even if you are not a touchy person. One should be willing to get out of their comfort zone and offer their friend a hug when struggling. Helping others enliven their moods is likely to uplift your moods as well.

Intimacy Touch

In romantic relationships, touches that communicate love play a critical role. For instance, the simplest of touches can convey a critical meaning, such as holding hands or placing your arm around your partner, which communicates that you are together. According to recent communication studies, adults place more emphasis on nonverbal cues than verbal cues when communicating. In the earlier stages of dating, men tend to initiate physical contact in line with societal norms, but in later stages, women initiate contact. Women place more premiums on touch compared to men, and even the smallest of gestures can help calm women. They were upset.

Arousal Touch

Arousing touches are elicited by intense feelings and are only acceptable when mutually agreed upon. Arousal touches are meant to evoke pleasure and involve kissing, hugging, flirtatious touching, and are often intended to suggest sex. One should be careful about their partner's needs. One can greatly improve their communication skills and relationships by considering the nonverbal messages you send via touching behavior.

Additionally, our sense of touch is intended to communicate clearly and quickly. Touch can elicit subconscious communication. For instance, you instantly pull away from your hand when touching something hot even before you consciously process. In this manner, touch constitutes one of the quickest ways to communicate. Touch, as a form of nonverbal communication, is an instinctive form of communication. In detail, touch conveys information instantly and causes a guttural reaction. Completely withholding touch will communicate the wrong messages without your realization.

Ways of Improving Touch in Appropriate Contexts

Pat Someone on the Back When You Grant Them Praise

If your colleague or friend has graduated, earned a promotion, or married, then pat them on the back. Giving a pat suggests that you are happy with the person and are encouraging them. Touch has a therapeutic value that relaxes the mind and the body and helps an individual feel secure and appreciated. At school, you must have felt valued and loved if you were patted on the back.

Initiate Discussions with a Touch to Create Cooperative Relationships

Studies have established that touching a person increases their willingness to cooperate and work with others. They were establishing physical contact with an individual that you wish to initiate a conversation with can help. Sometimes the target person may not realize that you touched them but will register subconsciously and establish a bond.

Extend the Handshakes

Shaking hands shows confidence and simplicity in interacting with others. Touch helps build trust between two people. Make your handshakes firm when shaking hands with people. It is also necessary to remember that some health conditions may make one shy away from shaking hands, and this includes hyperhidrosis, which makes the palms of the person sweat. With sweaty hands, the individual is likely to shun handshakes, and this has little to do with the context of the conversation.

Adjust the Touch-Type Concerning Context

As indicated, touch is highly contextual. For instance, the Japanese do not favor shaking hands, and a person in this environment will avoid shaking hands at all costs. In the American context, shaking hands is encouraged. For this reason, one should adjust their touch-type depending on the contexts. It might be welcome to continuously hold your partner's hands while the same is creepy when talking to a stranger or to a colleague at the workplace.

Another form of touch is tickling, mostly reserved for lovers, parents versus children, and peers. For instance, a mother may tickle her baby, which is a therapeutic touch and is permissible. On the other hand, children of the same age set may tickle each other, which is permissible. However, it is inappropriate to tickle an adult when you are not lovers, or the relationship between you and them is formal.

Touch as a Form of Abuse

Expectedly, there is a thin line between permissible touch and physical abuse. If not, certain one should avoid initiating touch unless fully certain its meaning to the target person. Pushing someone or pinching someone is considered a form of physical abuse. Kicking or striking someone as well as strangling, are forms of physical abuse.

- Touch as a game

In some contexts, a touch is a form of the game, especially teasing. Touch as a form of the game should only happen where the participants are peers and are receptive to it. For instance, your friend or classmate may blindfold your eyes with the palms of their hands from behind. The participants in this tease may touch each other. For instance, the blinded person may try to feel your arms or head to guess the person's identity. In this form of touch, the scope of teaching allowed is large and may be equivalent to that of lovers.

Chapter 19. Facial Expression As a Form of Body

Facial Expressions and Physiognomy

We want to understand by facial expressions all phenomena that we can observe in the face of a human being. By this, we mean both facial features, eye contact, and viewing direction, as well as psychosomatic processes, such as pale. Finally, we also include entire head movements with such. As a nodding, oblique (the latter, depending on the context, of course, the attitude can be assigned).

In general, we are concerned with the evaluation of congruence signals. As long as the facial expressions match the verbal utterances, we usually do not take them very well. When the incongruity is strong, it attracts even the most inexperienced. But the experienced can take note of a variety of facial expressions to perceive even slight disturbances or incipient incongruence (or, of course, first signs of relief, approval, etc.). Often only a barely perceptible grin indicates that someone is making a joke. Or it may be that a (questioning) raised eyebrow is the only indication of contradiction when the other one says, "Yes, I understand what you mean."

At this point in the seminar, the question often arises of how far one can manipulate his non-linguistic signals to what extent z.

For example, it would be possible not to let it be noted whether one grasps or approves of something?

Answer: Of course, anyone can learn to influence his body language to a degree.

However, it is particularly difficult to get the facial muscles under control. So, you can often observe that someone looks outwardly calm because he has learned to control his hands (for example, by intertwining his fingers to prevent him from playing around nervously). Nevertheless, an inner restlessness (if any) will express itself, and most likely, in the face. Why is the manipulation of our facial muscles so difficult? The word "manipulate" includes the word manus (lat., The hand). However, to be able to handle something skillfully, you have to know it well. We do not know enough about our facial muscles to get a grip on them. In general, we do not know how we look or how we affect others. Try it (right now) yourself! Check your facial expression.

A real experiment on this would look like this: You get a small pocket mirror, which you always have at hand shortly. Now and then, you will try first to feel your expression and then immediately see it in the mirror. Ask yourself before and while you look in each case: "How do I look now? How do I now seem to others?" (Or how would I act on others now?)

You will experience very exciting surprises, although they are not positively fascinating for everyone. Some people are horrified when they realize how often they have a discontented, disgruntled look around their mouths and eyes that they did not even realize! However, the less you know about his facial expression, the less you really know him, the less you can, of course, also manipulate him. That is, you have it.

A second mini-experiment that you can do immediately confirms this. After reading the instruction, close your eyes briefly and try to relax your face, especially the lips and chin, as much as possible. Observe and feel consciously what it feels like.

Stop.

Now three questions:

- Have you achieved relaxation?

- Have you got a feel for feeling your facial muscles?

- Were your lips laid together loosely?

If you answered yes to the last question, then you have confirmed what FELDENKRAIS (29) means when he says:

"How is it that such an important part of the body as the lower jaw is constantly held up? Muscles that work while we are awake, without even the slightest sensation that we are doing something to hold the jaw up?

To drop it, you even have to learn how to apply the muscle inhibitor. Suppose one tries to relax his lower jaw so much that he falls through his own weight and opens his mouth completely, so you will wonder how difficult that is. If it finally succeeds, one will notice changes in the facial expression and in the eyes. It will probably also be noticed later that one usually presses his lower jaw upwards or keeps his mouth firmly closed."

Did the little experiments teach you a little about how little you normally know about your facial muscles? Every actor who deals (or mainly) with pantomime knows the difficulties associated with the conscious creation of a desired facial expression.

Knowing the difficulties of manipulating one's facial expressions is essential if we want to control our facial expressions. With too much control, if they succeed, resulting in a robotic, non-living expression! But Information is also essential if we want to interpret the signals of others. Since the other person is just as unaware of his facial expressions, one can rely on the facial expressions in general quite well.

By the way, the study of the facial expression is divided into two areas, the facial expression itself and the physiognomy. Under the latter, one understands not the momentary, ever-changing expression but the facial features that a person has in general. I call that the "facial expression." If a person often expresses displeasure by squeezing his lips and lowering his mouth's corners, it does not surprise him if he has so-called mis-wrinkles after years. These are deeply scored "lines" that run down from the corners of the mouth. Anyone who looks at the young SCHOPENHAUER's face and then compares it with the old image can clearly see this (see also: "the compressed mouth").

The physiognomy also includes an interpretation of the facial or nasal form. Although the separation from the phrenology, which GALL (94) founded, is not clear. We will not practice physiognomy or phrenology.

Nevertheless, we cannot help but, for example, to register deep scored wrinkles when we consciously perceive. But even such a signal alone has no significance. To be sure, the wrinkling itself is unmistakable, so that we know that this man must often have his lips pinched and the corners of his mouth lowered, but we do not know why this happened. Of course, it may be that this human being is a "Griesgram" who does not like anything. But it may just as well be that this person has suffered a serious illness or a hard fate. Think of persons who have lost a loved one, to people who have spent years in concentration camps or to those who have been tortured (as is commonplace in certain parts of the world today), etc.

It has become customary to assume the following subdivision:

- Forehead area (including the eyebrows)

- Midface, i.e., eye, nose, and cheek area (for most authors, including the upper lip)

- Mouth (or lower lip) and chin area

The Forehead Area

It is believed that the forehead, with its wrinkles and eyebrows, provides information about processes of thinking and analyzing. Although this opinion seems to be a remnant of GALL's phrenology (94), I still hold the forehead's statements applicable. Nevertheless, of course, there is the demand for caution on the part of "scientificity" of such interpretations.

The Midface

The eye, nose, and cheek area are also referred to as the sense of sight. Most authors include the upper lip because they make more nuanced detail statements than we do. We usually only speak of the Lips or from the mouth, so that it is not so important in our frame, where you want to draw the border exactly.

The sense of sight is said to give us clues about taking on the outside world. It is because the eyes are the "window to the world." But they are rightly called the "window to the soul." So that we see that information from the inner life can also be seen in this area. It should also be borne in mind that the mouth also plays a key role in environmental uptake processes.

The Mouth and Chin Area

The mouth has developed from the Ur-Maw, which already has a very simple organism. It represents the relationship to the environment, in that the organism absorbs as well as eliminates it. It is easy for small children to see that they put everything in their mouths to grasp it. Therefore, it is not surprising that the mouth plays an essential role, both when it comes to not "let in" information from the environment and when one does not want to or is not allowed to express.

Next, assign the chin part (including the lower lip) the emotional and intuitive life, and, especially the chin, the assertiveness. A person who is about to assert himself vigorously will push his chin as a mimic signal. (While the assessment of the chin shape regarding the character traits of assertiveness belongs to the field of phrenology.)

And now, let's look at the interpretations of the three facial area turns.

Since we do not want to analyze the forehead's shape, we are concerned with the mimic expressions of forehead wrinkles, horizontal and vertical. Usually, horizontal wrinkles are accompanied by a lifting of the eyebrows. But there is also a barely noticeable lifting of one or both brows, which does not wrinkle.

Horizontal Forehead Wrinkles

As a rule of thumb, we can say that the horizontal forehead wrinkles indicate that the attention has been drawn heavily. However, this strong attention can have very different occasions. For example, Zeddies (94) calls the following:

- Fright.

- Anxiety.

- Obtuseness.

- Astonish.

- Amazement.

- Confusion.

- Surprise.

Again, it becomes clear that individual signals (usually) must be seen in association with others. It also applies within a category, such as facial expressions. For the forehead, wrinkles are automatically associated with the face's other muscle movements, which open eyes (or an open mouth) can lead to. Such a combination provides, for example, the following:

Horizontal wrinkles and open eyes. According to ZEDDIES (94), the two mean signals interpreted together: "The mental attitude lies in a waiting, attentive attitude to any circumstances that offer themselves to the consciousness."

Another possible combination of two mimic signals would be horizontal forehead wrinkles forming in conjunction with half-closed (= easy squinted) eyes. This combination can be observed if someone goes to great lengths to listen; in the case of the hard of hearing, for example, or in situations in which the volume of the transmitter (including technical sound sources such as a radio) is not sufficient. The vernacular describes this with the expression "the ears are pointed." However, this formulation not only describes "in a figurative sense" but also indicates physiological processes. In fact, when we tip our ears, we actually move our severely stunted ear muscles in a reflex that is pronounced in dogs, cats, and rabbits. An additional gesture and attitude change will often accompany the effort to "play" our "spoons."

Chapter 20. Manipulation In a Relationship

The culture romanticizes deceptive relations so much when talking about the love that it can be hard to recognize them for what they are. We have lots of literature suggesting that genuine relationships are about fixation, that pure love is all-out, and that infatuated people have no boundaries or separate lives.

While many people romanticize the concept of a deceptive relationship, we have to realize that it is not real love. Sometimes it may trigger a dramatic storyline and tension that keeps the reader engaged, but there is no fun living through a deceptive relationship that is romantic.

You may have been warned of manipulating people and the fact that coercion and mistreatment are worrying; the facts are that being in a relationship of control and manipulation that never develops into ill-treatment can also be terrifying and dangerous. Just because somebody does not harm you physically does not mean you cannot feel pain from their actions yet.

Being dominated or put down by a partner can damage our faith, make us feel fearful of relationships in the future, and leave us feeling lost rather than comforted, with various mental and emotional injuries with which we should not be burdened.

You may be familiar with the symptoms of a negative relationship. You might have met a partner, for instance, who required you to wear only certain clothing items or did not want you to visit your friends and family.

This person might want to know where you are going, what you are doing, and why you are just a couple of minutes late. Manipulators are frequently very anxious people, allowing nervous thoughts to pass through their brains and control their actions. We channel their intense fear and anxiety into hallucinations about what you might do if you are not around them. They will think about their worst fears and what you can do to damage them, so they will assume you are doing these things when you are not around.

Such things may spur them to hate you if you are not around. Sometimes it may seem flattering to have someone so concerned about you. You might think, "It is so sweet that they always want to know where I am, and I am safe," but it is not their intention when someone is going to take great steps to control you.

Unfortunately, they are not concerned about your well-being. Therefore, the manipulators are thinking, "I need to make sure I know where this person is at all times, so they do not do something that I do not approve of." Your presence is their assurance that you are not meeting their worst fears about the bad things that you are doing to them when you are not both of you together. In this case, they will not be addressing your needs. The manipulator behaves only to serve the interests of his own.

A manipulator will never tell you that but will only be worried about improving the way they look to you. They are always going to use this technique to make sure you feel guilty. They will make you feel guilty if you do not respond for 20 minutes, instead of admitting that it is acceptable for a person not always to write back immediately. They would view you as if you did something wrong or disrespectful to them because, at the time, you were not around your phone or too busy to answer first.

Marriage should feel better, not confining, scary, or distressing, and having an accomplice will make you happier, not more sorrowful. There will be hard times in life. Your mate may not be understood, and they may not understand you. On the way to making you stronger, these challenges should be pure obstacles. There shouldn't be a healthy relationship that continuously drains you and tears you down, making you feel constantly exhausted.

Signs of a Manipulative Relationship

Most of us have had terrible things happening in our lives—enough terrible things that the prospect of a hero sweeping us off our feet and protecting us from any problems for whatever remains of our lives can sound extremely tempting. For this reason, we are sometimes looking in the wrong places for security, empathy, and care.

Reconsider whether your partner's support thoughts include stopping you from making your own decisions and living your own life. This partner secures you by assuming responsibility for your maxed-out accounts. Or perhaps speaking to a partner you have been struggling with does not pay special attention to you; they are trying to make you have no choice but to put all your faith in them and no one else.

A true partner knows they cannot protect you and what it holds from everyday life—they can just support when you need them. If you run into a money-related issue at some point, a trusted partner can help you pray an overabundance of unopened bills—give help, but do not take control of the situation. They will not take your passwords or insist that only a small amount of money per month be allowed until you have paid off all of your current debt. A right partner is going to offer help yet realize you need to manage your problems.

One typical manipulative relationship is making us feel guilty when we see friends and family members. Suppose we imagine someone trying to cut off their partner from their emotionally supportive network. In that case, we envision something similar to the contemptible husband in a movie made for TV that threatens his better half that she will never talk to her closest friend again. Nevertheless, deceptive spouses can also inconspicuously isolate you from your support network.

A shrewdly manipulative person will not outwardly discourage you from seeing your family because it can be an obvious sign that you should be running in the opposite direction. We will make the coercion more subtle, rather than slowly dragging you out of your life, rather than an outright ban. If your partner can convince you to apologize for an action that you know you have not done wrongly and that you are doing, your manipulative partner will realize that he or she can force you to do whatever they want you to do.

Each time you go out with your buddies, your partner can sulk until you blow off other friends just to save the tension. Perhaps your partner will make negative remarks about your loved ones until you begin to believe that the thoughts they have about these people are valid.

You may even have a hobby or an event you enjoy trying to get your manipulator to stop doing it. They will ensure that you know that your interest is idiotic and will ridicule you until you give it up.

The scrutiny of a controlling partner may not always appear as such. It can be framed reasonably and rationally, implying that your partner is just trying to help you. They might even tell you they are trying to help you.

At school, they will research your decisions. Some of their sentences may include: "Why do you choose to use it for your presentation? You are not thinking about what the boss will think? They are going to question your spending habits and how you are going to buy things with questions like, "Did you have to buy another shirt?" Manipulators are going to spin their words, so it is not clear that the choices you make are wrong, but a seed of doubt and insecurity is being planted.

All partners, however, examine each other periodically. Our loved ones are still supposed to look for us, and sometimes we need others to help us make choices or point out bad habits. Remember, always test this person's true purpose and determine why they had wanted you to change your actions.

Sometimes a manipulator may ask for access to your personal belongings in a relationship, but they will not grant you the same rights. We may know all your secrets, but we rarely trust you.

They are not just less likely to share, and they are not helping you.

This type of behavior demonstrates that the other person dominates. Your partner does not reserve the right to search your emails or texts or asking for your passwords because they say they are concerned that you may be cheating. There is a distinction between having insider facts and having healthy independence from your partner, and when you are in a relationship with someone, you do not have to surrender that.

Every so often, sincere couples healing from a disaster would require the weakened spouse to view each other's messages as a form of transparency. If this is not an agreement you have worked out directly with your partner, it is incorrect.

By emotional influence, coercion is all about influencing the way someone else thinks and acts. Coercion is veiled with emotion, or at least what appears to be a sort of empathy. Most of the time, this is a calculated attempt by the manipulator concerned to relate to the victim.

We must recognize the impact it has had on us to overcome this manipulation completely. If you want a healthy relationship with someone, we must look at all the ways we have been affected by their relationship. It may be the first sign that there is a manipulative relationship if that impact is negative.

Most manipulative people have four standard attributes: they know the weaknesses.

- They use your vulnerabilities against you.

- They persuade you to surrender something of yourself to serve them through their quick plots.

- If a controller triumphs in manipulating you, he will likely repeat the crime until the mistreatment is stopped.

- They are going to have a lot of different reasons for keeping you around and controlling you.

One might just be because a past relationship damages them. We may have confidence issues that have made it difficult for them to be transparent and consider other partners. This situation can make them feel like they need to manipulate you to keep you loyal to them.

Understand Your Rights in a Relationship

It can be difficult to understand how to get out when someone is in the midst of an abusive relationship.

Manipulators are good at creating uncertainty, so they can also avoid blame for trying to control others instantly. Recalling your rights is the way to ensure that you are safe.

These are the things you completely have the right to take away and should never allow another person to take away. If you can remember these consistently, manipulation will be easier to confront as it happens, and it will be easier to recognize when a conversation may be toxic.

Then again, you may give up these rights if you convey vulnerability to other people. Our common, main human rights are the following: you deserve respect from others, especially those you respect.

Your thoughts, feelings, and emotions can be expressed.

You reserve the right to understand your own needs, share them with others, and do what you need to do to meet those needs, as long as you do not take anything away from others.

Chapter 21. How to Know if Someone Is Lying Through Body Language

Psychology of Lying

Almost everybody tells a lie once a day or gets lied to. Lying is a part of being a human being with the motive to protect himself against certain situations or to praise oneself. The reasons for lying are endless. Can you remember the very first time you realized that you were lying, or you were lied to?

There is a series of ideas as to why people lie, ranging from saving the hurting of oneself or something else, or with the motive to achieve personal gains. However, science has a different perspective on why people tell lies and the different types of lies. Nobody likes to be lied to, and it's not surprising to find that most liars do not like to be considered as liars.

You wouldn't have any trouble in believing anybody in a perfect world, but unfortunately, it's not perfect, so you need to be cautious about whom to believe and who not to. There are professionals primarily in law enforcement that are trained to detect liars. You don't have to have access to the polygraph machines so that you can understand who is lying to you and who is not. There are many behavioral clues that you could use to know who is telling the truth and who is not.

Detecting deceit will give you the rare opportunity to choose your associates wisely without having to say a word. The body goes into an immense ball of anxiety when a person lies. The trained eye will be able to detect these small variances that occur. Although words may speak their version of the truth, the body never lies. Deceit is the act of covering up the way you truly feel through seeking control. Often, that control is executed in a sloppy manner, thus leading to dominant cues that signal deceit. Whether it's a large lie or a little white lie, the results of dishonesty come with a variety of consequences.

Essentially, people lie as a subconscious form of protection. They are either hiding their negative behavior or protecting their reputations. Even when used to exaggerate a story, they may be attempting to protect the fact that their life is truly boring. They want others to find them enjoyable. Thus, various lies are told.

In general, lying requires more cognitive effort rather than telling the truth because you must work harder and strain to make your information or statement sound authentic. After you have settled on the path of lying, you must remember all the facts, but how? You already changed all facts. Having presented you with the small background about detecting lies, the following are now the various ways you could identify a person lying to you.

Some Liars Are Always Tense and Nervous

It takes a great deal for a liar to pull together fake points to convince you. However, this is not the case with professional liars. These know how to do it just right. But for those who are not used to telling lies, you will quickly notice that their body language is betraying them. On the other hand, a person who tells the truth looks relaxed and happy as far as the story that she is telling is not a sad or painful one.

Some Talk Unusually Slow

If you have ever observed or listened to somebody telling a true story, you might have realized that his or her speech is normal. However, some liars would tend to take quite long before they can respond so that they have a chance to edit their story. They act as if they are trying to be consistent and avoid negative comments. But for other people, it might be hard to detect when they are telling lies, especially salespersons; this is because they have recited lines they keep on mentioning every day with their numerous encounters with customers. You need to keep check of these factors when you are speaking to a person so that you can analyze them and determine when they are telling a lie.

The Hands of a Liar

When people are gesturing and using their hands while telling their stories, this is often seen as a truth-telling sign. However, if the gesturing comes after telling the story, this is often a sign of lying. The mind is so preoccupied with coming up with a story and realistic details that make sense that the mind is too preoccupied to gesture with their hands at the same time that they are talking. Granted, not all people use their hands when talking, but many people do, and this is a simple tactic that the FBI uses and focuses on determining whether someone is lying.

Breathing

Another good indicator if someone is lying is if their breathing suddenly changes. If you ask someone a question and their breathing changes while answering, this is a good sign that they are lying. When somebody is lying, their heart rate upsurges and they turn out to be nervous. It makes them breathe quicker and harder.

Too Still

Another good sign that someone is lying is if they are too still. It is normal for us to move around a bit while talking. It could be shifting in our seat or from foot to foot. Glancing around, hand movements, etc. However, when someone is noticeably too still, this can be a sign of deception. People are often aware that their body language can give them away if they are lying. They think that being fidgety and moving around will give them away. Instead, they do the opposite. They focus very hard on remaining very still so as not to seem fidgety. However, this has the opposite effect than what they were thinking.

Gut Instinct

Lastly, but most importantly, follow your gut instinct. It is probably one of the best ways to figure out if someone is lying to you. People are often very distracted when trying to determine if someone is lying because they focus too hard on the little signs that are supposed to tell you if someone is lying. Frequently, just listen to that other person and then ask yourself if you believe them. We instinctually know when something is "off" about someone. Sometimes we can't even accurately explain what it is or why we feel that way, but we know when something is not genuine. It could be the pitch of their voice, their facial expressions, etc.

Watch the Eyelids

If someone closes his or her eyelids for a long time, it means the person is trying to avoid eye contact. If the person blinks more than three times, it is a sign of nervousness and apprehension that you will catch him or her. If someone uses the hands to cover their eyes, this is another sign that they want to 'block-out' the truth.

Pointing of Eyes

Our eyes point at things we find attractive or where our body wants to go. If you are talking to someone lying, the person will continuously look at the door or watch, signaling the desire to cut short the conversation because they are fearful you will catch the lie.

Avoiding Eye Contact

Breaking eye contact is the most basic way to identify a lie. Someone who has complete confidence about what he or she is saying will never avoid eye contact. However, if someone is lying, he or she will avoid eye contact.

Facial Expressions

Observing facial expressions can help you detect a lie. The most common facial expressions observed in a liar are, dilated pupils, the appearance of lines on the forehead, narrowing of the eyebrows, and blinking eyes. Sweat on the forehead and an angry expression are common with these facial expressions.

Dilated Pupils

Pupil dilation indicates tension and concentration. When someone gets worried about exposure, the pupils unconsciously dilate as they think of ways to hide the lie. If you are talking to someone but unsure if the person is honest or not, look at the person's pupils for answers.

Several key facial indicators may tip you off to whether a person is lying to you. Though none of these are necessarily conclusive in and of themselves, learning to notice these indicators will be your ally when determining if someone is less than trustworthy.

Lines on Forehead

Someone lying may have lines on the forehead because of the stress the person has to bear as they seek ways to cover the lie.

Apart from the facial expression, we can also observe many other gestures in a liar.

Clearing of Throat

If someone is lying to you, he or she will probably clear his or her throat more than once as a nervous tendency to distract from the stress of telling a lie.

Backward Head Movement

When someone is telling a lie, the head could possibly move backward. This gesture occurs as the lying person tries to avoid the source of anxiety because people tend to distance themselves from things they dislike.

Hard Swallowing

The throat of someone who is lying may become dry, and additionally, they may become self-conscious of their swallowing and breathing so as not to give away their deception. Therefore, it is common for a person to swallow hard to bring moisture back to avoid clearing their throat. It is common for people trying to hide a lie.

Statement Analysis to Determine Lie

Analyzing someone's lie through his or her statement is the last step in lie detection. Sometimes what people say does not support their body language. It allows you to detect lies. People often stammer or talk at a fast pace as a way of trying to avoid discovery.

For instance, if you suspect your classmate stole your money and ask her about it, you notice darting eyes and nervousness in her tone. Her body language does not support her statement that she did not steal the money. It means she is lying and has stolen it or knows who did.

No matter how good a person is at lying, if the person's body language is not supportive of their statement, that person is lying. To identify a liar, analyze someone's body language and determine if it matches the person's statement. If the two contradict, you may have a liar on your hands.

You now have a complete idea of analyzing your target by studying body language, expressions, and gestures. It is just one way, however, to analyze people. If you wish to analyze people more efficiently, then you can use the information you gathered from your body language observations. It will give you a complete understanding of your target's state of mind, personality, habits, tendencies, thought patterns, and general operation mode.

Chapter 22. How Body Language Improves Your Mindset

Our body language is the way we speak with our outside world—and the more significant part of us don't understand, we are doing it! Body language phenomenally affects the center of who you are as an individual. It impacts our posture and physiological well-being, yet it can likewise change our psychological viewpoint, an impression of the world, and others' perception of us.

How Our Body Imparts

We utilize our body language to communicate our musings, thoughts, and feelings; we synchronize body developments to the words we express. We impart purposefully through activities like shrugging our shoulders or applauding just as through inadvertent correspondence like twisting in on ourselves or guiding our feet an alternate way toward the individual we talked about. Before spoken language was made, our body language was the primary technique for correspondence. Our body is our major method to speak with life!

How Can It Influence Our State of Mind?

Our body language is how we interface with our outside world, yet it is likewise how we associate with ourselves. How would you treat yourself? Do you slouch over when you walk, or do you walk tall and satisfied? It is true to say that you are thankful for each development that your body makes for you?

Most likely not; we regularly underestimate our body; we frequently decide to condemn it. Body language can impact our physical body and posture. However, it can likewise change how we are feeling. Having a great attitude can affect misery and cause us to keep up more elevated levels of confidence and energy when confronted with pressure.

An up and coming field of psychology, known as installed comprehension, asserts that the association between our body and our general surroundings doesn't merely impact us. However, we are personally woven into the way that we think.

Four Different Ways You Can Change Your Body Language

The followings are four ways you can change your body language.

Flip Around That Glare!

Grinning and snickering is infectious! A complete report on smiling found that a grin which draws in the mouth and moves the skin around the eyes can enact the cerebrum examples of positive feelings. So, grin and grin frequently! Regardless of whether you are having an awful day, grin at any rate! It may very well assist you with turning the day around!

Collapsing Your Arms

The intersection of the arms is a resistance system to ensure the heart and lungs. We regularly do it when we feel shaky, anxious, or disturbed. The physical obstruction gives others the feeling that we are cut off and detached from them.

The intersection of the arms is a broad idea to be an antagonistic body posture anyway. A few investigations have indicated that crossing the arms can cause individuals to progressively industrious when they feel like stopping.

If you believe you need a little additional lift to take a stab at making some regular mindset boosting homegrown cures like Hyperiforce. It contains concentrates of the bloom hypericum frequently utilized as a treatment for low mind-set and gentle nervousness.

Force Presenting

One of the significant specialists in the zone of body language is Amy Cuddy. She made members remain in high force stances and low force models for two minutes before sending them into a top weight talk with the condition. She estimated levels of the pressure hormone cortisol and the predominance hormone testosterone. The outcomes demonstrated that those remaining in high force present had expanded testosterone degrees and lower cortisol levels than those in little force presents.

Quit Slumping

It may appear glaringly evident; however, slumping not just influences your spine. It can likewise change your state of mind! Indeed, slumping can prompt back agony and an irregular spine arrangement. Intellectually, it can leave you feeling miserable, lacking vitality, and shut off from others. Sitting and standing up straighter can assist with settling back torment just as lift your life and state of mind.

Changing your posture can be trying for your body from the outset, particularly on the off chance you are accustomed to slumping over for significant periods! You may feel muscle hurts in the neck, back, and bears—don't stress, this will pass!

Meanwhile, I'd suggest utilizing Atrogel, a natural relief from discomfort cure containing new concentrates of arnica blossoms.

Improve Your Posture to Improve Your Temperament!

Body language likely isn't the first sport you'd think to look at when experiencing a low state of mind. However, investigating our body language can reveal to us how we are truly feeling. Our body language has an immediate connection to our temperament, similarly that our mindset influences our posture.

Simple ways you can fix your posture to adjust your state of mind:

- Smile when you are having a terrible day!

- Unfold your arms when you feel anxious and permit yourself to be available to circumstances.

- Turning the palms of your hands forward when you walk will urge the shoulders to unwind back as opposed to moving advances.

- Power present before pressure instigating situations like prospective employee meet-ups.

Body Language Signs When Someone Hides Something from You

Untrustworthiness. It happens in many connections—and a great deal of the time, it accomplishes more mischief than anything. It's once in a while ever astute to keep insider facts from your accomplice in a relationship. You never need to keep your accomplice in obscurity about a lot of things in your lives together. That is simply out and out insolent. It shows that you don't regard your accomplice enough to recognize that they are deserving of reality. You are saying that they aren't sufficient to be determined what's genuine—and that is, in every case, terrible in a relationship. You generally need to confess all to your accomplice, particularly about vital issues encompassing your relationship.

Be that as it may, a considerable deal of us are childish. Here and there, reality can be difficult to stomach. Now and then, a fact can place us in an extreme condition of a burden once it's uncovered. So, a great deal of us will turn to lie just to spare our butts. Your man may be blameworthy of doing as such. He may be keeping you out of the loop about something that he ought to be opening up to you.

What's more, that is hazardous for a relationship. You can't hope to make your link work if you're not being taken care of the entirety of the best possible realities. You generally need to ensure that you know all that is going on to don't wind up getting tricked or bushwhacked by anything.

Men aren't generally the best verbal communicators. You may likely know this at this point. Be that as it may, he consistently communicates through his body language and physical developments. His intuitive may be disclosed to you many things about himself without seeing it in any event. You simply need to willingly volunteer to ensure that you spot out the signs when they present themselves. You need to ensure that you keep steady over things in your relationship.

Getting and Understanding Nonverbal Signals

Lauren murmured. She'd quite recently gotten an email from her chief, Gus, saying that the item proposition she'd been taking a shot at would not have been closed down. It didn't bode well. Seven days prior, she'd been in a gathering with Gus, and he'd appeared to be extremely positive about everything. Of course, he hadn't looked, and he continued watching out of the window at something. In any case, she'd recently put that down to him being occupied. Furthermore, he'd said that "the task will most likely stretch the go-beyond."

On the off chance that Lauren had discovered somewhat progressively about body language, she'd have understood that Gus was attempting to reveal to her that he wasn't "sold" on her thought. He simply wasn't utilizing words.

The Most Effective Method to Read Negative Body Language

Monitoring negative body language in others can permit you to get on implicit issues or awful emotions. Along these lines, in this area, we'll feature some negative nonverbal signs that you should pay individual minds to.

Troublesome Conversations and Defensiveness

Troublesome or tense discussions are an awkward unavoidable truth grinding away. Maybe you've needed to manage an annoying client or expected to converse with somebody about their terrible showing. Or then again, perhaps you've arranged a significant agreement.

In a perfect world, these circumstances would be settled tranquility. Be that as it may, regularly, they are entangled by sentiments of apprehension, stress, preventiveness, or even resentment. However, we may also attempt to shroud them; these feelings regularly appear through in our body language. For instance, on the chance that somebody is showing at least one of the accompanying practices, he will probably be withdrawn, uninvolved, or miserable:

- Arms collapsed before the body.

- Insignificant or tense outward appearance.

- The body got some distance from you.

- Eyes depressed, keeping in touch.

- Keeping away from Unengaged Audiences

At the point when you have to convey an introduction or to work together in a gathering, you need the individuals around you to be 100 percent locked in. Here are some "obvious" signs that individuals might be exhausted or unbiased in what you're stating:

- Sitting drooped, with heads sad.

- Looking at something different, or into space.

- Squirming, picking at garments, or tinkering with pens and telephones.

- She was composing or doodling.

Step by Step Instructions to Project Positive Body Language

When you utilize positive body language, it can add solidarity to the verbal messages or thoughts you need to pass; on and help you abstain from imparting blended or befuddling signs. In this segment, we'll portray some fundamental postures that you can embrace to extend fearlessness and receptiveness.

Establishing a Confident First Connection

These tips can assist you in adjusting your body language so you establish an extraordinary first connection:

- Have an open posture. Be loose; however, don't slump! Sit or stand upstanding and place your hands by your sides. Abstain from remaining with your hands on your hips will cause you to seem more significant, conveying animosity or craving to rule.

- Utilize a firm handshake. However, don't become overly energetic! You don't need it to get unbalanced or, more regrettable, excruciating for the other individual. On the chance that it does, you'll likely seem to be impolite or forceful.

- Keep in touch. Try to maintain eye contact with the other person for a couple of moments, one after another. It will give her that you're right and locked in. Be that as it may, abstain from transforming it into a gazing match!

- Abstain from contacting your face. There's a typical discernment that individuals who contact their appearances while addressing questions are being untrustworthy. While this isn't in every case valid, it's ideal to abstain from tinkering with your hair or contacting your mouth or nose, especially if your point is to seem to be reliable.

Chapter 23. Proxemics

Now, imagine that you are standing in front of someone. You can see that they are crossing their arms with hands hidden behind them, their eyes shifting nervously from you to veer off to the left now and then. They shift their weight from foot to foot and struggle to maintain eye contact. Something about the body language of this person makes you uneasy, but you cannot place it. They keep their distance from you, and every time you approach closer, you notice that they are likely to move away.

Body language is good at giving us feelings that tell us to be on edge, offended, or relaxed, but if you do not know what you are reading, you will struggle to understand why you feel that way. It can be difficult to know what someone intends to not put meaning to what they are doing. You can have a general idea of how you want to respond, but it can be incredibly beneficial

Proxemics refers to the distance between yourself and someone else—it is the usage of space between yourself and the world around you. Naturally, people put varying degrees of space between themselves and others. When you are looking to understand proxemics, the best way to do so is to consider it a judgment of the relationship between yourself and those around you. You can also judge others' relationships based upon the distance they put between each other, both vertical and horizontal.

The Use of Vertical Space

Vertical space is what it sounds like—it is the space relative to your position height-wise. When someone utilizes vertical space, they attempt to make themselves taller or shorter, depending on the context. Those who want to make themselves taller may want to be an authority or otherwise as someone that is deserving of respect and compliance. They may even use this space when they are trying to look at others who are taller than them—they simply tilt their heads back to look down their nose at the taller person to create the same impact.

When you make yourself smaller, you typically want to be seen as less dominant for some reason. You may be attempting to shrink down to speak to a child to be understood truly, for example, or you may be lowering yourself to make yourself seem more submissive. In particular, people will pull their chins inward when they want to be smaller because they will then be required to look up through their eyelashes at the other person, even if the other person is taller.

The default, eye level, is deemed to be the most respectful—it marks you and the other person as equals deserving of the same respect and consideration.

The Use of Horizontal Space

In horizontal space, you are looking at how near or far people are to each other. You will use this when you are picking apart the relationships of others. There are four distances used between each other, ranging from intimate distances to public distance.

- The intimate distance: This refers to being as close as possible to the other person. When you are in this position, you are usually touching without trying or close enough to do so. It is typically for young children and parents, or for lovers that are comfortable being this close to each other. Generally speaking, this zone is only about 18 inches away from you.

- The personal distance: Slightly further away than the intimate distance, the personal distance covers about 18 inches away up to about 5 feet around you. It is what people are talking about when they say that you are invading their personal bubbles. This zone is usually reserved for those you like or feel comfortable with, such as friends and family members or children who are too old to be within the intimate zone. The closer you can get to the center, the closer your relationship with that other person.

- The social distance: This is a bit further out. It is the distance you naturally try to maintain with strangers around you or interacting with someone else you do not know. Typically, this is between about 5 and 10 feet. You will use this when you are out and about unless you have no choice otherwise. When you are forced to encroach on this distance, you will most often make it a point to ignore the other person in an attempt to ignore the fact that they are violating those personal boundaries, such as sitting on the bus.

- The public distance is even further out. It refers to anything beyond 12 feet and is reserved for instances in which you speak out toward a crowd. You want to be loud enough that everyone in the crowd can speak, so you want to ensure that people are a bit further away from you so they can see and hear you easier. It is reserved for lectures in classrooms, for example, or in performances.

Chapter 24. Muscular Core, Posture, and Breathing

The best way to find out is to copy your subject's muscular core state. Just look at how their muscles are arranged and try to set yours the same way. There's a good expression, "to carry oneself," and your goal will be to carry yourself just like them. Your copy doesn't have to be identical, just close enough. Hence, you feel close enough to themselves. Imitate them as close to perfection as your present acting skills allow (to be a good judge of character, a good analyst, you don't have to be a good actor, but it helps—remember Sherlock Holmes and his transformations?) It isn't hard—just contract whatever they have acquired and kept it that way!

Now, as we learned to carry ourselves like our subject of study, we must learn to walk like them and breathe like them, or at least pretend to do it, deep inside.

Much can be learned from a human posture and walk: people with bad eyesight recognize and spot their relatives and friends by their silhouette, their stance, their walk in the crowd of hundreds of people, alone, as easy as a person with keen eyesight would. Can you stand or sit as your subject does and feel as comfortable as they seem? Can you breathe like them, at the same rate, with the same depth, following the same intervals?

Try and practice it alone at first, looking at a video of someone else. Soon you'll be able to perform it mentally, running the process almost entirely in your imagination. As soon as your musculature and posture imprint feels identical to that of your subject, as soon as your collective breath sounds like one, it's time to analyze their non-verbal message.

Are they demonstrating the will to move closer, shorten the distance between you—or are they trying to distance themselves from you? Is their posture open towards you (face, chest, and groin unobstructed by limbs) or closed from you? (Folded arms, crossed knees, etc.) If their posture is closed, don't jump to conclusions: they may position themselves this way merely for comfort, not because they'd like to lock themselves away from you. If your object's posture is closed and is comfortable—they are likely an introvert. With extroverts, expect abrupt changes in posture, quick movements ahead (lean towards the person they're speaking to, or reach for them), meant to shorten the distance between them.

Body language is a nation-specific feature of communication—in some countries, it's hardly used, while in the other two conversing's, people may resemble two windmills. Still, you can generally detect the heat of discussion by the amount and smoothness of gesturing, even when watching the speakers from a distance. The rougher, sharper gestures become, the less controlled they are, the higher the conflict's likeliness.

A conflict is something often provoked by the opposition, or a third party, with intent to unsettle us, upset us, or make us lose our temper and act out. Our goal in this situation will be to retain control of ourselves. It doesn't mean suppressing our anger or bottling our frustration. It means dissolving the heat of emotions in the cold presence of our reason. It means starting with controlled breathing, restrained posture, and slow relaxation of the muscle core, resetting it to absolute calm.

A person in control is not someone gritting their teeth, holding reins back—it's the person showing calm restraint and conscious choice of their words and actions. Remember the monkey and the computer? The last one is the analyst; the first one lives for battle and spots a good fight mile away. There's a good use for this quality, too: your instincts will tell you when the situation is about to heat up a bit too much, so your reason could be there in time to prevent unnecessary drama before it has a chance to happen!

The point is neither of the two parts of one's consciousness must be restrained or removed from the interaction. When the reason is cast aside, no civilized communication is possible: any conversation will quickly derail and devolve into something childish, silly, and virtually useless for any purposes but socializing itself. If the moving part is suppressed, the person starts feeling discomfort.

It is a significant point. It happens to be twofold: whenever you spot manifestations of discomfort in yourself or your object, you will know it happens because the primal part, the emotional aspect, is subdued by reason. It may occur when the person's reason doesn't want to give something away, yet their body—heartbeat, breathing, perspiration—seems eager to betray them. Hence, they try and shut it off using reason, forcing themselves under control for some time, after which their animalistic part will inevitably act out. You must have seen how leaving the room after a difficult meeting. Usually, people will be overly childish and agitated. They even exclaiming loudly, pushing each other. At the same time, others are craving some sort of physical gratification. It is all the backlash of self-control imposed by reason. Then it is lifted.

Hence, to stay comfortable, to remain in full control of oneself—which is something you want to practice to become a good restrained analyst—one must never suppress their inner feelings! It's hard to give advice on how your computer could keep your monkey in check, as this is a personal thing, inherent to your character. There's a huge number of venting and confidence-building techniques out there, and you're free to try them all! Just remember this simple rule: by indulging a specific whim of your animal, you grow it, not reduce it. For instance, aggressive behavior does not deplete aggression. On the contrary, it increases your aggressiveness—the same as being afraid will not deplete your fear.

Still, techniques help you drop the level of aggression and overcome fear, from the essential things like counting to ten, naming objects around you mentally, or drinking a glass of water—down to counseling and transcendental meditation. In this book, we'll merely say the solution is out there, and self-control is essential if you want to stay an involved yet unbiased party.

On the other hand, this is what you want to notice in the behavior of your subject: not their controlled, reasonable actions, but their slips, their subliminal telltales, the small movements, expressions, and changes in posture that happen without the subject noticing. How to interpret this body language? The problem is that it's inherent to a particular culture and varies from one individual to another.

Many sources claim they're able to teach you some kind of universal list of telltales. One that enables you to tell the truth from lies, present you with recipes of telling an act from the real deal. But these sources are at best-generalized information. It is sometimes applied to many people. Enough to make it seem true, but not to be applied to just everyone. The truth is, only your own experience, attentiveness, and insight will help you to read another person's body language, for there are as many body languages as there are different people.

For instance, when someone is trying to touch or hide a part of their face—lips, the nose, an ear—it's typically considered a sign of secretiveness, the telltale of a person lying or trying to hide some information from the listener. In many cases, it's indeed so—and still, be careful not to call someone a liar just because they tend to rub their three-day stubble while they're thinking.

Another popular facial feature to be pointed out as a telltale: a genuine smile would cause crinkles around eyes, while a fake smile normally wouldn't. Yet again, in many cases, it may be true—we often hear about "someone smiling while their eyes remain cold." Then again, the experiments show the "smiling eyes" can be faked more or less quickly, and if you were to encounter a sociopathic person, someone good at mimicry—you'd never catch them faking a smile.

Approach tendencies in your subject's posture may mean aggression—or they could mean affection, and only your judgment may discern between the two. If your issue demonstrates avoidance tendencies—this, yet again, could mean an entire spectrum of emotions: apathy, fear, disgust, mistrust, submission, meekness, and so on.

A good analyst would always view the non-verbal signals of their subject as a part of the bigger picture, applying to them the knowledge of this person as a whole. Even a habit as simple as biting one's fingernails—are you sure I bite mine when I'm nervous? It may happen a person tends to stick their thumb in their mouth while they're thoughtful, relaxed, their attention directed inward—miles from feeling nervous!

Always remember: what you see is only half of the picture. Another half, no less important, is what you hear.

Chapter 25. Hand Gestures and Arm Signals

It is important to read gestures in the context of other aspects of body language, but we will explore ways of reading gestures. We all talk with our hands often. For some people, the gesturing matches their message well. Some people do not deploy hand gestures while others overuse hand gestures. Most hand gestures are universal. A person that does not use hand gestures may be seen as indifferent.

For this reason, the audience may feel that one does not care about what the other is talking about. If your hands are hidden, then the audience will find it difficult to trust you. If one's hands are open and the palms wide enough, the individual communicates that they are honest and sincere.

Furthermore, randomly throwing hands in the air while talking may suggest that one is anxious or panicking. Extreme anger will also make one throw their hands in an uncoordinated manner. For further understanding, take time and watch movie characters quarreling, and you will note that most people being accused of something will randomly throw their hands in the air. It is something that they have little control over because most of the body language happens at the subconscious level of the mind. Randomly throwing hands in the air indicates that one is overwhelmed with emotions or has given up defending their position in the argument and has left the argument to the individual who started it.

Additionally, one may point at an object or a person. Pointing as a gesture helps the focus of the speaker and the audience to the focused area. During your school days, you probably saw your teacher's point in a particular direction without speaking until the talking students had to stop. As such, pointing at specific students drew the entire class's attention to their direction, making them become the center of attention, and they had to do a quick self-evaluation and stop talking. All these illustrate that body language communicates tone and emotions just as verbal communication.

Furthermore, pointing while wafting the index finger indicates a warning. When one points the index finger at someone and wafts it up and down, then you are denoting a stern warning and judgment to the individual. It is the equivalent of saying, "this is the last warning." Your parent or teacher may probably have a point and waft gesture to signal a warning that what you are doing is wrong and that you should stop. You might have observed that the police or the lead actor uses the index finger to warn someone in movie characters. The finger signal singles out the individual and reduces the focus to just one aspect of behavior that the speaker wants the target person to understand.

If one spreads all the fingers and holds them together against those of the opposite hand, it indicates strong personal reflection, such as praying or remembering the departed soul. The same gesture can be used when one is focusing the mind during meditation or yoga. The holding of each of your fingers against their peers. On the other hand, it may also indicate feeling humble and thankful for everything. For instance, followers of the Catholic faith frequently use this gesture when praying. The gesture shows humility and thankfulness.

Sometimes one may tap on the head once or continuously. When one taps on the head using a hand or a finger, it indicates the individual is thinking hard or trying hard to recall something. For instance, when speaking and you try to remember what another person said, you might use this gesture. Children often tap their heads once or continuously using one finger or the entire palm to signal attempts to recall something. The gesture is equivalent to saying, "Come on, what it was?" or "Come on, what was the name again!" It is a prop to recall hard.

Similarly, a fully raised palm with fingers spread may indicate that one should stop. When stopping the vehicle on the roadside, one raises one of their palms high up, and it is taken as a sign to stop. The same is true in the sporting environment where raising one palm high up commonly communicates that the playing should stop. When arguing with your partner, if they raise one of their palms, it signifies the other to stop arguing or stop whatever action they are doing.

If one claps, the palms together may indicate applauding the message or the speaker. When the speaker is done speaking, the audience may clap their hands together to mark the message's appreciation or both the message and the speaker. However, when the hands are spontaneously and violently clapped, then it is a message that the audience should stop because what they are doing is unethical or irritating. At home, one of your parents probably clapped their hands suddenly and violently to make you stop as well as draw attention to their presence, especially where you were playing loudly around the house.

Relatedly, if one interlocks one hand against those of the other hands and folding them. The application of this gesture indicates that one is attentive but unease at the same time. During an interview, meeting, or a class session, the audience is likely to interlock their fingers and fold them. In a way, the interlocking of the fingers is supposed to offer assurance to the affected person that he or she is safe. One is likely also to use this gesture when he or she is mentioned negatively. Think of how you reacted when you were mentioned among noisemakers or workers having challenges following the company's rules. Most probably, you interlocked your fingers and folded them.

Additionally, if one feels shy or uncertain, the individual is also likely to interlock their fingers and raise the interlocked fingers when speaking. The gesture in this context appears to give some prop for the affected individual enabling them to navigate the anxiety. The gesture in this context is not just about communicating the affected person's physiological status but as a coping mechanism of sudden anxiety and discomfort of the individual.

Still on body language and focusing on gesture, if one raises both hands behind the head and interlocks the fingers, it acts as a cushion for the head. The gesture indicates that one is feeling casual, tired, or simply not tasked by the current conversation. The gesture may also suggest that the individual is feeling tired by the discussion or the activity. Think of how you react when feeling exhausted when talking to a friend or after watching a movie. You probably raised both of your hands behind the head and interlocked the fingers to act as a headrest. In most cases, when one invokes this gesture, the individual is likely to let the mind allow other thoughts to escape from the current conversation.

Correspondingly, there is the gesture where one lets one of their palms to brush down their faces. The gesture is used to signal deeper thinking, process new contradictory information, or accept humiliation in front of the audience. The gesture suggests surrender. It indicates yielding to inner thoughts or views from the audience that one may have initially opposed. At one point, the class or your friends cornered a speaker facing the speaker to pause and take a minute to admit that he or she may have overlooked some facts about the issue. Probably, the speaker used this gesture to indicate defeat.

On the other hand, to indicate rejection or strong disagreement. It is with both hands with palms broad are waved in an alternating manner to create the letter X. You probably drew the letter X using both hands to indicate that you disagree\what is being proposed in class. For instance, as a kid or as a student, you probably drew letter X to signal rejection that you will not follow instructions when the teacher sarcastically indicated that you should not follow his instructions. The sign also indicates retreat to your inner world to avoid listening or watching what the speaker wants.

For accentuation, when hands are open with palms down, at that point, one is communicating that he or she is certain almost what they are talking about. In case your palms are confronting each other with the fingers together. At that point, you're communicating that you just possess the skill around what you're talking about almost. At that point, there's the approximation gesture performed by holding the hand horizontally with palm down and with fingers forward. After that, tilting the hand to the correct and the cleared out. The guess signal shows that an explanation is to be taken a near appraise of the truth.

Equally important, the gesture with a gentle rocking from left to right means that it is not so good or not so bad. The same gesture indicates that an event is equally likely to end in one of the two ways suggesting that it can go either way. The gesture can signal the other person when a match is going, and the friends are watching in the house, and they do not want to wake up the child through loud talking.

Similarly, the beckoning sign has the index finger sticking out of the clenched fist and palm facing the gesture. Then the speaker's finger moves repeatedly towards the gesturer as to invite something nearer. The beckoning sign has the general meaning of commanding someone to where you are standing. The beckoning sign is often performed with the four fingers using the entire hand, depending on how far the sign's recipient is. Depending on the circumstance, when performed with the index finger, it can have a sexual connotation.

If one feels that the speaker is not making sense, they are likely to keep their fingers straight and together while holding them upwards with the thumb pointing downwards. Then the fingers and thumb snap together to indicate a talking mouth. The gesture suggests contempt for a person talking for an excessive period about a topic that the gesturer feels is trivial. In Asian cultures, the gesture is used as a reaction to a dry joke. The gesture may also indicate that one is blabbering.

Also, there's the check signal that's caught on by servers around the world to flag that a supper supporter wishes to pay the charge and get out. The signal is showed by touching the record finger and thumb together and signifying a wavy line within the air associated with marking one's title. Drawing a checkmark within the discussion utilizing the fingers communicates that the person needs to pay the charge.

Chapter 26. Different Types of People and How They Fit In the Social Circle

All of us are full of different flaws that make us feel ashamed. We do have strengths that we want to brag about in front of everyone. Some of us prefer to stay natural in their everyday life while others love to take up their favorite persona to get through different hurdles in their lives. Some people like to make their way by deception, lies, and manipulation, while others prefer to face stumbling blocks but refuse to deviate from the right path. Whatever our choice of being a person in our lives is, the goal mustn't be of hiding our weaknesses and dark spots if we have any. We must allow our flaws to be a part of our personality. We should celebrate our flaws. It is what being human is about. When a person takes up a fake persona, he forgets that the people loving him are loving that persona that he has taken up and not that person who is in hiding under the fake personality. The real success is that people start loving us because of what we are and not because of what we are trying to become.

The Joker

The first category is a joker. The foremost feeling on hearing the word joker is of a person who is cracking jokes and laughing his heart out even during sober conversations. Jokers love jokes, costumes, and makeup. Each makeover gives them a new look and personality. They love to hide their real looks and nature from others. Generally, jokers are considered harmless, but things get different if we bring to mind batman's joker. A scary and nutty person comes to mind who is evil personified. That joker is always bent on inflicting the greatest pain on the people surrounding him. Can you think of a person who fulfills the above personality traits? Do you know anyone who laughs too much, always cracks jokes or tries to tease others while laughing it out? Beware! Jokers are masters of disguise.

The Smart One

Smart people can mold themselves according to the situation. They learn or are naturally gifted to adapt to changing circumstances. Smart people always remember to read other people's styles to gain more knowledge about them. They tend to see through the motives behind their acts and their hidden desires to work with them and gain benefits. Smart people are good at conveying their messages in an effective manner and without making the slightest buzz. They know how to express their feelings clearly, which is the most important thing when it comes to building and strengthening a relationship.

Similarly, smart people are very successful in their businesses or jobs. They work hard to learn how to read people, and the rest gets automatically easy for you. You can tell if a person is smart by looking at how they behave with you and other people around him. One important point to note is that smart people are very good at taking care of their interests, even at others' cost.

The Worker

Workers are the people who belong to a specific social class that is known for doing jobs for low pay only to live hand to mouth in their lives. The jobs they do low demand skills and labor and also have low literacy requirements. This category of people also lives off on social welfare programs. Working-class people mostly remain preoccupied with their day-to-day expenditures. They don't have time to take up different personas and disguises. Also, they are not smart enough to get a job done in the easiest way possible. Their brains are generally wired to do it the hard way. These people typically wear their hearts on their sleeves. They are easy to predict and are simple to understand.

The Loyal

These people are hard to find but exist. They are reliable as well as truthful. If a person is loyal to you, he shares affection with you and will not leave you when life gets hard for you. Loyal people think from their hearts and always work to benefit the people who are close to them. Just like the working class, loyal people are easily predictable and trustworthy.

The Strong

Physically strong people generally have a happy temperament. A strong person has higher levels of physical and mental strength. They don't have self-pity; that's why they are confident and good at judging people and dealing with them. Before they judge other people, they try to judge themselves. Besides, they have higher levels of self-restraint. Their nerves are powerful; that's why they are patient. They also are good listeners and observers. Their physical and mental strengths make them very good at reading other people and reaching an educated judgment. They don't hesitate to ask for help when they are in need, and also, they are open to helping others.

Different Types of Personalities

People are driven by their nature when they do this or leave you wondering why they did something that looked unwanted to you. It is perfectly normal if you think you need to understand someone a bit more than you already do. This someone can be a loved one or a person at our workplace. We have to accept the reality that people are not perfect. We are different, and it is this difference and diversity that makes this world a colorful and interesting place to live in. When people stay true to their role, they tend to contribute their bit to this diverse world. Imagine if we were all created in the same way, how the world looks like then. It would be boring.

Take an example of diversity. When a car hits a motorbike in a road accident, many people gather at the site. Most of them are on-lookers who are just investigating what happened. Some mourn the wounds of the injured while some call the ambulance. Only a handful of them step up and help the injured recover their senses. They try to administer to the first aid and take care of them until the ambulance arrives at the site. It is not that those people leap into a house on fire without thinking about their lives. We react differently to different situations. Our fears and desires trigger these reactions. Sometimes they motivate us, while at other times, they just demotivate us.

In analyzing people, you should know the people around you. What they do and how they react to different situations. Knowing their personality types and the fears that guide their behavior can improve how you interact with other people. It helps you read people more efficiently so that your interaction with them becomes smooth and your analysis of people broadens and deepens. Besides, you can track down your personality traits as well as faults. Let's roll on and take a look at different types of people in the world.

The Reformer/Idealist

The Reformer is a perfectionist. They have principles and are conscientious. These kinds of people have specific ideas to follow, and they come down hard on themselves and other people. They just love to keep them at pretty high standards. They are dedicated and responsible besides having perfect self-discipline.

They are usually successful in life because they tend to get lots of things to happen in a short time, and that too in the right way. They are always looking forward to setting themselves on the right path by eliminating their weaknesses. (9 Personality Types—Enneagram Numbers, nod)

The Performer

As the title suggests, these kinds of people will always be setting goals for themselves. They are highly target-oriented individuals, and they believe in doing rather than sitting on the couch and thinking day and night. They are always striving for success. This drive makes them pretty excellent at doing things right. You can find them in a big company, a shop or on the street selling vegetables or fruit. Wherever they are, their eyes are always on the horizon. They have dreams of success, and they are in the world to make them happen. These kinds of people are considered as role-models by many other people.

They have the fears that drive them toward the top. What makes them perfect is their urge to become somebody. The fear of dying as nobody makes them state-conscious. Instead of discouraging others, they respect the opinion of other people. (9 Personality Types—Enneagram Numbers, nod)

The Observer

These kinds of people spend time thinking and are of an introvert type. Their focus always is on gaining knowledge. They also prefer reading their personality instead of reading others. They remain absorbed in themselves and love to play with different types of concepts. They usually despise worldly attractions like big mansions, cars, and social status. They are always busy searching for themselves. They prefer to observe what is happening in their brains. You can see that these people will lock themselves in their rooms for hours as they love to understand how things go. This exclusive behavior allows them to concentrate on what they do. That's why they are usually considered experts on what they do. As they don't have the social skills needed to keep relationships healthy, they get overlooked most of the time.

The Adventurer

These kinds of people are fun-loving people. You will see them engaged in enjoyable pursuits, and also, they are often in an upbeat mood. They thrive on pleasure and adventures, which makes them a positive person. They tend to avoid negativity at all costs, which helps them fight off pessimism and stress well. They are also very optimistic and don't let tough challenges mar their optimism. They are the ones who always find that silver lining in dark clouds. They stick to that silver lining and turn negative situations fast and well. (9 Personality Types—Enneagram Numbers, nod)

Also, they are highly inconsistent. As they are fun-oriented, they remain in a particular work until the fun factor is alive but shoot out of it once they are bored, no matter if the work is complete or not. Completing projects poses a big challenge to them; that's why they struggle to succeed in the practical world.

The Warrior

As the name suggests, these kinds of people love to throw and take the gauntlet. They are strong and have dominating personalities. You can say they are born leaders and are confident. They are real alphas. They hate to depend on other people and also don't like to reveal their weaknesses. Instead, they use their strengths to cover those people who are around them as their family and friends. They are always ready to take charge of any situation, no matter how thundering and dreadful it is. They love to be the masters of their fate, and they also prefer to take control of people and circumstances.

Chapter 27: Conclusion of Body Language

If your mind is reeling from all the information shared so far, brace yourself. You see, this is an exceedingly vast topic. It is an essential topic because communication is one of the essential parts of our lives. How we communicate impacts our relationships, whether private, personal, or professional.

As with anything else, the impact can be positive or negative, so knowing what your body is saying on your behalf is of the utmost importance. The value in this book is not in learning all you need to know about this subject. It is in understanding that there is so much to know and that you can learn it over time by paying attention and putting in some effort.

Imagine that you are a very shy person who has amazing ideas for inventions or songs or movies, or whatever. Now, imagine how hard it would be for a very timid person to get those great ideas across to the right patent attorney, the right musician, or the right producer if they could barely speak above a whisper when they were nervous.

If they finally did get a meeting with their target audience, how would it look if they averted their eyes and crossed their arms over their body the whole time? Do you think they would be taken seriously? What is the possibility that they would win an influential person in a position of influence over under those circumstances?

There is nothing wrong with any personality type, but if you have a timid personality, know what your body language is saying on your behalf. If that is not what you want to convey, you can learn better behaviors that reflect what you want to say.

What of the person who is the opposite? What if you were naturally loud, bordering on boisterous, and the more nervous you became, the louder you seemed to get?

Being aware of how your volume affects others, you might try to tone it down a bit, but those who are naturally boisterous tend to have "big" body language as well.

If you walk into a room and begin to grip and shake hands as if you were arm wrestling, you would naturally start your event with mistrust and wariness as to your motives though you said very little at a modified decibel.

Here is one last word of caution about becoming a student of body language; never to use one cue to determine what a speaker means. Several factors are involved in each person's dynamic, and all must be considered before making an important determination.

Factors that could possibly affect someone's body language might include a physical or mental disability or limitation, a person's culture or background, or even a current health crisis.

Be aware that you can be influenced by body language with or without your consent, and you can influence others by your own body language, whether you are aware of it or even whether or not you mean to.

Body language is a powerful tool. Understand it and that understanding thoughtfully.

Chapter 28: Dark Psychology

It is the study of the human condition because it involves people's psychological nature; that is, they prey on other people with criminal activities and criminal motives. Illegal reasons and unlawful purposes lack instinct and social science theories. All human beings may harm other humans and creatures. Although many people have suppressed or sublimated this trend, some have acted on these impulses. Dark psychology attempts to understand the thoughts, feelings, perceptions, and subjective processing systems that lead to predatory behavior contrary to the contemporary understanding of human behavior. Dark psychology assumes that crime, deviance, and abuse are purposeful and have rational, goal-oriented motivation 99.99% of the time. It is the remaining 0.01% of the dark psychology part of Adler's theory and teleology. Dark psychology assumes an area in the human mind that enables some people to perform cruel behavior without a purpose. In this theory, it is called a dark singularity.

Dark psychology believes that all humanity's malicious intentions towards others vary from minimal ambiguous and short thoughts to purely psychotic deviant behavior, without any rationality of cohesion. That is called a dark continuum. Dark psychology calls it the confounding factor. The mitigating factor is the promoter and attractant close to the mysterious singularity. The heinous behavior of people falls on the dark continuum. A brief introduction to these concepts is as follows. Dark psychology is a concept that the author has struggled with for fifteen years. It was only recently that he finally conceptualized the human condition, philosophy, and psychology definition. Dark psychology covers all the people who connect us to the dark side. All cultures, all faiths, and all humanity suffer from this well-known cancer. From the moment we are born to our death, there is a latent side within us, which some people call evil. In contrast, others define it as crime, immorality, and pathology.

Dark Psychology introduces a third philosophical construction, arguing that these behaviors are different from religious teachings and contemporary social science theories. Dark psychology believes that some people will act the same, not for power, money, gender, retribution, or any other known purpose. They commit these terrible acts without aim. Simply put, their use does not justify their methods. Some people assault and hurt others because of this. There is this potential in all of us. The area the author explores may be to harm others for no reason, no explanation, or purposelessness. Dark psychology believes that this dark potential is very complicated and even confusing to define. Dark psychology assumes that we all have the potential for predator behavior and that this potential can enter our thoughts, feelings, and perceptions. As you will read through this manual, we all have this potential, but only a few of us will make a difference. All of us once had the thought and feeling of acting cruelly. All of us have thought about hurting others seriously and without mercy.

You are honest with yourself. You have to agree with the thoughts and feelings you once thought about committing heinous behavior. Given this fact, we consider ourselves to be a kind species. We want to believe that these thoughts and feelings do not exist. Unfortunately, we all have these ideas, and fortunately, no action has taken against them. Dark psychology constitutes that some people have the same thoughts, feelings, and opinions but act deliberately or impulsively. The apparent difference is that they operate independently, while others only have brief thoughts and feelings about it. "Dark Psychology" believes that this predator style is purposeful and has a specific rational, goal-oriented motivation. Religion, philosophy, psychology, and other dogmas have made convincing attempts to define dark psychology. Most human behaviors related to evil practices are indeed purposeful and goal-oriented. Still, dark psychology believes that persistent behavior and goal-oriented motives seem to be blurred in a particular field.

From thought to pure psychosis, dark psychology has suffered continuous damage without any apparent rationality or purpose. This continuum, the dark continuum, helps conceptualize the philosophy of dark psychology. Dark psychology addresses human psychology or the general human condition that allows or might even promote predatory behavior. In many cases, this behavioral tendency's specific characteristics lack the rational motivation of universality and predictability. Dark psychology believes that this general human condition is different or an extension of evolution. Let's look at some basic principles of development. First of all, consider that we have evolved from other animals. At present, we are a model of all animal life. Our frontal lobe makes us apex creatures. Now let us suppose that being advanced creatures does not entirely separate us from animals' instincts and predatory nature.

Chapter 29. What Is Dark Psychology?

The idea of psychology is to help people by helping them understand themselves. Dark psychology is about using the mental weaknesses that people have to get people to do what you want them to do. I know it sounds cringe worth to many people, but this is not nearly as bad as you think it is. The fact is that everywhere around, the tools of dark psychology are chipping away at your mind. Facebook ran a test on its users by curating their content and measuring their mood. They wanted to see how showing people more negative content would affect their news by showing them more positive content. Magazines and advertisements like to play on your need to keep up with the Joneses or not lose something. In doing so, you are drawn into whatever they are selling. The news feeds a looping heap of controlled opinions to try and make you agree with the viewpoint you already share. The world is full of psychology being used darkly, and most of the time, you are on the receiving end of it rather than getting the benefit of it.

That is about to change. Dark Psychology is about recognizing the compulsions, needs, and desires that we all have, which can be used to get what we want.

What Do We Mean by That?

Whether it is a fear of loss, a desire to keep up with the Joneses, or a need to feel wanted or feel right, these things guide our decisions and impulses, whether we like them or not.

Alternatively, whether we want them to or not, people act against their interests every day simply because they are in an emotional state that guides your actions. When someone finds out these emotional triggers, it is a matter of time before they can start to guide your actions, control your behavior, and even manipulate you.

There can be nothing worse when people have figured out your emotional triggers and begin to play them. Whether it is a parent or a stranger, you can feel yourself often taking action and not even certain why you feel drawn to taking action just knowing that you have to, or want to, or that it is something that must be done. No, you cannot wait and Dark Psychology is the tool that sets this into action. It is the tool that shines a light on finding all these mental triggers in yourself and others.

It also recognizes that as amazing as our brains are, they take many shortcuts in the name of efficiency, which leaves them vulnerable to some of the simplest attacks. Ideally, our minds should not make us feel sad simply because we had a negative thought, and yet, this happens all the time. We're wandering around, having a good time, a good day. Someone says something or does something, maybe even inconsequential, and yet suddenly, our mood is shifted, and we have to fight to get back to balance. Our brains, however, are just working to be efficient; they are not working to be perfect. And when you understand that, you know that there is a huge opportunity to be had when dealing with people. More importantly, you understand that there are something's that you need to learn to safeguard yourself.

You have desires and wants, needs, and how far you are willing to go to have those things met. Do you know? What are your buying triggers? What are your emotional triggers? You have them, but are you completely aware of them. What makes you stressed, confused, angry, happy, and excited? All of these things are inside your mind? They are inside everyone's mind. When you know how to access them, you will suddenly have greater freedom, happiness, excitement, and possibility in yourself and others. Because finally, you will be bringing your desires to life by getting others to see and want to help.

We are going to address manipulation—one of the keys to dark psychology. Manipulation is different from persuasion, influence, sales, and other such things. It is often about getting people to take action by playing on their weaknesses. We will talk about the ethics of manipulation, what you need to think about, and the "Right now" is essential to set the stage for what you can expect and learn the handful of psychological techniques and methods that will allow you to control people.

Dark Psychology is a tool, like a hammer. You can use it to build things or use it as a weapon to hurt people. We are making no moral judgments and go about using these skills. But the most important thing is for you to learn these techniques to make sure that you have a better understanding of yourself and what people are using against you.

The world can be a dangerous place knowing these techniques and understanding how people can manipulate you or fundamentally transform how you respond to people and how you engage with them. You will recognize when people are trying to use your emotional states and trying to take advantage of you. You will also learn how to use these techniques in ethical ways so that you can guide people to take the best action for themselves or the action you think they should take. Beyond everything, you will discover through the dark psychology what exactly is triggering your behaviors and, in part two, how to change those triggers if they are not going to be helpful or serve you in the way that you want them to.

Dark Psychology involves the use of mind tricks, which is in between deception and persuasion. The psychological mind tricks might sound outrageous, but it works well. They are being used to mislead people to think that what they know to be right is wrong, and what they believe to be wrong is right.

In a simple term, dark psychology allows humans to be willing and deliberate to harm others through their decisions and actions; sometimes, this might not be physical. However, some emotions are groomed from a very early stage of an individual's life. For example, a child grows to learn how to cry so that the adults around will make themselves available for their bidding. We can call this crying a manipulative tool for the child to be enabled to control people around. As a child grows up, if such as a child is not being cautioned on what he's doing, the so-called innocent childish behavior would now become a dark way of controlling people to do what he/she wants.

Dark psychology is the study of how a person thinks and sees a need to understand the intent behind actions and words. In general, it illuminates the dark side of human nature. In dark psychology, the effect is experienced by both the victim and the perpetrator. The personality traits which are considered as dark include narcissism, psychopathy, and Machiavellianism.

In a simple term, an excessive admiration of oneself in an obsessive manner towards appearance is referred to as narcissism. Narcissists usually feel superior. They do not subscribe to the rule of giving and take in a normal relationship. They are good at blaming others whenever there is an issue. A common feature is to be an extremely self-centered individual. Narcissists have a public appetite for control and power. They control people by making them think that they are looking out for them. They are also very smart such that they get involved in your day to day activities in life without being noticed. Above all, they are Keen liars and master is the lie skills.

Psychopathy is a trait that is associated with not being sensitive to other people. A psychopath will almost not have empathy for other people. Psychopaths are usually bold, confident, and fearless. They are risk-takers and extremely charming.

On the other hand, the third personality trait is known as Machiavelli's; the term is used to describe someone who lacks emotions and desire to achieve something at the expense of other people's feelings. This can be done through deceit, manipulation, or going against some moral rules. An individual who scores highly in Machiavelli's test is usually referred to as a "High Mach." These people are always around us, sometimes in our workplace or as a neighbor. They are hard-working people who are smart and are unapologetic about stepping on other people's toe. This set of people are opportunists and can emotionally detach themselves from situations they are in. Due to this ability, they are capable of involving themselves in several sexual several encounters. They can stand a chance of being good teammates but certainly not a good friend.

This knowledge of dark psychology is to protect yourself from those personalities when you come across them. Dark psychology cuts across all human conditions in which are universal. It studies how the state of humans relates to their thoughts, feelings, and perception. The general assumption here is that every human has the potential to be violent. Learning this concept is of two-folded benefits. First, it helps individuals accept that they tend to become evil, so the knowledge of this will prevent it from erupting. And secondly, it gives everyone a reason to struggle to survive.

The following concept I will be talking about is Neuro-Linguistics Programming (NLP). This is a technique used in restructuring people's minds on how to get rid of bad habits, how to become productive, and how to make them effective in general. You can use this technique to connect sense, mind, behavior, and language. This method is designed so that you tend to control people without them even being aware of what you are doing to them.

Neuro refers to the nervous system, which is made up of the mind and all other senses. Your nervous system functions when you interact with your environment or people. That's why when you listen more to people, you get to understand what is being said. When you pay more attention to what happens around you, you know and see more things about people around you.

Chapter 30. Explication of Dark Psychology

Several skills are essential in analyzing people. The first and perhaps most important skill is having an understanding of human nature and normal human behavior. If you do not understand how humans behave under normal circumstances or what motivates most people, you are unlikely to interpret others' actions and intentions correctly. Just as a judge relies on their sense of how people typically behave and what motivates them in their judgments, so too must you develop an understanding of the typical spectrum of human behavior to analyze someone properly.

Of course, human beings can behave in highly original ways, making analyzing them difficult at times. Although human beings frequently behave in typically human ways–like being jealous of others' success or envious of a colleague who just married a beautiful wife–sometimes people can surprise you. Indeed, some people never feel jealous or envious of others. Most poor people do not steal even though they may need this because it is not part of their character. Frequently the most significant, most flamboyant thief is the person who already has all that they need.

To analyze people, you are going to have to start with knowing how humans are generally. It includes understanding the spectrum of human emotion, the behaviors linked to these emotions, and the things that motivate people to do this. Everyone wears a mask, which means that sometimes the intentions of others are not always clear. But even with this mask, people can reveal their emotional state to you, the things that make them happy, and the things that make them sad.

We all wear a mask, but perhaps only FBI agents are so skilled that they never give you some clue. A spontaneous laugh, a twinkle in the eye, a giddy tapping of the foot: These are unconscious signs that men and women give of how they feel. Analyzing men and women will require understanding human behavior and interpreting what people say and do.

Non-Verbal Communication

Non-verbal communication refers to the little clues that others give us that convey essential information outside of language. Human beings are social animals, meaning we evolved in settings where we were generally close to one another rather than alone. For this reason, we developed the ability to perceive and interpret the signals that others send to indicate their emotional state, thoughts, and motivations.

It is easy to pay attention to words when we are attempting to analyze others. Still, because language is not always an accurate indication of how people feel, it is essential to pay attention to the non-verbal cues others send. These cues can include facial expression, body distance, and the position of hands, quick movements of the hands or the feet, and the like. These non-verbal cues are not specific to human beings. Non-human primates are excellent examples of how animal societies can be built without speech. From bearing of teeth to the tail position, apes have a language comprised entirely of non-verbal cues.

Differentiating Fake From Real Emotion

Analyzing others will require developing the ability to distinguish exact sentiment from a false one. Human beings know that others observe and interpret them, at least the intelligent ones do, so they have become adept at hiding their feelings. A typical example of this is someone who smiles even though they are not happy. Still, this hiding of emotion can mean angry when one is hurt or vulnerable. Human beings wear masks to protect themselves, as you must if you plan on defending yourself from practitioners of dark psychology. But protecting yourself also means analyzing people appropriately, and this means determining which emotions are real and which are not.

The practitioner of dark psychological tactics perceives you as prey, so they pay very close attention to your words, actions, and non-verbal cues: virtually anything that indicates what's going on inside. You may put a wall to make your emotions more difficult for the predator to access, but you will most likely say or do something to reveal the truth. This is just as true of the predator as it is of you, the prey. They can put on a façade of smiles and pleasantries, but sometimes all it takes is one fierce look to reveal that their intentions are not so friendly.

We see this all the time in films and television shows. The new neighbor seems nice, but the camera shot reveals their subtle change in expression when your back is turned. They are not so neighborly. Their goal is to steal your husband and wreak havoc in your life (in the case of the standard Lifetime Original Movie). To protect yourself, you need to use your understanding of human nature and analyze it to figure out what is going on. Is there a discrepancy between the surface emotion and the events taking place? Perhaps the other person is smiling, but you heard that they lost their house and are short of funds. Would most people be so giddy in this situation?

An essential part of distinguishing real from fake emotion is deciding whether the surface or "fake" feeling makes sense, given what you know. Human beings are good at being emotionally aware by dint of being so communal. A person can hide what they feel, but it may only take a brief glimmer of real emotion for you to establish the rule of what is real in this person and what is not. The other person drops their mask for a second and notes what the natural person beneath looks like.

Tips to Identify a Liar

Anyone who has spent time around a pathological liar knows that little tricks can be used to tell when fibbing. Pathological liars are often highly friendly people who love to talk and always have something to say. It is this still having something to say that gets them into trouble. If you are suspicious that the person you are speaking to is a pathological liar, pay attention to the factual aspects of the things they say. This will become natural in time as you become aware the person is lying. You will make a mental note about facts like a specific monetary amount of something, a date, or a restaurant's name because you know these things may potentially be false.

Paying close attention to the details is the first step in identifying a liar. The second is knowing when to face the liar with the facts. It may not be a good idea to confront them pointedly, as you may decide. If they said they went to a particular restaurant, ask them what they had to eat—baked chicken and mixed vegetable stir fry. The next day, s/he asks them how the steak was. If they say, it was beautiful when you have caught them. They did not go to the restaurant at all. A pathological liar tells so many lies that they cannot keep track of them.

Chapter 31. How To Use Dark Psychology

How Can Psychology Improve Your Life?

The following are some of the top ten realistic uses for psychology in regular life:

1. Get Prompted

Whether your purpose is to stop smoking, lose weight, or examine a new language, psychology training provides pointers for buying motivation. To grow your motivation while drawing close to a project, make use of some of the following tips derived from research in cognitive and educational psychology:

- Introduce new or novel factors to hold your interest high.
- Vary the series to help stave off boredom.
- Study new matters that build on your present understanding.
- Set clear goals that might be at once related to the assignment.

2. Enhance Your Management Abilities

It doesn't count number in case you're an office supervisor or a volunteer at a neighborhood teenage activity group; having true leadership abilities will, in all likelihood, be vital sometime in the future for your existence. Now, not all of us are born leaders, but some easy suggestions from mental studies can improve your leadership capabilities.

One of the most famous research papers on this topic looked at three distinct management styles. Primarily based on the findings of this look at and subsequent studies, practice several of the following when you are in a management function:

- Offer clear steering but permit group contributors to voice opinions.

- Communicate approximately possible answers to troubles with contributors to the group.

- Focus on stimulating ideas and be inclined to praise creativity.

3. Come to be a Better Communicator

Conversation involves a whole lot more than just the way you speak or write. Research indicates that nonverbal indicators make up a big portion of our interpersonal communications

Some key strategies encompass the subsequent:

- Use proper eye contact.

- Start noticing nonverbal indicators in others.

- Learn to use your tone of voice to boost your message.

4. Learn To Better Understand Others

Just like nonverbal communication, your capacity to apprehend your emotions and the feelings of those around you perform an important role in your relationships and professional lifestyles. The time emotional intelligence refers to your potential to apprehend each of your emotions in addition to those of other human beings.

What can you do to emerge as more emotionally stable? Recall a few of the subsequent techniques:

- Cautiously assess your very own emotional reactions.

- Record your enjoyment and emotions in a journal.

- Try to see situations from the angle of a different person.

5. Make Extra Correct Selections

Studies in cognitive psychology supply a wealth of statistics about choice making. By making use of those techniques for your lifestyles, you can discover ways to make wiser choices. The following time you want to make a huge decision, strive the usage of several the subsequent techniques:

- Try using the "Six Thinking Hats" technique with the aid of searching on the situation from multiple points of view, including rational, emotional, intuitive, creative, advantageous, and Dark views.

- Recall the capacity prices and blessings of choice.

- Appoint a grid evaluation approach that offers a score for how a selected decision will fulfill unique requirements you may have.

6. Enhance Your Reminiscence

Have you ever wondered why you can remember the precise information of childhood events yet forget the call of the new customer you met yesterday? Research on how we form new reminiscences and how and why we forget has caused some of the findings that can be implemented without delay in your daily life.

What are some methods you can grow your reminiscence of electricity?

- Awareness of the data.

- Rehearse what you have discovered.

- Do away with distractions.

7. Make Wiser financial decisions

Nobel Prize-winning psychologist Daniel Kahneman and his colleague Amos Tversky performed a chain of research that looked at how humans manipulate uncertainty and danger while making decisions.

One looks at located that workers could extra than triple their financial savings by making use of some of the following strategies:

- Don't procrastinate. Start investing savings now.

- Commit earlier to dedicate quantities of your future profits to your retirement financial savings.

- Try to be aware of non-public biases that may result in Dark money choices.

8. Get Higher Grades

The subsequent time you are tempted to whine about pop quizzes, midterms, or finals, consider that research has confirmed that taking checks helps you better consider what you have learned, even if it wasn't on the test.

Every other study discovered that repeated check-taking might be a higher reminiscence aid than studying. College students who were tested repeatedly have been able to remember 61% of the content while looking at the group recalled the most effective 40%. How can you observe those findings to your lifestyles? While seeking to research new data, self-check frequently to cement what you have learned into your memory.

9. Become More Effective

Occasionally, it looks as if there are hundreds of books, blogs, and magazine articles telling us the way to get more completed in an afternoon. However, how much of this advice is based on real studies? For example, think about the variety of times you have ever heard that multitasking can help you become more productive. Studies have discovered that trying to carry out multiple missions at the same time severely impairs pace, accuracy, and productiveness.

What classes from psychology can you operate to boom your productivity? Consider several of the following:

- Avoid multitasking while running on complex or dangerous obligations.

- Cognizance at the venture at hand.

- Eliminate distractions.

10. Be Healthier

Psychology also can be a useful device for improving your ordinary health. From approaches to encourage workout and better nutrients to new remedies for melancholy, the sector of fitness psychology gives a wealth of beneficial strategies that can help you to be more healthy and happier.

Some examples that you may practice at once in your very own existence:

- Research has shown that both daylight and synthetic mild can reduce the symptoms of seasonal affective sickness.

- Studies have demonstrated that exercise can contribute to more mental well-being.

- Studies have determined that supporting people apprehend the dangers of bad behaviors can lead to healthier choices.

Chapter 32. Delving Into Dark Psychology

Some of the best science fiction that has ever been written has surrounded the subject of mind control and its ability to control our world. However, it can still sound like a futuristic event. However, many neuroscientists are continuing to create a digital interface specifically designed to connect to the brain, which has continued to make progress in recent times. Even though this advanced technology is still unreachable, it has made plenty of headway where we could see mind control gadgets popping up everywhere shortly.

Currently, a technology known as brain-computer interfaces, or BCIs, has only been in the development stage for individuals who have fallen victim to injuries, debilitating such as being paralyzed. A great example of this is a paraplegic by the name of Dennis DeGray. Neuroscientists at Stanford University assisted DeGray in creating a major breakthrough and a typing world record involving mind control.

DeGray's success partially stems from the assistance of Jaimie Henderson. Henderson, a neurosurgeon at Stanford, successfully implanted two electrodes arrays the size of a tic-tac into DeGray's brain. DeGray's brain activity is then monitored by the electrode arrays, which helps decode electrical brain signals that neurons fire deep in the brain's motor cortex. The results achieved were beyond impressive and allowed for the early steps of achieving independence for many currently fully or partially paralyzed people. With a lot of interest pointed towards this ability to control the environment through a BCI, many researchers hope that future demonstrations can further the technology in the future ahead. It could even be as soon as the next 5-10 years that we could see more of it being integrated into people's lives.

Besides the research and development being conducted at Stanford, another company seems to be taking it one step further. Neural ink, founded by Tesla and SpaceX CEO Elon Musk, has become dedicated to creating BCI that they have labeled as "neural lace." To date, Neuralink has already raised close to $30 million for funding the project.

Nevertheless, like anything connected to the internet, one has to be extremely careful and diligent in the security and safe handling of all devices so that the device's security does not become compromised. We saw this occur when the Mirai botnet practically destroyed many internet areas that created attacks that used Denial of Service. Once a person's brain is implanted and connected to an internet device, this is when an entirely new level of security issues could occur, including a possible 'brain jacking.' Not only for security purposes, but it also could lead to many questions about ethical responsibility. For example, if a brain-controlled machine breaks the law, then who is arrested for it? Problems like this would need to require in-depth discussion before our future becomes a place where mind control is used for everything. However, in the short-term, an interface that is a less invasive brain-computer is already in use and which have significantly lower risks.

Many headsets have been developed and used in many drone races successfully as well as controlling Mind Desktop, which is a brain interface that is generalized for the use of Windows. With these devices, they bring less of a risk than implanting a chip into your brain. Not only that, but they do lack a few things too, especially with performance. This is seen with Mind Desktop, where a character is typed in 20 seconds. Regardless of that, they are still pretty cheap because of their use of electronics that have been modified. Therefore, if you currently have Mind Desktop, you are using an $800 "electroencephalogram" (a medical device used to measure brain activity) for a fraction of the real machine's cost.

When it comes to external BCI challenges, they mostly surround the skull, brain coverings, and scalps density and thickness. These characteristics prevent us from snooping on the brain's neurons with accuracy, which is what we think is essential for a BCI system to be high performing. As far as the future is concerned, we can only get remotely close to the information found on neurons is if we get an implant placed inside.

With many researchers making attempts to build a better BCI, other researchers have continued with their BCI implant technology. However, they have been experiencing technical issues of their own, which they will need to overcome. First, they hope to obtain an increased amount of views from their sensors, which will increase their ability to decode faster brain signals a lot more accurately. Plus, there remains the question of getting these outsides of the laboratory so people can use them.

These BCI's need to be constructed not to require a technician or some third-party intervention is of high importance since the main goal includes restoring people's independence while being paralyzed. This is why researchers are continuing to address these issues actively.

The erasing and implanting of memories seem to be only capable in movies such as Total Recall, Dark City, and Inception. But this idea no longer sounds as farfetched as we once thought since many people do not even lose sleep over the fact that it could happen someday. But now we can begin to see a brighter future with ontogenetic and how it continues to tamper with memory to bring it to light eventually. Although ontogenetic is still a relatively new procedure in the experimental stage, it has broken some laboratory ground. It uses light to activate or inactivate neurons that are highly specific by way of light-sensitive channels. For these to be used, they also require sensitive proteins. A few of these proteins include halorhodopsin or channelrhodopsin, which are added to the subject. These proteins are found naturally in many organisms. They need to be inserted genetically into an organism like in a rat or mice in the laboratory. Once injected, the neuron will fire every time the light is activated. When the light is on, the light enacts discretionary particles' progression, such as calcium or sodium, making the neuron produce an activity potential.

This system has been utilized in mice to control their eating or drinking propensities. The mice are hereditarily built to have these light-touchy proteins, and a wire is embedded into their cerebrum. Specialists demonstrated that the mice would keep eating while the light is turned on, regardless of whether they do not feel hungry. The best way to prevent the mice from eating is by killing the light. By basically turning on or off a light, one can control a neuron from terminating, bringing about certain and automatic conduct changes. This procedure can be utilized to figure out which neurons are required for specific activities. Likewise, researchers would now be able to figure out what capacity a neuron has by initiating it or deactivating and watching the impacts.

There have been a few speculations that caffeine may avert memory deficiencies by restraining the adenosine A2A receptor. A recent report demonstrated that the actuation of adenosine A2A receptor in the hippocampus, utilizing ontogenetic, was sufficient to weaken spatial memory in mice. This investigation not just exhibits the relationship between caffeine and abatement in memory misfortune; however, this additionally demonstrates the likelihood of erasing and hindering recollections in mice utilizing ontogenetic. Another investigation demonstrated that if neurons in the thalamic core reunions were initiated utilizing ontogenetic, the working memory in mice indicated deficiencies. As this system turns out to be further developed and used, researchers will frequently have a superior comprehension of which neurons influence memory and how they influence it.

Ontogenetic was utilized to take a gander at the impact of core cucumbers (NAC) on the "cocaine-setting related" memory guideline. They found that when the NAC neurons were enacted, the mice basically "overlooked" that cocaine was situated in that district. The researcher likewise saw that the actuation caused a diminished number of c-Fos+ cells in the VP, which has recently been related to a "decline in medication chasing." They presumed that these neurons were significant for the directing prize looking for conduct brought about by cocaine. This might be significant for deciding how a habit is shaped and maybe helping expansion issues.

This demonstrates the significance of certain natural triggers for medication addicts. If ontogenetic can help cancel the recollections engaged with the situations, it can have exceptional consequences for how we treat chronic drug habits. Not exclusively would memories be able to be deleted, yet false recollections can likewise be included. A recent report demonstrated that when dentate gyrus neurons were enacted, mice solidified in a spot where they had never been stunned, indicating dread. This dread was not there earlier, yet after the light was demonstrated, these mice had recollections of dread in a novel spot.

Even though ontogenetic is genuinely new, it is rapidly being consolidated into numerous tests. It is enabling us to all the more likely comprehend what impact enacting or deactivating neurons has on conduct. Unmistakably it is conceivable, at any rate in mice, to cause a mouse to do certain things utilizing optogenetics; we can even eradicate recollections and "make" new ones. One day those science fiction films may not look so inconceivable.

I do not mean the enthusiastic control intentionally used to get our particular manner. I mean the capacity to get others to figure out how we do and concur with us, just by the sheer quality of psyche.

Consider despots who can bewilder hordes of individuals with quality of speech while on the ascent to control. Analyze the content sometime in the not too distant future. You think it is difficult to see in what capacity numerous individuals moved toward becoming influenced around then. Consider a well-prepared canine or horse and the association with their proprietor. A steed is more grounded than the proprietor, and a canine normally increasingly deft, yet they obey directions. Consider the impact of "charm." How does a specific entertainer hold a crowd of people while similar words or activities by another entertainer are less captivating?

Are these things the aftereffect of the idea structure billows of extraordinary power, created by a solitary individual who empties their feelings into the conveyance and into that idea structure cloud? Rather than a few contemplations, social events to cause a solid cloud can include a solitary individual who has excellent conviction and self-conviction blended with crude feeling produce their cloud that overwhelms the psyches in the crowd?

In most close to home connections, there are fluctuating degrees of control, some favoring one individual one minute and the other the following minute. Equalization is accomplished at the point when intense feeling bolsters amazing personalities.

Chapter 33. The History of Dark Psychology

Human mythology is riddled with tales of ghosts and creatures that behave in such drastic ways. The very description sends chills down the adults' length that listened to such stories as relayed by past musicians and bards. The creation of monsters advises us that perhaps the universe is not as secure as it might seem from within our window. Beasts live among us and render our lifestyles as something to be protected against, as anything to be covered.

Maybe a creature crawls out of the closet while you rest in your room or slips in from a backdoor that you failed to lock. Perhaps you assumed you were over there, but as it enters your door, you listen to footprints crackling upstairs and a soft voice roaring. You see a bushy, tail-like foot poking out beneath the bed or a claw. You notice a massive, vicious laugh while running for life. You sprint into the shower, and the door is locked. It's not necessarily a stellar exit strategy as there is no window in your toilet, but you didn't know where to get off. Maybe the beast is on the escalators. You don't know where everything is. But after that, you push the above head bathroom light chain and see that you are the monster.

Monsters exist among humans and are medically related to as H. Sapiens... sapiens. Aliens from some other world did not commit actions of murder, theft, and ruin. They were living things who decided to commit these crimes, and today they also live among us. There is indeed a term in behavioral genetics, the so-called dark chord. Applies to the three characteristics of psychopathy, narcissism, and sociopathy, such as factors are deemed especially harmful, so distinguishing such people from the general public is necessary, or would it be?

Since ancient times, an argument could be made that human beings accept their character's horrific components. Today we believe in everyday practices of ancient history, such as orgiastic religious practices, human sacrifice, and ritualized murder as brutal acts of the past that indicate a better forgotten time. Still, it has been argued that these acts represent social and cultural outlets for the black universe that lies beneath the beautiful surface of the human outside.

Societies were then explicitly organized. This would be up upon you to determine whether things are more comfortable today or bad. As tacky as the past, as mentioned earlier, practices may have been, their career status within their living area represented an acknowledgment. That human being had a wrong side to their personality. It was great to give outlets to this dark side than to let it explode and simmer in unexpected ways. For what do today's gang stalking, serial murder, cybercrime, and narcissistic and antisocial acts portray, but living things give in to ends of themselves because they have already expressed themselves in other ways?

The argument is not to assert that living things must consider to give in to their so-called dark tendency of singularity, but to recommend that the contemporary art of mind control represents a variety of activities expressed in ancient society in unique ways. Although the conversation of societies' tradition of providing into their character's dark sides may seem incidental to the discussion of mind control, few things could be essential. A significant phase in planning for defense lies in understanding anyone, you know, maybe the perpetrator of these black arts. It could be someone you already understand.

History of Dark Psychology Study

The 2 social scientific patterns that proactive solutions-day dark psychology are undoubtedly abnormal psychology and psychology for individuals. Irregular psychology is a psychology experiment concerned with psychological illness-related habits of behaviors, emotion, and behavior. These emotions, thoughts, and actions can precede a psychiatric disorder and are usually thought abnormal. As psychology tends to construct a relatively linear dichotomy between normal versus strange behavior, a sociological factor will come under the scepter between irregular or atypical behavioral forms instead of actions assumed to be inside the usual spectrum.

In the early late nineteenth century, person psychology was founded on human conduct driven by the purposeful activity compared to latent libido and sex impulses that describe Freudian psychoanalysis. While we have already addressed in some depth the degree to which individual acts are not consciously driven. May thus be viewed as non-purpose, person psychology allows for implicit or involuntary motives. It just appears to recognize them when non-Freudian, benevolent, and even not always implicit.

For example, as a motivating factor for action, Alfred Adler focused many of his texts on superiority complexes. He found that people who handled the situation in angry or otherwise unbecoming ways were generally inspired by a sense of inadequacy, which is a certain sense caused them to "act out." Now in some people, an inferiority complex as an enthusiastic may lie beneath the surface. However, others may be fully aware that they have a feature of themselves. They are not completely satisfied and trying to compensate.

When creating dark psychology as an outgrowth of internal mental ideas compared to Freudian psychoanalysis concepts, it may be simpler to assume. That human beings usually act with conscious, deliberate motivations instead of being consciously or unconsciously inspired by sexual urges, such as the well-studied complex of Oedipus (the desire for a man to kill his father and sleep). To truly comprehend the historical growth of dark psychology as a research field, it is crucial to realize that individual psychology's philosophy requires non-completely aware motives to explain why human beings tend to act in such a cruel fashion. Even so, the theory of dark psychology supposes that humans are capable of a dark universe, engaging in harmful actions that have no purpose at all.

The research and therapy of psychological disorders have been around as a field of study since the Ancient Egyptians. We have more data from the Greek period, partly because we are closer to the Greek philosophy period in time than we are from the Egyptians. This group just seems to reach the concept of pathology with a fascinating avidity. The research of what we term pathological psychology today existed in the 18th and 19th centuries and earlier in asylum and hospices that diagnosed people and women with rare mental disorders, but the discipline as we now know it dates from the 20th century.

Indeed, in the 19th century, trepanation, exorcism, and being burnt on the stakes as a witch were the standard remedies for pathological mental conditions. Trepanation relates to drilling a hole in the brain to expel malignant spirits from their grip over the head. It is claimed by others to be the earliest surgical technique we have historical evidence. Trepanation was already performed in the 19th century. Today, there are proponents of the procedure, though their appeals usually fell on deaf ears.

Exorcism also looks at how society viewed odd habits and emotions in the current age. Indeed, many practices that we consider to fall inside the normal range today have been considered mental diseases up till the early 1980s. Exorcism, although maybe less brutal than trepanation, represented the perspective that an evil force or demon inhabited the individual who possessed the weird thoughts and actions. All this has been a transmission from the individual's malevolent encouragement to anything else, whether something else was an informant of evil or an agent of evil.

One line of thinking recognizes Satan as the manifestation of human potential to act in a manner "strange" or, more accurately, evil or cruel. It is hard to say whether their ideas of ghouls, demons, values, or even of Satan himself embody that people beings were produced to commit acts of possession. They could be better described as stories intended to fool children or teach them valuable life lessons of good and evil. Of course, exorcisms are still happening today; individuals who assume evil acts come from ownership.

If you believe that the evil committed by human beings comes from a source outside the human being, then the dark psychological theory because it currently stands may be somewhat contrary to what you believe. However, a locally crucial in dark psychology is the idea that humans can behave without purpose in a remarkably violent and cruel manner, only as an augmentation of something obscure that dwells inside us. It is up to you to ascribe this type of conduct to Satan as a component of your religious views.

Of course, 19th-century and later abnormal psychologists did not fully recognize this idea of an independent factor for the conditions they were seeing. So treatments such as trepanation or exorcism would've been disturbing or at least pointless to them. As we commented on earlier, scientists shifted away towards the dogmatic beliefs that dominated their careers, ideologies that mostly had more to do with theology than with the professions' empirical compendia. There is nothing intrinsically inconsistent with religious belief, of course. Still, a practitioner who is inexperienced with human anatomy if he is not permitted to examine q cadaver is probably to follow a religion that is not advantageous to him (or herself) or you.

Abnormal psychologists started to question why humans were inspired to behave abnormally. The Devil or the Demons were not entirely acceptable responses. Most of these research groups in psychological disorders were psychiatrists and psychoanalysts who undertook detailed studies of these subjects based on a new, more free understanding of health matters. Though the word dark psychology did not emerge until later in the mid-twentieth century, narcissists, sociopaths, and those who we might identify today as possessing mental illnesses were conducted already throughout the 19th-century studies.

Abnormal psychology of that time would have followed the trend of what we now understand as Freudian psychoanalysis, with Alfred Adler's writings representing one of Freudian's first significant departures. Although Adler is a virtually unknown figure today, his biographies from the generations 1912-1914 provided the basis of many concepts that permeate today's psychological field. His writings were translated into English in 1925. And his personality beliefs and where they derive from predominate in advance psychotherapy and psychoanalysis.

Adler focused on resignation, compensation, and overcompensation as the 3 external factors that shaped personality development. His theories parallel those of another essential psychologist, Abraham Maslow, who acknowledged Alder's influence on his work. Although Adler himself didn't even write about "dark psychology," his theories helped shape this topic's development as a departure from pre-existing psychoanalytical theories.

The analysis of dark psychology can be new. Still, it reflects a spectrum of habits that have been associated with individuals from the very start. The dark area of psychology provides the illusion of a transient research domain. The word and the principles connected with it are more widely available to the people. This has turned dark psychological into a topic that remains beyond the radar of those who may be victims of perpetrators exploiting their resources to damage impact.

Chapter 34. Advanced Techniques to Manipulate Human Psychology

Sources tell us that it is concealment—hiding in the shadows, knowing when to strike. It is also a false front, hiding true intentions. When we are talking about this level of deception, we are talking about hiding aggression. When we take, there is a certain level of aggressive behavior that happens. A small part of manipulation is hiding that aggressive behavior so that the victim sees only good nature.

This is accomplished in various ways and means, one being knowledge. When we allow another to know us, we display vulnerability along with strengths. The experience of these personality traits can give the manipulator the ability to maneuver around without any alarms going off.

- The effectiveness of manipulating those strengths and vulnerabilities arrives when the dark practitioner knows what is vulnerable and inspires pride.

A reoccurring ideology that drives us to war takes into consideration that the action is more negative than positive. We want to avoid it. The manipulation process sees pride in all of us and plays to that pride. It is our strength. For example, when used to drive an army to slaughter others, the intention of our satisfaction has been manipulated to enforce the agendas of others.

- Often, the practitioners of dark psychology use aggression and fear to drive us. The less dark side still falls into the category of knowing what weakness is. That weakness leaves the individual open to control.

How the manipulator uses that control determines the severity of manipulation. There are positive versions of manipulating others, like convincing someone that they are not doing well and needing help. We, however, are looking at the darker side of this. The manipulator uses their control skills to get what they want—and the cost does not apply.

- There are many ways to move another into a place of being controlled. From the positive to the negative, psychological manipulators utilize all tactics.

When positive reinforcement is used, the charm is displayed. A forced smile or laughter can trigger laughter in all of us. As when we were infants, we copy what we see. When we see tears, we want them to stop. When we see a smile, we find ourselves smiling as well. Using positive reinforcement, the manipulator can shower money, charm, and gifts to get us to feel something. The usage of these things allows control of us on an instinctual level. We follow those who tell us what we want to hear.

- Psychological manipulation can also implement negative reinforcement. This is a form of deflection—the substitution of one thing for another.

Often, we have things we need or have to do, and we do not want to do them. The psychological manipulation of negative reinforcement uses that power of negativity to lure the subject from their original need, pushing them toward something they want to be done instead. The long game, a slow play of putting tasks into another's life and then controlling those tasks so that the manipulator can get what they want, is an extraordinarily useful and subdued tactic. Sometimes only partial reinforcement is required to gain control. We are talking about elevating the fear or doubt regarding the tasks needed to be done. The partial is the extended play. It knows that in the end, the victim will lose. It knows that by planting small seeds now, victory will eventually happen. It knows that we all have our weaknesses and that by planting even a tiny seed, we can take someone to that weakness. An individual trying to work toward something they already were shaky on or had doubts about will listen to the lie and flow with that idea, and use it to their destruction.

- The partial manipulator only needs to put the thought in mind, knowing the weakness is already there, and utilizing it will take their prey to a destructive end.

Psychological manipulators flat, outright punish. From an actual physical lashing to the victim's passive-aggressive playing, punishment is beneficial when one wants to control another.

- We skulk and cry and yell and nag and go completely silent. This is the blackmail of the manipulator. It inspires guilt in us. That "wanting to be the better person" rises to the front, and we do what the manipulator wants. When the manipulator sets free the crocodile tears, we have no idea if they are real or not. The degree of crying is not up to us to determine. Only the manipulator knows if the tears are legitimate or not. In this case, the trap is often sprung from the victim's side. They walk up to the hurt individual to help, only to find that the manipulator is just lying in wait to strike.

- One extreme version of manipulation is violence.

Violence triggers something inside us. We often do anything to avoid it. The manipulator knows that power strategically applied can make us go into a state of avoidance. There incites the control, physical violence can have mental scarring, and the manipulator causes the scarring. It places power in tactical places to get the result they want.

Some would say this is the darkest of the dark. Taken to the individual, this can mentally damage them for an extended period, if not permanently. Placed on a world stage, it can lead up to the physical conflict of genocide.

- Mostly, it is about gain. Manipulators of the dark want to gain something. When we speak about improvement, we are talking about power and influence, control and manipulation over others. The trophy is up to the individual. This can be everything as to gaining affections, to money, and even to life itself.

It is about gaining for their reasons and gratifications. The taking of others and making the power and control their own. Selfishness to the extreme. The mind of the dark practitioner sees the ultimate win as the gain over others. They have power. Superiority is the power over another, and taking of someone else's power makes them feel superior. This is a tremendous driving force behind the manipulator. Often, in the case of immature individuals driving manipulations toward superiority, any is pushed aside for just the feeling of being superior. In relationships, it is about control. The manipulation of power can put one in control. Although we have looked at the vampire and energy role, we know who has control.

This feeling of control can be overwhelming to the mental state of the dark. Almost drug-like, it is a feeling of emotion that is more logical. Management is one of the most straightforward manipulation tactics to achieve with only logic to guide. It drives not only the victim but the manipulator as well. Psychological manipulation can also be about self-esteem. The self of the manipulator is always in question. This is one of the reasons they manipulate, to define themselves. How easily they can manage, another can tell the dark that they are better than others. That weakness and strength can be measured in the tactical playing field of the hustle.

- The dark psychological manipulator is bored most of the time, more than most. The psychological manipulator will often use manipulation to determine the validity of feelings and emotions.

This boils down to that manipulation applied in relations with others helps the manipulator regulate reactions to validate or not validate their own emotions. The manipulator measures the self and their self-esteem by how others handle their self-questioning. This happens when the practitioner does not have a grasp on what emotions are. They look at their feelings as invalid and manipulate the situation in such a way as to validate them. We are stuck with ourselves, and we cannot get away. Psychological manipulators validate or invalidate themselves by the tactical controlling of others. It is an exciting way of viewing life, although we all idolize one form of manipulation.

- **The con aspect.** One common form of manipulation is the convincing of another to make their money's yours. This is a hidden agenda of the criminal. This form of mental manipulation preys mostly on the elderly and the rich. However, we all can fall into this form of manipulation. We choose to spend on, and we do not respond to a state of psychological manipulation.

Something happens when the buck is passed over, we go from manipulation into action, and something drives us. It is within us, and it is outside forces that drive. What causes this drive and the drive itself is called Persuasion.

The manipulation process in dark psychology usually is not a single move. It is a complex series of actions, often with the outcome only known by the manipulator. The motivations of manipulators are as convoluted as human nature.

Chapter 35. Mind Control

Mind control is an aspect of manipulation that is similar to brainwashing. The main difference is that the individual might only want to control your mind at the moment. Maybe they want to get you to do something that will benefit them temporarily because they are opportunistic individuals. Since there is not much time to take over a person's mind when you are engaged in a simple conversation, there are some very detailed techniques that a manipulator will use to attempt to gain control of your mind. As you explore these techniques, you will also learn how to combat each of them. The stronger your reason is, the better you will ward off the people trying to harm you.

Compensating for Lack of Physical Prowess

Someone might try to control your mind because you secretly intimate them. Because someone does not appear physically threatening, a manipulator will be quick to move forward with mind control by seeing how much they can change your thoughts. The mind control gives them the same type of satisfaction they would receive if they were physically controlling you. Because the latter is a lot more prominent, the idea of controlling your mind is also a lot more appealing. You will find that manipulators are very discreet about this.

They might remark on how strong or tough you are, building you up based on your physical characteristics. Even a simple comment about you being tall can be enough to let you think that they respect you because you have more physical prowess than they do—this is what they want you to think. Instead of backing down, which you will think they are doing, they make you more vulnerable by making you comfortable.

When you believe that someone sees powerful traits in you, you will be less likely to assume that they have bad intentions. Surely because they appear to respect you, they won't deceive you, right? Always make sure that you remind yourself anyone can fool you at any time. It is hard to keep track of everyone's true intentions, especially when they have mastered the art of mind control.

What You Can Do: Remain firm in your core beliefs. Even if you believe that the individual respects you and what you stand for, always remind yourself of what you hold dear to your heart. Staying true to who you give you little reason to change your opinions on a whim. Remind yourself that the person trying to control your mind is very insecure.

Using Hand Placement as a Decoy

Have you ever noticed that people normally place their fingers on their heads when thinking very hard? In moments of concentration, you have probably done the same thing. This is a subconscious mind control technique that is often used by manipulators. When they want you to rethink something, they might place their fingers on their head to coax you into doing the same. With the help of muscle memory, your brain will be receiving a message that it needs to think harder.

It is an interesting technique because it is so subtle. You surely would not notice it if you were not looking for it in the first place. As you become better at reading body language, you will become more aware of moments when the person you are talking to is merely using a decoy movement as an attempt to control you. Do your best to break the mirroring effect that typically happens during a conversation. Keep your arms in a neutral position by your side.

Manipulators get nervous. They probably get very nervous and will do the best they can to hide this from you. As soon as you notice their fingers move up to their head, imagine that they are nervous that they won't be able to pull off this attempt at mind control. Pride yourself in your ability to pick up on it before it affects you—this will keep you strong.

What You Can Do: In an attempt to break their cycle, you can make a comment that indirectly refers to them concentrating. Something like, "Oh, is that what you were thinking?" is a way to make manipulators second-guess their abilities. If you let them know from the start that you are not automatically going to agree with what they are saying, this will be your way of standing your ground.

Convincing You of Psychic Powers

The person who is manipulating you is not any more powerful than you—repeat this to yourself often. Even though many mind controllers are portrayed as psychic beings, this is not the case for most. A successful manipulator is usually just very good at picking up on your body language and context. There is nothing psychic about it, though it can feel that way at times.

Being misinformed that someone is psychic and can read your mind at any time is intimidating. These are your private thoughts, and you do not want anyone intruding upon them. The good news is that you never have to let this happen. You are still in control of your inner thoughts, and what you share with the world is always going to be your decision. Anyone who tries to force you or to coax you into sharing something you do not want to does not have your best interest at heart.

The mention of psychic abilities might come up as a joke. For example, the manipulator will joke around with you while mentioning that you don't need to say much because they already know what you are thinking. You can laugh this off, but you can also remain firm in believing that this isn't true. With the way you portray yourself, you can get them to think anything you want.

What You Can Do: Always be aware of your intention during every conversation. If you are presenting yourself in a certain way, the manipulative person will pick up on it. Try your hardest to practice standing neutrally and speaking neutrally. When you can master this concept, it will be a lot harder for them to read you.

Surrounding You with Other Manipulative People

This is an incredibly dangerous mind-control technique because it closely ties in with the idea behind brainwashing. The more people that you believe are on the same page about something will make you want to agree with them, too. If a manipulator can find other people who want to manipulate a vulnerable person, you might become an easy target for a bad situation. They will gang up on you in a way that is subtle yet effective. You do not have to put up with this. Knowing who you are as a person will protect you in many ways.

There will be times when a manipulator will only "scout" for like-minded individuals that believe in the point they are making. Unknowingly, they might recruit innocent bystanders to further lead you into thinking that you must agree with them. The people that also fall victim to these traps might be people you love and respect. This is why it might be tempting to give in and to just "go with the flow." It is what the manipulator wants you to think. They want others to know that it is easier to go with a mass opinion than form their own.

What You Can Do: Speak up when you disagree with something. This is difficult because you do not want to cause conflict or controversy, but it becomes necessary to protect yourself. A disagreement does not always have to turn into an argument. If you approach the situation maturely, you can simply speak your mind to get your point across without requiring validation. You can provide this for yourself. Remind yourself that it is not other people's opinions that matter most. Your view of yourself dictates your self-esteem.

Believing it Won't Happen to You

Because a mind controller works hard to use other people, you might assume that they would instead do this to strangers or bystanders. One of the most challenging realities to face is that these individuals are more likely to attempt the act of mind control on a loved one. This happens because the task seems a lot easier—they already know you well. Instead of having to figure out the things that get under your skin, they have an idea of what to say and how to persuade you. Realizing this can be very hurtful, especially when you have many trusts invested in the person.

"I would never do anything to hurt you" is a promise that is often broken by a manipulator. With mind control, they are directly going against that promise, even if it doesn't feel hurtful at the moment. When someone does not respect you for who you are, they will do anything to change you. Suggesting you should get something else to eat or that you should shop elsewhere for clothing are two simple examples of how manipulators can use their conviction to change you.

You might not believe that these little changes mean much, but when you add them up, they can completely transform who you are as a person. It is not a great feeling to realize that you no longer recognize who you are. As upsetting as it is, you have to work on rebuilding yourself and getting back to your roots. It is normal to feel betrayed because this is what the manipulator has done to you—betrayed your trust.

What You Can Do: Never let your naive thinking get in the way of your rational thinking. You are not immune to the mind control that goes on around you. Your strength does not necessarily protect you from the intentions of all manipulators. By keeping yourself humble, you will always be on alert for the red flags presented by those who wish to change your mind.

The Blank Stares of Intimidation

Making a statement to someone and receiving a blank stare in return is intimidating for many reasons. One of the most prominent is that you do not know what they are thinking. It scares you because you might not know what to say or do next. A manipulator will use this technique to control your mind after you have said something vulnerable or profound. This will make you second-guess if what you said was "wrong" or incorrect somehow. You will end up prioritizing their feelings over your own.

They might follow this instance up with a statement that seems wise or all-knowing. When you combine the two actions, you are sure to believe that they can read your mind or that they know something you don't know. Both possibilities are unsettling in their ways. When you feel a negative emotion, understand that this is what your manipulator wants you to feel. They want to catch you off-guard and make you question everything that you have confirmed in your reality. By slowly breaking you down and staring at you blankly, you will get the idea that you came to this conclusion independently. It becomes maddening when you do not realize what is happening to you.

Chapter 36. Mind Control Techniques

Mind control involves using influence and persuasion to change the behaviors and beliefs of someone. That someone might be the person themselves, or it might be someone else. Mind control has also been referred to as brainwashing, thought reform, coercive persuasion, mental control, and manipulation, just to name a few. Some people feel that everything is done by manipulation. But if that is true to be believed, then important points about manipulation will be lost. Influence is much better thought of as a mental continuum with two extremes. One side has respectful and ethical influences and works to improve the individual while showing respect for them and their basic human rights. The other side contains dark and destructive influences that work to remove that human rights from a person, such as independence, rational thought, and sometimes their real identity.

When thinking of mind control, it is better to see it use influence on other people to disrupt something in them, as their way of thinking or living. The influence works based on what makes people human, such as their behaviors, beliefs, and values. It can disrupt the very way they chose personal preferences or make critical decisions. Mind control is nothing more than using words and ideas to convince someone to say or do something they might never have thought of saying or doing on their own.

There are scientifically proven methods that can be used to influence other people. Mind control has nothing to do with fakery, ancient arts, or even magical powers. Real mind control is the basis of a word that many people hate to hear. That word is marketing. Many people hate to hear that word because of the negative connotations associated with it. When people hear "marketing," they automatically assume that it refers to those ideas taught in business school. But the basis of marketing is not about deciding which part of the market to target or deciding which customers will likely buy this product. The basis of marketing is one very simple word. That word is "YES."

If a salesperson asks a regular customer to write a brief endorsement of the product they buy, they will hopefully say yes. If someone asks their significant other to take some of the business cards to pass out at work, they will hopefully say yes. If you write any blog and ask another blogger to provide a link to yours on their blog, they will hopefully say yes. When enough people say yes, the business or blog will begin to grow. With even more yesses, it will continue to grow and thrive. This is the very simple basis of marketing. Marketing is nothing more than using mind control to get other people to buy something or do something beneficial. And the techniques can easily be learned.

The first technique in mind control is to tell people what you want them to want. Never tell people to think it over or take some time. That is a definite mind control killer. People already have too much going on in their minds. When they are told to think something over, they will not. It will be forgotten, and then it will never happen. This has nothing to do with being stupid or lazy and everything to do with just being way too busy.

So the best strategy is to take the offensive and think for them. Everything must be explained in the beginning. Never assume that the other blogger will automatically understand the benefits of adding a link will be for them. Do not expect anyone to give a demonstration blindly. And merely asking for a testimonial, while it might garner an appositive response, probably will not garner a well-formed testimonial to the product. Instead, be prepared to explain the blog, show examples, and offer compelling reasons why this merger will benefit both parties. Have the demonstration laid out in great detail with notes on what to say when and visuals to go along with the letters, so all the other person has to do is present the information. Offer the customer a few testimonials that have already been received and ask them to choose one and personalize it a bit. Always be specific in explaining what is desired. Explain why it is desired. Show how this will work. Tell the person how to do it and why they should do it. If done correctly, it will feel exactly like one friend advising another friend on which is the best path to take. And the answer will be yes, simply because saying yes makes so much sense.

Think of the avalanche. Think of climbing all the way to the top of the highest mountain ever. Now, at the top, think of searching for the biggest, heaviest boulder on the mountain. Now, picture summoning up superhuman strength to push this boulder, dislodging it from the place it has rested for years and years. Once this boulder is loosened, it rolls easily over the edge of the cliff, crashing into thousands of other boulders on its way down the mountain, taking half of the mountain with it in a beautiful cascade of rocks and dirt. Imagine sitting there, smiling cheerfully at the avalanche that was just created.

Marketing and mind control are very like creating an avalanche. Getting the first person to answer yes might be difficult. But each subsequent yes will be easier. Always start at the top, never the bottom. Starting at the top is more complicated. It is more likely to come with more negative responses than positive responses in the beginning. But starting at the top also yields a much greater reward when the avalanche does begin. And the results will be far greater than beginning at the bottom of the mountain. Yes, the small rock is easier to push over. Then it can be built upon by pushing over another small rock, then another. This way can work, but it will take much longer than being successful at the top. No one ever went fishing for the smallest fish in the pond or auditioned for the secondary role just to be safe. Everyone wants that top prize. Do not be afraid to go for it.

On the other hand, never ask for the whole boulder the first time. Ask for part of it. This may seem directly contradictory, but it is not. Always start with a small piece. Make the beginning easier for everyone to see. Let other people use their insight to see the result. When the first bit goes well, then gradually ask for more and more and more.

Think of writing a guest spot for someone else who has their own blog. By sending in the entire manuscript first, there is a greater risk of rejection. Begin small. Send them a paragraph or two discussing them with the idea. Then outline the idea and send that in an email. Then write the complete draft you would like them to use and send it along. When asking a customer for a testimonial, start by asking for a few lines in an email. Then ask the customer to expand those few lines into a testimonial covering at least half a typed page. The customer will soon be ready for an hour-long webcast extolling the product's virtues and your great customer service skills.

Everything must have a deadline that exists. The important word here is the word 'real.' Everyone has heard the salesperson who said to decide right away because the deal might not be available later or another customer was coming in, and they might get it. That is a total fabrication, and everyone knows it to be true. There are no impending other customers, and the deal is not going to disappear. There is no real sense of urgency involved. But everyone does it. There are too many situations where people are given a fake deadline by someone who thinks it will instill a great sense of urgency for completing the task. It is not only totally not effective but completely unneeded. It is a simple matter to create true urgency. Only leave free things available for a finite amount of time. When asking customers for testimonials, be certain to mention the last possible day for it to be received to be able to be used. Some people will be unable to assist, but having people unable to participate is better than never beginning.

Always give before you receive it. And do not ever think that giving is fifty-fifty. Always give much more than is expected in return. Before asking for a testimonial from a satisfied customer, be sure to make numerous acts of exceptional customer service. Before asking a blog writer for a link, link theirs to yours many times. This is not about helping someone out so that they will help you. This is all about being so totally generous that the person who is asked for the favor cannot possibly say no. It might mean extra work, but that is how to influence other people.

Always stand up for something much bigger than average. Do not just write another blog on how to do something. Use a critical issue to take a stand and defend the stance with unbeatable logic and genuine passion. Do not just write a how-to manual. Choose a particular idea and sell people on it, using examples of other people with the same idea living the philosophy.

Never feel shame. This does not mean being extremely extroverted to the point of silliness or having a total lack of conscience in business dealings. In mind control, shamelessness refers to a full, complete belief that this course of action is the best possible course. Everyone will benefit greatly from it. This is about writing the best possible blog ever and believing that everyone needs to read it to improve their lives. It is about believing in a particular product so deeply that the feeling is that everyone will benefit from using it. Knowing deep inside that this belief is the correct belief ever and everyone should believe it.

Mind control uses the idea that someone's decisions and emotions can be controlled using psychological means. It uses negotiation or mental influence powers to ensure the outcome of the interaction is more favorable to one person over the other. This is what marketing is: convincing someone to do something particular or buy something in particular. Being able to control someone else's mind merely means understanding the power of human emotion and playing upon those emotions. It is easier to have a mental impact on people if there is a basic understanding of human emotions. Angry people will back down when the subject of their anger is not afraid. Angry people feed upon the fear of others.

Chapter 37. Influence People With Mind Control

A mind controller approaches the victim with the sole intent of cloning themselves, making the other person think like them. This is a complicated thing to do, so, to achieve it, one has to possess an inflated ego, lack doubts about themselves, and have a high sense of entitlement. All of us are susceptible to manipulation, and what matters is how much effect the mind control will have on us.

Psychologists studying mind control have found out that the entire process seems to adhere to a typical structure. This conclusion was made after a study was conducted on multiple marketing and networking companies which used mind control to persuade clients to purchase their products. One of the remarkable similarities is that all new members joining the companies underwent pre-planned training to recruit more people and convince potential customers to buy their products. The training sessions are meant to make the employees think like the company wants and use a mind twist to convince people.

Let us now look at the mind control process in detail:

Step 1: Understanding the target

Before anything else, the manipulator will seek to establish a bond or connection with their potential victim. Good intent, or friendship, will be the first step because it makes the victim lower all their social and psychological defenses. Once the controller gains the target's trust, they start reading them to devise the most effective method to invade them. The reading aims to tell whether their victim is susceptible to their manipulation. Just like any project manager, they do not like wasting time on a subject they suspect might outsmart them and lead to failure.

Multiple clues are used to scan the victim. They include vocal style, body language, social status, gender, emotional stability, etc. A person's traits can be used to decode the strength of their defenses. All this time, the manipulator will be asking themselves questions like, "Are you introvert or extrovert?" "Are you weakly?" "Are you emotional?" "Are you self-confident?" Humans give a lot of information about themselves when interacting with each other. This is something that the controller knows all too well. From these signs, they can quickly tell if the person is cooperating. They will look at body posture and immediately analyze the victim. Excess blinking might insinuate that a person is lying. Arms folded across the chest might show a lack of interest or insecurity. Taking enormous strides while walking might portray fear. As you can see, the body releases so much data at any given time that it is essential to be aware of the signs that you are giving out

When the attacker has collected enough data from the target, they now understand their interests, strengths, weaknesses, routines, and so on. Using this information, they can decide on an entry point, which will allow for easy and accurate manipulation. They also determine whether the target is worth the effort. If they see one as a favorable target, they move to the other step in the mind control process- unfreezing factual beliefs and values.

Step 2: Unfreezing Solid Beliefs and Values

All of us have some beliefs and values engraved deep within. Most of them are the principles that were instilled in us since childhood, and others have been acquired from experiences are we grow older. We rarely let go of them, but revise them as we proceed. Most of them make up our identities, so we do not like them being interfered with. If these principles are threatened, contradicted, or questioned at any point in time, our natural reaction is to defend them through all means possible. However, if a good-enough reason is given to us, so we voluntarily question them ourselves; we undergo a process known as "unfreezing."

Tons of reasons can lead us to unfreeze: a breakup, the death of a loved one, religious interference, getting evicted from our houses, to mention but a few. These situations force us to seek answers to complex cases, which goes as deep as questioning our sole beliefs and values. Take this, for example:

Way back when I am a teenager, we had some family friends who were solid Christians. It happens that my best friend, who was my exact age, came from this family. His name was Sam. Sam used to tell me about the Bible and its teachings, trying to convince me to accept salvation and live according to its instructions. I remember asking him why he was so insistent on this issue. He would respond that all problems were solvable with saving and that life was much more comfortable and happier. Fast-forward about fifteen years, Sam's mother was diagnosed with breast cancer. They tried all forms of treatment available at the time, but the cancer would grow back. One day, while talking to him about the issue, he looked at me with a pale face and said, "I think what they say about Christianity is not real!" Unsure about what he had just said, I asked him why he thought so. He responded that they had met tens of spiritual leaders for prayers, but his mother's cancer was only getting worse. What's worse, she would not live for more than a year.

Sad as Sam's story is, it makes us realize that some situations in life might force us to question the vital principles that we grow up with. In this case, my best friend had come to doubt the very same religion that he once felt had automatic solutions to all of life's problems. In the very same manner, a manipulator will dig deep into their victim's life to understand their vulnerabilities and exploit them fully. These people will say anything they think their targets would love to hear. Once the victim swallows the manipulator's comfort, there is a shift in power dynamics, and the target is now ready for the manipulation.

Step 3: Reprogramming the Mind

The mind control process seeks to separate the target from their initial beliefs and begin reprogramming their mind. The reprogramming is meant to install the manipulator's beliefs and values into the victim's mind. Apart from distancing the initial principles, the controller also tries their best to make them look wrong or harmful, or the cause of past mishaps in the victim's life. If the victim absorbs this reprogramming, their defense is lowered to zero, and they now become a robot that is ready to accept any operating system that is offered.

During the reprogramming phase, the attacker will ensure the victim has minimal contact with the outside world. They make everyone else appear insignificant to the victim because this raises their opportunity to deposit their malicious principles. This behavior is typical in cults, mostly crafted to sway their followers from mainstream human life. Some cults go as far as controlling their followers' food intake as a way of weakening them. The psychology behind this idea is that a weak person will always turn to the person they feel has the power to protect them or alleviate their suffering. The same happens in relationships, where one partner plays the controlling role. The victimized one has no choice but to adhere to the other. You might wonder why some people put up with violent partners. Still, so far, you must already understand that the problem is more profound than it appears. If you control a person's mind, you can control their lives.

Once the victim has been reprogrammed, the manipulator moves into the final phase of the mind control process known as "freezing."

Step 4: Freezing the New Beliefs and Values

Once the victim has been fed with contrasting principles by the offender, the offender applies tactics to cement the new beliefs into their brains. This is what psychologists call "freezing." The freezing bit is necessary because the controller is aware of the person's original ideas that might clash with their initial ones. As such, they need to force the victim to choose their malicious principles over their old ones. To do this, they might apply any of the following methods.

One of the methods is using the reward/punishment approach. When the victim acts according to the manipulator's demands, they are rewarded. Hopefully, you see the similarity between the freezing process and dog training. The dog is given treats when it follows the trainer's instructions. The trainer aims at solidifying the new skill in the dog by rewarding it. In the future, if the dog is instructed to do the same thing, it will not hesitate since it has been made to think that obeying the command is useful and attracts a reward. The same applies to mind control; when the victim follows, they are made to feel that what they did was right and deserves a reward.

Punishments are the second most-applied approach in the freezing process. If the victim deviates from the controller's commands, they are punished. If we go back to a cult scenario, they usually have defined punishments for violations of terms. During the Holocaust, for instance, any Germans who failed to hail Hitler were punished through imprisonment or death. In the same way, any German who was suspected of protecting the Jews was shot. Hitler understood that by punishing anyone who went against his rules, he would force every German to help him attain his ethnic cleansing objective. The psychological trick used in these situations is that the victim is made to see punishment as justice being served for breaking the rules.

Mind controllers' final method to solidify their manipulation is to transform their victims into their agents. Better put, once the controller feels that the victim's pseudo personality has materialized, they use them to distribute their worldviews. We said that the mind controller's list is to create a replica of themselves in the other person. Therefore, once the controlling process is complete, the victim starts living like the attacker without realizing it. Depending on the manipulation's nature, the victim might also be used to recruit more victims into the oppressor's way of thinking and living. This is especially true in the context of marketing and networking. From this explanation, we can readily tell why a wife is likely to be violent towards the kids if the husband is violent. The kids are also expected to be violent towards each other or their friends. The process of mind control is slow, but once it solidifies, it can result in devastating effects.

Chapter 38. Dark Persuasion

Whenever folks try to provide meaning to the notion of demeanor, their responses always come in various forms. Even though some could put their thoughts on the ads and advertisements which are everywhere in contemporary society, advocating you to patronize a specific product or service over the other others' heads fall back into the politicians who attempt to modify the minds of Republicans simply to get yet another vote in the polls. Both instances are right since they are messages targeted at altering the understanding of this topic. The purpose of diversion between ordinary persuasion and dim persuasion is the dark persuasion doesn't necessarily have a moral rationale.

Even though a standard persuader might attempt to convince someone for this individual's own great, a dim persuader does so together with motives that are not always great for another individual. They try to obtain a total grasp of the individual they would like to convince and take pains to do this since they understand the greatest motivation.

While persuasion consistently has ethical consequences, a dim persuader doesn't concern themselves with those consequences. In reality, they are mindful of these, but decide to put their eyes on their goal (s) rather than persuasion as a mental phenomenon in an individual's regular life. It's either that you're the person attempting to convince someone else or you're being persuaded. What makes the distinction between dark and ordinary is that the motivation for this. In mass media, politics, legal and advertising conclusions, persuasion comes to play all of the time. The results of instructing it in such areas are set utilizing persuasion to determine the topic of influence.

There are a few clear and crucial differences between behavioral and other brain control varieties, like brainwashing and hypnosis. Even though these two demands that the topic should be isolated from modifying their thoughts and individuality, persuasion doesn't require isolation. To be able to reach the target, manipulation is utilized on a single individual. Although persuasion may also be performed on a single topic to make them change their thoughts, there's also a chance of using it on a vast scale to alter the heads of an entire group or a whole society.

Because of this, persuasion is a much better mind control procedure and maybe more harmful since it can alter the minds of lots of people at precisely the same time rather than the head of only one individual at one time. Many people produce the error of believing that they have immunity to the consequences of persuasion because they think that they will always have the ability to observe every sales pitch that comes in their way.

They think they'll always have the ability to use logic to grasp what's happening and find a logical decision for this. As a result of how people aren't ever likely to fall for whatever they hear, this might be accurate if they utilize logic. It's likewise feasible to steer clear of persuasion since the debate doesn't augur nicely with the individual's beliefs, whatever the strength of this debate. Some individuals understand how to use clear messages to inspire people to market the industry's newest gadgets or goods. This information action is quite delicate, so the topic won't always recognize it; therefore, it's going to be rather difficult for them to continually have the ability to decide the information they will get.

Every time is said, it's extremely probable that you think about it in a terrible light. That is because it is inclined to automatically consider a conman or salesman who's always attempting to make them modify their view, and that will finally push them till this shift is reached. While black persuasion is notable in earnings and conning clinics, also, there are ways that persuasion may be used permanently, such as in diplomatic relationships between global bodies or at public service attempts. The difference only lies in the method by which in which the practice of persuasion is attracted to perform.

Dark Persuasion Methods

When an individual is prepared to modify the head of the topic by devoting them to do anything against their first frame of mind, the persuader will get some nicely laid out methods to help them reach their targets. Every day that passes, the goal will face various kinds of persuasion. Food manufacturers aim to receive their goal to test the recipes that are new or have them adhere to the earlier ones, even while studios may flaunt their most recent blockbuster films about the faces of the aims. In any situation may be whatever merchandise they're promoting, their principal intent is to generate more revenue, and that's the reason they're attempting to convince you. They couldn't care less about how this may affect you, and that is why they need to be quite careful and proficient in the art of subtle persuasion to make sure they don't deceive you off or make you plump.

As there are also lots of different brands attempting to convince you, they need to locate an exceptional approach to impress their perspectives on you. As a result of the effect of info on a vast selection of individuals, the methods used in it's been a topic of research for several decades, dating back to early times. That is because the influence is a really helpful instrument in controlling a large assortment of individuals. Beginning in the early 20th century, the proper analysis of those techniques started to grow. Bear in mind that the objective of attempting to convince people would be to push a compelling debate in an audience and have the positive.

They'll then internalize this information and embrace it as their fresh mindset or even means of life. Because of this, there's a great need to find very prosperous persuasion methods. Three dark persuasion methods are of fantastic value through recent years. We will go over those three:

Create a Need

This is only one of the most profitable methods of obtaining an individual to change their perspective or lifestyle. The individual hoping to convince a goal will create demand or concentrate on a demand that the topic already has. If that is achieved suitably, it's the capacity of enticing a fantastic deal to your goal. This signifies that to become prosperous, the persuader should interest in the demands that are far more significant to the goal.

This could be their requirement to fulfill their fantasies of fostering their self-esteem. It might also function as a desire for love, food, or shelter. This method will work out nicely since there's not anyway the topic isn't likely to require one or more of these items or need of anything at all for that matter. As there's not always, the goal is not likely to get dreams and ambitions. The persuader will probably simply find strategies to produce the sufferer understand how they can easily help the sufferer attain those dreams. The persuader can also tell their goal the goal will probably recognize their visions if they make certain adjustments to their faith or outlook.

As stated by the persuader, doing this will provide the target with a greater prospect of attaining success. For example, a young guy who wishes to get romantic with a woman may inform her that he'll help her boost her grades and eventually make her parents happy by obtaining a. Still, only when she's friends with his or her although this woman may believe she has finally discovered the salvation she desires, the simple truth is that the young guy is not very curious about how she plays in college. Her teenagers are just a lure for obtaining access to sexual activity.

Appealing to Social Needs

Another technique the persuader may utilize is identifying the goal of social demands. Even though this might not yield as many outcomes and the goal's main requirements will, it's still a powerful instrument in the hands of the persuader. Some are naturally attracted to audiences and want to be desired. They always wish for certain things, not because they want them, but because it includes certain prestige, making them feel like they belong to a bigger course. The idea of appealing to your target's societal needs is what's accessible through several TV advertisements where audiences are invited to purchase a product so they won't be "left behind." When they could recognize and allure to the societal needs of their goal, the outcome is that they can achieve a new field of the goal's interest.

Making Use of Loaded Words and Images

When an individual is hoping to convince someone else, they need to be cautious with their selection of words because words could make all of the difference. When there are many means to say something, one way of stating it might be more potent than another. When it's related to persuasion, among the essential things is understanding how to say the ideal thing at the ideal moment. Words are the most effective tools in communicating and understanding the perfect call-to-action phrases.

Dark persuasion is just one of the most effective dim psychology theories, but regrettably, it's always overlooked and suppressed. This might be because, unlike many different head control procedures, persuasion renders the goal using a selection. At another mind control procedure, the aim is forced to enter. Occasionally, this is achieved by placing them into isolation to ensure, in conclusion, they don't have any say in the procedure results. Regarding persuasion, the chips have been laid bare (though with the ulterior purpose in dim persuasion), so the goal is made to make the choice they think will fit them best.

Chapter 39. Dark Persuasion To Lookout For

After looking at the different types of persuasion and what they all mean, you may see why dark persuasion is such a bad thing and can be harmful to the victim. Recognizing the different techniques that the manipulator may use can make it easier to understand when used on you.

So, how exactly is a dark persuader able to use this idea to carry out their wishes? There are a few different types of tactics that a dark manipulator is going to use. Still, some of the most common options include:

The Long Con

The first method that we are going to look at is the Long Con. This method is kind of slow and drawn out, but it can be effective because it takes so long, and it is hard to recognize or pinpoint when something went wrong. One of the main reasons that some people can resist persuasion is that they feel that they are being pressured by the other person, making them back off. If they feel that there is a lack of rapport or trust with the person trying to persuade them, they will steer clear. The Long Con is effective because they can overcome these main problems and give the persuader precisely what they want.

The Long Con will involve the dark persuader to take their time, working to earn their victim's trust. They will take some time to befriend the victim and make sure that their victims trust and like them. The persuader will achieve this with artificial rapport building, which sometimes seems excessive, and other techniques will help increase the comfort levels between the persuader and their victim.

As soon as the persuader sees that the victim is adequately readied psychologically, the persuader will begin their attempts. They may start with some insincere positive persuasion. The persuader will lead their victim to choose or do some activities that will benefit the persuader. This is going to serve the persuader in two ways. First, the victim starts to become used to persuasion by that persuader. The second is that the victim will start making that mental association between a positive outcome and the persuasion.

The Long Con will take a long period to complete because the persuader doesn't want to make it too obvious what they are doing. An example of this is a victim who is a recently widowed lady who is vulnerable because of her age and from their grief. After her loss, a man starts to befriend her. This man may be someone she knows from church or even a relative. He starts to spend more time with her, showing immense kindness and patience, and it doesn't take too long for her guard to drop when he comes around.

Then this man starts to carry out some smaller acts of positive persuasion that we talked about before. He may advise her of a better bank account to use or a better way to reduce any monthly bills. The victim will appreciate these efforts and the fact that the man is trying to help her, and she takes the advice.

Over some time, the man then tries to use some dark persuasion. He may try to persuade her to let him invest some of her money. She obliges because of the positive persuasion that was used in the past. Of course, the man is going to work to take everything he can get from her. If the manipulator is skilled enough, she may feel that he actually tried to help her, but the money is lost because he just ran into some bad luck with the investment. This is how far dark persuasion can go.

Graduality

Often when we hear about acts of dark persuasion, it seems impossible and unbelievable. They fail to realize that this dark persuasion isn't ever going to be a big or a sudden request that comes out of nowhere. Dark persuasion is more like a staircase. The dark persuader will never ask the victim to do something big and dramatic the first time they meet. Instead, they will have the victim take one step at a time.

When the manipulator has the target only go one step at a time, the whole process seems like less of a big deal. Before the victim knows it, they have already gone a long way down, and the persuader isn't likely to let them leave or come back up again.

Let's take an example of how this process is going to look in real life. Let's say that there is a criminal who wanted to make it so that someone else committed the crimes for them. Gang bosses, cult leaders, and even Charles Manson did this same thing.

This criminal wouldn't dream of beginning the process by asking their victim to murder for them. This would send out a red flag, and no one in their right minds would willingly go out and kill for someone they barely know. Instead, the criminal would start by having the victim do something small, like a petty crime, or simply hiding a weapon for them. Something that isn't that big of a deal for the victim, at least in comparison.

Over time, the acts that the manipulator can persuade their victim to do will become more severe. And since they did the smaller crimes, the persuader now has the unseen leverage of holding some of those smaller misdeeds over the victim, kind of like for blackmail. Before the victim knows it, they are going to feel like they are in too deep. They will then be persuaded to carry out some of the most shocking crimes. And often, by this point, they will do it because they feel like they have no other choice.

Dark persuaders will be experts at using this graduality to help increase the severity of their persuasion over time. They know that no victim would be willing to jump the canyon or do the big crime or misdeed right away. So, the persuader works to build a bridge to get there. By the time the victim sees how far they are, it is too late to turn back.

Masking the True Intentions

There are different methods that a persuader can use dark psychology to get the things that they want. Disguising their true desires is very important for them to be successful. The best persuaders can use this approach in various ways. Still, the method they choose is often going to depend on the victim and the situation.

One principle used by a persuader is that many people will have a difficult time refusing two requests when they happen in a row. Let's say that the persuader wants to get $200 from the victim, but they do not intend to repay the money. The persuader may begin by saying that they need a loan for the amount of $1000. They may go into some details about the consequences to themselves if the persuader doesn't come up with that kind of money sometime soon.

The victim may feel guilt or compassion for the persuader, and they want to help. But $1000 is a lot of money, more than the victim can lend. From here, the persuader is going to lessen their request from $1000 down to $200, the amount that they wanted from the beginning. Of course, there is some emotional reason for needing the money. The victim feels like it is impossible to refuse this second request. They want to help out the persuader, and they feel bad for not giving in to the initial request when they were asked. In the end, the persuader gets the $200 they originally wanted, and the victim is not going to know what has taken place.

Another type of technique that the persuader can use is known as reverse psychology. This can also help to mask true intentions during the persuasion. Some people have a personality that is known as a boomerang. This means that they will refuse to go in the direction they are thrown away and instead will veer off into different directions.

If the persuader knows someone more of a boomerang type, they can identify a key weakness. For example, let's say that a persuader has a friend attempting to win over some girl they like. The persuader knows that the friend will use and then hurt that girl. The girl is currently torn between a malicious friend and an innocent third party. The persuader may try to steer the girl in the direction of the guy who is a good choice, knowing that she will go against this and end up going with the harmful friend.

Leading Questions

Another method of dark persuasion that can be used is known as leading questions. If you have ever had an encounter with a skilled salesman, verbal persuasion can be really impactful when deployed in careful and calibrated ways. One of the most powerful techniques that can be used verbally is leading questions.

These leading questions will be any questions intended to trigger a specific response out of the victim. The persuader may ask the target something like, "how bad do you think those people are?" This question will imply that the people the persuader is asking about are bad to some extent. They could have chosen to ask a non-leading question, such as "how do you feel about those people?"

Dark persuaders are masters at using leading questions in a way that is hard to catch. If the victim ever begins to feel that they are being led, they will resist, and it is hard to lead them or persuade them. If a persuader ever senses that their victim starts to catch what is happening, they will quit using that one and switch over to another. They may come back to that tactic, but only when the victim has quieted down a bit and is more influenceable again.

The Law of State Transference

The state is a concept that will take a look at the general mood someone is in. If someone is aligned with their deeds, words, and thoughts, this is an example of a healthy and harmonious state. The law of state transference will involve the concept of someone who holds the balance of power in a situation and can then transfer their emotional state onto the other person they interact with. This can be a potent tool for the dark persuader to use against their victim.

Initially, the influencer will force their state to match the state that their target naturally has. If the target is sad and talks slowly, the influencer will make their state follow this format. The point of this is to create a deep rapport with the target.

After we get to this state match, the influencer will alter their state subtly and see if they have some compliance for the victim. Perhaps they will choose to speed up their voice to see if the victim will speed up as well. Once the victim starts to show these signs of compliance, the influencer is at the hook point.

Chapter 40. Subliminal Persuasion

Subliminal persuasion means an advertising message displayed below the threshold of awareness or consumer awareness to persuade or help people change their minds without making them aware of what is going on. This is about affecting individuals with more than words. Some subliminal persuasion methods impact our stimuli with smell, eyesight, sound, touch, and taste.

There are 3 subliminal methods of persuasion that affect everyone. They are:

Building a Relationship

Building a relationship makes the other person feel comfortable. This will open up the individual even more. This can be accomplished through a healthy observation that matches their mood or state. This helps create confidence.

Power of Discussion

The power of discussion and convincing a person is connected to an advertiser's conversion. The correct words and inflections help you to be openly straightforward.

Suggestive Power

Associating useful and desirable stuff in a discussion or interaction enables an individual to become more open to fresh thoughts.

Suggestion and Emotional Intelligence

This stage may be described as having one central and dominant idea focused on the participant's conscious mind, which was to stimulate or decrease the various regions' physiological performance within the participant's body. Using different nonverbal and verbal suggestions was increasingly emphasized to convince the participant easily.

Achieve Optimal Persuasion With Subliminal Psychology

When you can expertly utilize a person's subconscious depths, your control over them is easy and vast. Subliminal psychology is one of the most effective ways to do this. This is an advanced technique, so do not expect to become effective overnight, but know that with time and dedication, you will be able to start putting subliminal messages into the minds of those around you. Once you can do this, you will control what they think and the actions they take. Essentially, you become almost like a puppet master for those around you.

Subliminal Message Techniques

This type of message or affirmation presented either visually or auditory sent in a way below what is considered normal for human visual or auditory perception. For example, a record might be playing on repeat, but you cannot hear it with your conscious mind. However, deep in your subconscious, you hear it and fully register everything that it is saying. In most cases, the messages used are meant to control you in some way or suggest that you do something.

For example, subliminal messages are commonly used in today's world to promote smoking cessation or weight loss. In general, you listen to recorded tapes with a specific message when you are sleeping. Your unconscious mind gets the message, but you never really hear it as your conscious self. Either way, research shows that it can be an effective tool to change your smoking or eating behaviors. You can use a similar technique to help change how people think to make them more vulnerable to the types of persuasion you prefer to use.

This is an effective way to control both your mind and others' minds, but it can be obvious when you do not use the techniques properly. As you read into the primary techniques, pay close attention to how you might introduce a person to them. This is important. Ultimately, your relationship with the person you are seeking to control will determine which of these techniques works the best.

Subliminal Messages During Sleep

This is one of the most common ways to use these types of messages. Most people will use them for themselves in this manner, but you can also use them with people you live with. For example, once you know your spouse is asleep, play a subliminal recording for about one hour. This is all it takes to get your message across.

Now, you must know for sure that they are sleeping, or else you could do more harm than good to your persuasion efforts. When you create your recording, use a calm and steady voice. State precisely what you want the person to do. Use no filler words. Use a maximum of 10 words and simply repeat it for an hour. Then, once the person is sleeping, play the recording at a very low volume close to their head so that their unconscious mind hears it.

Subliminal Flashes

These do not take as long as they are not as risky as the above method. These are a type of visual subliminal message. You can create the flashes to say what you want. What is nice about this technique is that the messages flash so quickly that the conscious mind often does not see what it says. Only the subconscious can understand and record it. So, you can get some control over a person's mind without them knowing what you are attempting to control.

Unless the person you want to do this with knows about subliminal psychology, you can just tell them you want to show them something you created. It is best to do this on a computer so that the screen is large enough to read and keep their full attention during the flashes.

Mixed Subliminal Messages

You can insert subliminal messages into the music or audiobooks that someone listens to regularly. Some programs can do this, so you do not have to be a tech expert to take advantage of this method. Just like with the subliminal messages during sleep, you will use a calm and steady voice. You want the messages to mix into the audiobook or music without being detected. Remember, the subconscious mind will pick up on it even when they cannot hear it when they are awake.

Just make sure to use these messages in something they listen to daily, or almost daily. They must hear it regularly to gain the most control.

Subliminal Notes

This is the easiest method, but it is also the simplest to figure out if you are not careful. You can put messages inside messages throughout your home. For example, when you create the grocery list, add something else you want but do not usually shop for. This puts the thought in the person's head when they are reading the list. This is ideal for smaller things that you want to persuade someone to think or do. So, keep it simple and use this method periodically. Unlike the above methods, it is not a good idea to use it every day.

Chapter 41. Psychological Manipulation

Today, the greatest battles are not fought on battlefields but in our minds and hearts!

And one of the biggest and strongest reasons for an inner battle is psychological manipulation. The biggest problem with psychological manipulation is not only the fact that we are often not prepared to deal with it but also the way we respond to it. And then, our greatest enemy, beyond the manipulator/oppressor, will become ourselves!

One of the main characteristics of psychological manipulation is that the manipulator (who can be a father, a mother, a brother or sister, a romantic partner, or a friend) exercises great control and power over us. And in that instant, our life becomes a real hell, and we live in tremendous anguish.

However, it is crucial to know that we are not, and should not be, impotent in this situation. There are various ways of combating these techniques of psychological manipulation.

The first step is to achieve consciousness, that is, to become aware of these techniques. Take a closer look and learn more objectively how your handlers "work" so you can protect yourself in the future. There are several Manipulation Techniques. See some of them below:

Psychological Manipulation Technique 1: Emotional Blackmail

Emotional blackmail is one of the oldest and most used manipulation techniques employed by human beings. But how does this work exactly?

Many people succumb to this trick because they feel they have no choice. At this point, phrases such as "If you cared about me, you would do this for me" are very common and make the manipulated person feel "forced" to make decisions they do not want. The target will make them anyway just to please the person who manipulates.

To avoid this manipulation technique, you will have to develop a strong sense of yourself, which involves knowing who you are, what your responsibilities are towards others, and who your true friends are. Usually, manipulative and blackmailing people tend to stay away from people with strong and solid personalities. Always remember: you always have a choice, and it is you who decides what you do with your life and how you want to react to the world.

Psychological Manipulation Technique 2: Focus on Negative Aspects

Some people like to put a "brake" on another's ideas and brilliant projects by emphasizing everything that could go wrong with them. These people often push him to doubt his projects and all the good things they would bring if they were put into practice. And at these times, the manipulators offer an endless list of questions that will only serve to create and raise doubts in their target's mind and heart.

For example, if you tell someone, you are thinking of traveling somewhere for a month to relax or go on vacation. If that person does not feel comfortable with the idea for some reason, they will probably react to your news by talking about the big travel hazards and the endless number of negative things that can be expected at the airport, etc.

At such times, if there is no apparent reason for such a reaction from the other person. If you are comfortable with your decision, bearing in mind that it will not harm you or others, choose not to listen to them and follow through with what you have decided.

Do not be overly swayed by this negative thinking pattern. If we think about something a lot, we attract it. If you put it in your head that something bad will happen and focus on it excessively, it is very likely to happen because the thought has life and is a great magnet.

Psychological Manipulation Technique 3: Teenage Rebellion

Unfortunately, sometimes the manipulative person adopts a childlike attitude to respond to his decision or something you have said to him.

For example, you want to leave your home and live independently. At first, it may even seem like everyone is happy and comfortable with your decision. But with time, as soon as you start looking for the perfect apartment, things start happening one after another. Some personal crisis occurs in the family, your mother or father suddenly (re)starts smoking, etc. These are adult people, but they adopt the behavior of a teenager and rebel against the idea.

The easiest way to deal with this is to make them see that their efforts to make you give up are worthless and that you will go ahead with your decision.

At first, it can be challenging and hard for you, especially if you have been exposed to this type of psychological manipulation for a long time. But as time goes by, it will become much easier, and you will see that even the people who manipulate you will come to respect you much more.

Psychological manipulation can be done throughout life, but always remember that you have the power to break this vicious cycle, and above all, remember that only one person can change your life: You!

Love and life together can be sources of well-being, pleasure, and support or a dead-end in which you feel suffocated and as if you are in the dark. The worst is that in many cases, these can be combined in a single day. Both feelings and problems begin when the relationship shifts rapidly. You find yourself immersed in a constant storm of feelings. This mainly happens to those who do not know how to escape such situations.

Many people are immersed in insane and toxic relationships in which they suffer psychological abuse of various kinds. They receive continuous damage to their integrity and honor and levels of disrespect that seem crazy when seen or heard from outside. Still, to the person who is now accustomed to suffering, they do not even produce a minimal reaction in their daily lives.

Love is not an excuse to hide the emotional pain that another person can cause us. It is our responsibility to ourselves to learn how to defend our rights and enforce them. Beyond your insecurity, the parental patterns that you picked up in your childhood, and all the mechanisms of self-deception that you can activate so as not to see reality, at the bottom of your being, you know how to differentiate what is right and what hurts you. That said, sometimes we need someone to tell us in a neutral and unbiased way that we have the right not to put up with what we know we do not deserve. Present a list of the main techniques of manipulation in unhealthy couples.

Manipulation to maintain social control: This technique usually begins in a very subtle way. The couple criticizes friends, family, work colleagues, and anyone in your social circle until they can completely annul the other's social network in such a way that the only source of effort and social support is the couple. This is manifested through jealousy: "If you love me, you would prefer me over your friends," etc. Emotional blackmail: This mechanism is famous for being used between pairs of individuals. It is also widely used by almost everyone, and you likely know it very well. It is about using phrases to handle guilt and repentance as a tactic to get something or as an impediment so that the other does not do something or does not abandon the manipulator. The manipulative person usually uses phrases like: "If you do that, it means you don't love me," "I do not want you to suffer, I would never do that to you," "I want the best for you, even if you let me destroy my life," "If you let me die," etc.

Chapter 42. Psychological Manipulation Technique

What Are Manipulators Looking For

Deceptive people in general: sociopaths, narcissists, liars, and so-called emotional vampires, and it is more a practical question to consider them than a theoretical one. For this purpose, if you've been victims of them at times, it's easier for you to identify and precede them now.

However, it can be said that deceptive people's aims are very straightforward, instrumental and that they follow a specific pattern. Most of them include:

- **Cancel your willpower**: they're trying to sow suspicions and want to bind you to their safety.

- Destroying your self-esteem: bringing a spoken word into the wheel of all you do or have done. We are not helpful and just want to point out the shortcomings.

- Passive-aggressive revenge: By avoiding you, they threaten you. They neglect you when you need them; it's enough to ask something, to get to stand up and not even speak to you.

- Prevent reality: they enjoy confounding people and creating misunderstandings and discussions. We step back after provoking a debate, loving the rants of others.

-

What Are the Psychological Manipulation Techniques?

Gaslighting

Gaslighting is one of the most subtle methods of deception. "It's never happened," "Imagine you" or " You're kidding?" These are some of the words that they use to manipulate and confuse our perception of reality, making us believe things have changed.

This instills an intense sense of anxiety and uncertainty in the victims, to the point of causing them not to trust in themselves, their memory, their understanding, or their judgment.

Projection

The manipulator transfers the negative characteristics to another person or shifts blame for his actions. This is being used heavily by narcissists and psychopaths, saying that the wickedness surrounding them is not their fault but anyone else's.

Meaningless Conversations

The conversation lasts ten minutes. Now is the time for you to leave the conversation. Manipulators say ridiculous things, offer illogical excuses, refer to past events, and throw smoke in the eyes...

We generate discord and misunderstanding. We are doing monologues, and they are trying to confuse you with their gab. Some advice? Get straight to the point and then better if you can leave after 5 minutes. Your feelings would be thankful.

Generalizations and Denigrations

They make generic, vague, and abstract statements. They may seem intellectual. In reality, they are just elusive. Their conclusions are too general; their goal is to demean your e debilitate your opinions.

For example, "you always want to be right," "anything annoys you," "never once you agree." Keep calm. You can opt for irony, with a simple "thank you," or you can ignore them with a curt, "I think you're a little upset. We'll talk later."

Absurdity

Remember that they try to undermine your morals and cause you to question what you believe. They can put words you have never said in your mouth; they will make you think you have the superpower to "read your mind." But that's not the case, and they are just tricks and deceptions. You can help yourself with simulated defeat. Tell them they are right for them to believe it, but stick to your position. You can also respond to their blackmail with an "okay" or with harsh sentences.

The important thing is that you take your self-esteem out of their hands. Remember that they want to demoralize you so that they can control you. After making you weak, the task will be much easier.

Good Mask

"Yes, but..." If you manage to buy a house, they will tell you that it is a pity that you do not yet have a place by the sea; if you are dressed more elegant than ever, they will tell you that another pair of earrings would have been better for you. If you have written an impeccable report, they will tell you that the staple is not well fixed.

But don't let yourselves be influenced: you know what you are worth! Your successes and virtues are worth more than their manipulation techniques. Don't give them any credibility and hang out with people who spend more time pointing out the positives and encouraging you; those who compliment you when you deserve them and who make constructive, non-destructive criticisms.

Positive Reinforcement

Through positive reinforcement learning, behavioral performance is linked to achieving a good outcome. This does not have to be an entity, not even tangible; in many cases, food, liquids, a smile, a verbal message, or the presence of a friendly emotion are likely to be seen as favorable reinforcement.

A father who congratulates his young daughter if she uses the toilet correctly promotes positive reinforcement learning; the same thing happens when a business offers cash incentives to its most successful workers. When we get a bag of potato chips after placing a coin into a retailer.

The definition of "positive reinforcement" refers to the reward that accompanies the action. In contrast, positive reinforcement is the process that creates the connection the learner produces. Nevertheless, the words "reinforcement" and "reinforcement" are frequently used interchangeably, possibly because such a distinction does not exist in English.

From a technical point of view, we can conclude a favorable variance between a particular response and an appetizing stimulus in positive reinforcement. The knowledge of this risk motivates the subject to act to get the reward (or strengthening).

Negative Reinforcement

In comparison to what occurs in the positive, the instrumental response in the negative reinforcement includes the absence of an aversive stimulus, i.e., an event or condition that motivates the subject to avoid or attempt not to come into contact with it.

In behavioral terms, the reinforcement of this technique is the absence or non-appearance of the aversive stimulus. As we stated earlier, the word "negative" refers to the fact that the reward does not consist of obtaining inspiration but in the absence thereof.

This type of learning is divided into two processes: training to escape and train to prevent it. The conduct precludes the presence of the aversive stimulus in the negative reinforcement of avoidance. For example, when an agoraphobic individual avoids using public transport to escape the fear this presupposes, it is reinforced negatively.

On the contrary, the escape is the disappearance of an aversive stimulus present before the subject executes the behavior. Some examples of negative escape reinforcement include an alarm clock that stops by pressing a button, a mother buying a request for her child to stop weeping, or taking a pain reliever to relieve pain.

Brainwashing

The concept of brainwashing is very close to that of 'mind control.' It is an idea without a strictly scientific basis that suggests that the will, thoughts, and other mental facts of individuals can be modified through techniques of persuasion that would introduce unwanted ideas into the psyche of the 'victim.' If we define the concept in this way, we see that it has a marked similarity. However, the term "suggest" is less ambitious.

Although the idea of brainwashing is not entirely wrong, this popular concept has some scientific connotations which have led many experts to reject it in favor of more modest ones. The instrumental use of the term in legal proceedings has contributed to this, particularly in child custody disputes.

Mind control is also known as brainwashing, coercive persuasion, mind control, and mental manipulation. All these terms mean a process that a group or individual systematically uses to force someone to do what they want through thinking of that person. In the majority of cases, these systematic processes are realized without the conscious knowledge of the person.

There are times when we can use mind control over ourselves for a variety of reasons. Self-hypnosis is in this category. We use this kind of mind control, which is voluntary on our part, with our conscious consent, to reinforce a positive idea or to change our minds.

However, this is not the same as the "mind control" phase, or it involves brainwashing. These phrases mean that a person's mind is systematically changed without knowing it, either in the agreement or against his will.

They are carried out through unethical, manipulative tactics, and other means, all designed to control someone's mind. In such cases, they are realized so that one person or group can take full control of others' thoughts and actions. So, when the terms "mind control" and "brainwashing" are used, it is said that specific tactics are used to take control of another at the expense of the manipulated person.

This is interesting because the idea of brainwashing falls under the category of social influence. This is because the concept of brainwashing is used to induce a victim's mental manipulation. This means that brainwashing and mind control are used to completely change how someone thinks and perceives things concerning their beliefs in a particular social device. This is achieved by using various means to change a person's attitudes, behaviors, and thoughts. The person is like a puppet who does everything the manipulator wants.

Chapter 43. Covert Emotional Manipulation

Covert emotional manipulation is used by people who want to gain power or control over you by deploying deceptive and underhanded tactics. Such people want to change the way you think and behave without realizing what they are doing. In other words, they use techniques that can alter your perceptions in such a way that you think that you are doing it out of your own free will. Covert emotional manipulation is "covert" because it works without you being consciously aware of that fact. People who are good at deploying such techniques can get you to do their bidding without your knowledge; they can hold you "psychologically captive."

When skilled manipulators set their sights on you, they can get you to grant them power over your emotional well-being and even your self-worth. They will put you under their spell without you even realizing it. They will win your trust, and you will start attaching value to what they think of you. Once you have let them into your life, they will then begin to chipping away at your very identity in a systematic way. As time goes by, you will lose your self-esteem and turn into whatever they want you to be.

Covert emotional manipulation is more common than you might think. Since it's subtle, people are rarely aware that it's happening to them, and in some cases, they may never even notice. Only keen outside observers may be able to tell when this form of manipulation is going on.

You might know someone who used to be fun and festive. She got into a relationship with someone else, and a few years down the line, she seems to have a completely different personality. If it's an old friend, you might not even recognize the person she has become. That is how powerful covert emotional manipulation can be. It can completely overhaul someone's personality without them even realizing it. The manipulator will chip away at you little by little. You will accept minute changes that fly under the radar until the old a different version of you replaces you, build to be subservient to the manipulator.

Covert emotional manipulation works like a slow-moving coup. It requires you to make small progressive concessions to the person that is trying to manipulate you. In other words, you let go of tiny aspects of your identity to accommodate the manipulative person, so it never registers in your mind that there is something bigger at play.

When the manipulative person pushes you to change in small ways, you will comply because you don't want to "sweat the small stuff." However, there is a domino effect that occurs as you start conceding to the manipulative person. You will be more comfortable making subsequent concessions, and your personality will be erased and replaced in a cumulative progression.

Covert emotional manipulation occurs to some extent in all social dynamics. Let's look at how it plays out in romantic relationships, in friendships, and at work.

Emotional Manipulation in Relationships

There is a lot of emotional manipulation in romantic relationships, and it's not always malicious. For example, women try to modify men's behavior to make them more "housebroken";

that is just normal. However, certain instances of manipulation where the person's intention is malicious, and he/she is motivated by a need to control or dominate over the other person.

Positive reinforcement is perhaps the most used covert manipulation technique in romantic relationships. Your partner can get you to do what he wants by praising you, flattering you, giving you attention, offering your gifts, and acting affectionately.

Even the seemingly nice things in relationships can turn out to be covert manipulation tools and props. For instance, your girlfriend could use intense sex as a weapon to reinforce a certain kind of behavior in you. Similarly, men can use charm, appreciation, or gifts to reinforce certain behaviors in the women they are dating.

Some sophisticated manipulators use what psychologists call "intermittent positive reinforcement" to gain control over their partners. The way it works is that the perpetrator will shower the victim with intense positive reinforcement for a certain period, then switch to just giving her normal levels of attention and appreciations. After a random interval of time, he will again go back to the intense positive reinforcement. When the victim gets used to the special treatment, it's taken away. When she gets used to standard therapy, the special treatment is brought back, and it all seems arbitrary. Now, the victim will get to a place where she becomes "addicted" to the special treatment. Still, she has no idea how to get it. Hence, she starts doing whatever the perpetrator wants, hoping that one of the things she does will bring back the intense positive reinforcement. In other words, she effectively becomes subservient to the perpetrator.

Negative reinforcement techniques are also used in relationships to manipulate others covertly. For example, partners can withhold sex to compelling the other person to modify their behavior in a specific way. People also use techniques such as the silent treatment and withholding of love and affection.

Some malicious people can create a false sense of intimacy by pretending to open up to you. They could share personal stories and talk about their hopes and fears. When they do this, they create the impression that they trust you, but their intention may be to get you to feel a sense of obligation towards them.

Manipulators also use well-calculated insinuations to get you to react in a certain way at the moment to modify your behavior in the long run. Such insinuations can be made through words or even actions. In colloquial terms, we call this "dropping a hint." People in relationships are always trying to figure out what the other person wants out of that relationship, so a manipulative person can drop hints to get you to do what they want without ever having to take responsibility for the actions that you take because they can always argue that you misinterpreted what they meant.

Dropping hints isn't always malicious (for example, if your girlfriend wants you to propose, she may leave bridal magazines out on the table). However, malicious insinuations can be very hurtful, and they can chip away at your self-esteem. Your partner can make insinuations to suggest you are gaining weight. You aren't making enough money or implying that your cooking skills aren't any good. People use hints to get away with "saying without saying," any number of hurtful things that could affect your self-esteem.

Emotional Manipulations in Friendships

Covert emotional manipulation is quite common in friendships and casual relationships. Companies tend to progress slower than romantic relationships, but that just means that it can take a lot more time for you to figure out if your friends are manipulative. Manipulation in friendships can be confusing because even well-meaning friends can come across as malicious. That's because there is a certain social rivalry between even the closest friends, which explains the concept of "frenemies."

Manipulative friends tend to be passive-aggressive. This is where they manipulate you into doing what they want by involving mutual friends rather than directly coming to you. Passive aggression works as a manipulation technique because it denies you a chance of directly addressing whatever issue your friend is raising. So in a manner of speaking, you lose by default.

For example, if a friend wants you to do her a favor, instead of coming out and asking you, she goes to a mutual friend and suggests that she asks you on her behalf. When a mutual friend approaches you, it becomes very difficult for you to turn down the request because of added social pressure. When you say no, your whole social circle now perceives you as selfish.

Passive aggression can also involve the use of silent treatment to get you to comply with a request. Imagine a situation where one of your friends talks to everyone else but you. It's going to be incredibly awkward for you, and everyone will start prying, wondering what the issue is between the two of you, and taking sides on the matter.

Friends can also covertly manipulate you by using subtle insults. They can give you back-handed compliments that have hidden meanings. When you take the time to think about what they meant by the compliment, you will realize that it's an insult in disguise, which will bruise your self-esteem and possibly modify your behavior.

Some friends can manipulate you by going on a "power trip" and controlling your social interactions. For example, there are those friends who insist that every time you hang out, it should be in their apartment or at a social venue of their choosing. Such friends often intend to dominate your friendship, so they are keen to always have the "home ground advantage" over you. They'll try to push you out of your comfort zone just so that you can reveal your weaknesses, and you can then become more emotionally reliant on them.

Manipulative friends tend to excessively capitalize on your friendship, and to a disproportionate degree. They will ask you for lots of favors with no regard for your time or your effort. They are the kinds of friends who will leverage your friendship every time they need something but then make excuses when it's their turn to reciprocate.

Emotional Manipulation at Work

There are many reasons why your colleague may want to manipulate you. It could be you are on the same career path, so he wants to make you look bad. It could be that he is lazy, and he wants to stick you with his responsibilities. It could also be that he is a sadist, and he just wants to see you suffer.

One-way people at work exert their dominance over others is by stressing them out and then, almost immediately, relieving the stress. Say, for example, you make a minor error on a report, and your boss calls you into his office. He makes a big fuss and threatens to fire you, but then towards the end, he switches gears and reassures you that your job is secure as long as you do what he wants. That kind of manipulation works on people because it makes them afraid and gives them a sense of obligation at the same time.

Some colleagues can manipulate you by doing you small favors and then reminding you of those favors every time they want something from you. For instance, if you made an error at work and a colleague covered for you, he may hold it over your head for months or even years to come. He is going to guilt you into feeling indebted to him.

Chapter 44. Covert Emotional Manipulation Tactics

Dark Psychology also spends time looking at Covert Emotional Manipulation. It is more commonly referred to as CEM. CEM is a way to gain real power over someone without them, even realizing it is happening. You will be so enthralled that these sneaky tactics will have you doing things you would not usually agree to.

We have already talked about manipulation, but there are so many different forms of it, which is pretty important. It allows criminals and people with mal intent into your life and breaks you down mentally. The effects of this type of manipulation can last forever if you are not careful. As noted, it is insanely subtle, which means looking for the red flags are very important.

Covert Emotional Manipulation looks different depending on the people involved. Often, the victim will be slowly made to feel like they can't do anything without the other. It is a strange sort of codependency that happens over time. This happens without manipulation on occasion; the difference is when your partner intentionally gets you to behave or think differently.

It may start with offers of help for simple tasks that you usually do on your own. They may follow it up with a critique to make you question your ability to do it. It starts small, but they will continue to poke at it until you start to believe you can't do it on your own truth. You can see it worked into all kinds of things and a ton of relationships.

Depending on who you have allowed doing this to you, it could be mostly harmless. On the other hand, many people with less than genuine intentions could take this to an extreme. This type of manipulation can turn it to flat out brainwashing. In that case, you may lose your free will forever.

People that use CEM against other people pay great attention to detail. This can be endearing as it appears as if they are learning about you. In reality, they are observing your behavior, understanding what makes you tick. This will grant them access to how to manipulate your emotions subtly to get what they want. They are truly hunting for your weaknesses.

The heinous people and criminals that do this in life are calculating. They tend to have bigger plans, and you are simply playing a role. They have no care or regard for how you feel or for the damage they are causing you. All they can see is the outcome that they are striving for. Finding that they are unable ever to sustain relationships is not surprising because of the selfish nature of how they are wired.

As time goes on, CEM turns into something else. What started as little jabs that looked like they were made from love become something much darker. As you start to lose control and bend your will, the aggressor will pounce. They can become domineering. Also, they will begin to tear you down piece by piece to gain complete control.

Playing with someone's emotions is a great way to gain control over them. Some people would rather bombard someone with love to get them to do what they want, rather than being crasser or crude about it. Love bombarding is very typical of the narcissist. It is its form of manipulation, and it can be downright cruel in reality.

You will feel like the most important person in someone's world. You will go along with what they say hook, line, and sinker because you truly trust in what they say. Once this person has you there, they can easily force their will and beliefs onto you. Fighting against this is extremely difficult for some people.

Becoming solid in your belief system will make it more difficult for someone to pray on your emotions. Another way to combat this dark tendency is to work on really knowing yourself. When you spend the time meditating, self-actualizing, and maintaining control of yourself, it is much easier to fend off attacks on your emotions.

When someone manipulates your emotions, it can have a detrimental impact on the rest of your life. Narcissists and Psychopaths cannot often have true feelings. They are shut off, in a way. So, them playing with yours is a simple way to gain control of you and the situation they are in. Practicing NLP's art can also give you signs of when these types of people are trying to harm you.

Gut feelings and red flags should be paid attention to. Naturally, we have instincts, and sometimes something just feels off from the beginning. Maybe you meet someone, and they seem just a little too perfect, or you just feel a bit uncomfortable around them, don't disregard these thoughts and feelings. We are wired to sense danger. This is not just the physical danger that we sense but also an emotional and mental danger. The phrase "go with your gut" is a good one that can help you avoid unpleasant situations.

Chapter 45. Brainwashing

Brainwashing is a particular form of manipulation or control over someone else used through very specific means. Usually, when you use brainwashing, you refer to a particular pattern typically used in hostage situations to try to get the other person to give in to control. Brainwashing most often occurs in the context of trying to get someone else to conform to something new. The purpose of brainwashing comes right down to thought reform—when it is used, the entire purpose is to get compliance and reeducation to encourage someone to become someone they are not. We will also take a look at the most common steps to going through the process.

Defining Brainwashing

Perhaps the first reported source of brainwashing was recorded during the Korean War. During this time, it is said that several American prisoners of war were held in prison camps and were brainwashed into believing that they had engaged in germ warfare and pledged allegiance to communism. When this happened, they were effectively stripped of their identities, forced to comply, and denounced everything that they had known of their past lives. They had their thoughts rewritten through coercion and threat.

Brainwashing is a form of influence designed to be invasive and forceful to break down others' minds. They eventually comply in hopes of protecting themselves from being hurt worse. It becomes self-preservation to do whatever they are told to do to protect themselves. As a result, they are willing to take on complex personas that are entirely dictated by the captors.

The Science of Brainwashing

Brainwashing is believed to work because the agent, that is to say, the person doing the brainwashing, is gaining complete and utter control over the target. This person is being brainwashed in the first place. This makes it so that the agent has complete power over everything and anything related to the individual. The agent gets to determine when needs can be met and how they are. Over time, the result is a systematic destruction of everything that goes into making that person who they are. Over time, because they can't meet their needs, they feel like their identities are destroyed to the point of no longer being viable. Over time, through torture, coercion, and control, brainwashing can occur. Typically, however, it should be noted that the individual's old identity can be returned over time. After leaving the dangerous situation, it is possible, with therapy, for the old identity to be returned.

Using Brainwashing

When brainwashing happens, it is usually done through several steps designed to be as effective as possible. These steps are brutal, but that is the entire purpose of it all. It is designed to be brutal so that it can have its intended effect. Let's go over the steps that go into this method now.

1. Assault on identity: The first step is designed to help to break down the self. It is an assault on your direct identification. It is designed to make you feel like you are not who you are. Typically, in the actual context, the agent will deny everything. They will directly contradict anything that the individual may say is true. As this happens, the individual is repeatedly attacked to the point of exhaustion and eventually even giving in to what the other person said.

2. Guilt: The individual has to be made to feel guilty. This is done so that the individual is more likely to give up his or her identity. When that entire identity is wrapped up in guilt, it is easier to get rid of it and pretend that it is not there than it is to do anything else. By rejecting the identity entirely, the individual is even closer to being brainwashed.

3. Self-betrayal: The stage in which the agent gets the target to agree with what has been said. The agent wants the target to recognize that he or she is bad and that it is time to denounce who they once were. They need to feel like they were wrong to have the opinions that they can do better.

4. Breaking point: That betrayal culminates in what is known as the breaking point—the point at which the individual just cannot cope any longer. At this point, the target goes through what is commonly referred to as a nervous breakdown—sobbing, depression, and generally just not coping well. They may be in the middle of a psychotic episode or may have other problems going on as well. They believe that all hope is lost, and that is the key to the whole process.

5. Leniency: When all seems beyond help, that is when the agent can get in and take control. Usually, with a small kindness—offering a bit of leniency or otherwise offering a drink of water, and that small kindness is enough to make the individual feel indebted.

6. The compulsion to confess: At this point, the target realizes that they have hope. All is not lost, and they can do what it will take to protect themselves. So, what they do is they confess. They want to try to channel and relieve their stress and guilt, so they confess.

7. **Channeling the guilt**: At this point, the target assumes that they are just wrong. The target assumes that they are wrong for some reason, and want to get rid of that sense—which gets connected to their guilt. They wrap all of their guilt about identity together to release it.

8. **Releasing the guilt**: The target realizes the problem is not with him or her, but rather with the guilt and beliefs. They do not have to be permanently bad or problematic—they can get better and do better to release the pain and escape. So, they do this through confessions.

9. **Progress toward harmony:** At this point, the target can begin making a move toward what they perceive as salvation or goodness—they can rebuild themselves to be good. In doing so, in deciding to assimilate and comply, they can make the abuse stop. In denouncing the past, the target can begin choosing the new belief system, making a conscious choice to assimilate and comply. As a result, they conclude that this new identity is reliable and safe, and they follow it.

10. **Final confession**: Finally, the new life is clung to. All old beliefs are rejected, and the individual pledges allegiance to the new life instead.

Chapter 46. Brainwashing Technique

While we are focusing more on the dark psychology that comes with manipulation, you will find examples of manipulation that can occur in our daily lives. Often we don't think that we are doing it at all. We think of manipulation to get what we want from other people, but sometimes we do it to save others' feelings. For instance, how many times have you lied to someone to let them know they looked good in something, even though you didn't think so. You did this to spare their feelings, whether they are a family member or a close friend!

Even though the point of doing this was good, you still were looking to save yourself. You didn't need to be the one who said something means about the other person and how they looked. This kind of manipulation can be seen as a good thing, though, because it was done to spare the other person's feelings in the process.

With that in mind, we will take a brief look at some of the most common manipulation techniques available to us to get what we want. You are sure to recognize at least a few of these as ones that you have used at some point or another in your life, even if you did not think of it as manipulation at the time. Some of the most common manipulation techniques that you can use includes:

Lying is something that we have all done at one point or another. We do this to confuse the other person, make sure that others believe something we want, or even get ourselves out of trouble. You may decide not to go to a party one night because you don't want to go, so you say you had something with family come up. You don't like the gift, but you smile and tell the giver that you love it. We have all used lying at one point or another, and it is considered a type of manipulation. When it comes to a dark manipulator, though, lying will be done in a deliberate way that helps them succeed while ensuring that the other person gets harmed.

Another method that you can use is going to include not telling the whole story. You can imagine yourself as a teenager with this one. Your parents asked you where you were, and you say at the mall with Susan and Sally. But you leave out the fact that the boy they don't like, John, was there as well. You technically were at the mall with your friends, but you leave out the part of the story that will get you in trouble or make someone else mad.

Punishment. This is often reserved for the dark forms of manipulation, but it will still be used on occasion. Without thinking of it as manipulation, we may punish someone else when they don't do what we want. How often have we used the silent treatment against a friend or a spouse who didn't do something that we wanted?

None of us want to end up being the one to blame for something even if we were the ones who did it. We will try to get out of it by denying that anything happened at all. With another tactic known as minimizing, we may admit that something did happen. Still, we will downplay the actions and make it feel like the other person was overreacting and misreading the situation. How many occurrences have we said something we didn't mean. When the person came back to get mad at us about it, we turn it around and minimize it by saying they didn't hear the words the right way. These are probably the two methods of manipulation that we use the most to help keep us out of trouble as much as possible.

Another option that you can work with is going to be known as spinning the truth. This is something that we see all of the time with politicians. It is done so often we can usually see it happening ahead of time. The spinning of the truth will be done to turn some lousy behavior into something that doesn't seem as bad to others. This takes a bit more work to accomplish because you have to think on your feet and develop something plausible. Still, the point is to change up the story to change your perception from other people.

Even though we are not fond of it when other people do this to us, we can all admit that we have played the victim at one point or another. We know that people are more likely to feel bad when we can come up with a sob story. Maybe we try to make one particular person feel bad about how they treated us, and we will do it in front of others so that we can get what we want. Other times we may come up with a big sob story to get out of a group thing, out of late work, and more. The point here is to turn ourselves into a big victim, even though we don't deserve to have that kind of attention or that title.

Positive reinforcement is something that every parent who has wanted to keep their sanity and who has wanted to make sure that their children will follow the rules and behave will use at one point or another. This is where you will reward the behaviors you really like, the behavior you want to make sure sticks around. This can include paying a lot of attention to the target, excessive charm, and expensive presents.

Think of it this way. When your toddler is learning the rules, it is often more efficient to convince them to listen and do what they should when they get a reward. Whether it is a sticker chart, a reward of a toy or some candy or lots of praise, you will find that the more consistent you are with these, the more the toddler will continue to follow the rules. This is precisely how the idea of positive reinforcement is going to work whether you use it on a child or an adult with manipulation.

Diversion can be another way to focus on yourself and work to make sure that the other person doesn't catch on to your true meaning. How many times have you felt that someone was trying to get at your lie or coming close to figuring something you had hidden? Then you would divert the conversation away? No matter how firm they tried to get back to it, you would just push it all back at them or turn the conversation over to a new topic to get the results you wanted and keep the target away from guessing your true intentions.

Sarcasm is a technique that we have all used at one point or another, especially when we want to feel frustrated about something. We may not be able to explain things to someone else. This is going to be done in a way to make us feel more superior to other people and to lower the self-esteem of the victim. Whether we are doing it with friends as a joke or using it against someone else we want to belittle to make ourselves feel better, sarcasm is something that we are all going to be pretty familiar with.

Guilt-tripping is an excellent way for us to make sure that we can get what we want from other people. We will say things like the other person have life easy, really selfish, or don't care about us. This will make the other person feel bad and like something they did was wrong, even if they were trying to help you out with something, and they are more likely to want to try and help you some more.

How many occurrences have we all tried to use some form of flattery to get what we want from other people? This helps us get on the other person's right side, and all it takes is flattering the target praising them and using all our charm. No matter who they are, the target will be happy to get all of this praise and compliments, and it will help lower their guard a little bit in the process. This is a great one that can be used when we want to get a new job or gain up in our position when an opening happens.

As you will notice, there are many different methods of manipulation that we can use in our daily lives. It doesn't seem to matter whether we are using them just to help us get by or if we are trying to use them to help us be dark manipulators and always get what we want, no matter the consequences. How many of the methods on the list have you used at one point or another in your own life to get what you wanted?

Chapter 47. Hypnosis

What is Hypnosis

There have been many definitions of what hypnosis is. The American Psychological Association has defined hypnosis as a cooperative interaction where the hypnotist will give suggestions to the person; he picks which he or she will respond to. Edmonton said that a person is simply but in a deep state of mind when undergoing hypnosis. Hypnosis is, therefore, when a person enters a state of mind in which a person finds himself or herself vulnerable to a hypnotist's suggestions. Hypnosis is not new to us because many people have seen it in movies, cartoons, or been to magic shows or performances where participants are told to do usual acts, and they do it. For sure, some people believe that hypnosis exists and would do anything to avoid being a victim, while others believe that its fiction.

Induction

Induction is considered as stage one of hypnosis. There are three stages in total. Induction aims to intensify the partaker's expectations of what follows after, explaining the role they will be playing, seeking their attention, and any other steps needed during this stage. There are many methods used by hypnotists to induce a participant to hypnosis. One of them is the "Braidism" technique, which requires a hypnotist to follow a few steps. This technique is named after James Braid. The first step would be to find a bright object and hold it in your left hand and specifically between the middle, fore, and thumb fingers.

The object should be placed where the participant will fix their stare and maintain the stare. This position would be above the forehead. It is always crucial that the hypnotist remind the partaker to keep their eyes on the object. If the participant wonders away from the object, the process will not work. The participant should be focused entirely on the item. The participant's eyes will begin to dilate, and the participant will start to have a wavy motion. A hypnotist will know that his participant is in a trance when the participant involuntarily closes his or her eyelids when the middle and forefingers of the right hand are carried from the eyes to the object. When this does not happen, the participant begins again, guiding that their eyes are close when the fingers are used in a similar motion. Therefore, this puts the participant in an altered state of mind. He or she is said to be hypnotized. The induction technique has been considered not to be necessary for every case. Research had shown that this stage is not as important as already known when it came to the induction technique's effects. Over the years, there have been variations in the once original hypnotic induction technique, while others have preferred to use other alternatives. James Braid's innovation of this technique still stands out.

Suggestion

After Induction, this follows the suggestion stage. James Braid left out the word suggestion when he first defined hypnosis. However, he described this stage as attempting to draw the partaker's conscious mind to focus on one central idea. James Braid would start by minimizing the functions of different parts of the partaker's body. He would then emphasize using verbal and non-verbal suggestions to get the partaker into a hypnotic state. Hippolyte Bernheim also shifted from the physical form of the partaker. This well-known hypnotist described hypnosis as the Induction of a particular physical condition, which increases one's susceptibility to the participant's suggestions. Suggestions can be verbal or one that doesn't involve speech. Modern hypnotist uses a different form of suggestions that include non-verbal cues, direct verbal suggestions, metaphors, and insinuations. Non-verbal suggestions that may be used include changing the tone, mental imagery, and physical manipulation. Mental imagery can take two forms. One consists of those that are delivered with permission and those that are done none the less and are more authoritarian.

When discussing hypnosis, it would be wise if one would be able to distinguish between the conscious mind and the unconscious mind. While using suggestions, most hypnosis will try and trigger the conscious mind other than the unconscious mind. In contrast, other hypnotists will view it as a way of communicating with the unconscious mind. Hypnotists such as Hippolyte Bernheim and James Braid, together with other great hypnotists, see it as trying to communicate with the conscious mind. This is what they believed. James Braid even defines hypnosis as the attention that is focused upon the suggestion. The idea that a hypnotist will be able to creep into your unconscious mind and order you around is next to impossible as according to those who belong to Braids school of thought. The determinant of the different conceptions about suggestions has also been the nature of the mind. Hypnotists such as Milton Erickson believe that responses given are normally through the unconscious mind. They used the case of indirect suggestions as an example. Many of the nonverbal suggestions, such as metaphors, will mask the hypnotist's true intentions from the victim's conscious mind. A form of hypnosis that is completely reliant upon the unconscious theory is a subliminal suggestion. Where the unconscious mind is left out in the hypnosis process, then this form of hypnosis would be impossible. The distinction between the two schools of thought is quite easy to decipher. The first school of thought believes that suggestions are directed at the conscious mind will use verbal suggestions.

In contrast, the second school of thought who believe that suggestions are directed at the unconscious mind will use metaphors and stories that mask their true intentions. In general, the participant will still need to draw their attention to an object or idea. This enables the hypnotist to lead the participant in the direction that the hypnotist will need to go into the hypnotic state. Once this stage of suggestion is completed and is successful, the participant will move onto the next stage.

Susceptibility

It has been shown that people are more likely to fall prey to the hypnotist tactics than others will. Therefore, it will be noted that some people can fall into hypnosis easily, and the hypnotist does not have to put so much effort. At the same time, for some, getting into the hypnotic stage may take longer and require the hypnotist to put quite the effort. While for some, even after the continued efforts of the hypnotist, they will not get into the hypnotic state. Research has shown where a person has reached the hypnotic state at some point in their lives. They will likely be susceptible to the hypnotist's suggestions, and those who have not been hypnotized, or it has always been difficult for them to reach that state. It will be likely that they may never be able to get that hypnotic state.

Different models have been established to determine the susceptibility of partakers to hypnosis. Research done by Deirdre Barrett showed that there are two types of subjects that considered being more susceptible to hypnosis and its effects. The two subjects consist of the group of dissociates and fantasizers. Fantasizers can easily block out the stimuli from reality without the specific use of hypnosis. They daydream a lot and also spent their childhood believing in the existence of imaginary friends. Dissociates are persons who have scarred childhoods. They have experienced trauma or child abuse and found ways to put away the past and become numb. If a person belongs to this group finds him or herself daydreaming, it will be associated in terms of being blank and fantasizing. These two groups will have the highest rates of being hypnotized.

Types of Hypnosis

A hypnotist can use different types of hypnosis as a participant. Each of them will use different ways and will help with certain issues. Some types of hypnosis will assist in weight loss, while others will help a participant relax.

Traditional hypnosis

This type of hypnosis is very popular and used by hypnotists. It works by the hypnotist, making suggestions to the participant's unconscious mind. The participant who is likely to be hypnotized by this does what he is told and does not ask many or frequent questions. If one was to self-hypnotize themselves, they would do this by using traditional hypnosis. As we have said, this type of hypnosis is very popular, and this could be attributed to it not requiring much skill, and it is not technical. The hypnotist will just have the right words and just tell the participant what to do. This might pose a problem to the hypnotist where the participant is a critical thinker and can analyze a given situation.

Neuro-Linguistic Programming (NLP)

This type of hypnosis gives the hypnotist wide criteria for the methods they can use in hypnosis. The hypnotist can save time during the process as the hypnotist will just use the same thought patterns to create the problem in the participant. For example, if it is stress, the same thought pattern causing this stress will be used to counter the stress.

NLP Anchoring

To understand how anchoring works, think of a particular scent. The first time you had that scent, you were going through some feeling in which the unconscious mind attached these feelings to that scent. Through this, the scent will become the anchor for those particular feelings. Every time you heard the scent, those feelings come rushing back, triggered by the unconscious mind. This type of NLP has been useful to hypnotists in the process of hypnosis. If you won a prize or some money, for example, the hypnotist will try and recreate those feelings you had when you won the prize. While recreating these feelings, the hypnotist will ensure the participant does an action during this process. Each time the subject does the said action, they will be reminded of those feelings.

This type of NLP can motivate a person to accomplish their goals, for example, if they are trying to be healthier or lose weight. The hypnotist will create a positive anchor that is in line with the mental image of the participant. The mental picture will be that of a sexy slim body. This image will be used as the motivator to start losing weight.

NLP Flash

This technique should only be done by a certified professional because it is considered very powerful and used to alter thoughts and emotions around the participant's unconscious mind. It is deemed to be helpful to persons who experience chronic stress or are addicted to a substance. Here is what the hypnotist will do; he or she is addicted to a substance instead of it, causing some feelings of happiness the act will now cause feelings of pain.

Where the person had chronic stress, the cat will bring a sense of relaxation. Those addicted to substances such as cigarettes and alcohol will now feel pain when they take these substances, which can effectively help them get over their addiction.

Chapter 48. Hypnosis Techniques

Once you have mastered the process of hypnosis that can often be called the long process, you can begin to use another powerful form of hypnosis to your advantage, instant hypnosis. These techniques play with the basics of the mind and what can happen to everyone from time to time daily. Have you ever gazed out of the window and simply watched the rain come down? What about listening to music that makes you feel soothed and relaxed? Maybe watching a favorite movie or television show, and you just feel yourself tune out. Often when this happens, you may not even notice that your brain has checked out. You're comfortable, relaxed, and completely absorbed in what you are doing. It happens every day and has three characteristics that are telltale signs.

1. Increased focus and concentration.

2. Increased relaxation of the body.

3. Increased access to the subconscious mind.

Hypnosis simply uses this natural state of things to put your subject into that state of mind as quickly as possible.

The Handshake Technique

This technique requires that you and the subject have some trust between you. As you will reach out your hand to shake with and then pull sharply towards yourself, you will forcefully, but calming say the word sleep as you do this. If you don't have a little trust built between you, this could just as easily backfire and make the subject tense when you pull them in. How does this technique work so easily? It works by using two different methods of inducing hypnosis: moving the subject off balance, so the brain does not have time to compute a response and giving the forceful suggestion of sleep, which seems like a good idea to the brain. People are far more suggestive than they think, and that is how this simple but powerful instant technique can work.

Falling Backward Method Technique

This form of instant hypnosis again works in the process of putting someone off balance and giving them a suggestion to follow. Instead of pulling them forward towards you, however, the subject will tip slightly backward. By following simple steps, this process can put your subject under in less than a minute:

Step 1: Ask your subject to stand with their feet together and their arms hanging loosely at the side. As they get into a position to explain what you will be doing with them step by step to know what is coming next, you will let them also know this will test their relaxation reflexes.

Step2: Move to stand directly behind your subject and place both hands on their shoulders.

Stand close enough to control them as they fall, but not close enough so that they will fall directly on you. Control the fall but don't take too much weight.

Place one foot in front of the other, and you will be able to keep the right balance to hold their weight as they fall back. Tell the subject this is just a trial run.

Step 3: Ask your subject to relax and explain that you will pull them a few inches back but that you will not let them fall. Place a strong emphasis on this fact that you will not let them fall and ask them to stay relaxed and bend their body at the ankles only, not at the waist, knees, or anywhere else.

Step 4: With your hands still on the subject's shoulders, ask them to close their eyes and pull them back only a few inches. A space of two or three inches is sufficient. Remember not to jar of force them, but allow them to gently tip backward and then rock them forward again. Keep your hands firmly on their shoulders and stand the client upright again, ensuring they regained their balance.

Step 5: If your subject seems relaxed, move on to the next step. If not, assure the subject that they have done well, and repeat the earlier step again to make certain the subject knows what to expect. You may find that certain nervous subjects might require several attempts before they're fully comfortable.

Step 6: After having them fall back, you can sit them down and use a short and brief deepening technique to make sure they are deep in hypnosis. This is usually done simply using phrases such as "move deeper and deeper into hypnosis, relax" repeat this as needed to make sure that your subject is deep into hypnosis.

The Eye Test

To confirm for both you and the subject that a state of hypnosis has been reached with an instant technique, you want to use this simple process. With your subject comfortable and sitting, follow this process:

Step 1: "You feel your eyes are very heavy and completely relaxed. Each muscle around them is now relaxed. This makes your eyelids very heavy."

Step 2: "On the count of three and not before, I will ask you to open your eyes. When I ask this, you will not be able to. You are so completely relaxed that your eyelids are too heavy. You will not be able to open your eyes because your eyelids are so heavy, and you are so relaxed that you will not even try to open them."

Step 3: "Your eyelids are closed. Heavy. Sealed shut, and you can't open them."

Step 4: "One. Your eyes are closed; your eyelids are heavy. You can't open them, not even if you try. You simply can't open them. They are too heavy, so very heavy."

Step 5: "Two. You cannot open your eyes."

Step 6: "Three. Your eyes are tightly closed. Try opening them. You cannot open them, right? Your eyelids are too heavy. Stop trying, just simply relax your eyes again, no more trying to open them. As go your eyes, so you should go your body. Relax."

When you are doing this process, you do not allow your subject to try opening their eyes for more than a second or two. If you give them too much time, they will eventually be able to force their eyes open, and once they have done that, they will come out of hypnosis. If they can open their eyes right away without any effort, they have not been put under, and you will have to start again. If this does occur and open their eyes, simply tell them it's okay and that their eyes were not relaxed enough, so you will begin again. Remember to keep a festive air.

Relaxation Technique

Therapists usually ask you to make yourself feel at home and be comfy during an introduction meeting. They may even provide you with a soft couch to lay on. Why? Are they just being courteous? The truth is, it's more than that. Therapists use relaxation as a common method to induce hypnosis. If you are relaxed, you will likely fall into a trance quicker, and your mind becomes more open to accepting suggestions. Listed are some of the usual methods to promote relaxation:

- Be comfortable.

- Lay down.

- In your head, start to count down.

- Control your breathing.

- Tense your muscles and then relax.

- Speak in a calm, soft tone.

Handshake Technique

The father of hypnotherapy, Milton Erickson, became famous for using a handshake technique to get a person into a hypnotic trance. Handshake is a common greeting, but in hypnosis, it can be more than just a gesture. Hypnotists do not just shake hands in a normal way. They interrupt the subject's mind by grabbing his wrist or pulling him forward to break the balance. Because the pattern established by the subject's mind was interrupted, the client's subconscious mind will suddenly be open to suggestions.

Eyes Cues Technique

The brain has two spheres – the conscious and creative side (right) and the practical and subconscious side (left). When we are in a conversation with someone, we look for feedback to know how they feel or react to what we say. Watch your subject's eyes. Are they looking to the right? Or are they looking to the left? Remember, when they're looking to the right, that suggests that they are conscious of the current situation. If they are looking to the left, that means they are in subconscious thought.

Visualization Technique

You can use visualization to induce your subject into a hypnotic trance and make suggestions. For instance, ask your subject to visualize a room that they know very well. Instruct them to visualize each detail in that room: the windows, the smell, the lighting, the color of the wall, the texture of the floor. Then, ask them to visualize a room they do not know, such as your office. As they struggle to remember the exact details of the room they are less familiar with, they open their minds to suggestions.

Arm Levitation Technique

You can perform this by asking your subject to close their eyes. Then, ask them to notice the difference between their arms. They might say their arms are heavy or light. Subconsciously, they will enter a trance and lift their arms or make their mind believe they have lifted their arms. Either way, induction is a success.

Sudden Shock/Falling Backwards Technique

As with the handshake technique, a subject in shock can enter into a trance. You might have heard about "trust falls." The feeling of falling backward can put the body into shock. Thus, it opens the mind to accept suggestions. Of course, you must catch your subject and be very careful not to drop him/her.

Hypnotic Trigger Technique

There are several forms of hypnotic triggers. A trigger lets the subconscious remember a desired feeling or action that is suggested while under hypnosis. Here are some examples:

- Finger snap
- Clap
- Sound of ball
- Opening eyes
- Standing or sitting

Touch Technique

In this technique, the hypnotist or psychiatrist will put the subject into a relaxed state of mind. Then, gently, the hypnotist will tap the subject's hands with his/her own with slight pressure. With a pen held directly in front of the subject, they will follow it with their eyes while visualizing a perfect place in their mind. This technique needs to be repeated several times during each session. Every after the session I have with this technique, I am always relaxed and feel better.

Chapter 49. Mind Controls Hypnotism

How to Hypnotize People

Talking about any professional hypnosis instructor, they notify their clients that a successful hypnotherapist is usually confidential. Ideally, you motivate confidence in your clients with the method of 'Personality Assurance.' In other words, the clients get to the state, whereby they feel better when you are around. Of course, this is the same when you invent the method of delivering speeches to hypnotize your audience. To start with, you need to cultivate confidence in your ability when with the audience. You portray a nervous mood at the same time.

Ideally, you tend to put your client/audience in the state. They feel like you cannot find them in the room; you portray the narratives in their minds. This could be done with the ideology of focusing your attention so carefully to ensure that your words have a real effect on their perception, consciously, and unconsciously. Changing the functioning of your immune system or blood circulation tends to be done by a competent hypnotist.

A good narrator must understand the idea of you wanting to be sufficiently convincing your listeners to concentrate on what you say. This is necessary because you need them to disassociate themselves from their concerns and situations to travel to different times, places, and opportunities with you. So, at least for a while, you tend to make them understand the benefits of implementing the new ways of seeing reality.

Helping people learn new ways of responding to life, with the aim of not letting low confidence, phobias, and attention mess them up is so useful for 'Therapy hypnosis.' You concentrate your audience's attention so selectively when you speak with power that they become hypnotic rather than purely aware of the essence of their living. Therefore, this kind of education seems more profound for people.

Avoiding the Boredom Trance

However, it appears that various kinds of trances are in the crowd. You tend to hypnotize the audience by making them be in the state of leaving the room psychologically when you aren't inspiring them. Instead, the groups will try not to obey your concept and try to avoid your voice. In most cases, they begin imagining what they will do for the day, what their next social arrangements will be like, or even what they will cook for lunch. The audience/participant tends to be disassociating, but not in the ways we would like. However, it appears that the specific technique to guide your audience in the proper direction seems to be available.

Crowd Hypnosis

Professional public presenters tend to captivate the audience with thoughts and words. Also, what they will use are the anticipation, vocabulary, narrative, and initial pace. This means that implementing the ideas for their audience to act on in the future will be their ideal objective. This method tends to be very useful when it comes to hypnotizing the audience. This means that the hypnotic speakers don't give just facts. Instead, they serve the audience with an experience that will improve how they feel, think, or even behave.

Prepare Your Speech With Words That Appeal to Feelings

'Nominalization' happens to be the term in which the people who have to travel inwards to communicate with personal meanings are called. This idea helps in hypnotizing the audience. These happen to be words like mighty, lovely, devotion, wisdom, power, and so on. What's just needed is that you ensure that you align the terms with what you mean. Ideally, such correctly used terms need to contain more than mere concrete words, but words evoke feelings.

Paint Vision of Hearing Minds Through Combining Senses

We portray a paradise-like experience to someone, the moment we hypnotize them. And indeed, in pictures, words, sounds, feelings, tastes, and as well as emotions, we dream. You need to tell what you've seen, felt, heard, and tasted when you say a story about something that has happened to you when giving speeches.

Ideally, an address becomes more elegant with the implementations of this sensory appeal. For instance, "When I heard a sickening scream, I was carrying a huge bag through the mall, I turned around and saw two giant guys trying to mug an old lady who pushed them into the realm" sounds more appropriate. Compared to this, "I went to the shopping center and witnessed a serious physical conflict."

Tell All Your Stories to Hypnotize

When there are great stories to tell, tell your viewers/audience overwhelmingly, even at the moment when you're giving a talk about molecular biology.

Fascinate With Your Voice

Think about words that have significance and relevance. So, in other words, you need to speed up with your voice at times. Then sometimes slow down a bit. Perhaps, this shouldn't happen every single time to avoid getting upset. You need to reduce the speed you implement in your words when you make an argument of significance. Then, also, you can even talk to a real hypnotist calmly and on slow delivery, periodically.

Use Suddenness

We tend to go into a hypnotic spell when we're shocked or surprised, not only when we loosen up.

Humor, as it is, tends to amuse someone. So, great speakers implement the idea of using humor because it is hypnotic. There tends to be a punch on a punch line in some other perspectives, and that is because it is surprising. Mainly, the shock is often used by the hypnotists from different stages to track subjects quickly into a hypnotic state.

Be Powerful

You can create a hypnotic state for people by merely exerting power over others. Look at how people are likely to follow a person who appears to be powerful blindly. When you do this, you can get a following, and the people following you will do what you say because they want to please you and stay in your presence.

You can use this technique among your friends, family, coworkers, and any person you have a pre-existing relationship with. You want to exert your power over time so that it does not feel too aggressive. Once you notice you have followers, start small with what you are asking. They will do it without even thinking twice about it. Over time, you can ask for larger things, and you will have no trouble getting them.

Mirroring

Now, the powerful approach works for people, you know, but what about strangers? This is where mirroring comes into play. This allows you to quickly develop a rapport with someone once they see you both have someone in common. This can almost put them into a trance because they will naturally like you and want to please you since they will perceive both of you as very similar.

To successfully use this technique, pay attention to the stranger's common phrases and body language. Look at their behaviors. Exhibit these things back at them. As you continue your interaction with them, it will not take long to notice the similarities. You do not even have to lie about things you have in common. Simply mirroring their language and behaviors is enough to get them under your spell.

Use Stories

The good stories can put people into a trance-like state. Think back to when you were a kid, and your parents would read stories to you before bed. This would induce a deep state of relaxation. The same is true when you are an adult.

As you are talking to people each day, add in some anecdotes. This shows you personally and can even give you a sense of power and authority. You want people to visualize what you are saying, so use imagery to tell your story.

For example, you want a person to move something breakable because you just do not want to risk it. Do not just ask them to move it carefully. State that you do not want the vase to be dropped since it can shatter. They will visualize the vase shattering, forcing them to not only be careful when moving it, but they will volunteer to do it. They will almost see completing the task successfully as a type of personal challenge.

Lengthy Speeches

When you want to induce hypnosis on a large group, lengthy speeches are how to do it. Think about the television evangelists you have seen. They essentially use this form of hypnosis to get people to hand over thousands of dollars every time they hold a service.

When they are delivering their speech, they take a few pauses. They use varied voice tones to annunciate points and keep people completely engrossed in what they are saying. They know what their message is, and they repeat it frequently. However, they often use different phrasing, so no one in the audience ever feels like something is being forced on them.

It is not uncommon for them to tell you exactly what to do without directly telling you to do it. When you're in this type of situation, you are so enamored with the speaker that you will do just about anything they ask. They always present their lengthy speech, and then they just pass the collection basket. They do not ask you to donate because they know you will. After all, you feel dedicated to them.

You can use this technique too. You do not need an auditorium for it either. If you need something from a person or a group of people, plan out a speech. Make sure that those you are talking to feel empowered throughout the lesson. By the time you get to the end, you have already subconsciously implanted in their minds what you want. You will not need to ask for it. You will just get it.

For example, you want people to invest in your new business idea. Give them a speech about the business, about how much starting it would mean to you, and then insert a bit of a sob story about how this is your dream. Still, financially, you cannot swing it. After listening to your dramatic speech, they will feel compelled to invest.

Stacking

This is a hypnotic technique that works because you nearly overwhelm the people you are talking to. With this technique, you essentially bombard people with information. They are learning so many new things that they do not have time to sort through it. They do not feel they need to check facts because you are speaking with such authority that they automatically believe what you are saying. By the time you end your thoughts, you have essentially put them into a trance.

Cold Reading

This is something that psychics use to convince people that they can read their minds and predict their future. You will start by making a vague statement. For example, if you know a person to be shy, you will state this. You know it is accurate, and they will elaborate, giving you further information. You will use this additional information to make other predictions essentially. Once a person feels that you have this almost clairvoyant ability, they are more prone to believe anything you tell them.

Chapter 50. Dark NLP

'Neuro-Linguistic Programming' (NLP) is like a user manual for the brain that helps you communicate the unconscious mind's goals and desires to the conscious self. Imagine you are in a foreign country and craving chicken wings. You go to a restaurant to order the same, but when the food shows up, it ends up being liver stew... because of a failed communication.

Humans often fail to recognize and acknowledge their unconscious thoughts and desires because many get lost in translation to the conscious self. NLP enthusiasts often exclaim, "the conscious mind is the goal setter, and the unconscious mind is the goal-getter."

The idea of being your unconscious mind wants you to achieve everything that you desire. Still, if your conscious mind fails to receive the message, you will never set the goal to achieve those dreams.

NLP was developed using excellent therapists and communicators who had achieved great success as role models. It's a set of tools and techniques to help your master communication, both with yourself and others.

NLP is the study of the human mind combining thoughts and actions with the perception to fulfill their deepest desires. Our mind employs complex neural networks to process information and use language or auditory signals to give it meaning while storing these signals in patterns to generate and store new memories.

We can voluntarily use and apply certain tools and techniques to alter our thoughts and actions in achieving our goals. These techniques can be perceptual, behavioral, and communicative. They can be used to control our minds and those of others.

One of NLP's central ideas is that our conscious mind has a bias towards a specific sensory system called the preferred representational system (PRS). Phrases like "I hear you" or "sounds good" signal an auditory PRS, whereas a phrase like "I see you" may signal a visual PRS.

A certified therapist can identify a person's PRS and model their treatment around it. This therapeutic framework often involves rapport building, goal setting, and information gathering, among other activities.

NLP is increasingly used by individuals to promote self-enhancement, such as self-reflection, confidence, social skill development, but primarily by communication.

NLP therapy or training can be delivered in language and sensory-based interventions, using behavior modification techniques customized for individuals to better their social communication and improved confidence and self-awareness.

NLP therapists or trainers strive to make their clients understand that their view and perception of the world are directly associated with how they operate in it. The first step toward a better future is a keen understanding of their conscious self and contact with their unconscious mind.

It is paramount to first analyze and subsequently change our thoughts and behaviors that are counterproductive and block our success and healing. NLP has been successfully used to treat various mental health conditions like anxiety, phobias, stress, and even post-traumatic stress disorder.

An increasing number of practitioners are commercially applying NLP to promise improved productivity and achievement of work-oriented goals that ultimately lead to job progression.

Here are some prominently used NLP techniques.

Anchoring

Try this yourself! Think of a gesture or sensation on your body (pulling your earlobe, cracking your knuckles, touching your forehead), and associating it with any desired positive emotional response (happiness, confidence, calmness, etc.), recalling and reliving the memory when you experience those emotions.

Content Reframing

This NLP technique is best suited to combat negative thoughts and feelings. With these visualization techniques, you can alter your mind to think differently about situations where you feel threatened or underpowered.

Rapport Building

Rapport is the art of generating empathy in others by pacing and mirroring their verbal and nonverbal behaviors. People like other people who they think are similar to themselves.

When you can subtly mirror the other person, their brain will fire off "mirror neurons" or "pleasure sensors" in their brains, making them feel a sense of liking for you.

Dissociation

The NLP technique of dissociation guides you in severing the link between negative emotions and the associated trigger. For instance, certain words or phrases may instantly bring back bad memories and make you feel stressed or depressed. If you can successfully identify those triggers and make an effort to detach those negative feelings, you are one step closer to healing and empowering yourself.

Future Pacing

The NLP technique of leading the subject to a future state and rehearsing the potential future outcomes to achieve the desired result automatically is called future pacing. It's a type of visualization technique or mental imagery used to anchor a change or resource to future situations by imagining and virtually experiencing those situations.

Influence and Persuasion

This is the most ambivalent NLP technique and houses a gray area between dark psychology and psychotherapy.

NLP is primarily focused on eliminating negative emotions, curbing bad habits, and resolving conflicts. Another aspect of NLP deals with ethically influencing and persuading others. Now pay attention to the word ETHICAL here.

How to Use NLP as a Useful Tool to Manipulate?

Your intentions are the only North Star in a dark and lonely ocean. It is the only thing that sets NLP apart from manipulation by serving as a useful tool to remember the actual purpose of using NLP. Studies show that your brain subtly works towards achieving them when innately aware of your goals, even when you aren't actively thinking about it. It is known as "diffused thinking" when you allow your mind to wander freely, making connections randomly. It's a process that encompasses all parts of the brain and is commonly used to solve problems and difficult concepts.

The true motive can sit undisturbed, deep in your subconscious, while your brain works around it, trying to develop ways and plans to achieve it. NLP is a set of skills that allows you as the user to be in control of your own conscious and unconscious mind.

However, that doesn't mean that NLP is unsuccessful if the user's intentions are immoral. It is possible to imbue those habits known to be practiced by historically unsavory characters, such as criminals and terrorists; thus, the patient can be fashioned into the next revolutionary terrorist who ushers in a new era completely reinvents modern violence as we know it. This is an example of the more extreme cases. Subtler manipulation, the kind that may not make headlines and morning news, can be equally deadly.

For example, consider this hypothetical scenario between two rival law firms competing for the same large client. Law firm A plans to manipulate the client's choice by presenting their rival law firm in a bad light. This is done by hiring a programmer to sit in on the regular therapy sessions of law firm B's top attorney and subtly twist the patient's view of his/her relationship with their spouse, thereby planting subconscious suggestions of problems in the relationship that do not exist. This technique would fall under the category of manipulation in court, with or without NLP.

Another instance of manipulation your brain doesn't commonly recognize because humans are sympathetic creatures is the emotional manipulation done by beggars. Though there is a percentage of 'honest' beggars, who are truly homeless and struggling to survive, there is a great majority of those whose trade is begging.

It is quite popular in the South Asian region, and the manipulators often don patchy clothes and have dirty faces. They use words and behaviors to play on the emotions to convince people that they need money. Many even go the extra mile and hire children for the day, just to rub it in. The manipulation is done so well that whether they have trained themselves in NLP techniques or not, they are very good at it.

On the other hand, NLP programmers hired to hold regular workshops in businesses (such as our hypothetical law firms, for instance) use it as a tool to help boost employee motivation, and encourage them to pick up new skill-sets that have been attributed to highly successful individuals, in a bid to improve general worker productivity and employee attitude in the company. It is a technique that has shown positive results.

Similarly, as it is used in business purposes to inspire workers, it is also commonly employed by a door-to-door salesman to sell as many products as possible and earn higher commissions.

Personal programmers work with their clients to help them repair relationships with their friends and family, rectifying and solving conflicts. NLP is also clinically utilized in curing mental illnesses like PTSD, GAD, phobias, anxieties, paranoia, and even substance abuse.

There are many more instances where NLP is employed, for good and bad, but the prevailing truth of the matter is that NLP itself is not guilty. Like any technique or product, there are users and abusers.

The thing being abused is innocent of the crime of the abuser. It's NLP abusers with evil, nefarious motives that have brought a bad name on the personal development and psychotherapy technique so well-intended by Brandler and Grinder.

Chapter 51. The Positive and Negative Aspects of Neuro Linguistic Programming

There are both positive and negative parts of neuro phonetic programming or NLP. Tragically, not many individuals have a complete comprehension of this term, even though they are dependent upon it each and ordinary. More critically, many organizations, associations, and people who realize how to control this idea, regularly do such with exploitative aims.

NLP is the investigation of how verbal correspondence impacts the human cerebrum. The words that you hear are answerable for forming your discernments, thoughts, and even your activities. This is the essential thought behind uplifting feedback. In contemplates, uplifting statements have been appeared to make significant enhancements in mentalities and practices. Neuro etymological programming characterizes why this works.

On the other hand, negative words additionally sway the individuals who hear them. Individuals who are continually encompassed by antagonistic individuals will regularly fall prey to their negative talk. Expressions of demoralization will, as a rule, cause an individual to take on a naysayer mentality. This makes it almost certain that the individual will surrender before attempting. Something else to consider is how your own words may make you stay dormant in certain life territories. You must be cautious about discussing these things on the off chance that you are attempting to create change in specific examples or practices. Your cerebrum will accept a follow up on the very words that you express.

The absolute most noteworthy experts or NLP are significant promoting and publicizing organizations. They realize that their words can shape popular suppositions and free activity. To get mass-market consideration for explicit merchandise, a significant number of these elements will make individuals partner industrialism with satisfaction. Individuals at that point start to accept that they should purchase items to feel glad.

When you have an away from how verbal correspondence influences your practices, it is critical to be progressively cautious about the words you express and the organization you keep. You can likewise play a progressively active job as an audience. Individuals who listen inactively to verbal messages are unmistakably progressively liable to being influenced by them.

When you realize what neuro phonetic programming or NLP is and how it tends to be utilized, you can become much progressively amazing in your dynamic. You will be able to begin utilizing positive words to fortify yourself and the people around you. You will furthermore turn out to be progressively capable in endeavors to prevent you or to persuade you to burn through cash on superfluous things. This is genuinely one of those occurrences in which information is power.

How Negative Thinking Can Affect Us

Negative reasoning influences us inwardly, however, genuinely. To be sure, negative considerations have genuine implications past simply the idea itself. How might you use neuro etymological programming and entrancing to break liberated from this?

Neuro semantic writing computer programs are methods by which you can truly be instructed to "retrain" how you think. A specialist prepared in NLP can assist you with rethinking and repeat contemplations, and think about them from an alternate perspective, so you truly start to think in various manners that are increasingly adjusted and positive - and without a doubt, progressively practical.

This is an extremely positive advance to take because so regularly, negative considerations are "outside of any relevant connection to the issue at hand" based on what is truly occurring.

Negative Thinking in Every Day Situations

Suppose, for instance, that you've been doled out a venture grinding away, and you're sure you can do it. You complete the activity, and you've done quite well. In any case, you notice one modest mistake. In a split second, you start to converse with yourself adversely, disclosing that you took care of the activity inadequately, even though the one small mistake isn't huge and won't sway on the nature of the undertaking generally. So while your supervisor is stating, "Incredible employment!" you may be stating to yourself, "No, it's most certainly not. I'm so dumb. I will lose my employment on account of that botch."

How Reasonable Is That?

A certified NLP Practitioner may challenge you with this: "All in all, your manager has advised you will lose your employment since you committed one little error?" How will you respond? You'll think, "Obviously not!" and understand that your supervisor is revealing to you that you've worked superbly. Like this, neuro etymological programming truly shows us how to retrain our musings in a progressively adjusted and positive manner, given a target assessment of the natural conditions.

Presently, I don't get this' meaning regarding how you can abstain from following this example by and large? All things considered you make a stride back and take a gander at the task with target eyes. Impartially, without that negative self-talk, you can see that genuinely, you worked superbly and committed one little error. What's more, even though you need to abstain from committing errors, they do occur.

So a good repetition of your underlying response - that you took care of the activity inadequately - may be to state, "I worked admirably and committed one little error. I will focus next time and make an effort not to commit a similar error, yet I can at present be pleased with what I did, all things being equal." You can likewise disclose to yourself that because your supervisor is content with what you did, you ought not exclusively to be glad for what you've done, however. You can be secure that your activity is protected. Truth be told, what is sensible and present and is considerably more precise as self-talk than your past explanation.

Chapter 52. Understanding Body Language

What is Body Language

We sometimes do things unconsciously, much like a nervous habit, such as tapping your foot or rubbing your hands together. Though we may not be aware that we are doing these things, others see these habits and read into them. We may be seen as nervous or agitated by others due to these unconscious behaviors that we are prone to.

At other times, we might engage in an action or pose with a specific intent consciously chosen. We can choose to turn our bodies towards someone we are busy talking to seem more attentive. Imagine your first job interview: you cautiously keep yourself from twitching, rubbing your face, or reclining. You have been made aware by various knowledgeable people such as school counselors and career guides to be aware of these interview bombs. Knowing how bad these make you seem, you learn not to engage in this form of body language.

We can lie with a written and spoken language. Usually, we lie to avoid getting into trouble. Likewise, we can also lie in our bodies. We can project a disingenuous body image and has been carefully polished to accomplish a particular appearance. I imagine that several of us have been caught in a scam at some point in time. This is an ideal example of how intelligent users of body language can manipulate it to convince us of their honesty. We get people to believe us based on what we show and not what we say.

In expressing emotions, the facial expression is essential. It combines the cheeks' movement, nose, lips, eyebrows, and eyes to show a person's various moods. Some researchers showed that body and facial expressions complement each other in interpreting emotions. Some experiments recognized the influence of body expression in identifying facial expression, which means that the brain simultaneously processes body and facial expressions.

Body postures can also detect emotions. If an individual is angry, he will try to dominate another person. His posture will show such approach tendencies. If he is fearful, his approach will be that of avoidance. He will feel submissive and weak.

Even gestures have different interpretations. For instance, if an individual folds his arms during a discussion, it's going to mean that he's unwilling to concentrate on the speaker or features a closed mind. If he crosses his arms over the opposite, it means he lacks confidence and is insecure.

Simple hand gestures show that the individual is self-assured and confident, while clenched hands can mean either angry or stressed. If he wrings his hands, it means he is anxious and nervous.

Finger gestures show the overall well-being of an individual. In some cultures, it is acceptable to point with an index finger. Handshakes also show the levels of emotion and confidence of individuals. They are popular in some cultures. In Muslim cultures, a man cannot shake or touch the hands of a woman. In Hindu cultures, a man greets a woman by keeping his hands together, like praying.

When it comes to learning how to read body language, the main goal is to determine if the person in front of you is genuine. Body language clues are incredibly crucial when deciphering someone's innermost thoughts, personality, and even intentions. In many ways, body language teaches you to become a human lie detector. Humans can be great liars, but while we may have been able to trick our mind into saying words we do not mean, we cannot trick our bodies into executing the lie flawlessly.

Reading body language is an excellent skill to have in job interviews when trying to solve a crime or resolve conflict. Being able to see beneath the surface into what is going on inside someone's mind will help you make better, more informed decisions.

What makes body language so tricky to master is deciphering body language cues within the right context. For example, when a person crosses his or her arms in front of the chest, you could construe that as negative body language, perhaps an indicator that the person is not happy to be here. However, depending on the context, it could also mean that the person feels cold, uncomfortable, or frustrated. Not accounting for a situation can lead to misreading of body language cues and a wrong conclusion.

Most people generally display a few categories of body language:

Dominant: Dominant body language comes into play when someone wants to be in command. The most standout cue for this category of body language is standing tall, with chest puffed out.

Attentive: This shows someone's interest and engagement with the conversation or situation.

Bored: A typical representation of this body language is the lack of eye contact and constant yawning.

Aggressive: An aggressive person will display threatening body language cues.

Defensive: A defensive person will look as if he or she is protecting or withholding information.

Closed Off: You can recognize a closed-off person by noticing if he or she is shutting you off by crossing his or her arms and guardedly standing farther away from you.

Open: This body language is friendly and welcoming.

Emotional: We usually display this body language when we feel heavily influenced by current feelings and typically have to change moods.

The Power of Body Language

Body language extends beyond more than just the four types. It can also be divided into positive and negative body language. Positive body language draws people towards you and creates a sense of belonging and accomplishment. This includes encouraging smiles, firm handshakes, making eye contact, facing someone with your body in a neutral position, and using an encouraging tone of voice.

Negative body language is based on avoidance. It includes turning your back on someone, not facing the speaker, looking down, using a soft and insecure tone of voice, and avoiding eye contact. When someone uses this body language tells, we begin to assume the worst about that person. We see them as being dishonest, uninvested, and disinterested.

Knowing these two forms of body language, which would you choose to look at? In all likelihood, you would prefer seeing positive body language. We want to feel acknowledged and valued during our communications with other people. Seeing someone face you, look you in the eye, speak in a clear tone without hiding their mouth, and have a natural appearance due to their open posture is very encouraging and ensures that communication can happen harmoniously and smoothly.

Yet, we often use negative body language when we feel intimidated or unsure of a situation. Being skilled at using your body language would help you achieve more favorable outcomes from your daily interactions and communications.

According to Guilbeault (2018), body language's power lies in that it can help you gain things you want, such as friends or jobs; however, it can also make you lose the things you want negative body language forms. It can cost you your job, friends, and even intimate relationships. Without even opening our mouths, we can attract or repel people.

Body language can build trust, which is the crucial ingredient in all relationships, whether for work, companionship, or intimacy. Using the power of body language, you can lead a more productive and successful life. Hence, it is well worth learning how to recognize body language and its meaning in others and ourselves.

Characteristics of Body Language

In general, body language manifests an individual's emotions, meaning another person can perceive it.

First, it is understood that the signal from the body language to the receiver can be highly complicated. An individual's body language consists of multiple body parts moving or not moving together. All must be taken into account to interpret a specific person's emotion. A specific facial expression taken out of context from the person's other bodily reactions will give an incomplete or otherwise misleading analysis of their emotions.

Another characteristic is that the projected emotion from body language is perceived automatically in a way similar to speech. This characteristic makes nonverbal interaction spontaneous. There is often little need to interpret further what an individual means with their body language.

A third characteristic is that young individuals can acquire and develop body language very easily and rapidly. Children learn what gestures and facial expressions mean from their parents, friends, and even strangers who interact with them. The ease of acquiring knowledge of body language can make children carry on specific body language into their maturity.

Deciphering Body Language

To understand and use body language, you have to learn how to read it in action and view it holistically as an overall picture of what a person is trying to communicate. If you want to begin controlling your body language, you'll have to understand how it all works together in the field as well. Somebody crossing their legs away from you could mean they are shy, it could mean that they are closed off to you, or it could just mean they need to pee desperately. To be able to read what they are feeling, you need to notice how they use the space around them, group behavioral actions into clusters (clusters are multiple body language cues placed together, so if they cross their legs away from you, cross their hands, and face in a direction away from you, it isn't looking good!), and to place them into context.

Actively Listening

Suppose you are looking at somebody's posture or trying to pick up the micro-expressions in their face that occur at one-fifth of a second. In that case, you might be closer to understanding how they feel, but you might also be ignoring something more obvious. The whole point of studying body language is to understand better what people think to build a better connection. The point isn't to make you paranoid that they are continually deceiving you. It's to make you less paranoid about what they are thinking.

Proxemics

Proxemics is a fancy word used in the body language community to mean the study of personal space and proximity. You can't indeed read someone's body language without noticing where they concern you in space.

Someone seems to be paying attention to you. They have open body language. They are even pointing themselves towards you– so they're paying attention to you, right? Well, maybe not if they're on the other side of the room and not moving any closer towards you.

When it comes to reading other people, some aspects of personal space are apparent. If someone is close, it will mean they are or are trying to be more intimate. However, with some people, especially men, there is a tendency to be territorial and to feel they have more access to your personal space than you might feel comfortable with. You can use these cues to determine if someone is aggressive, friendly, or flirtatious. By reading the rest of someone's body language, you can see if they are leaning towards you to be friendly or assertive. It is quite risky to invade other people's personal space to get an advantage over them. In general, try to avoid getting too close to someone unless they invite you to by touching you or speaking at a lower volume that requires you to lean in.

Chapter 53. Deception

What is Deception?

The definition is a theme that usually resonates within the spectrum of dark psychology. Throughout the years, it has been defined as any particular act used by a particular manipulative individual to instill certain beliefs within the victim that are usually false or only those possessing partial truths. It is usually placed in the same category as deceit, mystification, and suffrage. Deception is not usually an easy theme to understand since it involves many different things like, for example, distractions, propaganda camouflage, and concealment. The manipulator is often able to easily control the subject's mind since the victim is often led to placing immense trust in this manipulative individual. The victims often believe in whatever the manipulator will say and might even be basing plans and shaping their world base on the things that the manipulator is feeding their subconscious mind. This strong element of trust towards the manipulator can quickly fade away once the victim realizes what is going on. Because of this very reason, a certain level of skill is needed for deployment of this theme, since only then will a manipulator be able to skillfully change the focus of suspicion towards him and onto the victim's paranoia.

In most cases, deception will often present itself in relationship settings and lead the victim to have dominant feelings of distrust and betrayal between the partners in the relationship. This usually happens because deception is a theme that violates most of the rules of most relationships, together with having a negative influence on the expectations that come with the relationship. When getting into relationships, one of the usually ordinary things is always the ease of having an honest and truthful conversation with their partner. If the then learns that one of them is beginning to show signs of deception, they might have to learn the different ways of using misdirection and distractions to pry out reliable and truthful information that they need from them. The trust would have gone into a permanent rift that will not be easy to come back from since the victim will always be questioning everything that the partner will say and do, wondering whether the story is true of fabricated. Most relationships will end as soon as the deceptive partner is found out.

As we described earlier, this form of communication relies on lies and certain omissions to make the victim believe whatever he is being led to believing by the deceptive individual. This is the case; there are five main types of deceptive tactics that are seen to exist. We shall briefly touch on each one to better understand this theme.

Concealments

Probably taking home the medal of most used type of deception, concealment is basically when the deceptive individual knowingly omits information from his often relevant and important stories to the context. They can also engage in certain behaviors that would signal to hide relevant information to the subject at that particular time. A skilled manipulator is experienced enough to know that he will have to be clever to know that it's safe not to be directly in their approach but rather insinuate the lie leading the victim to their own conclusion, which is predetermined.

Exaggeration

What can be said about this? This is where an individual, in a sense, stretches the truth a bit too much with an intended goal of leading the story towards a direction that best caters to their needs. The manipulator will make a certain scenario appear more severe than it is to avoid lying directly to their victims. This is usually done to let the victim do whatever it is they want.

Lies

This is one tactic that we, as humans, use daily for one reason or another. We are often inclined to lie as a way to avoid some form of penalty. For example, if you work in the bank and you run late because of something minor, you will be inclined to lie to your boss to keep him from cutting you lose. What then can be said to be the meaning of this? This is where an individual gives information that is all south of the actual truth. They will present this completely fabricated truth to the victim, and they will believe it.

Equivocations

This is where an individual will knowingly make a statement of a contra dictionary nature intended to lead the victim to the path of confusion on what is exactly seems to be going on. This clever tactic will allow the manipulator to save his image if he is later discovered.

Understatements

This is where an individual minimizes aspects of the truth in the particular story being told at the time. They will often approach a victim preaching how something isn't that big of a deal when it is of the utmost importance.

What drives a manipulator to the deployment of the theme of dark psychology? According to research done over the years, there are usually 3 main things that motivate an individual to use deception on others. These three motives are under the umbrella of close relationships. They include self-focused motives, relationship-focused motives, and partner-focused motives. Let's look first at the motives focused on the partner. The victim will use deception in this kind of motive to avoid harming the subject or their partner. They may also use front to protect the relationship between the victim and an outside third party, avoid worrying about something about the subject, or keep the subject's self-esteem intact. Such motivation for deception will often be seen as both relationally beneficial and socially polite.

Deception's self-focused motive. This one is not considered noble as the first one and is therefore considered more inferior to the other techniques. Rather than worrying about the victim and how they feel, the manipulator will simply think about how they feel and their self-image. The manipulator uses deception to protect or enhance their self-image in this motive. To shield the victim from criticism, embarrassment, or anger, this form of deception is used.

Finally, we shall look at the relationship-focused motive of deception. The manipulative individual will use this deception to limit any harm that could come to the relationship simply by avoiding the trauma and conflict of relationships. This form of deception sometimes helps the relationship, depending on the situation. It may be the cause of harming the relationship because it will make things more complicated. For example, if you choose to hide how you feel about supper because you don't want to get into a fight, the relationship might be helpful. On the other hand, if you have an affair and choose to keep this information to yourself, it will only complicate things in the end.

Primary Components of Deception

As much as it may be difficult to clarify which factors show clear deployment of deception, some subtle components are immediate identifiers of these themes. The victim will come to be aware of these factors only when the manipulator dispatches a direct lie. Let us now dive deep into the particulars of said components.

Disguise

The first component we shall unravel is that of disguises. What usually goes on here is that the manipulator works tirelessly until he successfully creates the impression of being someone they are not. Manipulators often resort to this tactic if they want to hide something about them so deep that no one ever finds out. This could be a dark secret or just something as harmful as someone's name. This component's popular belief is that it is simply a change of clothes, just like in the moves. However, it goes far beyond this in that it also involves a complete change of one's persona. Having a rough idea of how discuses work, let us look at a few examples of how it can be used in the process of deception.

The first instance is where the manipulator changes himself to another person so as not to be discovered. An individual will do this with a view to maybe be able to get back into a particular crowd of people who are not very fond of him, revamp their whole personality to make someone like them, or further their own goals. In some instances, disguise may be used to refer to the hiding of one's true nature in the hopes of maybe hiding the effect that appears to be unpopular with that proposal. Disguises usually have adverse effects because it is generally hiding one's true intentions for a victim. When information is withheld in this fashion, it often clouds the victim's judgment. The victim ends up having the feeling of being in control of their decisions when they have been swayed towards the directions' manipulator. This is seen mainly in a political setting.

Camouflage

This is where individual works tirelessly to hide the truth in one way or another, leaving his victim clueless as to what exactly is going on. This is characterized by the manipulator's use of half-truths when divulging certain information to his victim. The victim will only be aware that camouflage has taken place when the actual truths are brought to light. A skilled manipulator with a lot of experience using camouflage is more likely to bra undetected in performing certain actions.

Simulation

The third component of deception is what is commonly referred to as simulation. This is simply the process where the victim is shown continuously subject matter that is false in every way. Further on, we get to see that simulation consists of 3 other techniques that can be used. They are mimicry, distraction, and fabrication.

Fabrication is when the manipulator takes something found in actual reality and chafes it to become this completely different thing. The manipulator will seek to either give detailed events that never happened or add some exaggerations that either make it sound better or worse than it sounds. The core of their story, however, is usually true. If the teacher gives them a bad grade, these manipulators may further the story by stating that they were given the bad results on purpose. The reality is that the manipulator did not study for the test hence his bad grade.

Mimicry is another tool that manipulators use when deploying these tactics of deception. The manipulator here usually portrays a persona that is quite close to their own, but not their own. They may present an idea similar to someone else's and give him credit for thinking about it first. This form of stimulation may be able to take pace through visual and auditory stimuli.

The last tool we shall look at is that of distraction as another form of simulation in deception. This is where the manipulator tries to get the victim only to focus their attention on everything else but the truth. How is this usually done? This is generally achieved through baiting or the offering of something more tempting than the reality itself.

Chapter 54. Dark Cognitive Behavioral Therapy

" A small behavioral change can also lead to embracing a wider checklist of healthier choices" - Chuck Norris.

What is Dark CBT?

To understand Dark CBT, we first must realize the necessary cognitive behavioral therapy and its approach to mental health and healing. Dark CBT is founded on the tried and true CBT principles employed by therapists everywhere. That is why it is guaranteed to work. Learning about CBT and then applying them as you see fit to unknowing subjects makes you very powerful.

Gain a thorough understanding of how to use CBT and maybe even use it upon yourself for practice. From there, you can begin leveraging Dark CBT as a clandestine healing method or weapon on those around you.

History of CBT

CBT was first developed by a psychologist named Aaron Beck in the 1960s. Beck noticed that his patients had internal monologues, where they spoke to themselves in the privacy of their minds.

Beck began to have his patients analyze their automatic thoughts and report them. As his patients became more conscious of their ideas, they realized how these thoughts could make or break their success. Some thoughts made them make poor decisions or drew them to untrue assumptions that made them feel bad for no reason. Other studies helped them overcome problems and feel better about themselves. By gaining awareness of their thoughts by reporting them verbally to Beck or writing them down throughout the day, his patients were able to gain more control over their thinking.

In time, Beck was able to teach his patients to harness their thoughts and become more self-aware. He taught them to think differently to feel better. He noticed that changes in thinking led to changes in behavior and emotions. Correcting flawed thinking was what helped his patients heal faster.

Since Beck's initial observation, CBT has grown by leaps and bounds. It is now better understood and has become a significant part of psychotherapy. All therapists are aware of CBT, and most therapists employ it to some degree in their practice. There are many forms of CBT, but they all have the same premise and the same goal, putting them under the enormous Cognitive Behavioral Therapy umbrella.

Now we have developed Dark CBT. Dark CBT operates on the same principles as CBT. However, it is more clandestine. Rather than using CBT on yourself or a willing psychotherapy patient, Dark CBT is something you can use on anyone without their awareness. You can apply CBT concepts to change someone's thinking to suit your needs. You can also use it on yourself, emphasizing becoming successful and achieving what you want in life. Dark CBT goes beyond simple healing and instead gives you the power to shape your life and your relationships as you desire.

Your interest in using Dark CBT may be purely altruistic, as you seek to help others who won't help themselves. Or you may have a more nefarious interest in using it to get your way and to manipulate others. How you use Dark CBT is up to you entirely, but the wealth of opportunity that Dark CBT provides you with is astounding.

Dark CBT is a relatively new method. It has not been applied to many study groups or researched extensively. Therefore, there is room for growth and experimentation in Dark CBT. You may find new applications or new ways of performing Dark CBT that is already unheard of. This is a new field that you can certainly expand and make your own. Supplement your Dark CBT with simple CBT methods and experiment with trial and error. You may just find your type of therapy that works well for you, based on the incredible techniques included and in basic CBT.

Why Use CBT?

There has been much success using CBT to treat difficulties in people's lives, ranging from depression to alcoholism to drug dependency to relationship problems. It can help people quit bad habits and feel better about themselves. It can also help people learn how to cope with their mental ailments to feel better. Even people who are not mentally ill can benefit from using CBT thought processes to tackle challenging problems in their lives, such as marriage difficulties, difficulties with communication, anger management issues, and even financial struggles.

The great thing about CBT is that it is possible to use on yourself. With the help of a CBT journal, you can document your thoughts and emotional reactions to events in your life or emotional wounds you are trying to overcome, or bad habits you are trying to break free of. Then, you ask yourself questions that lead you to change how you look at the situation, wound, or habit. You write down your new mental approach and new emotions now that you are using different thinking. You will notice a drastic improvement in your feelings and outlook on life. Suddenly, you won't have so many difficulties in life, and your problems will become so easy to solve that they will practically disappear before your eyes.

Dark CBT is incredibly useful for two reasons. The first is that Dark CBT is focused on personal gains and success. Rather than just healing your annoying thinking habits, you learn to become a massive success at anything that you wish. You can make yourself invincible if you teach yourself to believe that you are capable of anything. You can also create a monster by teaching someone else to feel the same way.

The second is that Dark CBT is sneaky. So even if someone is not interested in changing his thinking, you can still use Dark CBT on him to achieve the results that you desire. You will enjoy success, and he won't even know what has happened to him. You can fix people who refuse to get help or change people who stand in your way. No one will guess what you are doing. You simply seem to be an interested friend or loved one, trying to help someone think more realistically or positively.

What Separates Dark CBT From Regular CBT?

We already talked about this a little bit. But we want to stress that Dark CBT is the same as regular CBT. Its uses and applications are a bit different, however. That is the only thing that separates the two types of CBT.

Regular CBT is used in therapy or by individuals who are actively interested in changing their thinking. People use CBT knowingly and willingly. Their desire to change can make CBT very useful. You will find that you can use CBT to correct your problems, or you can visit a therapist who will set goals for you and help you adjust your thinking. The entire process is transparent and known to all parties.

Dark CBT is more opaque, hidden by a veil of deception. The subject of Dark CBT most likely is not aware of what is going on. Dark CBT is significant because it is subliminal, and it makes someone think that there is something wrong with him so that he strives to change it. You never reveal that you are the therapist here. You are also never asked to perform Dark CBT on anyone. This can be unethical, but again, you are using Dark CBT at your own risk.

Dark CBT is not evil in and of itself. It can be used for evil, but that is your call. The altruistic and positive applications of Dark CBT can be especially useful if you choose to make someone better through Dark CBT. You can help people who can't help themselves and who are resistant to getting help. You also create your success, furthering your own goals, and getting ahead in life. You don't have to become a monster and use Dark CBT to hurt people to gain from it. Using Dark CBT as a way to help others can improve your own life because it will heal your relationships and make people like you more. People will associate you with feeling better and liking themselves more, so they will want to spend more time around you. And everyone knows that being liked by people gets you what you want.

Even if you do choose to use the darker applications for Dark CBT, you won't ever get caught. People will not be aware of what you are doing. Therefore, you won't hurt your subjects or destroy relationships. You also won't get into trouble because you are not doing anything illegal.

Chapter 55. The Art Of Using Your Mind to Succeed

Many people want to learn about dark psychology because they want to do better in their careers. They aren't content working the job they already have: they want to prove themselves capable of more.

But somewhere along the way, we figure out the truth: that getting ahead in our careers isn't necessarily a matter of skill but manipulation and persuasion. As you know, dark psychology is the best and most legitimate way to learn these skills, and now it's time to learn how to use them specifically in a work setting.

We have to think in a more challenging way about how we interact with our co-workers. For instance, let's say we have a female early 20-something analyst amid a post-graduation down-cycle who has encountered many challenges both professionally and personally since starting work a few years ago.

She frequently finds herself wanting to connect with people who are perceived to be more advanced in their careers or whose interests are different from her own. Identifying why you are attracted to certain people is a valuable skill for early-career practitioners. It likely contributes to her success as an analyst. If she wants to get ahead, she should follow along with all the directions in these pages, where we speak to dark psychology in the workplace directly.

Personality is an incredibly crucial subject for the workplace context because it is an environment where you have to interact with many different kinds of people, many of whom—you will soon find out—you don't know that well as people.

Dark psychology is broader than neurolinguistics programming, but NLP is where all of our tools and techniques of in-depth communication and manipulation come from. NLP is where the three significant steps of manipulation and mind control originate from:

- Establish your state control and perceptual sharpness.

- Imitate the unconscious cues of communication of your subject so that they incorporate you into their mind.

- Use one of the techniques.

People continuously think without even realizing it because most thought is unconscious. NLP is how we take advantage of most studies' cold nature to tell people's minds to change the structure before they even know it.

NLP's topic is vital for discussing workplace personalities because NLP has five main categories for the kinds of characters' people have. In the jargon of NLP, these "personalities" are actually called metaprograms. You would do well to identify the important people at your workplace within these metaprograms. Take advantage of your perceptual sharpness to ascertain this information.

As we have told you before, getting information about the subject is everything. But it is also true that our brains need to sort all the information we get into categories to understand the world better. These metaprograms do that job for you.

Metaprograms are more useful than personalities because they are more objective. They also focus on the motivations people have and how they use logic rather than their mannerisms or less essential behavior patterns. Metaprograms do not merely describe how much you like attention or how nervous or relaxed you are. You may notice some aspects of each metaprogram that overlap with these traits. Still, metaprograms are more specific than these less useful terms.

These NLP-styled personalities are not only a way for you to get more information about your co-workers. Remember the second step of NLP's mind-reading and manipulation: you have to imitate the communications cues the subject shows you. When you do this, you make them unconsciously see you as being like themselves. That means if you take on the traits of your co-worker's metaprogram, you make it easier for you to succeed in this step.

The last thing for you to know about metaprograms, in general, is that they are sorted in dichotomies. A dichotomy is a contrast between two items that are different. But while you should choose just one from each dichotomy in each metaprogram, you must remember that people are not as simple as being A or B. Any time we have a dichotomy—in any situation—picking one of the two is just a category you can use to simplify things and think of them differently. But you should not think of them as being always or exclusively one of the two. People are much more complicated than this.

Our first metaprogram is between the dichotomy of options and procedures. People who are on the options metaprogram don't like being limited or being told what to do. They want as much freedom as possible, and they like to think about things from a general perspective rather than getting in the weeds. On the other hand, people on procedures need to understand every small detail whenever they get into something new. Procedures people hate the feeling that they are missing something. When an element is skipped, they fear they are missing something important.

The second metaprogram is external and internal. This metaprogram is concerned with people's incentives. External people want to be told by others when they do good work, and they want to be notified when they do bad work, too. Internal people don't want to get outside opinions about their work, though. They feel they know when their work is good or not, and hearing what other people think is just a bother.

The third dichotomy in metaprograms is proactive and reactive. These metaprograms describe how someone deals with the future. Reactive people look at a calendar and are always thinking about how the work they are doing. Now fits into the picture of all of their work. This can be a hindrance because they believe so much about planning to lose sight of what they are trying to do right now. Proactive people, on the other hand, hate thinking about the future or planning ahead. They only care about the here and now.

Our second-to-last is toward and away. This metaprogram is about goals and deterrents. All of us have things we look forward to in the future, but toward people are chiefly concerned about their goals, and they don't look behind them at all. Away people are the exact opposite of this. They can have issues looking ahead because they spend so much time thinking about what is behind them.

Finally, we have sameness and difference. Sameness people have a love for familiarity: they spend their time around things they already know. Things they don't know will make them fearful, so these people avoid them at all costs. On the other hand, different people are always craving new experiences to have new people meet, fresh foods to eat, etc. If there is something they haven't experience yet, different people want to share it.

These are the five significant dichotomies in metaprograms. Whoever the co-worker is who you want to use our dark psychology tricks on will want to sort them into these metaprograms. Now, when you use the Aristotelian technique of envisioning the future, you have a more objective stand-in for the person you will interact with.

When we imagine someone in our heads, it isn't always accurate to how they are. NLP's metaprograms are useful because they make us think carefully about our subject's kind of person.

Metaprograms are particularly useful for the work environment because they force us to think about the people we work with more objectively. When you do Step 1 and prepare to get into the co-worker's mind with Step 2, you can use these metaprograms to paint a fuller picture of who you will use dark psychology on.

Since these are often just people we interact with exclusively in work environments, we can be surprised by how little we might know about them from a metaprogram standpoint. If you are honest with yourself as you sort them into these dichotomies, you might realize you don't know very much about them at all. When this turns out to be the case, don't just go along with the dark psychology technique anyway. There is no point in doing this when it won't always work—you can't adapt to the social cues of a person you don't even know yet.

That's why from here, you will have to do more intel-gathering on them first before you can even move on to Step 1. Step 1 can't successfully happen until you know the person and how they fit into all the metaprograms. Until you do that, you won't be able to properly imagine your interactions with them for Steps 2 and 3.

With that said, after you get to know the co-workers' metaprograms, let your senses do all the work in perceptual sharpness, use our exercises to prepare your state control, and imagine the interaction in your imagination, you are ready for Step 2.

For Steps 2 and 3, things go about the same when you are dealing with someone from your workplace. However, some techniques seem tailor-made for use in the work setting. We will go over these before moving onto our big lesson on neurolinguistics programming in psychology.

We will cover three big dark psychology techniques for the workplace before diving into the world of NLP. Social framing is a technique in which we paint a picture for the subject where adopting a particular behavior or idea will help them with social climbing.

Our social lives are one of the most important things to us as humans. That's why framing the truth about the subject's social environment is such a powerful tool for manipulating and mind-controlling people. As long as we make them believe they get a social reward for doing what we say, they will jump at the opportunity.

Executing this technique is simple. Assuming you have already mentally sorted these techniques into the proper metaprograms, controlled your state, and paid close attention to your senses.

Chapter 56. Dark Personalities

Dark psychology is not a single, universally applicable medical diagnosis that can be applied across all cases of deviant personalities. In fact, there are a wide variety of ways that dark psychology may manifest itself in someone's psychological and behavioral makeup. There is no absolute division of one deviant personality type from another. Many bizarre personalities with prominent dark psychology features may display more than one manifestation of dark psychology.

We will explore three types of dark psychology personalities. It is important to remember that although the internet has spawned a massive growth in problems resulting from dark psychology, these traits have been part of human culture since ancient times. One of the dark psychology profiles we will explore here, Machiavellianism, takes its name from a medieval politician. Another narcissism takes its name from an ancient mythological character. Together, the three dark psychology profiles talked about here—psychopathy, Machiavellianism, and narcissism—make up what is known as "the Dark Triad."

The Dark Triad Personalities

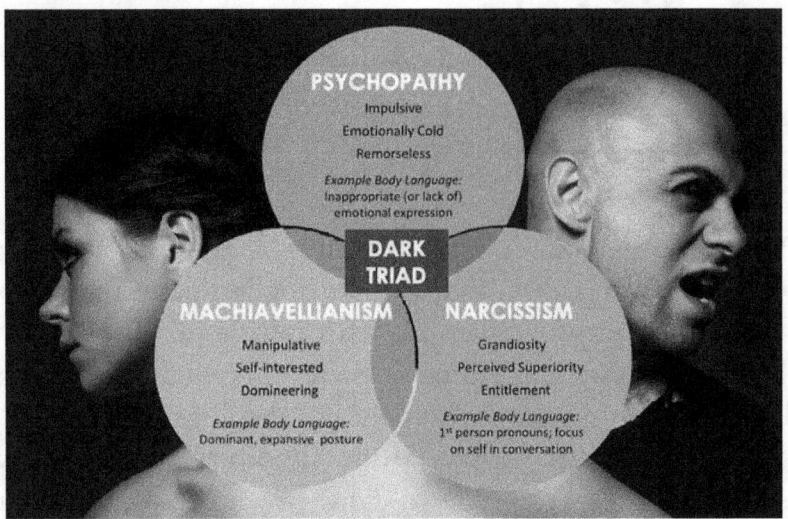

Narcissism

The term "narcissism" originates from an ancient Greek myth about Narcissus, a young man who saw his reflection in a pool of water and fell in love with the image of himself. In clinical psychology, narcissism as an illness was introduced by Sigmund Freud and has continually been included in official diagnostic manuals as a description of a specific type of psychiatric personality disorder.

In psychology, narcissism is defined as a condition characterized by an exaggerated sense of importance, an excessive need for attention, a lack of empathy, and, as a result, dysfunctional relationships. Commonly, narcissists may outwardly display a too high level of confidence. Still, this façade usually hides a very fragile ego and a high degree of sensitivity to criticism. There is often an enormous gulf between a narcissist's highly favorable view of himself or herself, the resulting expectation that others should extend to him or her favors and special treatment, and the disappointment when the results are quite negative or otherwise different. These problems can affect all areas of the narcissist's life, including personal relationships, professional relationships, and financial matters.

As part of the Dark Triad, those who exhibit traits resulting from Narcissistic Personality Disorder (NPD) may engage in relationships characterized by a lack of empathy. For example, a narcissist may demand constant comments, attention, and admiration from his or her partner but will often appear unable or unwilling to reciprocate by displaying concern or responding to their partner's circumstances, thoughts, and feelings.

Narcissists also display a sense of entitlement and expect excessive reward and recognition, but usually without ever having accomplished or achieved anything that would justify such feelings. There is also a tendency toward excessive criticism of those around him or her. Combined with heightened sensitivity when even the slightest amount of criticism is directed at him or her.

Thus, while narcissism in popular culture is often used as a pejorative term and an insult aimed at people like actors, models, and other celebrities who display high degrees of self-love and satisfaction. NPD is a psychological term that is quite distinct from merely having high self- esteem. The key to understanding this aspect of dark psychology is that the narcissist's image of himself or herself is often completely idealized, grandiose, and inflated and cannot be justified with any real, meaningful accomplishments or capacities make such claims believable. As a result of this discord between expectation and reality, the demanding, manipulative, inconsiderate, self-centered, and arrogant behavior of the narcissist can cause problems not only for themselves but also for all people his or her life.

Machiavellianism

Strictly defined, Machiavellianism is the political philosophy of Niccolò Machiavelli, who lived from 1469 until 1527 in Italy. In contemporary society, Machiavellianism is a term used to describe the popular understanding of people who are perceived as displaying very high political or professional ambitions. In psychology, however, the Machiavellianism scale is used to measure the degree to which people with deviant personalities say manipulative behavior.

Machiavelli wrote The Prince, a political treatise. He stated that sincerity, honesty, and other virtues were indeed admirable qualities. In politics, the capacity to engage in deceit, betrayal, and other forms of criminal behavior was acceptable if there were no other means of achieving political aims to protect one's interests.

Popular misconceptions reduce this entire philosophy to the view that "the end justifies the means." To be fair, Machiavelli himself insisted that the more critical part of this equation was ensuring the end itself must first be justified. Furthermore, it is better to achieve such ends using means devoid of treachery whenever possible because there is less risk to the actor's interests.

Thus, seeking the most effective means of achieving a political end may not necessarily lead to the most treacherous. Also, not all political fortunes that have been justified as worth pursuing must be pursued. In many cases, the mere threat that a particular course of action may be followed may be enough to achieve that end. In some cases, the betrayal may be as mild as making a credible threat to take action that is not intended.

In contemporary society, many people overlook the fact that Machiavellianism is part of the "Dark Triad" of dark psychology and tacitly approve of the deviant behavior of political and business leaders who can amass great power or wealth. However, as a psychological disorder, Ma- Machiavellianism is entirely different from a chosen path to political power.

The person displaying Machiavellian personality traits does not consider whether his or her actions are. The most effective means of achieving their goals, whether there are alternatives that do not involve deceit or treachery, or even whether the ultimate result of his or her actions is worth achieving. The Machiavellian personality is not evidence of a strategic or calculating mind attempting to reach a worthwhile objective in a contentious environment. Instead, it is always on, whether the situation calls for a cold, calculating, and manipulative approach or not.

For example, we had all called in sick to work when we just wanted a day off. But for most of us, such conduct is not how we usually behave. After such acts of dishonesty, many of us feel guilty. Those who display a high degree of Machiavellianism would not just lie when they want a day off; they see lying and dishonesty as the only way to conduct themselves in all situations, regardless of whether doing so results in any benefit.

What's more, because of the degree of social acceptance and tacit approval granted to Machiavellian personalities who successfully attain political power, their presence in society does not receive the kind of negative attention accorded to the other two members of the Dark Triad—psychopathy and narcissism.

Psychopathy

Psychopathy is defined as a mental disorder with several identifying characteristics: antisocial behavior, amorality, an inability to develop empathy, establish meaningful personal relationships, extreme egocentricity, and recidivism, with repeated violations resulting from an apparent failure to learn from the consequences of earlier transgressions. In turn, antisocial behavior is defined as behavior based upon a goal of violating formal and/or informal rules of social conduct through criminal activity or through acts of personal, private protest, or opposition, all of which are directed against other individuals' society in general.

Egocentricity is the behavior when the offending person sees himself or herself as the central focus of the world, or at least of all dominant social and political activity. Empathy is the ability to view and understand events, thoughts, emotions, and beliefs from others' perspectives. It is considered one of the most essential psychological components for establishing successful, ongoing relationships.

Amorality is entirely different from immorality. An immoral act is an act that violates established moral codes. An immoral person can be confronted with his or her actions with the expectation that they will recognize that their actions are offensive from a moral, if not a legal, standpoint. Amorality, on the other hand, represents psychology that does not realize that any moral codes exist, or if they do, that they have no value in determining whether or not to act in one way or another.

Thus, someone displaying psychopathy may commit horrendous acts that cause tremendous psychological and physical trauma and not ever understand that what he or she has done is wrong. Worse still, those who display signs of psychopathy usually worsen over time because they cannot connect the problems in their lives and the lives of those in the world around them and their own harmful and destructive actions.

The Dark Triad in Practice

The professional workplace has acknowledged the presence of people exhibiting Dark Triad characteristics.

The following diagram illustrates that they are tolerated for their efficiency and their ability to get things done but contrasts that ability with the adverse effects it has on their ability to form personal relationships:

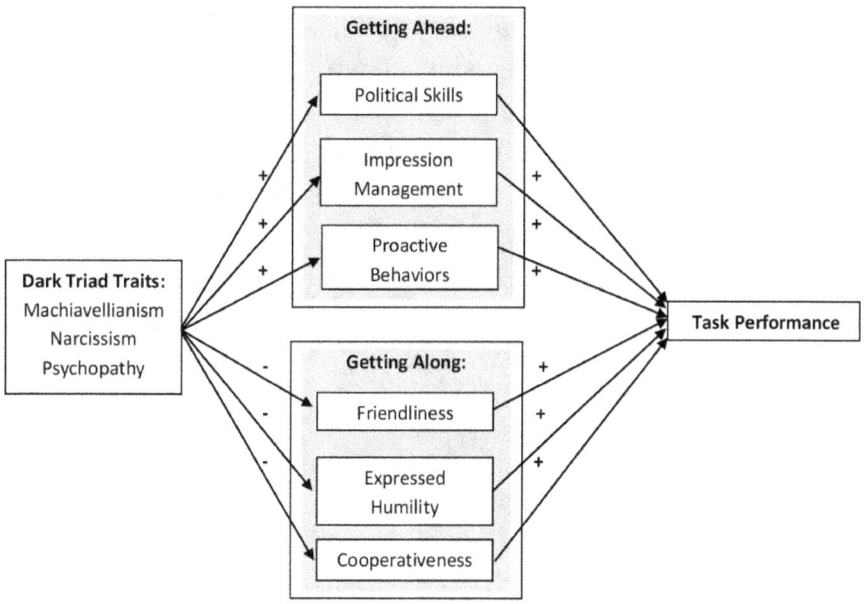

(Benjamin McLarty, Mississippi State University, 2015)

The remainder will discuss a wide variety of people and situations where you may find one, two, all three, or some combination of these Dark Triad personalities working in concert around you.

The clinical descriptions are easy enough to categorize. In isolation, it can be reasonably straightforward to separate one type of dark psychology from another. The real world is a lot messier. Many of us have grown accustomed to so-called "toxic relationships," whether they are relationships with our partners, co-workers, family members, bosses, or political and community leaders.

Also, dark psychology manifestations are often far more mundane than the dramatic examples we see in major television and film productions about serial killers and other criminals' romantic lives. The more we accept these relationships, as usual, the more difficult it will be to identify them as problematic.

Remember that psychological, emotional, and social predators do not think of themselves as sick. Their lack of morality and empathy, and their adaption from a very early age to live according to rules and methods you may find wrong, can make their presence intimidating. However, you should also remember that even when their amorality and lack of empathy may allow them to enjoy it. An unfair advantage in relationships, their mental capacities result from underdevelopment, not a higher evolutionary state.

Chapter 57. The Dark Triad

The dark triad is a psychology term that refers to a person's behavioral characteristics, which is, in most cases, defined as narcissism, Machiavellianism, and psychopathy. Some people rate it as a mental disorder and some as a disaster that just dawns on someone changing their behavior and how they relate to others. Dark triad generally affects a person's personality, making them take advantage of others. People with these traits tend to be manipulative, deceptive, and egoistic. They attempt to brainwash others to gain success and fame.

Politicians are, on most occasions, the worst group of people affected by this personality disorder. Their lives are full of lies, ego, and manipulation. To gain power, most of them only deceive other people to get public support and seem successful. Many people fall victim to the dark triad because they are not well exposed to the point of understanding what it is. They cannot easily tell when this is being used against them.

Persons with dark triad personalities have no empathy for others. They always attempt to have everything for themselves, ignoring other people's importance around them. Narcissists still want to be regarded as the most influential people in society. They want to be praised and admired all the time, a kind of behavior that only manipulates others for the benefit of their interests.

You may be tempted to think that these people are insane. From my perspective to some extent, they are. No one in his normal state of mind would want to have everything go their side at the expense of others. To these people who possess a Machiavellianism trait, they always want to win and be declared successful. They go as far as deceiving everyone around them to turn out the right person. They easily exploit the "less fortunate" in society to open their ways.

Apart from politicians, bloggers are another group of people that are overwhelmed by these traits. For example, in Kenya, we have Dr. Miguna, who is all over the social media busy manipulating people—the youth and young politicians being the most affected. He tries to make everyone his psychopath through his blogs, twits, books, and constant drama here and there.

Can we Say Dr. Miguna is insane? He is all over seeking fame and wants everyone to believe he is always right, and the rest are wrong. He manipulates everyone, and those who follow his steps end up being disappointed at the end. Once he gets what he is looking for, he turns against you and uses your negatives to manipulate others that are not in the same line as him. He comes up with dramas to attract attention and convince everyone to believe whatever he does.

While politicians everywhere are fighting him back, the youth become psychos by his blogs and believe that he is right because he is fighting politicians whom he claims to be narcissists. Not to be personal, I would like to say that if you research deeply into psychology, you will find most bloggers with the same interest showing narcissism, Machiavellianism, and psychopathy traits. They won't feel guilty or ashamed because they don't even notice that they are too much.

Anyone can be a victim of these traits. You may, at one point in your life, find yourself in a relationship with a narcissist. Before you notice it, you will be exploited and used by your partner. Your partner can be that antagonistic person that only feels superior to you and those around you. They will always want to be treated special and can exploit you to serve their interests. They often interact in a way that shows you are less important and not as good as them.

This kind of person usually wants to be listened to. They will prefer seeking attention than empathizing with you or even recognizing your needs. Everything they do is always for their benefit. They only concentrate on feeling better in the relationship and are never ready to give you a listening year. You have no say in their decisions because this makes them feel less important to you and don't respect their decisions.

To know that you are in a relationship with a narcissist, you will realize that your partner doesn't really care about how you feel. They only expect you to make them happy and superior without considering what you go through for them to be what they want. Failing to meet their interests makes them feel so low and unwanted in the relationship. They make you feel like you are of no good to them and that you don't deserve them.

They can also be antisocial and low self-esteemed. They will always think of their mistakes as the worst ever and that none can be compared. Whenever they fail in something, they will feel like they don't fit in society anymore and imperfect. They feel so drowned and depressed as a result of one mistake. This is always brought about by the fear of being a normal person.

On some occasions, narcissists attempt to praise themselves too much without realizing how majestic they can be. They never stop talking about their achievements and plans in life. They always talk about how intelligent and successful they are and even exaggerate what they are capable of. They always want people to believe that their success cannot be related to someone else's. Stopping them from doing this makes them feel stupid, and they can easily hate you for pinpointing their imperfections.

These persons' living standards are always set high by them, which is becoming realistic because they are in a way that has low standards. Their lives are usually filled with a fantasy about success, and they expect everyone around them to respect them because their destinies are thought to be successful. No one can ever change their perception in their minds without hurting them and making them feel useless.

At some point, these people are always depressed, and no one will ever understand the reason for their depression. Understanding them becomes difficult. If you are not a psychologist, you will always be brainwashed to serve their interests before noticing what you are getting yourself into. Other people can advise you, but you will not have the time to listen to what they have to say because you will have fallen victim to narcissism. The narcissist will, by that time, have full control of you.

You are always left torn between thoughts when it reaches a point that you no longer understand a friend or a partner who has a dark personality. Failing to listen to them makes them feel worse than other people while listening to you is useless to them, on the other hand. They never have time to listen to you but to seek the audience all the time.

Machiavellian leaders are the most dangerous leaders because they are always cunning and duplicitous. They always manipulate everyone from doing what they want, whether they like it or not, and never reveal any reason for their actions. They only do that when the favor is on their side. They always make people believe that they are the most intelligent and that no one's intelligence can be compared to theirs. Those who believe in this kind of leaders are never ready to listen to other people's advice unless they align with the Machiavellian heads.

Dark triad strikes too much due to several reasons and the following additional reasons.

1. The Understanding of Dark Triad Is Not Everybody's Cup of Tea

Not everyone has the psychology of understanding dark personality. This leads to many of us fall victim to dark triads without noticing it. We get manipulated easily and exploited to serve the interest of narcissists and Machiavellian leaders without a choice of thinking a second time or even the chance to take an alternative move.

2. The Fear of Standing Alone

Narcissists always manipulate the big number from being on their side and supporting their ideas. This has left many people stranded between thoughts because they fear being left alone for making an opposing decision. They fear of not getting back up from those around you led many people to fall, victims of the dark triad since they are forced to take steps they were not ready to take.

This usually happens with people who are often close to this kind of person or whose friends are involved with those with dark personalities.

3. I Don't Want to Lose a Friend

Many people tend to value friendship more than their own safety. They are too much into their friend's decisions and way of life that they even forget they are also important. Such people are the most common victims of the dark triad. They easily get exploited by their friends into doing what their friends want, what makes them happy.

In this case, when you're are friends with a narcissist, then you have no choice. You will always be a tool for happiness. You will be ready to listen to all sorts of boasting and exaggerated stories from your friends.

4. Investing Your Trust in the Wrong Person

On many occasions, we don't always know the right person to trust. Laying your trust in someone without considering their personality opens a gate for you to be used by narcissists. This normally occurs in relationships that are just beginning, and partners wish to travel miles away together.

Many fall into traps of their partners because they invest too much trust in them that they can never think of the negative side of them. This is what makes the narcissists overjoyed and leave them feeling so highly of themselves.

5. Believing Too Fast

These narcissists always have their stories told everywhere by them and by those who believe helplessly in them. They always catch the interests of those who believe in all stories they are told because they believe the people telling the story are always right, intelligent, and successful.

The narcissist always catches others' attention with their striking success that makes others believe in them desperately and follow their steps blindly without a third eye to see into the future and the consequences of following these people.

6. Most People Don't Care

The tendency of assuming everything said by those in authority is final is what makes us victims of manipulation and exploitation. Some of us don't even care about what is going on around them, and having no idea about it for them is even much better. Some say that something you don't know does not hurt.

People with dark personalities easily exploit such people because they know the favor will always be on their side no matter what. No one will stand against them because they don't even care in the first place.

7. Psychopathy

Being too possessed with someone is what leads you to become their psychopaths. You will always want to listen to what they say, and at the end of it, you will be convinced they are right, and anything said against them is wrong. You will feel pain when they are in pain are depressed when they are depressed because you have become their shadow. Whoever sees you see the person you have invested your personality in.

Conclusion

Now that you've learned some of the basic dark psychology disciplines, you have a great deal more power than you had before. At the very least, you will be better able to recognize controlling techniques and behaviors when other people try to use them against you. If someone is trying to manipulate or even persuade you, you can now see through their tricks and resist.

But you also have the unique opportunity to use dark psychology for your personal growth and improvement. Just because these tools and techniques are labeled 'dark' doesn't mean they're inherently destructive. Many techniques, including hypnosis and NLP, were first developed as self-improvement tools. Only when people learned how to turn these techniques against other people did they become relegated to the field of 'dark' psychology.

NLP, persuasion techniques, body language, and even hypnosis are all regularly taught in social spheres that we would not normally consider 'dark.' Athletes, business people, teachers and educators, actors, entertainers, and marketers all regularly use these techniques to improve their performance, increase their productivity, make themselves better negotiators, and yes, to convince others to do what they want. There's nothing inherently amoral about social influence, especially if the thing you're persuading the other person to do is good for them. Using NLP techniques to persuade your alcoholic partner to get help is hardly an act of evil or manipulation. Neither is learning to read your teenager's body language to improve your communication and defuse potential conflict.

With great power, however, does come great responsibility. Whenever you decide to employ any of these techniques against another person, always take a step back and ask yourself, "What are the consequences for the other person if I get my desired outcome? Will the other person be hurt? Will this put them in danger? Will this compromise their core values or beliefs in some way?" If the answer to any of these three questions is yes, you have to find another way to get what you want without manipulating tactics. All of the techniques that you've learned are extremely powerful. With patience and practice, they do work. Suppose you become skilled in any of these disciplines and decide to use them for the wrong reasons. In that case, you could cause some serious damage to another person's psychological well-being and risk losing your important relationships if someone else becomes aware of what you're doing.

I hope that, you re-enter your life as a more secure and empowered person. Psychological techniques are subtle and often context-based. It's normal to be clumsy when you first begin, and you should always be aware of how the other person is responding so that you can make necessary and appropriate adjustments to your techniques.

With these tactics at your disposal, you are no longer at the mercy of other people. If you find yourself constantly rubbing other people the wrong way, perhaps receiving labels like 'bossy' or 'pushy,' you now have a variety of subtler ways to get what you want. If you're someone that's constantly fighting and barreling over others, you know that sometimes being straightforward isn't the best option. Being too blunt can often backfire on you. Asking for what you need more subtly won't only get you more success in life—it may even make it easier for you to build healthy relationships with other people.

If you find yourself in the opposite position, these tactics can work for you, too. If you feel that you're just too timid to get what you want or find yourself easily pushed around by other people, you now have a way to succeed. Instead of running headlong into conflicts that scare you, you can try a different approach, one that may feel much more comfortable. As you start to achieve results, you'll probably feel a big improvement in your confidence. And the more confident you feel, the more comfortable you will be with straightforward communication, making you a much better communicator all the way around.

Most importantly of all, now that you are aware of dark psychology, those who would wish to do you harm have significantly less power over you. Suppose someone does try to manipulate, persuade, or use NLP against you in the future. In that case, you will be better able to recognize their tactics before something bad happens. And suppose you are currently in a relationship with a manipulative person. In that case, you now have a better idea of their tactics and therefore take steps to free yourself from their influence.

HOW TO ANALYZE PEOPLE

Introduction

NLP refers to the ability to sway interactions with other people. It has several different stages when used, beginning with establishing rapport and ending in getting the desired result. Ultimately, it is guided by non-verbal responses and reactions of the client, which can be used first to create rapport and sway the other person to do what is necessary.

NLP starts with developing rapport, which is typically done through mirroring and matching behaviors. You can cue the other person to begin identifying more with you when you use mirroring first. Following the other person's behaviors as a guide in interacting with him or her, you can begin keying into their desire to like you. They are more likely to identify with and trust you if you are mirroring them. It opens them up to the following step.

You will then be gathering information about the other person's mental state. It is using a study of body language or the way the other person may answer. When you understand the other person's mental state, you can begin understanding what their thought processes are, as well as the wording they use. It is where you start to understand the linguistic and programming parts of NLP. You can understand the other person's mind through understanding their words. You can begin to understand the mindset based on the wording, such as focusing on sensory-based metaphors or focusing on certain tendencies. You understand their programming by watching their body language with their words.

From there, it is time to start coming in on changing their minds. When the other person readily mirrors your interactions, you can begin speaking to the other person and mirroring the behaviors you want. For example, if you wish the other person to be more comfortable with spiders, you make a subtle body language sign that you are comfortable with when you mention spiders. You may learn in a little bit toward the other person, conveying that you are comfortable as you mention the spider. The other person should mirror your response, and as they do so, they tell their minds that there is nothing to fear, nothing to worry about, and that everything is fine.

This sort of process can then be expanded upon to be used for everything from depression to creating self-confidence in another person. It is, essentially, swaying the other person to feel more comfortable with things that may have been uncomfortable before. It allows you to sway opinions, behavior, goals, and more just by tuning into their body language, ensuring that you share rapport, and using that rapport to slowly mold the other person's mind to mimic the one you are attempting to create.

Historically, persuasion is rooted in ancient Greek's model of a prized politician and orator.

To make a list, a politician or speaker needs to master rhetoric and elocution to persuade the public. Rhetoric, according to Aristotle, is the "ability to make use of the available methods of persuasion" to win a court case or influence the public during important orations. On the other hand, elocution (a branch of rhetoric) is the art of speech delivery, including proper diction, proper gestures, stance, and dress. Although Grecian politics and orations seem clearly to be the genesis of persuasion, its use in the rapidly developing world of the twenty-first century goes beyond politics, oration, and other human endeavors.

In the business domain, persuasion refers to a corporate system of influence to change other people, groups, or organizations' attitudes, behavior, or perception about an idea, object, goods, services, or people. It often employs verbal communications (both written and spoken words), non-verbal communication (paralinguistic, chronemics, proxemics, and so on), visual communication, or multimodal communication to convey, change or reinforce a piece of existing information or reasoning peculiar to the audience. Persuasion in business can come in different forms depending on the need of the management. For instance, business enterprise sometimes uses persuasion in cases like; public relations, broadcast, media relations, speech writing, social media, client relations, employee communication, brand management, etc.

In psychological parlance, persuasion refers to using an obtainable understanding of the social, behavioral, or cognitive principles in psychology to influence the attitude, cognition, behavior, or belief system of a person, group, or organization. It is also seen as a process by which a person's attitude and behavior are influenced without coercion but through the simple means of communication. For instance, when a child begs his mother for candy and the mother refuses but instead proffers a better food for the child to eat while also encouraging him to grow more significant. The child gets excited and goes for the new alternative. In this way, the mother has been able to tap into his belief system without any form of duress. Hence, persuasion can also be used as a method of social control.

In politics and governing today, persuasion still retains its role as one of the essential means of influencing the populace's behavior, feelings, and commitment through the power of mass media. For instance, politicians sometimes use social media, television, radio, newspapers, and magazines to persuade people to sponsor their political campaigns. Persuasion in modern politics is also observed through the use of authority in such situations where opponents of one political party influence on cross carpet to the other party with different promises in the form of power and immunity. Also, the court still entertains the use of persuasion during the prosecution or defense of an accused.

Another way to see persuasion is through the intentional use of communication as a tool of conviction to change attitudes regarding an issue by transferring messages in a free choice atmosphere. The verbal, non-verbal, and visual forms of communication are manipulated just for the sole purpose of persuading an individual, group, or organization. Although communication is the most essential and versatile form in which persuasion is manifested, it is worthy to note that not all communication forms are intended to persuade. For instance, the celebration of a newly inaugurated president or governor circulated on the news cannot be classified as persuasion unless intended to impact the country's citizens or react in specific ways.

We go further to look at other possible definition of persuasion in the circular world.

Persuasion is a concept of influence that attempts to change a person's attitudes, intentions, motivations, beliefs, or behaviors. When a child begs his parent for candy and the parent says a big no to him, but the child insists on having candy even while knowing it might not be suitable for his health, persuasion is beginning to occur. The parent will try to proffer a better food for the child to eat instead of the candy. The child gets excited and goes for the new alternative. In this way, the parent has won a banter of persuasion.

On its own, persuasion is a branch of communication and popular as a method of social control. Hence, it is worthy of note that not all forms of communication intend to be persuasive. Persuasion is also a process by which a person's attitude and behaviors are influenced without harsh treatment by simple means of communication. Other factors can also determine a person's change in behavior or attitude, for example, verbal threats, a person's current psychological state, physical coercion, etc.

Having explained the meanings of persuasion, it can be observed that persuasion extends beyond a specific field as there is an intermingling of ideas from different study areas. However, communication and psychology seem clearly to be in use for persuasion to take place. While communication provides the model of how interlocutors in persuasion get messages understood, psychology provides the mental processes model during persuasion.

Now that we know both NLP and persuasion basics, we will now go more in-depth into detail about the subjects connecting to these two from this point and forward.

Chapter 1. Neuro-Linguistic Programming (NLP)

NLP is a fantastic art and science. It is an art since everyone gives what they are doing their own personal and stylish touch, which can never be conveyed with words or techniques. It is a science, and for outstanding results, there is a system and process to discover the models used for outstanding in-dividing in a region. This method is called patterning. In the field of education, guidance, and industry, the models, skills, and techniques discovered can increasingly be used to achieve more efficient communication, have substantial personal growth, and accelerate learning.

Have you ever done something so elegantly and successfully that your time will be cut short? Have there been moments when you were very pleased with what you were doing and how you handled it? The NLP shows you how to appreciate your achievements and arrange them to experience several more moments like this. It is a way of uncovering and unveiling your talent, a form of bringing out the best of yourself and others.

The NLP is a real ability that produces the outcomes we want in the world while at the same time valuing others in the process. It is the p of what distinguishes between the excellent and the nor-evil. It also leaves behind many extremely successful strategies on schooling, therapy systems, business, and therapies.

The History of NLP

The initial version of the NLP of today originated in the early 1970s. At the time, Richard Bandler was a student at the Santa Cruz University of California, met with John Grinder, assistant professor of linguistics.

Grinder, who was especially interested in advanced teaching techniques, was rapidly aware of Bandler's research and held a series of seminars in collaboration with him. Such seminars originally had the classification of group studies. But with growing Bandler and Grinder experience and expertise, the participants encountered more exciting transition processes ever. It culminated in an increasingly close relationship between Bandler and Grinder over the years.

They explored why well-known individual psychotherapists had so much success with their patients in their practice and on what basis this success was based. Several people treating the same patients with the same conditions have struggled to bring about these drastic improvements simultaneously. In Bandler and Grinder's original theory, they believed influential psychotherapists had a common or similar pattern of action in their work with people, based on which they might produce these excellent results. These standard or related behavior patterns are now known as NLP, or magic structure.

So, they started to investigate and evaluate the types of therapy used by the top therapists:

- Virginia Satir, an exceptional family therapist.

- Fritz Perl's, an innovative Gestalt therapist and founder of this direction of therapy, as well.

- Milton H. Erickson, a world-renowned hypnotherapist.

In doing so, the expectations of finding patterns and structures that could clarify these top therapists' success in coping with their clients were always driven.

Despite the three successful psychotherapists' diversity, after long and careful observation, Grinder and Bandler discovered that they used surprisingly similar basic patterns in their work with others. Grinder and Bandler put these basic patterns into writing, refined them, tried them out in their seminars with other students who agreed to do so. Finally, they developed an elegant model to achieve more effective communication, accelerated learning, personal change, and enjoyment, and joy in life. They called it NLP—Neuro-linguistic Programming:

"Neuro" because these are strategies that heavily involve the functions of our nervous system (brain + spinal cord + senses). The point is to perceive more precisely and more, to purposefully change unwanted feelings and behavior patterns in harmony with yourself.

"Linguistics" because it is also very much about the linguistic aspect. We maintain external communication with other people and internal communication with our fantastic "bio-computer"— our brain. Unfortunately, not all of the inputs that we make in this biocomputer are received. Therefore, advanced communication methods are also required here.

"Programming" means that we want to use systematic methods in all of this and not learn through trial and error. It's about discovering procedures and processes that can also be transferred to other areas and people. Many NLP techniques are content-free, which means that the same method can be used for headaches, a phobia, or to build an irresistible motivation. NLP describes procedures and processes that can and are effective regardless of the content.

Based on this approach, NLP developed in two complementary directions:

- In the first direction, as a process for discovering the pattern of brilliant achievements in every conceivable social area.

- The second direction is a compilation of effective ways of thinking and communication used by outstanding personalities in this field.

Beginnings of NLP

In the spring of 1972, Bandler himself offered a Gestalt therapy seminar, inspired by his studies' lack of real significance. It was possible for students in an advanced semester. He focused mainly on studying the therapeutic effects of gestalt work in a group and improving his theoretical skills in practice.

During these seminars, John Grinder became aware of Bandler's research, joining him and his exploration. From then on, both worked together on Bandler's workshops, with John Grinder, a beginner to counseling and psychotherapy.

Between 1972 and 1974, intense and productive cooperation took place, with Grinder benefiting from Bandler's knowledge of psychotherapy and Bandler's knowledge of linguistics.

This combination was particularly useful in modeling Virginia Satir's therapeutic masterpieces, Friedrich Perl's, and hypnotherapist Milton Erickson. When modeling, a person's unique skills are made learnable and accessible through systematic and accurate observation and questioning. Patterns and principles were developed so that interested people could also emulate the skills.

Bandler and Grinder were not primarily concerned with explaining something real but with discovering something useful for others. As proof of the success of their analyses and observations on Satir and Perl's, they saw evidence that in other people, they could achieve the same results as the person who modeled them.

In early 1974, both began designing the first meta-model structures with students held in Mission Street squat, Santa Cruz. To simply put, and the meta-model is a set of particular questions to uncover thinking processes and obtain in-depth knowledge. The starting point for research in the meta-model groups was that verbal communication between therapist and client is central to any therapeutic change work. Consequently, it was believed that common language patterns would crystallize and be cemented in Friedrich Perl's and Virginia Satir's verbal communication, making the dysfunctional processes conscious and causing change.

With John Grinder's linguistic context knowledge, both researchers succeeded in creating starting points for a model that allowed the targeted collection of information about a person's imaginary world. They modeled Perl's and Satir's critical linguistic skills and explained these constructs clearly and thus move them on.

From late 1974, Bandler and Grinder regularly participated in teaching seminars given by hypnotherapist Milton H. Erickson. Again, with the primary objective of researching Erickson's work with people, talking about his language patterns and actions. The findings were refined as with Satir and Perl's, reported in writing, tested for applicability in student groups, and integrated into the current knowledge base.

In 1974 and 1975, more formal communication models became the focus of group study. Since Perl's non-verbal actions often appeared to contribute significantly to the therapeutic impact achieved in addition to language behavior, the beneficial non-verbal elements were then specifically evaluated and attempted to address them. The resulting models were then used for both psychotherapy and daily contact.

Various types of procedures were used and revamped, leading, in addition to Perl's and Satir methods, to the current NLP shape. Bandler and Grinder published their first discoveries in four books from 1975 to 1977. These were:

In 1977, Grinder and Bandler held their first U.S. public seminars. The seminars were received very quickly. NLP's awareness has grown noticeably in the following years and is now used worldwide, especially in therapy, education, and management.

Bandler and Grinder developed reframing in 1982. It shows how one can contact unconscious parts, causing unwanted behaviors or disease symptoms. It enabled changes that were recently only conceivable under classical hypnosis.

1984 introduced the concept of submodalities, inventing one of NLP's most significant and impressive techniques. The submodalities represent a kind of brain programming language that everyone can use if they know the commands. People take information with their five senses, process it, and store it internally as events and thoughts represented in their senses, the so-called modalities. These modalities can, in turn, be specified more precisely, so it is possible to ask more precisely about an experience's inner picture. The fantastic thing about it is that it takes advantage of the fact that the human brain reacts to WHAT we think and how a person thinks, e.g., more in color pictures or black and white pictures.

James developed Time Line Therapy (Zeitlinie) in 1988. This method is particularly suitable for gently healing past traumatic experiences. Using the timeline, unconscious or repressed traumas causing physical or emotional problems can be found and mentally processed.

In 1990, Robert Dilts developed reimprinting to change our childhood's relational structures to limit beliefs and beliefs. An imprint is a decisive experience from which the person concerned has formed a belief or bundle of beliefs that are effective in his world. Such an imprint usually also includes an unconscious assumption of the role by other important people involved. The purpose of reimprinting is to find the missing resources, change the belief, and adapt the role model developed to the person's actual and acute circumstances.

Unlike popular belief, Grinder and Bandler did not create NLP alone. After thirty years of silence, a third colleague now goes public: Frank Pucelik.

Chapter 2. How NLP Works, Importance of NLP, and is NLP Effective?

How NLP Works?

If you are coming across this topic for the first time, NLP may appear or seem like magic or hypnosis. When a person is undergoing therapy, this topic digs deep into the patient's unconscious mind. It filters through different layers of beliefs and the person's approach or perception of life to deduce the early childhood experiences responsible for a behavioral pattern.

In NLP, it is believed that everyone has the resources that are needed for positive changes in their own lives. The technique adopted here is meant to help in facilitating these changes.

Usually, when NLP is taught, it is done in a pyramidal structure. However, the most advanced techniques are left for those multi-thousand-dollar seminars. An attempt to explain this complicated subject is to state that the NLP user (as those who use NLP will often call themselves) is always paying keen attention to the person they are working on/with.

Usually, many NLP users are therapists, and they are very likely to be well-meaning people. They achieve their aims by paying attention to those subtle cues like the eye's movement, flushing of the skin, dilation of the pupil, and subtle nervous tics. It is easy for an NLP user to determine the following quickly:

- The side of the brain that the person uses predominantly.

- The sense (smell, sight, etc.) that is more dominant in a person's brain.

- The way the person's brain stores and uses information.

- When the person is telling a lie or concocting information.

When the NLP user has successfully gathered all this information, they slowly and subtly mimic the client by taking on their body language and imitating their speech and mannerisms. They start to talk about language patterns that aim to target the client's primary senses. They will typically fake the social cues that will quickly make someone let their guard down to become very open and suggestible.

For example, when a person's sense of sight is their most dominant sense, the NLP user will use a very laden language with visual metaphors to speak with them. They will say things like: "do you see what I am talking about?" or "why not look at it this way?" For a person that has a more dominant sense of hearing, he will be approached with an auditory language like: "listen to me" or "I can hear where you're coming from."

The NLP user mirrors the body language and the other person's linguistic patterns to create a rapport. This rapport is a mental and physiological state that a human being gets into when they lose their social senses. When they begin to feel like the other person they are conversing with; it is just like them.

Once the NLP user has achieved this rapport, they will take charge of the interaction by leading it mildly and subtly. Thanks to the fact that they have already mirrored the other person, they will now begin to make some subtle changes to gain a particular influence on the person's behavior. It is also combined with some similar subtle language patterns, which lead to questions and a whole phase of some other techniques.

At this point, the NLP user will be able to tweak and twist the person to whichever direction they so desire. It only happens if the other person can't deduce that something is going on because they assume everything is happening organically or consent to everything.

In NLP, there is a belief in the need for nature's perfection of human creation, so every client is encouraged to recognize the senses' sensitivity and use them to respond to specific problems. NLP also believes that the mind can find cures for diseases and sicknesses.

Importance of NLP

NLP's effectiveness is focused on the idea that your mind and body are all the tools you need to improve your life and your world. It will help you to identify specific goals and act. And by analyzing your behaviors' changes, you can adjust them to produce better performance.

Some clinical studies suggest positive benefits to weight loss, reduced anxiety, and a healthy mood from Neuro-speaker programming. A specific investigation also reveals a positive impact on children's learning abilities with dyslexia, helping them improve their self-esteem by reducing their anxiety level. Here are the other importance or benefits of NLP:

As an adult, NLP lets you take responsibility for events that we feel we can't manage. A person can change his or her responses to past events and control their future through NLP. It is essential to be aware of people's body language in your inner circle and those you want to communicate with. NLP offers opportunities to use controlled and purposeful language. It helps you to monitor your life. With the same mind, you can't make the same mistakes and expect a different outcome. A Neuro-Linguistic (NLP) class is all about YOU; you are the subject. It is more important because it gives you more insight when dealing with individuals when dealing with yourself or yourself as an entity.

NLP helps you improve sales performance, income, health problems, better service to client, family, parenting, and all areas of your life. It allows you to become whole when your relationship with yourself and people is whole as an individual.

NLP helps you focus on your ideas, beliefs, and values. It allows you to understand your brain functions, how it develops patterns, how these behaviors become habits, how these habits become actions, and how these actions become outcomes.

The NLP application covers different professions and vocations in life. It is a highly competent tool for sales degrees, self-help and development experts, parents, teachers, communications, etc.

"You are all you ought to be, and all this is sufficient. Be proud of who you are and love who you are."

Is NLP Effective?

Based on valid, recognized, and established scientific research in sociology, linguistics, and psychology, NLP theories have been largely discredited as pseudo-science. The founders of NLP based their theories on sound scientific research. Still, the scientific community has repeatedly stated that the founders' comments and responses to inquiries have demonstrated that they do not understand the underlying theories they often cite in their work. Also, they have not produced any of their actual scientific evidence to support the claims made by NLP theorists or that their programming sessions bring about the changes they promise.

Mainstream psychology has established through clinical research, practice, and published works the reality of the subconscious mind and the importance of understanding its function to help alleviate, treat, or change harmful psychological developments in individuals. Cognitive-behavioral therapy (CBT) and traditional psychotherapy must meet with fairly rigorous professional standards and are based on proven methods and clinical psychology theories. At the same time, NLP's success record is less consistent and based more on anecdotal testimony.

NLP providers generally have a financial interest in promoting NLP's success, so their testimonials may or may not be accurate. Also, results among people who have completed NLP training sessions are mixed. Some studies have shown that patients who participate in NLP have improved psychological symptoms and a better quality of life. Still, most studies indicate little evidence that NLP can effectively treat any significant psychological disorders, such as anxiety, insomnia, or substance abuse.

However, while clinical studies have discredited NLP as a legitimate form of treatment for severe psychological illnesses, NLP continues to be part of the large, profitable industry that capitalizes on the demand for self-improvement literature. Tony Robbins, the contemporary self-help, self-improvement, and motivational speaking guru, trained with NLP's founders and continues to employ many of their ideas in his famous seminars.

Regardless of all the adverse press reports and scientific criticisms, NLP has spawned a global industry. Companies such as NLP Power, The NLP Center, The Empowerment Partnership, and the founders' own NLP University continue to advertise and promote their services on the internet and provide behavior modification training to a global audience. Many corporations and government agencies also send employees to NLP-based seminars to train leadership teams and sales staff. Thus, while the scientific foundations of NLP have been exposed and discredited, these organizations continue to attract followers and clients who see a benefit in the behavioral changes that result from associating with organizations that provide training in psychological and behavioral change.

Chapter 3. Components of NLP and NLP Techniques

Components of NLP

NLP's core philosophy is built on three essential components. From these components, other researchers and practitioners have expanded upon them. So long as these three components are respected, NLP is believed to work and be effective. To reach their maximum potential, practitioners need to pay close attention to how these pillars interact with one another.

Subjectivity

The first component, or core concept, is subjectivity. It is based on the fact that we all have different perceptions of the world around us. And while there are universal concepts that are believed and accepted, the fact of the matter is that we all have an experience that differs significantly.

Moreover, subjectivity is the basis of human experience. Therefore, we need to engage all of our senses to perceive the world as best we can. It is why educators who implement NLP seek to engage all five senses within the learning experience. That way, learners can get a good sense of the content they are trying to internalize.

Consciousness

NLP is predicated because the human psyche is built on a dual-layer of consciousness and unconsciousness. In this manner, the human psyche uses consciousness to express rationality for the things that we do daily. On the flip side, unconsciousness is the automatic manifestation of the built-in programming that we have accrued throughout your evolution.

Learning

Learning occurs when the conscious internalization of the world around us is achieved through the senses' perception. When a person can internalize content or their particular perception of the experiences they live, they can transform this into learning. It is why experience is crucial to the effectiveness of NLP. Unless a human is unable to experience the world, meaningful learning cannot fully take place.

NLP Techniques and How They Work

Neuro-Linguistic Programming (NLP) tells you that emotions and experiences guide people on their planet's view. It tells us that what you currently see isn't the critical world but a distorted representation supported your beliefs, perceptions, values, and other variables. NLP techniques will help you integrate aspects of your life, improve your quality, and understand how people work. Discover how to use these NLP techniques to enhance communication skills and emotional intelligence that you can use to regulate your life and mind.

Anchoring

The anchoring technique in NLP is important to tug up a particular emotion or put yourself into a specific psychological state, which may be used on yourself or somebody else. It works by integrating emotion with a physical movement, and the anchor laying dubs it. For example, if you decided to tug the thrilling feeling, you'd start by brooding about the days you have been euphoric. You'd wish to tell the account of what went on in your head that led to the present moment. Mention how it feels and enter an excellent deal of detail. Remember the instant, the emotions.

First, confine your right to your left index and middle fingers. Squeeze them twice. Mention your special moment on the second squeeze and strive to feature the feeling. Describe once more how you are feeling, how you think, and clap your hands twice. Let the nice and cozy feeling double once you clap the second time. Roll in the hay continuously for five times. You'll use those gestures to regain your feeling of happiness. You'd use a fast touch of the arm to secure them if you were to try this to a different man.

Meta Model

The methodology of the meta-model of NLP is usually wont to understand other individuals' concerns. It could even be wont to support others to possess a better understanding of their issues. The aim is to dismantle the conversation, assist you in achieving the basis explanation for the difficulty, and fix it. The response is consciously or unconsciously understood when someone features a question, but the only solution is some things that they are doing not like. The shortage of uncertainty allows the crisis to persist, anticipating that there'll finally be a replacement solution. You'll help them develop how by deconstructing the way someone explains their question.

Mirroring

One of the foremost relevant NLP strategies you ought to learn is mirroring. It'll be very beneficial to be good at mirroring. It's been quite hard to hate someone who knows the way to do that act. Moreover, it's the replication of the individual you interact with (i.e., his/her behaviors). While being subtle and typically subconscious, this simulation is complete. Copying somebody's speech patterns, visual communication, vocabulary style, speed, rhythm, pitch, voice, and volume are ways you'll do that.

Framing

The technique of NLP framing is employed to affect the rise or decrease of the emotional feeling significantly. It is an excellent way to use alongside most of the others. You are going to experience good and bad moments in life. These should enable you to be ready to learn and grow in your life. Nonetheless, memories haven't any feelings connected to them. Such separation occurs because memories and thoughts exist in several parts of the brain. Therefore, at present, you'll experience feelings, then you'll be ready to remember them. The hippocampus is that the brain part that's liable for LTM storage. The amygdala is the brain's portion that regulates feelings. The amygdala will offer you a fast-little reminder of what you feel once you recall a memory from the hippocampus. Simply because of that, the feeling that's important to a selected memory is often modified.

Pattern Interruption

Interruption of the pattern is usually wont to preserve words during a listener's subconscious. One great technique to pair with others is that this technique. To try this, you've got to draw the listener's thoughts into a series or pattern form. When the model gets out of control before finishing the shape, you would like to require them out of the template for a critical juncture. The listener's unconscious is meant to embody the pattern while the conscious mind is overwhelmed at that moment. You'll change the way you think that check out the past, and consider your life with a replacement way of thinking by learning NLP. It can help to enhance your communication skills and enhance your emotional intelligence.

Chapter 4. The Swish Pattern

The Swish Pattern is your answer to powerful and constant change. It is one of the most widely known and widely used NLP tools, and it helps people genuinely create their ideal self and eliminate negative behaviors. Using visualization, the Swish Pattern allows you to take the old images and behaviors you have developed over the years and replace them with powerful, dynamic. All-around better images and behaviors that work for the new ideal life you want to build.

First, though, you need to understand what visualization is:

Visualization

Visualization has gotten a bad rep, mostly because it has been tied up with Oprah's new age movement and the Law of Attraction. Everything can be yours if you just sit down and visualize that it is yours. And that is left behind many bitter and angry people who are ready to say visualization is not good. But, visualization is a tool used by athletes, politicians, and billionaire business people who want to get more and more from their life. Which is all to say many people are wrong.

One of the essential foundational tools for change when it comes to using NLP is visualization. To powerfully use all the NLP tools, you will need to understand what visualization is and how to use it, especially when using the Swish Pattern.

Power of Visualization

Dr. Biasiatto did a study at the University of Chicago, where he took three groups of people and tested their free-throw ability. He took note of each of their scores, and then he had one group practice their free throws for an hour every day for a month. The second group makes them visualize, making free throws for a little bit every day. In the third group, he had to do nothing at all.

In the end, the group that did nothing improved in no way whatsoever. The first group that practiced an hour a day improved their free throws by 24%. The visualization group was just 1% short of people who practiced for an hour a day. They improved at nearly the same rate as those practicing every day through merely the power of mental rehearsal.

Study after study has confirmed that the brain processes a visualized event the same way a real event happens. Athletes who visualize their playing see their muscle fibers activate and their brain process as if they are doing it. Some of the world's wealthiest and most influential people talk about using visualization to enhance their success, get better ideas, and achieve faster.

Visualizing is real. It works when you know how to do it. But, there are a few things that usually trip people up that do not have to trip you up. First and foremost, you do not have to be able to see anything. It is so important because many people think if they are not visual thinkers, then the visualization will not work for them, so they never try it.

Also, though, this will come if you practice visualization enough, your brain will learn to start creating images, and you'll feel a lot better about the whole process. But for many people, they are not visual thinkers, so they're initially just not seeing anything.

It's okay. You do not have to see anything to visualize (as weird as that sounds). Your brain will create experiences for you; if you focus on it, you will access other areas of your body, whether kinesthetic, verbal or anything else.

You will develop the feelings and the skills you are looking for. Now that you understand visualization, let us talk about the Swish Pattern.

The Swish Pattern

The Swish Pattern is a life changer that helps people with weight loss, smoking cessation, better habits, a healthy self-image, a more meaningful and better life. The thing is that you already have your ideal-self likely built inside of you. You know what your life would look like if you did not have your problems and what amazing things could happen with your life once those problems were solved.

You probably have a self-image of yourself that is far and away from your ideal, one that has been built by those problems weighing you down and working on you. It is these two images that you can leverage to make significant changes in your life.

Swish Pattern Step by Step

Step 1: Recognize Your Automatic Reactions

Images, thoughts, emotions, and a host of other things can cause you to have an adverse reaction. Whether you are reaching for a cigarette or a muffin, or it is making you yell and scream, or retreat and cower. We all respond to certain stimuli in remarkably consistent ways with our character that probably does not always help us be the best version of ourselves that we would want to be. You want to find that automatic response for whatever behavior or emotion or anything else that you want to fix. Once you do, you want to narrow down all the images, emotions, and anything else that forms in your mind when you respond in those automatic fashions.

You want to create an ideal image, a simple, powerful one that connects with your emotional state. It should be inspiring, exciting, and something that should make you want to change. You want to create this image focusing on your life would be like without whatever negative automatic response you have.

Once you have these two things, you want to create an image of yourself disassociated from both of these things, almost as if you're watching these two images from a distance, looking at them, admiring them.

Step 2: Determine the Cause of the Negative Image

As we said, you have automatic responses, and hopefully, you will have found them. Now, it is time to isolate what causes these automatic responses. Something brings these negative states to the forefront of your mind. Negative behaviors do not come from anywhere. Find that trigger. Ask yourself, "What Occurs Before This Negative State Begins?" This way, you can imagine the automatic response happening from the trigger and be prepared to create an alternative response to this event in the future.

Step 3: Prepare for Displacement

Take the positive image that you made initially, make it the size of a postage stamp in your mind, and place it on the corner of your developed negative image. You will want to notice a few things from its placement in the corner of the image. Its brightness, it is strength, and everything else that makes it stand out.

Step 4: Swish the Two Images

Now you are going to swish the images back and forth. Making a Swish sound can help because it gives your brain something else to engage with. Imagine the images switching places—the positive one growing more prominent, brighter, and more colorful. The negative one shoots off into the distance of your mind, disappearing and becoming nothing but a memory.

Notice how the further an image travels in your mind, the further the malicious behavior feels a part of you. More importantly, notice how, when the positive image gets brighter, your positive image can feel better.

Step 5: Repeat the Process

Keep repeating the swishing. Bring the old image back to the front of your mind; notice it as it loses color, as it gets blurry, as it begins to lose more and more of its power. You will notice the more powerful image continuing to glow brighter and brighter in the corner, almost as if it cannot be contained.

Keep the process going until the negative image has become tattered, black and white, blurry, and no longer packs the same emotions with it that it once did.

Step 6: Test It

Think about your negative emotion, think about the trigger, and find out if it is now replaced with that more powerful image that you want.

The Swish Pattern is a powerful tool, and it can completely liberate you from your negative behaviors and negative beliefs if you let it and you work it. It is there to help you genuinely transform how you live. You should notice improvement within a few days of using it, especially if you do it every day for a few days until it becomes part of your unconscious. There is no such thing as a transformation without actual work. You are going to have to work at it. The people who complain about the Swish Pattern do so because they thought they could do it once and forget it. But, that is not how it works. That is not how life works. But if you do it few a few days in a row, keep testing it; find where you're feeling weak with it. Within a week, you should see a clear improvement in your malicious behavior and see a positive transformation.

It works, and it works well. As you move through life, consistently trying to make yourself the best version of yourself possible, you will need to use this technique every time you want to end a malicious behavior. The more negative behaviors, beliefs, and emotions you can eliminate from your life, the better your overall life will be. The more you use this, the faster it will work, and the more powerful this technique will become in helping you create the behaviors and strengths you want in your life. You can install everything you want inside of you. You can make your life as exciting and memorable as possible.

The best thing about the swish pattern is that you can do it just about anywhere, and you can control the process. No need for audiotapes or some outside person guiding you through the process; no, you can be in complete control and have full power over yourself.

Start the process now and figure out what you want to change and what negative behaviors you want to eliminate from your life for good. Then create a list of desired behaviors and start to craft out everything that you want to do with your life and what your life will be like if you had these fantastic new behaviors instead of the negative ones you want to get rid of.

The more you design out your amazing future and your amazing life, the more you craft out the opportunity to create something marvelous for yourself to take over.

Chapter 5. Hypnosis

Hypnosis is a position of consciousness that involves focused attention, together with reduced peripheral awareness characterized by the participant's increased ability to respond to suggestions given. Every person has a waking state, a state when they know that they are awake, alert, alive, and in the universe.

What happens is that your attention becomes more and more focused, and your awareness of your environment diminishes. Your attention has more focused on what is inside and lesser on what is occurring outside. It makes you much more aware of your internal images, feelings, and thoughts and less aware of things going on in your surroundings. Usually, it's so pleasant for many people, enjoyable and very relaxing.

Highly imaginative people are usually easier to hypnotize: they have an intense experience of both nature and art. Psychopaths tend to be immune to hypnosis because psychopaths tend to have restricted emotions, but many people are easily hypnotized. Being in a hypnotic state is a regular aspect of human life. Often, creative people use guided imagination in their daily routine without necessarily realizing it as a hypnotic technique.

Three Stages of Hypnosis

Hypnosis is more of an ability than a disadvantage unless you are often hypnotically governed by an external force. Three stages are recognized in the hypnosis field:

Induction

It is the first stage involved in hypnosis. Before a subject undergoes full hypnosis, the subject is introduced to the hypnotic induction technique. For many years, hypnotic induction was used to put the participant into their hypnotic trance, but the definition has altered some modern times. Some of the non-state theorists have comprehended this stage a bit differently. Instead, the theorists understand this stage as the technique to enhance the subjects' expectations of what will happen—defining the role that they will play, getting their attention to concentrate on the right direction and any of the steps that are required to lead the subject into the appropriate direction of hypnosis.

Various induction methods can be applied during hypnosis. The most used method is the Braidism technique. The Braids technique has a few variations, like the Stanford Hypnotic Susceptibility Scale, which is the most applied research tool in the hypnosis field.

For you to apply the Braidism technique, you will have to follow the following steps:

- First, take any object that you can find bright, for example, a watch case, hold it between your middle, fore, and thumb fingers on the left hand. Hold the object somewhere above the forehead to produce a lot of strain on the eyelids and eyes. During the process so that the subject can maintain a fixed stare on the object at all times.

- Secondly, the hypnotist should then explain to the subject that they should keep their eyes often fixed on the object. The subject will also be required to focus theirs mindfully on the idea of that specific object. The subject should not be allowed to think of any other thing or let their mind wander, or else, the process will not be successful.

After some time, the subject's eyes will start to dilate. With some more time, the subject will begin to assume a wavy motion. If the subject involuntarily closes their eyelids when the fore and middle fingers of the right hand are carried from their eyes to the object, they are in a trance. If this is not the case, the subject will be required to start the process again: you should ensure that you let the subject know that they are to let their eyes close once the fingers are carried in a similar motion back towards the eyes again. It will get the subject to go into an altered state of the mind or hypnosis.

Suggestion

At first, the term suggestion was not used. Instead, Braid defined this stage as the act of having the conscious mind of the subject concentrate on one dominant and central idea. Braid did this to reduce or trigger the various regions' physiological functioning on the subject's body. Braid then started to emphasize applying various non-verbal and verbal forms of suggestion to get the subject into the mind's hypnotic condition. These would involve using waking suggestions as well as self-hypnosis. Hippolyte Bernheim, another hypnotist, emphasized the hypnosis process's physical condition over the psychological process that included verbal suggestions. According to Hippolyte, hypnosis is the induction of a physical state that is peculiar and which will enhance the susceptibility of the suggestion to the subject. He always stated that the hypnotic condition that is induced would assist in facilitating the suggestion.

Modern hypnotism applies various suggestions to be successful, such as direct verbal suggestions, insinuations, metaphors, non-verbal suggestions, and other figures of speech that are non-verbal. Some of the non-verbal suggestions that may be used would include mental imagery, voice tonality, and physical manipulation.

One of the distinctions made in the types of suggestions offered to the subject includes those suggestions delivered with permission and more authoritarian. One of the aspects that have to be considered regarding hypnosis is the difference between conscious and unconscious minds. Several hypnotists view this stage to communicate directed to most of the participant's conscious minds.

Susceptibility

It has been observed that people will react differently to hypnosis. Some will find that they can easily fall into a hypnotic trance and don't have to put much effort into the process. Others will find that they can get into the hypnotic trance, but only after a prolonged period and with some effort applied. Still, other people will find that they cannot get into the trance and, even after constant efforts, will not reach their goals.

One thing that has been found about the various subject's susceptibility is that this part remains unchanging. If you have gotten into a trance easily, you will likely be the same way for the rest of your life. On the contrary, if you have challenges teaching your hypnotic star of mind and have never been experiencing hypnotized, then it is probably that you never will.

Two types of victims are considered to be highly susceptible to the effects of hypnotism. These include:

- Fantasizers

- Associates

Fantasizers will have a high score on the absorption scales; they will block out easily the real world's stimuli without the use of hypnosis. They spend a lot of time daydreaming, they grew up in an environment where imaginary play was encouraged, and they had imaginary pals when they were in their childhood.

Associates will always come from childhood abuse or trauma; they found ways to forget their trauma and escape into numbness. When they daydream, it is more in terms of going blank instead of creating fantasies. Both dissociation and fantasizers score highly on the tests of hypnotic susceptibility.

Two groups of people with the highest hypnotism rates include those suffering from dissociative identity disorder and post-traumatic stress disorder.

Effects of Hypnosis

In a trance state, your ability to think logically and critically reduces. You tend to accept any information that is given to you without thinking if it's reasonable and rational or not.

People in a hypnotic state are suggestible. They tend to consent uncritically to any suggestions given to them. Even the strong-willed people can be hypnotized and made to do things that they wouldn't normally do.

Conscious decision making, independent judgment, and rational analysis are all suspended. It is a bonus for leaders who, after all, don't want their members thinking of themselves. Hypnosis is an incredibly powerful set of tools to influence others and manipulate others to do things that violate their ethics and morals.

What Manipulators Say

It is exciting that most leaders usually claim that people can't be made to do things against their will, even when applying mind control hypnosis.

The members are programmed to agree to whatever the leaders say. Therefore, the members will tend to accept the idea. Implicit in the idea is that if the person does something, they do it of their own volition.

When you make your own decisions, you believe more firmly and more committed to the outcome, and the actions and effects of your decision last longer.

Myths About Hypnosis

You should remember that hypnosis is not often a closed-eye process. It's not compulsory to have your eyes closed to be in a trance. Have you ever tried to be on a trip or journey, and when you reach your destination, you do not even remember much of the journey? That is an example of a trance that you were in.

People in a trance state who are driving while their eyes are entirely open and performing; if they see a person in front braking, there's no difficulty in braking themselves and doing what is necessary to avoid accidents. Many have the idea that there are unique hypnotic words to trigger trance. Hypnosis can be triggered in normal-sounding conversations, using the daily words.

Chapter 6. Brainwashing

If you talk to someone and ask them what they think brainwashing is, they may reply that they know because this is a topic that many people have heard about. But most people don't have a full understanding of how this kind of mind control can work. And if you are trying to fight off someone using dark psychology, you must make sure that you understand this topic.

Brainwashing will be the slow process of taking the ideas that a victim has about their identity and their beliefs and then replacing them with new ideas to suit the manipulator's purpose. Brainwashing can occur in a narrow and broad context. For example, a brainwasher could use the techniques to control one person or use those techniques to control a more extensive group's minds all at once.

The Process of Brainwashing

The starting point of brainwashing is the social circumstances and the mental state of the victim. It will be the basis for the rest of the process, and if the manipulator cannot figure this part out, then the brainwashing session won't be successful. Brainwashing is not a process that is going to work out for everyone. It will require an adequate identification of a person looking for something or someone who has a void they are trying to fill.

It brings us to an important point. Who is the ideal victim for a brainwasher? People who have had their existing reality shaken up because of some recent events are excellent brainwashers' targets. If you have lost someone you are close to or had another dramatic or traumatic event in your life, then you may be more susceptible to brainwashing.

Once the brainwasher has found their victim, the process of brainwashing can begin. Contrary to the popular image you may have in your mind about a brainwasher, this person will often come across as someone rational, friendly, and calm. Someone who seems to have their lives together in a way the victim wishes they could have their own. Visualize how it would feel if you were homeless and a celebrity you admired befriended you. It is often how the process of meeting the brainwasher is going to feel for the victim.

The brainwasher is going to get to work right away. The first step for them is to create a rapport and trust between them and the victim. It is going to be done with superficial and deep similarities. The superficial similarities could involve some surface-level preferences, something like enjoying the same food or sport as the other person.

They will then move on to a deeper level of rapport, some that could involve a more in-depth shared experience that they had in the past. The brainwasher will most likely fake these, convincingly, to create these bonds. If the victim shares with the brainwasher that they lost a close relative in the past, then the brainwasher is suddenly going to have a similar story to share with the victim.

This false connection and warmth emotionally are not the only thing that is going to occur. The brainwasher wants to cement that new bond as quickly as possible. It is not unconventional for them to provide favors and gifts to their victim. They could send them a gadget or some other item they may find useful. They may treat the victim to a meal. It is to create a sense of gratitude and indebtedness from the victim to that brainwasher. It is going to soften up a lot of the resistance that the victim may experience.

After the resistance has been stripped away a little bit, the other step will be a sort of romantic presentation. It will involve the brainwasher slowly and increasingly offer a solution to any problems that the victim recently opened up about. It is not going to be a big hard push or sell. Instead, the brainwasher knows how to do this in an offhand and casual way to make sure they don't deal with any negative experiences by pressing the victim. This solution will always be the personality, ideology, or cult that the brainwasher is working to make the victim convert.

When these steps are done correctly, the initial stages will leave the victim wanting more. The victim will want more information and more understanding of the solution that the brainwasher hints at. The brainwasher may even withhold some of this information initially, treating it as something that the victim needs to do some work to attain. Doing this is to push the victim to seek out and accept the information they are eventually going to hear.

After the victim has had some time being spoon-fed snippets of this belief system, and they have shown they will respond well to them, the brainwasher will be careful to reveal the right information at the right time. It is a concept that is called a gradual revelation or milk before meat. It will include the presentation of an easy to accept idea before the controversial idea is revealed.

For example, if the brainwasher is trying to convert the victim over to religious terrorism, they would not start with the terrorism part. They may initially start focusing on the fact that God loves the victim, something that the victim is likely to accept. The more objectionable ideas, such as God wants you to blow yourself up, are ones that are saved until much after in the process. Once the victim has accepted that last part, then this brainwashing session is at a point of no return.

In this situation, you may be curious why the victim is still engaging with the brainwasher, especially when these more objectionable ideas become apparent. There are three main reasons:

The brainwasher has worked on the vulnerable victim. They feel a strong sense of liking the brainwasher, and they want to get the brainwasher's approval.

The victim has invested some time, and in some cases, money, in the process up to this point. It is often known as the sunk cost fallacy. The victim will feel like it is terrible to throw away all the hard work and money they have put into the process.

During this process, the brainwasher has been amassing many sensitive and secretive information on the victim. The brainwasher is often willing to hold this information over the victim to keep the victim on the right path.

The Impact of Brainwashing

The above analysis that we did about brainwashing is going to show how severe this technique can be. It is changing the victim's beliefs and inner identity, and this can be a big deal. Sure, the manipulator will get what they want out of the process, but the victim will lose out on their real identity and often gets so far into the process that they aren't sure what went wrong.

Many different impacts will come with brainwashing after the process is completed. The first one is a loss of identity. Many ideologies and cults feature that the people who go through the initiation process are given a new name. It helps the psyche of the person to detach from their old identity altogether. They can believe things and even do things they would never have done in the past because that older adult they were no longer exists. When this process is carried out the proper way, it can leave a victim feeling like all the parts of their old identity are no longer real or permanent and that they have woken up from a nightmare.

Post-traumatic stress disorder, or PTSD, can sometimes be a hallmark of those who managed to escape or rescued from a situation where they were brainwashed. The victims of these brainwashing endeavors will show some of the same psychological and physical signs as war veterans who were right in the battle. The severity of this traumatic aftermath shows that this type of process, of the manipulator getting more control over the victim, could harm the victim as much as if they went to war.

Brainwashing is something that can have a lasting impact. There are plenty of examples of rescued individuals or who managed to escape from their brainwashing situation, who then went back to that situation of their own free will. Even when they were able to leave the brainwashing and controlling environment they were in, the legacy that came with that process was done so well and ran so deep in their mind that the victim wants to return to it. It shows the power of using this brainwashing process and how much a manipulator could gain.

Chapter 7. How to Use NLP for in Sales

We are all on sale, believe it or not. When was the last time you had to sell an idea you had to your boss or your colleagues or make a proposal to increase your project budget? When was the last time you had to convince your kids to do something they were supposed to do? Whether you sell a product, service, concept, or influence others to achieve the desired result, you sell.

The following 5-step sales process seems to be a simple framework to use and remember:

- Establish and maintain a rapport.

- Understand your client or potential client.

- Define the need/define the value.

- Need/value link to your product or service.

- Close the sale.

Neuro-linguistic Programming is the study of excellence and excellent communication and how to reproduce it. Your ability to communicate effectively is the key to your success in any business interaction. So, let's look at each step of the 5-step sales process and see how NLP fits in.

Establish and Maintain a Rapport

Keeping eye contact while talking or listening to another person is one way to stay connected. Leaning or bending forward and tilting a bit your head to the side while listening shows that you are entirely listening and engaged to the person you're talking to. Uniting and reflecting body, voice, and words is another way to create and maintain relationships. Any resistance you encounter means that you have not established enough relationships and an excellent indicator to go back and build an additional connection. Making a rapport is the first step to getting better results in sales or any communication interaction.

Understand Your Client or Potential Client

The best way to understand your client or prospect is to ask many open questions. Asking questions will allow you to know your client/potential client better and will allow you to identify if it is necessary for your product or service. Find out what is important to them, how they think and process information. Observe their eye patterns as they answer questions to see where they are going to access private information. Look at the main words you use most often. Do they prefer visual words and descriptors such as "I see, can I imagine," or do they incline to the auditory words "I hear what you think," "it sounds true." Or are they more appropriate with kinesthetic phrases like "I understand what you are saying"? I feel your passion. "If you understand the needs of the client or potential client and understand their communication style and preferences, you will be better prepared to communicate with them in a way that works best for them.

Define the Need/Define the Value

Once you have determined the need, you need to define a value. Do you realize it would be useful to solve your problem or improve the situation? Reinforce your value proposition by asking something like, "So it would be useful to answer that, right? Is it something that would interest you or not?" It is an important problem because they may have a need but see no value in solving it. Most sellers spend 80% of their time on people who don't buy. You want potential clients/buyers to buy while ensuring that the value solves their problem is crucial to your sales pitch.

Connect Need/Value to Your Product or Service

You don't sell a product or service in the sales process. You sell emotion. We believe it is our sound mind that makes the decision, but the fact is that all of our memories, feelings, and emotions are stored in our unconscious. Furthermore, the more significant part of our choices is made subliminally. Connecting with your client or client's sentiment is the key to your ability to close a sale successfully. For example, potential buyers looking to buy a new home can see the value of a locker room. You associate it with the sensation she will feel when she wakes up in the morning, approaches her, and feels good when she sees and chooses clothes quickly in the morning. This feeling will connect her to the house they are selling.

Close

If you have successfully followed steps 1 through 4, closing should be smooth. Just ask for a purchase or order. Take advantage of the sale to the end and look for a win-win opportunity.

Chapter 8. How to Use NLP in Relationships

In this part, we will know how NLP can be beneficial to healthy relationships. We will learn what excellent and fulfilling relationships are based on and built upon. We will explore techniques that can strengthen relationships and those that can help us establish healthy relationships. We will talk about the benefits or importance of our mental health and readiness before entering any partnership or relationship and possible outcomes associated with having and not having these factors.

Once you have decided what you want, now is the time to enter into a relationship and have covered your predetermining factors. Now you can begin to open up to the possibilities of finding the right person. Here is when rapport becomes essential. What is rapport? It's your similarities and likeness with someone you are interested in entering a relationship with. It's also the establishment of trust with that person. With rapport, many individual factors can be used for determining compatibility. Some of these are personality types, values, beliefs, culture, political ideologies, interests, religious beliefs, etc. Of course, physical characteristics, such as gender and body types, need to be considered. However, some features can't be overaccentuated because it will mimic the other and cause a loss of rapport.

The rapport established initially, the reasons for your attraction to your partner, and his or her attraction to you must be kept at the forefront of each partner's mind throughout the relationship. It all too familiar for people to enter relationships with guns blazing, meaning being the perfect partner, only to begin to relax and change once the relationship has been established. One partner, or both, will use all available techniques to get the other to enter into a relationship. Once they are in that relationship, the other partner believes they can initially tone down what they were doing. It is one of the typical reasons for relationships ending. Keep in mind, the reasons for someone falling for you are the same reasons that will make them want to stay with you. If you remove the reasons for their attraction, they have no reasons to stay with you. Often, we see children born of relationships used as new reasons, but this does not work. It leads the partnership to morph into, what be, a business relationship. There will be no real emotional connection in the relationship and, even though that couple may remain together, they will lack the comforts and fulfillment of needs they desire.

Now you have identified what you want, making sure the timing is right, and have met that special someone. Now, what do you do? You need to ensure that your significant other feels the same about you. There are several ways in which a person can see that they are loved by the other. These ways should be identified at the relationships beginning. A few methods are by what the other person buys and places he or she takes you. There are also things such as how they touch you, the looks they give, or what they say. Identification of these is essential as they can gauge the continuance of love throughout the relationship.

The best way to determine how you can best assure your partner that you love them is by doing what they tend to do for you. For instance, if your partner puts her arm around you at times to assure you of her love and affection, you can bet that if you do the same, she will believe that you do love and appreciate her. We don't tend to do things to or for others, especially those whom we care about the most, that we wouldn't want to be done to us. Although this is commons sense, it's also an excellent method to gauge or determine how your significant other feels about you. As the relationship progresses, this will come naturally and will take much less conscious effort. Be sure not to allow these things to stop just because the relationship is no longer new.

NLP has devised a few strategies to determine areas in relationships. Areas such as attraction, love, and desire are all strategized with NLP techniques. First, you must know your partner. It means that you should know what those subtle gestures and tones of voice your partner will display depending on how they feel. Know what your partner fears and what he or she wants. You will pick up ideas as to how to carry these things out by merely learning your partner. Be sure never to use this knowledge for manipulation. There isn't a positive outcome in relationships where manipulation takes place.

One technique you can use to ensure that your partner is in love with you and wants you is to remove yourself from his or her presence temporarily. It does not mean that you can tell your wife that you are going to the store for a lottery ticket to not return for a week. However, in short time frames, absence can signal want or lack thereof. Just like the cliché, absence makes the heart grow fonder; this is built on the same premise. When using these kinds of tactics, please never overuse them. Here is some advice. If you are an insecure person needing constant approval and reassurance that you are loved, you should take care of that issue before entering a serious relationship. If not, you will not be the right partner. If your shortcoming does not end the relationship, it could lead it to become a codependent partnership or, at the very least, a very unhealthy relationship. Again, you must first make sure that you are the right candidate for entering into a relationship before taking that other step.

With relationships, you are not merely selling yourself to another, and then the job is over. It's a continuing process forever. Never relax and believe that you have your partner and aren't going anywhere, no matter what you may or may not do. You should always be selling yourself, your worth, compassion, and desire for your partner.

Think of this; You meet someone at the beach or any spot you can imagine. You are both at that exact place at that same time. You may both have everything in common too. However, both you and the other person took different routes to that spot and lived through different circumstances while on the way. Even though you both find yourselves to be at the same point and with the same characteristics, you took different paths there. It means that it's likely that you are not both going to react or respond to every event the same, and those events may lead you to go in different directions. Another way to look at this; you may both like the same sports team. The difference is why each of you has this opinion of that team. One of you may be a graduate from that university, while the other just picked last season's champions. It probably means that the school's alumnus is less likely to decide that they no longer favor that team. Regardless of the possible ways, the ending remains the same. What does this mean? Are we all just merely at life's mercy and subject to emotional trauma at the drop of a hat? Not exactly. Although we may not be able to change the situation when finding ourselves here, we can know why. First, don't give up. Do whatever you can to carry both you and your partner through the tough spot in your relationship, and you may find that you both were able to beat the odds and remain together.

Let's look at what it means to have taken different routes. The recently mentioned scenarios were only metaphors. The location isn't an actual place but a specific state of mind and life situation. Regardless of the spectrum of commonalities you and your partner may or may not have, you both will respond and react to things differently. One of you may be able to brush something, such as a traumatic event, off, but the other cannot do that. Let's look at this. Both you and your wife have religious faith. It is one of the main commonalities you found of yourselves that led to your relationship. Then down the road, your wife either endures a traumatic event or meets an influential person, either causing a dramatic shift in her religious ideologies. What was once the main glue that kept you together has deteriorated to where there is no more left. Not only does she no longer agree with your religious faith, but her newfound beliefs also contradict what you believe. What do you do when faced with this situation? Both of you are firmly holding to your individual beliefs and not willing to waiver. Both accuse the other of being naïve. Neither of you is terrible people, but you are no longer finding the same rapport you once had.

You both joined the relationship only after taking the proper steps and exercised due caution in choosing the other as a mate. Even though this was done, life didn't care about that. Circumstances led to the separation of you and your partner's beliefs, and both of you are much too committed to your independent ideas to compromise them. Therefore, you are now at constant odds, and the negativity within the relationship grows stronger each day. One day, it will lead to resentment and even hate. You have taken the necessary steps in attempting to salvage the relationship to no avail. So, as the very last resort, you decide to part ways. It happens every day.

Like the baggage we carry due to prior bad relationships, we have lessons learned and unique ways of dealing with specific issues based on these lessons. The best thing to do is know what and how things are going, and this can give you a good idea as to what is about to come.

To conclude this guide, NLP is essential and beneficial in the relationship. It isn't just with the beginning of the union but throughout its entirety. You must first know yourself, and then using NLP; you can learn your partner. Knowing your partner can prove invaluable in maintaining a healthy and long relationship. Also, the relationship will be much more fulfilling to both parties. Remember that severe and personal relationships prove beneficial in many areas in life and isn't limited to just the partnership. It's beneficial for both of you as a couple, as individuals, and as part of society.

Chapter 9. NLP in Business

NLP enhances negotiation skills and selling skills. Clients who use NLP in the business report that their managers are excellent coaches, motivators, and influencers.

NLP multiplies excellence in any field. It is a skill known as modeling in NLP; it incorporates all other intermediate skills. It is beneficial in a business organization if, for example, business took good employees from each field and brought them together. The work done will be excellent.

NLP helps to improve communication while doing business. During communication, there is the use of verbal and non-verbal cues. Using NLP, one will be able to understand the spoken and unspoken language of clients and prospects.

It helps one to emulate the successful efforts of other businesses easily. NLP teaches one to understand how successful people work and converse. One can then emulate those using NLP strategies to copy those successes to fit their businesses.

NLP gives one sales staff mind-reading abilities. It enables them to understand non-verbal cues and eye movements, allowing them to answer clients' questions and provide useful information about the products. They also understand how a client feels about the product in question, making it easier for them to close sales.

NLP improves negotiation skills. Negotiation is a critical requirement in the business world—negotiation with vendors, employees' marketers, advertising firms, and many more. With

NLP negotiation skills, everyone in the business will be more effective and persuasive.

NLP boosts morale. Why wouldn't one's morale be boosted if everyone in the company or office knows how well and effectively you communicate? One can make themselves apparent as well as able to relate with everyone in the office. It makes the workplace much more fun since there is a better understanding of one another.

NLP is the best client service tool. NLP helps to understand clients' complaints and suggestions after a sale. One can discern if a client is complaining because of awful client service or if he or she is having a bad day. When one's client care can understand the client's non-verbal cues, he will be able to deal with the angry client and make them happy to come again.

NLP can be so useful in boosting your entrepreneurial pursuits. It helps build skills in teamwork, coaching, sales, productivity, personal development, and leadership. For NLP to be useful, there must be potential for growth, and human interaction should be present.

NLP is a useful tool when you are setting and working toward achieving your goals. When you are in a business state, you must set your goals, which are supposed to be achievable, intelligent, meaningful, and measurable. For instance, it will not be realistic for you to set a goal to earn millions of dollars within a month without having logical ways to achieve your goal. Thus, using NLP, it is possible to set and achieve goals for your business. Using NLP will help you change your way of thinking and speaking and motivate you to take appropriate actions toward achieving your goal.

When you are in a business, sometimes you become stressed, but if you apply NLP techniques, it is possible to have a happier and more fulfilling life. NLP includes studying successful people's steps to achieve success, and these successes can come out from any part of your body. These techniques will help you overcome phobias, speak with confidence in front of a large congregation, reduce anxiety, and learn how to be in a healthy personal relationship.

Brain Training Success Techniques

Avoid using weak words, such as try. The type of language you will use in your business matters, and you should avoid using vague language. "I will try to get that book tomorrow"—this sentence is not exactly whether you will do it or not. In a business, make your intentions clear, and avoid giving your clients unclear expectations. When dealing with your clients, only use action-based and positive language.

Away from or Move Toward

We all experience problems and obstacles as we move toward success. The way you tackle those problems matters. If you use NLP techniques, it becomes easier. Entrepreneurs have a way of solving their problems. They tend to break tasks, and then they apply logic to it. Then they look at it objectively by removing emotions from that particular problem. You are supposed to move toward the positive "I am capable of doing this. Although it is a difficult job, it is worth it.' And get away from negativity: "This is impossible. I am not able to do this difficult job."

Direction and Focus

NLP helps you use personality to create focus and direction from both a personal and professional perspective, perfect for direct reports in a coaching setting. It involves having an overview of different areas of both life and work, and this helps you have priorities and identify areas of neglect or drift. It enables us to agree to measurable objectives and actions, sharing benefits to both the individual and the organization.

Improving Personal Effectiveness

Improving personal effectiveness is effective in changing the long-term behavior of a person in the workplace. When employees understand one another, it becomes much easier to respond to one another's and the clients' desires and needs. It has been proven that well-functioning and healthy relationships are essential for success in one's personal life.

In conclusion, applying NLP techniques in your business will make you more successful. It is one of the exciting approaches to your problem, and it is worth trying. It improves your way of thinking and helps you achieve your goals.

How to Use NLP to Gain More Wealth and Get Better Results

It is every human being's wish to gain wealth and receive better results in life. We have different ways of doing so, and by using NLP techniques, it is possible to achieve that. These techniques help you to realize yourself and also the best way you can improve your earnings. Those ways are below.

One Can Make Money Using NLP, Using Various Methods

You Can Make Money with NLP as a Coach

Being a coach has many benefits. One can work from anywhere, work at their time, and work at their pay and price. Coaches help clients integrate their desired outcomes, set timelines and deadlines. Create goals, make them achievable, give advice, make the client see things that they cannot see by themselves, and help them stay accountable for what happens to follow up on what is happening.

One Can Also Make Money with NLP as a Practitioner

NLP gives you a tool to work well with people and almost everything that might be bothering them. It has been discovered that most people are looking for NLP practitioners, and one is very marketable. Being a practitioner helps people to:

- **Conquer fear and phobias**

They have different ways of helping people to overcome fear. Sometimes they expose their clients to what they fear most but in a safe and controlled environment. You will realize that you will learn how to combat your anxiety and fear, and after some time, you will be able to control it. Another way they use is teaching their clients the relaxation technique, which will help control both mental and physical feelings of fear. Some practitioners will suggest you seek medical help if you want to treat phobias, and after taking medication, that phobia will go away. Now you can live in everyday life.

- **Lose excess weight**

They usually suggest methods for us to lose weight. These methods include exercising and always practicing healthy diet habits. You are very aware that if you have too much weight, it can lead to you getting diabetes, affecting your everyday life.

- **Quit bad habits**

Habit is defined as a pattern of behaviors acquired through repetition. We have two categories of habits: good and bad habits. These bad habits make us not live a normal life, and this affects our productivity in life. These bad habits include smoking, gambling, etc. Smoking affects our life as nicotine found in cigarettes makes us addicts, and thus, for your body to operate normally, you have to smoke. There are several ways we can break these habits, but it varies from one person to another. It is broken using the following tips:

- **Identify the trigger.** It is the first step when you want to break the habit. Triggers include those things that go through your mind at that exact time. For example, reflect on what always goes through your mind when you are biting your nails.

- **Then try to replace bad behavior with a healthy one.** For instance, if you want to counteract smoking, try to find a new hobby you can practice during free time.

- **Avoid temptations.** Sometimes habits may be linked to a particular place or people. To break the habit, you have to avoid those friends, for instance, who are always drinking or gambling. That way, you can break the bad habit of drinking alcohol.

- **Keep your focus.** When you want to break a bad habit, you have to stay focused and committed to that. You should keep in mind that you are cutting the bad habit for your good. For instance, when quitting smoking, you are supposed to know that you are doing that to avoid getting diseases like cancer.

- **Never lose hope.** Hope is a pillar that keeps us moving. You should consider that you will face many obstacles when you are trying to leave a habit. Thus, you should have a plan to counter that if it arises. Do it once per day, and never give up.

- **Reward yourself.** When you stay away from a bad habit even one day, treat yourself. You buy yourself a new outfit, or you take a vacation. It will motivate you to keep avoiding the bad habit even though you are the one rewarding yourself.

- **Enhance confidence.** Sometimes we face situations that help us become confident. For instance, when you are having a staff meeting, confidence should be displayed. Practitioners help us boost our confidence by assisting us in identifying our weak points and strong points.

Here, people tend to confuse this with being a coach. A coach is different from a consultant in that a coach doesn't tell people what to do but helps clients find answers to their questions while consultants give specialized advice. For example, a business consultant helps his clients with concrete advice on how to grow their businesses.

You can also make money with NLP as an author. NLP training incorporates accelerated learning, NLP subconscious teaching principles, and layered learning. Becoming a published author increases one's credibility in the field, which will allow you to charge expensively.

You can also make money with NLP as a speaker. It again points to the knowledge one would have acquired from NLP. Suppose one continues with training beyond being a practitioner. In that case, they have the chance to enter a Master Trainer Development Program, where they issue all useful materials one requires to become a good speaker.

Chapter 10. Body Language and Behavior Imitation

Our non-verbal, or body language, is one of the most powerful communication methods we use in our day-to-day experiences. It is the mode of contact that ignites feelings and reactions on our "healthy point." Research has shown that understanding body language improves one's potential to effectively get out of any given situation, whatever one wants.

Have you ever encountered a couple sitting together and got a feeling of exactly how good or bad their friendship was in minutes? Have you ever questioned how you could arrive so quickly at this point without any prior interaction? Whether you are aware of it or not, we spend our days listening to people's non-verbal signals interpreted by their body language and drawing conclusions from our assumptions about them.

The body language shows that we conceal from the world in words and how we feel about ourselves, our relationships, and our circumstances. The individuals we associate with will evaluate our motives. The strength of our interactions, how masterful we are in any particular situation, our level of trust, and our real goals and aspirations by our eye contact, movements, body posture, and facial expressions.

The strength of body language is seen in the resulting emotional reaction. In nearly any case, emotions influence choices and reactions. Non-verbal signals activate emotions that define an individual's core properties, such as truthfulness, trustworthiness, honesty, competence level, and willingness to lead.

Understanding these signals will decide who we are going to meet, the work we are being recruited for, the amount of recognition we are having, and even those elected to powerful political positions.

Why do we not spend years studying and improving successful body language skills for such an immense skill? The fact is that most people undervalue the meaning of body language before they try a better interpretation of human conduct in an intimate relationship or in a competitive market situation to achieve an advantage.

Mastery in body language contains the keys for individuals to perceive the context of particular movements and body expressions and understand how to convey and express signals while communicating with others properly. As a result, there is a significant improvement in the general success of public interactions. The easiest way to continue this learning cycle is to study the simple understanding of the two core body language styles—open presence and closed presence.

The closed presence's body language form is illustrated in individuals who fold their bodies around the body's centerline, which runs straight down the middle of the body from the top of the head to the foot. The physical features that produce this form of appearance are feet positioned beside each other, arms held tight to the chest, hands folded across the chest, slight hand movements kept close to the body, shoulders rolling forward, and eyes fixed below eye level.

The world's signals transmitted by the body language form of closed appearance were a loss of confidence, low self-esteem, impotence, and lack of experience. In extreme cases, the message of needing to be invisible may also be produced. The consequences of this kind of body language on the person expressing can range from actually not having the best possible opportunity to a worst-case situation of harboring a self-fulfilling image of victimization.

By comparison, the accessible appearance is displayed in individuals that build a sense of dominance, control, and leadership by projecting mastery of confidence, achievement, energy, and ability. The physical features include feet held hip apart, freehand movements used in speech away from the body's middle line, elbows held away from the chest, shoulders pulled back, upright postures, and eyes fixed on their listeners' eye level. Such people are viewed as desirable, competent, intellectual, and are quickly seen as achieving success. We consider this form of body language as the "leaders' body language."

The aim is eye contact to enhance body language and to start expressing a transparent appearance. Face contact is one of the social devices that we enjoy most. Someone will alter the way others see them by making direct eye contact while communicating with others. Once people start looking straight into a victim's eyes, they are perceived as confident, trustworthy, and professional.

Hand gestures and facial expressions are the second degrees of improvement that one can create for a transparent face to be seen. Both methods of communicating improve the ability to and accurately convey information. Through skillfully using open hand motions away from the body and expressive facial expression, greater emphasis is produced when communicating through engaging the audience more physically and increasing the amount of knowledge provided during the conversation.

Body language mastery is essential to creating the most powerful presence in all human relationships. Individuals lacking this knowledge are vulnerable to confusion and find their attempts inadequate in expressing their thoughts. With the ability to distinguish between the various body language styles, everybody will achieve the competence required to excel in whatever pursuit they want.

Know and Understand Your Body Language

If you know it or not, body language is a significant force responsible for how everyone you encounter comes up with an opinion on you. Listening skills are a must and very necessary in many careers—particularly in careers where you support others to build positive relationships with clients. Whether you help people maintain their relationships, give people advice for business success or educate people about some other form of issue, they see your body language; displaying strong listening skills makes people feel relaxed.

Poor body language could result in something big being lost in you. It doesn't matter to you! Attentively and sincerely listen to every single word. It is the body language that makes you feel necessary to you and gives them the support they need. Understanding what the signs of a lousy listener are here is significant, and you will seek to rid yourself of all of these. When you have the habit of having your arms crossed around your stomach, whether you tap your feet impatiently, move whether turn and look away too much, or while listening, you tell the other person you're not interested in what he or she does. It will most likely lead to the termination of the partnership, which may cause significant business losses.

Ok, what would you do to continue transmitting constructive messages through your body language to the person you're talking to? You will first try to face the other party squarely on. Look not out to give a constructive signal. So at the moment of contact, we fall into the body's posture. You will take a transparent approach. You never have to leave your arms or legs folded; otherwise, the other guy would think you're not interested in listening to his point.

When you lean over when you speak to someone, your body language suggests you pay more attention to what he or she does. Leaning forward, by comparison, suggests you have little confidence whatsoever. The most pivotal aspect is eye touch. Seek to keep eye contact at all times. When you are looking down or turning down, it shows you have no interest in the topic and feel embarrassed.

However, the importance of a confident stance cannot be overlooked either. You don't want to be too uptight. You need not be too formal when talking to anyone, either. When you believe you have experienced significant defeats in the past due to your bad body language, you can instantly start following the above tips.

Behavior Imitation

Behavior imitation is something that can be used for good and for bad. Often, as children, we mimic the behavior of the people around us. It helps us to learn social norms. Also, it helps us feel like we fit into the crowd. Many traditions have been built off of people mimicking other people's behavior.

As we continue to grow up, we continue to imitate the people around us. Here again, it makes us feel as if we belong. Also, it can help us build relationships and understand the people around us more easily. While many people use behavior imitation for the right reasons, many others don't.

Criminals who are socially awkward tend to act like the people around them. It can make it harder to discern the good guys from the bad guys. It is a manipulation tactic that works quite well when people don't know how to behave appropriately. While some people are very good at mimicking those around them, it will be obvious when others try to do this. Cases of extreme social awkwardness will not allow the person to behave like those around them genuinely. It can be a tip to seeing what they may have planned after.

Another way that behavior imitation is prevalent with criminals is when they idolize someone or something. They will change their very persona to reflect that of which they admire. An excellent example of this is people that still follow the ideals of Adolf Hitler. The new generation of Nazis mimics the ways of old because they still believe his blasphemous thoughts to be true. It is truly scary behavior imitation.

Chapter 11. Using NLP to Manage People

When it comes to managing people effectively, it's essential that you first understand the non-verbal cues they provide to apply your skills toward influencing them. It is a necessary principle in using the NLP technique. Following are a few NLP techniques that can allow you to influence people's perception and thinking:

Deciphering Eye Movements

It is essential to realize and know the meaning of eye movements because each eye movement tells its tale. For instance, when searching for the right word or trying to remember a name, you automatically move your eyes in a certain way (most likely, squinting). Rolling the eyes signals contempt or exasperation.

Winking Indicates Flirtation or a Joke

Widening the eyes signals surprise or shock, even extreme excitement. The eyes can reveal much more about people's mental and emotional status, all on their own.

Once you understand what other people's thought processes are, you can accurately follow a course of action or dialogue which acknowledges the unspoken response, as signaled by the eyes. And as you may know, eye movements complement other communication forms such as hand movements, speech, and facial expressions.

Dilation of the pupils, breathing, angle of the body, and the hands' position—all these are complementary to the spoken message. Still, eye movement is essential in communication because every movement is influenced by particular senses and different parts of the brain.

Here is how you can generally interpret eye movement:

Visual Responsiveness

- **Eyes upward, then towards the right:** Whenever a person tilts eyes upward and then to the right, it means that the person is formulating a mental picture.
- **Eyes upward, then towards the left:** Whenever a person tilts eyes upward, followed by an eye movement to the left, it means the person recalls a particular image.
- **Eyes looking straight ahead:** Whenever someone focuses directly in front of them, this indicates that the person is not focused on anything in particular. That is the look often referred to as 'glazed.'

Auditory Responsiveness

- **Eyes looking towards the right:** When a person's eyes shift straight towards the right, it means the person is in the process of constructing a sound.
- **Eyes looking towards the left:** When a person's eyes shift straight towards the left, it indicates that the person recalls a sound.

Audio-Digital Responsiveness

- **Eyes looking downward, then switching to the left:** When someone drops their eyes and then proceeds to turn

their eyes to the left, this signals that the person is engaged in internal dialogue.
- **Eyes looking right down then left to right:** When a person looks down and then proceeds to turn their eyes to the left and then to the right in consecutive movements, it means the person is engaged in negative self-talk.

Kinesthetic Responsiveness

Here, the person looks directly down, only to turn the eyes to the right. That is an indication that the person is evaluating emotional status. It further indicates that the person is not at ease:

- Verbal responses

- Rhythmic speech

The idea here is not to be poetic as you speak, but to speak at a regular pace. The recommended pace of speaking is equated to the heartbeat, say, between 45 and 72 beats per minute. At that pace, you are likely to sustain the listener's attention and establish greater receptivity to what you're saying. While normal conversational speed averages about 140 words per minute, slowing down a little and taking time to pause is highly effective to sustain people's attention. Your regular cadence should be punctuated by fluctuations in tone and emphasis in order not to sound monotonous.

Repeating Key Words

When you try to influence someone, some keywords or phrases carry additional weight as far as your message is concerned. This speaking method is a way of embedding the message in the listener and subtly suggesting that your message is valid and worthy of reception. Repeating key words also suggests commitment, conviction, and mastery of the subject matter.

Using Strongly Suggestive Language

Use a supportive and positive language of what you are saying, using a selection set of strong, descriptive words or phrases. As you do this, you should observe the person you are speaking to closely, in a way that makes them feel as though you see right through them and aware of what they are thinking.

Don't be invasive about this or aggressive. Merely suggest that you have a keen appreciation of what makes people tick by way of your gaze. It places you in a dominant position, especially when accompanied by dominant body language, like "steepling." It helps to use suitable, complementary body language as you speak to underscore the message subtly.

Touching the Person Lightly, As You Speak

Touching the person as you speak to them draws their attention to you in a relaxed and familiar way. By employing this technique, you're preparing the listener to absorb what you say to them, a way of programming attentiveness. Those engaging in inter-gender conversations in the workplace should take great care with this technique, as it can lead to misunderstandings.

Using a Mixture of "Hot" and "Vague" Words

"Hot" words are those that tend to provoke specific sensations in the listener. When you use them to influence someone's thinking, it is advisable to use them in a suitable pattern. Examples of phrases containing hot words are: it means; feel free; see this; because; hear this. The effect of employing these words and phrases is that you're directing influencing the listener's state of mind, including how that person feels, imagines, and perceives.

You're also appealing to the sense most prevalent in the listener's perceptive style (as observed through the movement of their eyes). For example, the phrase "hear this" will appeal to those who indicate a tendency to respond most actively to auditory stimuli.

Using the Interspersal Technique

The interspersal technique states one thing while hoping to impress on the listener something entirely different. For example, you could make a positive statement like:

"John is very generous, but some people take advantage of him and treat him as gullible."

When someone hears this statement, the likely assumption is that you want people to appreciate John's generosity. That is likely to be the message heard, and yet, the subtext is that while John is generous, he is also considered gullible and, thus, at a disadvantage in life when it comes to other people. Your hidden agenda may influence the listener to think of John as gullible, which calls into question his judgment. So, emphasize the words "but" and "gullible."

The word "but" serves to transition the perceived compliment to John to an implicit slight. The techniques just described form strategies in the service of influencing people.

They're not intended to force a viewpoint or to control people's behavior for nefarious ends. These techniques are intended to modify undesirable behaviors, resulting in workplace difficulties, including staff failure to work well together or complete team projects.

They're also accommodating in relationships with young people and children, whether at home or in a learning environment.

Techniques of subtle manipulative effects like those described, though capable of influencing people and their behavior, don't amount to anything even approaching coercion. The person being spoken to chooses all responses and is merely influenced or steered toward those responses.

Chapter 12. Protecting Yourself From NLP Mind Control

Now we get how the whole thing works, we're not that fond of it, but we understand the basics. The main question now, though, is how do you guard against it? That's really what we've been trying to figure out this whole time. How do you prevent someone from pulling all that NLP mumbo jumbo on you when you're not looking? This part of the guide is for you because we have a few pointers for you.

Beware of Matchers

The first thing you're going to want to do is to take in and apply everything you've just learned. Remember all that stuff about matching and mirroring? Well, now you need to be on the lookout for it. When you speak to someone you think is trying to control you, make a point to note how they react to your body language. Are they sitting in the same pattern you are? Are they copying your movements as well?

If you're unsure, try testing it out by changing your posture and then wait to see if they mimic it. With pro NLP practitioners, the mimicking may be a bit subtler and a bit more delayed, but the unskilled ones are a total giveaway. They'll copy the posture right away, and automatically, you know what you're up against.

Now that you know, you can either call them out on their behavior or, if you want to have a little fun, start applying NLP on them to confuse them! Not only will you catch them off guard, but if you can pull it off, you can get them to tell you what their whole ploy was all about and who put them up to it. Total win!

Consciously Infuse Randomness in Your Eye Movement

When it comes to confusing your opponent and playing them at their own game, there is little going to give you the same amount of satisfaction as random play. Random eye movements are like going to the gym with your iPod on shuffle. Nobody knows what's coming on after. It's basically like trolling your manipulators in real-time, and it can be quite fun.

Any NLP user worth their salt is going to go in hard with the whole eye movement thing. It is because your eye movements tell them how you assess and store information, which is precisely why some people can tell if you are lying or cheating just by looking at your eyes. When they say your eyes speak volumes, this is what they mean!

So how do you avoid being read by an NLP practitioner? Simple, use random eye movements. As you are speaking, make a point to look left or right or up or down. You can even make a game of it. Left for complex sentences, down for every question, and simple sentences can go right or up, depending on whether they start with a vowel.

Pick Up on Ambiguity

One of the tricks that NLP kind of sneaks in from hypnotherapy is the full use of vague, unclear language. A great example of the use of this technique is Donald Trump's "Make America Great" Again Campaign.

Even though the now-president went around campaigning about making a better version of America, he never really broke down what that meant. It was such a hazy term that it could mean anything to anyone, and that was precisely what he wanted.

Whenever anyone starts using stuff like that on you, such as "release your inner troubles and feel the world move slowly around you in conjunction with your prospective earthly successes." What you're doing is allowing hypnotherapy to program your internal state in a specific form. It helps the other person when they then try to convince you to do something that benefits them.

Anytime you feel that someone is trying to do something like that to you, force yourself to snap out of it and ask specific questions, "What exactly do you mean by 'great'?" or "What potential are you talking about?" Take note; all you have to do is point it out. Once you've done that, you're home free!

Be Hypersensitive to People Permitting You to Do Stuff

The other thing you should watch out for? Permissive language. When a person says something like "you can do XYZ" or "Feel free to make yourself at home" or even something tempting like, "If you want, you can borrow the new Avengers movie from me," what they are doing is preparing you to enter into a trance state. You see, experienced NLP users never outright tell their subjects to do anything. They suggest, recommend, or allow. In this way, the subject feels like they are in control, whereas control was wiped out a long time ago in reality! So then, feel free to say no thanks!

Read Between the Lines

We're onto reading between the lines. You have to keep in mind that people who use or people who are using NLP to control you or to manipulate you tend to use specific controlled langue, and nine out of ten times, you are not going to know what hit you.

How do they do it? Double meanings. And you'll find them in the unexpected places, so skilled NLP users who are good at what they do know how to use double meaning infused sentences to get you to think the way they want you to. Imagine that you are the evil witch's neighbor from the Hansel and Gretel story; now you don't eat kids, but you do have a thing for snacks. Your NLP user, A.K.A "the evil witch" comes up to you and says, "Children make nutritious snacks, just in case you were wondering." Sure the witch claims she was talking about their production capacity, but what you heard and processed was something a little different, and already you're a bit more inclined to take a little nibble.

Be Attentive

You need to be very careful about how much attention you are paying to your surroundings and what's going on in them. We get you that you can't always be super alert, but you need to know that you are vulnerable when you aren't alert. For example, an essential tactic that employers use when negotiating salary packages is waiting until the employee in question seems a little off and then jumping in. Saying that they haven't negotiated a pay difference for Tom, Dick, and Harry and don't foresee a lot of change in the other employees. Not much change at all, they repeat. Automatically, now that you are asked how much change in salary you expect, you say not much change—congratulations! You've just been programmed!

Watch Your Mouth

Another important tip? Watch what you say. Master manipulators tend to create a false sense of urgency to make you feel that you have to do this particular thing by this specific time, or else something drastic will happen. You don't have a choice. You have to do this now! What do you do? Well, nothing. Yes, seriously, nothing. Never make any important decisions at the drop of a hat. Chances are you're not the president of the United States, meaning no nuclear codes lie with you, which of course, means that you don't need to make any immediate decisions without consulting people. You don't have to make any quick decisions at all.

Sit tight. Getting you to commit is a classic dark psychology move to create a sense of obligation after being exploited. Please don't fall for it!

Trust Your Gut

And your final rule, which also happens to be your most important, is to trust your gut. Your instincts know a lot more than you do, mostly because your subconscious mind is processing signs and symbols at a rate your conscious brain can't even begin to fathom. So if it is out there telling you that something is up and that something needs to be done about it, then you need to make sure that you are on your guard ready to get things done because, like a used car salesman, you are more likely than not in the hands of a master practitioner.

Chapter 13. Smart and Wise Goal-Setting Using Neuro-Linguistics

NLP or Neuro-Linguistic Programming explores how you think and feel. It examines the inner language that you usually use to represent your life experiences. It studies human interaction and achievement and uses this knowledge to help you achieve excellence in all aspects of your life.

The concepts behind NLP techniques are based on the fact that you already have the necessary internal resources and capabilities to effectively change your life and the lives of the people around you. NLP helps you in your goal setting and in taking the necessary actions to realize your goal.

Easy NLP Techniques to Help You Achieve Your Goals

Be Specific About the Things That You Want

It repeatedly reiterates what has been echoed: you must have a clear understanding of what it is that you exactly want. You need to have a noticeable or clear vision of what you are aiming for. Look at it this way; imagine you are sailing in the middle of the ocean. Without a clear vision of where you want to go and just going with the flow and where the water will take you, you will fail. If you are blindly going through life, how do you expect to get to where you want to go?

Ask Yourself What You Want

NLP recommends asking questions like: "If I continue doing the things I am doing now, where will I be a year from now?" "Am I happy where I am now and the direction I am going?" "If I am not happy, what should I do instead? What would make me happy?" When you can answer similar questions, it will be easier to identify what you want.

Create Mental Images of Your Goals

The moment you have established what you want to achieve, put them into writing. If buying your dream house, create images of the actual house, including the smallest details as design, location, and neighborhood. You must create powerful internal images and play them on your mind over and over. Be realistic and think about actual colors, what you see around, the smell of the flowers, or the sound of your neighbor's dog barking in the background. Create a "movie" in your mind. Go as far as seeing what you are wearing on that particular day that you are finally buying the house. Make the movie as detailed as possible, as if it is happening. It is bringing visualization techniques to a higher level.

Write Your Goals As If They Are Already Being Realized and Focus on Them

You might find it helpful to use words in the present tense and then create the images. You'll create a more powerful impact if you picture your goal like it is happening right this very moment. Keep in mind that NLP teaches you and allows you to move towards the things you intently focus on. By doing so, you are attracting success. This technique will enable you to influence what the universe gives you. You must maintain your focus on a clear positive image of what you want you to achieve, in this case, buying your dream house. Throughout your journey towards attaining your goal, you have to maintain your focus on that goal.

Use Your Goal As Your Motivation to Keep on Moving Toward It

Think of action items that will bring you closer to your goal. Devise plans of action on how you can continue to move forward. Imagine that you are already there at the "finish line" and look back at how you were able to get there. It might help if you imagine a physical mind with several essential points. It is the path that you have to take to reach the realization of your goal. There may be obstacles, but if you keep your focus on the result, you'll think of ways to overcome those obstacles and continue with your journey. Having a clear picture of the things you have to do to reach your goal helps you achieve it.

Look for a Role Model

Look for a person you can look up to and learn from. Read their success stories. Take pointers from them or if you cannot reach them, find resources that speak about them. Most stories of famous and successful people contain tips and guidelines on how they attained their current stature. Watch video clips, testimonies, and books about them. Learn from their life lessons and mistakes.

Act!

You have the goals, and you have established what you want to do, but you'll never achieve anything if you don't begin to act. Nothing and no one can achieve your goals for you, you have to act, and it is the first step you have to take. Act to begin moving towards the fulfillment of your goals. If you want to buy a house, start saving or considering taking on additional income sources. One small step is actually what you need to get you going.

Plan!

Once you have acted on your goal, you have to make sure that you have a concrete plan to achieve your goal. You have to have a timescale. As you move towards attaining your goal, continue to stay focused, and create positive images of the final goal in your mind.

Exude Positivity

Having confidence doesn't mean you won't fail. It means that while you might encounter challenges, you remain confident to push forward. You might commit a misstep, but if you use that as an opportunity to learn, then you'll get back on track.

Be Flexible

Things do not turn out the way you want to, even if you work hard at it. You need to keep on going, move forward, and try other options.

Keep on Going

You might fail along the way, and you might encounter rejection, but that shouldn't discourage you from continuing to follow your dreams. Keep on moving forward.

Chapter 14. Introduction of Persuasion

Persuasion is the ability to transmit ideas and disseminate them by those who act as recipients. It translates more effectively as the ability that human beings have through a relationship, to convince others. Persuasion is a tool that can be used in fields such as marketing, advertising, and commerce, basically sectors of the economy in which the public is sensitive to various interactions with environmental media and where the decision is the objective of who persuades.

How Does it Work?

Let us elaborate on a scene in which a seller wants his products to be acquired by the buyers; besides being useful, they must be attractive and, in one way or another, more desirable than that of the competition. It is achieved with persuasion, which attracts clients by offering the best product or service attributes, effectively providing comfort to the buyer by relating the most promotional aspects to the most personal. In turn, persuasion generates competition and demand in the market, generating dynamism of intentions and offers that fosters sustainable economies.

Another use of persuasion that we see in a society continually is in the application of the law. In a trial, the lawyers, using the law as the main tool, use the elements in their favor and persuade the jury and the judge that they are valid to win the case.

We are always waiting for others who live in our environment to reproduce or share our ideas; even unintentionally, people seek to persuade others to fulfill their ends. A wife who asks her husband to optimize expenses is trying to convince him that it is the best for both. Either way, each person's ideas will be interpreted as an intention for others to apply and build their ideas based on the initial idea. Persuasion can be so extreme that they can change the way a person thinks. It all depends on what the person who persuades another looks for.

Psychological Tricks to Increase Your Persuasive Power

Evaluate Context and Time

The foundation for increasing your power of persuasion is context and the exact time. The first requirement sets a standard for what is acceptable and can be done, while the right timing makes your chances increase or decrease considerably. Trying to persuade your boss to raise you well when he is nervous or talking about an important issue is not a timely approach. Therefore, having this notion of timing is critical in the persuasion process.

Remember That Persuasion Is Different from Manipulation

To manipulate is to coerce someone into doing something that is not in their best interest. However, persuasion is the art of persuading people to do something that is in their interest and benefits you.

Speak What People Want to Hear

You will not be able to persuade someone who has no interest in what you are saying. Generally, people are interested in themselves and spend most of their time thinking about money, love, or health. Therefore, to increase your persuasion power, it is necessary to learn to talk to people about themselves consistently. Remember: If you show interest in what they want and say, you will always have your attention.

Be Persistent

Have you noticed that historical figures who persuaded large masses achieved this with much persistence in their messages? If you focus on demonstrating value and staying focused, you are much more likely to get what you want.

Greet People Sincerely

We are all affected by compliments, whether we like it or not. And people tend to believe more in someone who gives them good feelings. So greet people when they deserve it, highlight their qualities and achievements. You will see how, practically and honestly, you will be able to persuade someone more easily. Investing in reciprocity is also very effective in this process; after all, when you do something for someone, that person feels compelled to do something for you too. It is part of the evolution of our DNA.

Create a Sense of Urgency

To increase your persuasive power, you need to create a sense of urgency in people by making them want something or act right now. If you're not motivated enough to want something right now, you probably won't like it in the future. Therefore, invest in your power of persuasion in the present, betting on the urgency of things.

Value the Images

Remember: what we see is more important than what we hear. Therefore, hone your first impressions to increase your persuasive power by increasing your ability to paint an image of experience you can offer others in the future.

Be Flexible and Communicate Simply

Have you noticed how flexible children are in their behaviors? They do everything, in every means they can to get what they want from their parents, and most of the time, they can. Therefore, adopting a rigid posture is never a good way to increase your persuasive power. Communicating is also another important point because the art of persuasion is to simplify something so that it is quick and straightforward to understand.

Chapter 15. History of Persuasion

The persuasion can be traced back to Greek origins. It was used as a tool by great orators to get their message across to the common folk. For a country that has created the political frameworks behind democracy, persuasion was immensity popular. If you have ever taken an advanced writing class that went over rhetorical analysis, you might recognize the three rhetorical modes of pathos, ethos, and logos. Aristotle billed these as the three main appeals that an orator could make to move their audience.

Its usage implies that the audience is a malleable entity, like putty. A skilled orator's words can manipulate the audience like a child might manipulate a piece of putty. Other times, persuasion is used to rile up an already popular cause, to begin with, but that had been up to that point undisclosed.

The three rhetorical modes are important because they represent three different attack vectors that a manipulator might use to persuade their audience. Again, any form of persuasion is a type of mental manipulation, but it doesn't become a psychological attack until it becomes malicious. In other words, there is a difference between plain old persuasive arguments and using persuasion to carry out dark psychology.

Regular persuasion is the type that might make you vote for a candidate or buy some product (though some would argue that modern-day advertising has dark psychology aspects). On the other hand, malicious persuasion might entice you to go against your set of morals and beliefs. This sort of persuasion is dangerous because an attacker's arguments may seem very convincing to you when, in reality, they are just cleverly designed to trick you. At the same time, the persuasion is being used to benefit someone else.

The dark psychology mindset tells us that there are people out there with less than kind objectives. They may be after your wealth, your emotional labor, your body, your mind, or just a few minutes of your attention. And all of this is theoretically possible through the levying of persuasive techniques. But first, we should talk about everyday persuasion in the traditional sense.

Modern-Day Aristotle

No matter what persuasive argument you come across, they will have all of the semblances of Aristotle's appeals, mixed in with a modern "secret sauce" that is unique to the persuader (and indeed the situation). It is still worth talking about persuasion and persuasive arguments because they are the cornerstone of all manipulation types. If a manipulator were a boxer, persuasion techniques would be like their left jab. Not as powerful as a KO punch, but still the punch that lands them the most points and slows down their opponent.

A modern-day Aristotle can be anyone. A politician, a used car salesman, even your mother is trying to convince you to move closer to home. All of these would be Aristotle's have something in common: they want something from you. And it is your job to decide whether their needs are genuine and desirable for all parties. They will no doubt stop at anything to convince you that they are. To do this, you have to separate their argument from the chaff. For persuasive techniques, the chaff is usually the bubbly language or the sharp edge in their arguments that cut you into you.

But beware. Just because it cuts you, it doesn't mean that it is deep or meaningful to you in any way. Many skillful persuaders will only pander to already preconceived notions that their audiences may have. They say something that they know their audience will like and instantly become that much more credible.

But someone trying to come up with a novel argument will first have to design a rhetorical strategy using any of the three rhetorical modes available. It is true whether they are trying to form an essay, a speech, or persuade you into doing something. The world of sales is chock-full of strategies used designed to get you to buy. A competent salesperson may try to get to know you first (especially if the purchase is large, like a new house or car). They wish to form a relationship on a first-name basis and then pose as a close friend.

In the world of sales, the only thing that matters is the purchase. If a client decides to buy, then whatever strategies used to make that sale are fair game. It opens the ground for deploying several different types of psychological tricks against the unsuspecting client. For example, a salesperson may introduce them to a high-end item that is purposely out of their buying range and then redirect them towards an item of similar functionality perceived as being more affordable.

A family looking to buy a new laptop for their college-bound son may be directed towards the expensive and latest Apple laptop product only to realize that it is well out of their budget. The savvy salesperson can then walk them to the Windows computers aisle and show them an alternative product that is the same color as an Apple computer but has a different operating system and is slightly less performative. Now, that other laptop may still be a flagship item and have a sizable price tag, but it is perceived as a good buy by the family because the salesperson showed them an item they believe to be state of the art.

Such tricks are less persuasive strategies than they are crude psychological manipulation. More psychological persuasion involves more trickery and deception—the type of things one would expect except dark psychology techniques. Indeed, the salesman trick of going high and then going low can pass as a type of emotional manipulation. It is subtle, but there is clear pandering towards what a client believes their money can buy them. First, they are shown what is considered to be the "it" product. But since they can't afford it, the salesman puts them on an emotional roller coaster of desire.

In a way, it is a projection of what the client believes they deserve. Sure, they can't afford the best, but since they feel like they deserve the best (and since the salesman believes they deserve the best), buying the other best product is an easy choice. And if they can afford the high-end object the salesman shows them first, their job is already finished. In other words, whether the client buys the expensive item or the lesser expensive one, the salesman still wins. It is a perfect example of a psychological manipulation that is difficult to detect in the moment's heat and has a high success rate.

Chapter 16. Six Principles of Persuasion

To learn and enhance the art of persuasion, you need to be aware of the underlying principles that will enable you to harness your influence. Generally, Human beings are a touchy lot; one wrong move and you're going to lose all ability to persuade people to join your team. You need to make critical decisions that are guided by the necessary fundamental principles. Reciprocity, consistency, social evidence, liking, authority, and scarcity are the six principles of persuasion.

Reciprocity Principle

Reciprocity does to others as you would have them do to you. Reciprocity calls for respect and kindness as you go about your everyday experiences. It's a good thing to show kindness to others that makes others feel better about your interaction. Besides that, your way of earning chips that you can cash in after is to do well. If you have been very nice and kind to someone else, you have a better chance that they will be nice and kind to you.

If you are hoping to persuade a person, you must decently behave towards them. Speak a word of kindness, give them a favor, or even buy them a gift. They will be more agreeable after when you need to convince them to do something. After all, you have proved yourself to be a kind human being who cares for him.

The Cohesion Principle

Consistency in persuasion works this way: once you have convinced them to agree to smaller ones, people are more likely to commit to bigger tasks or favors. That is, if you get them to spring a puddle for you, you can get someone to swim oceans for you. A few studies have been done to support this hypothesis. For example, in one study, a group of researchers asked some homeowners to put up a hideous Drive Safely billboard on their front lawn. Very few homeowners declared yes. However, the researchers had to take a different approach to the experiment: first, they got homeowners to agree to the small commitment to putting up a Drive Safely postcard in their home's front windows. Ten days after, they returned with the request for a billboard. This time, despite its lack of aesthetic appeal, more homeowners agreed to put up the billboard. The reason for this is that the homeowners subconsciously felt compelled to keep up with their earlier reaction.

The technique of foot-in-the-door compliance is premised on consistency. It means getting people to consent to a bigger request by first using smaller requests to check the waters. If you want to execute this strategy cleverly, your target will need to be trained to be consistent with their responses to your question.

The Liking Principle

If some people like you, they're more likely to fulfill your demands, no matter what that may be. A person who is unlike and who is also unlikeable will hear no more times than a well-liked person. But how is it that you get people to like you? The secret to being loved is a combination of three main factors, according to science. First of all, people prefer the ones close to them. You must find common ground with them to look close to the person you are trying to convince. For example, many foreigners have learned that learning and speaking the local language is the simplest way to become more likable. You also need and practice to be mindful of is flattery while making yourself more likable. If you are using it well, flattery will open many doors for you.

Citizens prefer those paying attention to them. If you want to ask someone to do something for you, start by offering them a genuine compliment first. Just because this is called flattery doesn't mean you need to be effusive about it. Too excessive in your praise will be counterproductive to your need to be liked. Last but not least, be the kind of person that is usually pleasant and cooperative in achieving mutual goals, and you will be one step closer to being pleasant. If you're always stepping on the toes of others to get what you want, you'll have very few friends, and this won't help your case when you need to convince someone in the future. Remember, being pleasant and cooperative doesn't imply being a doormat. Sometimes, it merely means putting some little effort into helping a person achieve a vital goal. For example, if a colleague struggles with a due report, offer to help them with the printing and mailing process. It's not a lot of work, but you're going to go from an uninvolved, unwritten colleague to a kind and helpful colleague. You can cash this chip after if you wish.

The Authority Theory

Compared to a complete newbie, a person who is an authority figure in a particular field will have an easier time influencing others. If you want to persuade or influence more people to do something specific, you need to build your credibility by making yourself seem like you have expertise in whatever field you play. This principle is a key reason why professionals in their field display their diplomas. Think about it—when, for example, you step into a therapist's office, you would probably deliberately look out for the sort of qualifications they have hanging on their walls. If your therapist has many credentials displayed in this way, you will probably feel a sense of comfort in their expertise and experience. As such, you'll quickly accept and follow any advice they have for you. Essentially the therapist has managed to influence you without even saying a word.

It's a fact that if you're the only one talking about it, your authority won't be taken very seriously. As such, you have to make sure, so to speak, that you recruit others to beat the drums on your behalf. Subtle ways exist to do this. You can identify a field in the office you are passionate about and become that field's office guru. It could be Microsoft Excel or Reporting for some people. The guy known as the Excel office guru will have a much easier time getting things out of people because they already know he knows what he's talking about. He has also proved to be likable and helpful by solving all of their problems with Excel, and his colleagues may want to pay him back in some way. You don't need to learn Excel to make your mark around the world.

Scarcity Principle

The laws of supply and demand are easy and straightforward in economics: when supply is low and demand is high, prices rise. To translate this, the value of scarcity builds. If you are a business person who wants to persuade people to purchase your product or service, it highlights that the product is on offer for only a limited time. Furthermore, let the clients know that they will lose significantly if they do not access this product on time. If the marketing message is packaged in this way, more people will be rushing to beat the time limit on your product.

It is essential to become a scarce product yourself in the business and personal relations world. If you're not there for others whenever they need you, you'll quickly lose your worth. If you want to remain your aura of mystery and power around you, you must learn the art of being inaccessible and unavailable. When you appear, your word will be respected more than a person's word that continuously appears and speaks out of all importance and meaning.

The Consensus Theory

People look at others similar to them in everyday interactions for clues about what to do or say. An individual who is a good influencer knows that buying into their idea is all it takes is one individual, and the whole crowd does. There are different ways you can apply the consensus principle to your benefit. For example, in an office setting, you can get a part of the staff to agree to a cause and champion that causes their colleagues to do so. These colleagues are more likely to be convinced of the worthy cause because their peers have said so.

For example, if you've ever purchased anything from Amazon, you might have seen that it includes a part showing the other items purchased by clients who ordered the product you just purchased. How does that segment affect you as a buyer? More often than not, you'll probably consider buying those other items because they were bought by these clients who have similar tastes and needs to yours. Initially, you may not have planned to buy the additional items, but just the fact that others did it will make you think you also need to. That is, in effect, the principle of consensus.

Chapter 17. Theories on Persuasion

There are a few different theories on persuasion that we should start to understand. Before we talk about these, let's take a more in-depth look at what processes persuasion might be done through. How can we completely change the way we are thinking or feeling based on another person's ability to alter our feelings? There are a few core elements to what persuasion is and what you can use to define this process.

Persuasion is when a message is transferred from one person to the other. This message might be a way of life, such as religion. Have you ever seen signs of someone wanting to share their religion with you? Maybe they have passed free information like brochures or mini booklets to get you on their side. It is an example of how others might try to convince you of their messages. They will be using symbols and words to try and get you to understand where they are coming from. Some will go as far as to scare you as well, making you think that something bad might happen to you if you choose not to follow what they're stating. Persuasion goes as far back as human history does. Some methods of persuasion have been natural in our society. There are other times when persuasion has been a little more forced. Perhaps it is a physical skill ingrained in the anatomy that we use to help us survive. It could simply be a survival tactic or deeply ingrained in our society and the language we use.

Persuasion is always going to be more positive when you can give the other person their freedom to choose. When you take that freedom away and become more forceful, this can turn into manipulation, brainwashing, and other dark psychology methods. We will break all three of these down for you to better recognize the different levels of persuasive behavior. First, let's start to talk about some other theories about how and why persuasion can be so effective.

The first one is conditioning theory. It explains how prolonged exposure could be "conditioning" us to fall more efficiently for a message. It is something easily seen on the level of advertisements. Think of a brand, specifically maybe a candy brand that you like. Whatever this is, recall the last time you saw an advertisement for it. They will use signs of the actual product and what this might look like. In a commercial, they might show someone eating it with the same branded colors in the background. Maybe they have a simple phrase or logo that you remember immediately without even trying. Then, you make your way to a grocery store and see this same product with the same colors and are more inclined to purchase this because you have already been conditioned to do so. If you had never seen an advertisement for the product, you might not notice the display of candy sitting there when you walk in the store, but they have already planted this idea in your head, so you're way more willing actually to purchase this.

The other theory that we have is the cognitive dissonance theory. It states how we will always be looking for ways to connect our thoughts and behaviors with reality. Even if you have thoughts different from what you do, your brain will look for ways to justify this kind of behavior. For example, let's say that you are overweight, and you don't want to be. You'd love it if you could lose thirty pounds. However, you continue to eat unhealthy junk food and skip the gym every day. Your actions are not aligning with your beliefs, and this creates cognitive dissonance. It is essential because it will show how your brain can be persuaded easily even when you know certain information isn't true. Your brain wants your actions to match your beliefs, so it will convince you to do one of two things. You can either find that motivation to go to the gym and eat healthier and then your actions match your beliefs of wanting to lose weight. Alternatively, your mind might instead convince you that there is nothing wrong with being unhealthy. You might assure yourself that what you are told about your health is all a lie, or maybe that you don't deserve even to have a healthy body. Whatever it is, your brain is going to try and fill in those blanks and make you believe something that isn't entirely true, all so that your actions align with your belief. It is something that might end up hurting others in the long run. Think of a crazy cult leader. They will have things that they believe, and after a while, it might not be just enough for them to be the only ones to believe this. Instead of changing their mind about their beliefs, they might try to convince others to believe the same thing in an attempt to validate their perspective. It can be toxic and damaging behavior, but it is something that our brain might naturally do.

These theories are essential to understand because they will start to give you a little insight into how or why someone might be trying to convince themselves or others of their message. We will talk about the basic persuasion techniques that people use soon, but we must first understand the motive. If you can't discover a motive behind someone's persuasion, then they might not necessarily be trying to be manipulative, intentionally or not. Always ask, "Why are they doing this?" whenever you might be questioning someone's goal for whether or not they are manipulative.

Chapter 18. Persuasion Techniques

Persuasion techniques also have their level. Whether you are a beginner, an intermediate one, or an advanced user of persuasion of techniques, you should be able to discern when to apply these techniques to maximize their effectiveness.

Basic Persuasion Techniques

By Association

It is one persuasion technique commonly used by people who are in the early stage of improving their influencing skills. With this technique, you try to link the particular service, product, or idea with another thing that is already liked by your target audience. Association is a powerful technique, although it does not explicitly claim that you will achieve these things.

Let's take an example—associating the concept of 'family' with the brand such as Coke through emotional transfer has been an effective tool for many years. The term 'victory' has also been associated with another brand, 'Nike.'

By Bandwagon

Another persuasion technique that can be used by newbies is the Bandwagon method. What you want to achieve is to make other people realize that 'everyone else is already doing it, and so should you.' Most people want to have a sense of belonging, and they do not want to be left behind. So, in this technique, your ultimate goal is to make sure that your prospect is ready to hop on the bandwagon with you.

By Testimonials

OK, this is probably one of the most common methods, yet it works well despite being around for decades. It is because people tend to pay extra attention to celebrities. Whether we admit or not, following a celebrity or being a fan is one of the guilty pleasures anyone can have. When big brands use celebrities, famous athletes, and models, it is easier to influence people into trying the same product.

By Using Humor

Many of the ads that we usually remember are because of the humor injected into it. When we see them, we laugh, and we feel good. Thus, it becomes a great persuasion tool. When you associate your product or service with something that makes people 'feel good,' it becomes easier to influence them. It performs or works when it comes to relationships too. When you can be intelligently funny to someone, it becomes a lot easier to influence him or her to continue to like you.

By Repetition

As they say, repetition is the key to retention. To influence and persuade people, you should be able to repeat your message subtly and in various ways. Have you ever experienced humming or singing an ad jingle in your head? You may not like the product itself, but since you see the ad almost every day over the Web, on TV, or even in print ads, something about it sticks. When it sticks, it becomes a lot less complex to influence the person.

By Experts

It is a form of testimonials too. Commonly, people would look at the logical reasoning or expert claims behind a particular item. If you are an expert in one area, it would be easier to find an expert testimonial. For instance, if your prospective clients are parents or moms—then the expert should be a mom as well who is known in a particular field.

By Bribery

Yes, we all love freebies, don't we? It is one technique you can employ, as well. When you want to influence people, give them more than they expect—discount, promo, holidays, etc. Influencing people also means giving them good value for money, good returns on their investments, etc. As you hone your skills, you will then influence more effectively using the succeeding techniques.

Intermediate Persuasion Techniques

By Being Charismatic

For instance, if you present yourself to be bold, confident, strong, and sleek, you could expect people to listen to you more. Like, if you get persuaded into buying something if the endorser itself is someone that tickles your fancy.

By Presenting Novel Ideas

People love new things. It is no longer surprising that people place great faith in technological advancements. One method to influence people is by presenting an idea that is new to them. Giving something novel gives them that sense of pride in being one of the first to get it.

By Using Rhetorical Questions

One of the most useful or effective ways to elicit reactions from people is by asking them questions. Questions such as, "Do you want to become a millionaire before you hit 30?" "Do you want to live debt-free?" "Do you want to be as stunning as Monica Bellucci?"—these are all set up to build alignment and to establish rapport before the sales pitch takes over. Usually, these are the type of questions that would capture the attention so that your prospect would stay longer and listen to the sales pitch.

By Nostalgia

It is the opposite method of #9 By Presenting Novel Ideas. In this method, you try to influence people by making them excited about the 'good old days.' As changes come rapidly, some people get tired of it and want to get back to the days when life is simpler. A good example is the revival of the Nokia 3310 in this time of advanced smartphones or that easy-to-prepare food that brings back childhood memories.

By Offering Simple Solutions

We live in a complicated or complex world, and people are continually seeking simpler solutions. If you intend to influence someone or a target market, offer relief by proposing a simple solution to any problem. For instance, advertisers like the concept of 'one-stop-shop' for any particular service, enabling consumers to address their multiple needs in one place.

By Showing Slippery Slope

It is quite similar to using 'fear' as a weapon for influence. Instead of predicting positive results, you can influence people by showing them the looming dangers of not acting and deciding immediately. For instance, to influence and persuade people to invest, you could show the possible scenarios when the recession kicks in. Anything that could give them a picture of what could happen if they do not do something can be used in this technique.

By Presenting Scientific Evidence

In this method, you get to present facts that would eventually influence someone to decide instantly. Many people tend to consider themselves 'people of Science,' or those keen on knowing one product's scientific principle before buying them. For case, if you are trying to sell a collagen-based skincare product, you need to explain the role of collagen and what it does in the biological makeup of the skin. By showing pretty girls using it in ads may not be sufficient.

You will learn the techniques that influencers of the advanced level users. Note that you do not have to jump to this list right away. You can utilize any from the recent list to know which suits your style best.

Advanced Persuasion Techniques

By Analogy

A good analogy helps in influencing people and creates a sense of truthfulness, which helps establish your credibility. A weak analogy, on the other hand, can instantly break interest. When using this method, make sure the comparison is still logical and not over the top.

By Understanding Group Dynamics

It is a more intense version of the 'Bandwagon' technique. Understanding the specific beliefs of a group of people will help understand the influence method to use. For occasion, if you are selling a high-end product, you would certainly look for a market that can afford them. However, you can also capture the market that aspires to be part of the group.

Ad Hominem

It is a Latin phrase that means 'against the man.' In this technique, you do not influence people by attacking a product, but the maker itself. This method is also referred to as 'attacking the messenger.' It takes skills and a colossal amount of research to do this. Incorrect use of this method may lead to other complex problems, so use this with care and discretion.

By Scapegoating Method

It is one powerful method that politicians of today make use of influence voters. They tend to highlight the failures of former politicians or leaders to capture the trust of the voters. Another example is when they blame a particular person, organization, or race for a problem.

One clear example here is when politicians vying for a position in an incoming election would blame the undocumented immigrants for the rising unemployment rate. Unemployment itself is a complex matter that is bound by multiple factors.

Knowing the Right Timing

Timing is of the essence even when it comes to influencing. You need to know what is happening around you, current affairs, and current problems that need immediate solutions. For instance, an ill-timed proposal can instantly go up in smoke when people find the timing irrelevant.

Card Stacking

In this method, you do not tell the whole story but only select the parts considered favorable to your audience or target market. While this could work well, it is imperative to know how you could justify the 'hiding' of the facts. Again, as this is a tricky method, you need to be 'great' to make it work.

As you can see, there are 'dirty' tricks that people can do to influence people. While they are entirely incorrect, it takes a great deal of care, courage, and common sense to use them. If you are not exactly comfortable using advanced techniques, you can still use the beginner and intermediate methods.

Remember, each one of us has an influencing style that we are most comfortable with. Evaluate yourself and find your own. If you have finally grasped how you could do better, it's now time to learn how you could increase your influence in this digital era.

Chapter 19. Difference Between Persuasion and Manipulation

Many people fail to recognize the nuances between manipulation and persuasion. Although both seek to convince someone else to do something else, they are quite different in enough key ways to be classified entirely differently. One is only beneficial to the manipulator (manipulation), while the other ideally, should benefit both people. Because of these key differences, manipulation becomes far more insidious than persuasion. The manipulator sees the other person as a tool, a means to an end, whereas the persuader sees the other person as a partner.

Defining Persuasion

Though persuasion involves changing someone else's mind, it is not necessarily a bad thing—there are plenty of ways to use persuasion innocently or benevolently. Persuasion is any method that will actively change the thoughts, emotions, actions, or attitudes of another person toward another person or thing. This change is seen as a persuasion. It can be done inwardly toward oneself by changing one's attitudes or being done to other people.

Usually, persuasion is used as a form of influence—it is everywhere. It is present in ads, politics, schools, professions, and just about everywhere you could think of. If you can think of something, chances are there is some persuasive layer to it somewhere and somehow.

When persuading someone, four key elements must be present. These four elements are:

- Someone who is doing the persuading

- The message or the persuasion

- A target recipient for the persuasion

- A context that the persuasion is received

Each of these four key elements must be present for something to be considered persuasive. Of course, this means that manipulation would fall within the category of persuasion as well.

Defining Manipulation

In psychology, manipulation is a type of influence or persuasion, but unlike regular persuasion, manipulation is covert, deceptive, or underhanded. It means that, unlike regular persuasion, which seeks to be most honest, manipulation is often untrustworthy. The manipulator will have no concern about lying about the situation or attempting to coerce the target into believing something, so long as he gets what he wants.

The manipulator seeks only to serve himself further—he does not care about the target and does not care about hurting the target. The target is seen as little more than collateral damage—a necessary to get the desired results. As such, manipulation tactics are often quite exploitative and almost always meant to be insidious and harmful.

Successful manipulation requires three key concepts to happen. These three are:

- Concealing the intentions and behaviors while remaining friendly upfront

- Understanding the ways the victim or target is vulnerable and using those vulnerabilities to the manipulator's advantage.

- Being ruthless enough to not care about the harm caused to the victim

Manipulation can take several different forms, but most of them follow the covert, harmful, and causing no guilt to the manipulator.

Key Differences

Ultimately, persuasion and manipulation are quite similar: They are both forms of social influence, but that is where the similarities end. While persuasion is generally positive, even within dark psychology, manipulation is not. Manipulation is harmful, ruthless, and insidious in every way, shape, and form.

When you are trying to choose whether something is manipulative or persuasive, there are a few questions you can ask yourself to decide. This simple test can allow you to analyze what you are doing and say to ensure you are making the best choices. If you are not looking to manipulate, but the questions tell you that you are erring on the manipulation side, you know to tone it down slightly, lightening up on the manipulative factors. These questions are:

- What is the intention that has led you to feel the need to convince the other person of something?

- Are you truthful about your intention and the process?

- How does this benefit the other person?

The persuader will be attempting to convince the other person from a good place—they intend to help the other person somehow. While they may benefit too, they are primarily looking out for the other person's best interest. For example, you may try to convince someone to buy a specific car because it will work better for their family than the person currently looking at. It would be seen as persuasion—you are offering facts about the other car and showing how it would likely serve the person longer and better.

On the other hand, the manipulator is not concerned with the other person's needs—the manipulator will attempt to push for whatever benefits them the most. There is no good intention, and there will likely not be much truth either. It is also not likely to benefit the other person in any way and may even be detrimental. For example, the manipulator may try to sell a car that is no good for the buyer simply because the other car may be worth more money and therefore net a much higher commission. The car is not likely to be very good for the buyer's needs, but that is not the manipulator's concern. The manipulator would see that as something the buyer should know on his own and not bother pointing out how the buyer may be making a bad decision, even if the manipulator knows it was wrong.

Chapter 20. Factors That Influence Persuasion

Before you attempt to persuade anyone, some groundwork goes into the process that must be done beforehand. You will not just walk up to a stranger in the street and try to convince that person that they should buy a house or even a piece of paper from you. You have not assessed that person to determine if they need what you are selling or if that person has the means to buy the item. That scenario is farfetched, but the same principle applies to any situation where persuasion is being used.

You need to put thought into how and why you will approach the person or group of people you would like to persuade. The first factor that needs to be assessed is how easily this person or group can be persuaded. You need to know how much work needs to be placed into making the individual(s) see things in the way you do.

The first factor that determines how easy and straightforward it will be to influence other people is whether you are part of their group. Groups can mean several things. Groups can mean family, workplace, gym, or even a social media group. Being part of the group you would like to persuade does the job that much easier because you are seen as one of them. That relatability makes you more trusted. You also have insider knowledge of what makes the group tick. You know their views on particular matters and are less likely to step on toes when implementing the art of persuasion.

Certain qualities make certain people easier to persuade compared to other people. A person's mental health is one of those qualities. Persons who suffer from depression and other mental health issues are more easily swayed to see things from someone else. It is largely because this person is likely to be lacking in aggression and has low self-esteem, both qualities that also make a person more easily persuaded. It is a point that can tip the scale in any direction, though, as a person with a mental health issue might agree with you to avoid the conflict if they do not but are not convinced or persuaded to your point of view.

As it relates to a lack of aggression, people who are typically not prone to showing aggressive tendencies are more agreeable and less likely to challenge the point you bring across to them. People with low self-esteem do not hold themselves or their abilities in high regard. Therefore, they value the opinion of other people more than their own. As a result, they are typically easier to persuade. Slouching posture and the confidence in a person's tone as they speak are indicators of self-esteem levels. If a person is upright and open in their body posture and speaks with high confidence, this person likely has high self-esteem, while the opposite is true for low self-esteem.

People who are socially inept as also easier to convince compared to social butterflies. People who are impaired when it comes to social interactions typically place the burden of the conversation on other people and are less likely to express their opinions freely. This increases the chances that they can be persuaded without challenging the person who is persuading them.

Once you have determined why a particular individual or group needs to be approached for persuasion, you need to figure out how you will cross that bridge to start the process of persuasion naturally. Coming across as awkward or unsure will immediately put your target's guard up, hence making it less likely that you will sway them to your point of view.

If you are not part of the group that you would like to persuade, you need to get the right introduction into that group. Walking or calling will likely not work as we are naturally suspecting people we do not know. This person does not know you or what you stand for and, therefore, will not trust what you have to say. It is why salespeople who cold-call have so much trouble getting a foot in to make the sale. The potential client does not know or trust the salesperson.

Getting someone that the target already knows and trusts is better for forming that bridge. People tend to think that the connections of the people they already know and trust are likely trustworthy because people tend to form connections with people who hold similar views and beliefs.

Sometimes though, it is not possible to get an introduction through a mutual connection. Therefore, as a persuader, you need to be still able to finesse your way into building that connection with the intended target from scratch. Even though cold calling is a sales strategy that many salespeople hate participating in, many salespeople find great success with the technique because they have mastered making the potential client or client comfortable in their company and, further, trusting the message delivery. This mastery comes from having great listening and communication skills.

The first thing that effective listening does is to allow the persuader to observe the target's language. Language, in this instance, refers to the jargon that the target understands or recognizes as applicable. A computer salesperson will have to learn a particular language that includes memory capacity, hard drive space, and monitor resolution. He cannot hope to sell anything to a computer fanatic if he does not understand these terms and others related to computers.

A master persuader knows how to ask questions that allow him or her to gather information about the one to be persuaded and then listens effectively to gain pieces of information that can make it easier to persuade the target. For example, a door to door salesman can walk up to your door to make a sale. However, if he wants to have an effective campaign, he will not just start selling to you. Even if you want or need the product or service that he is selling, you will be wary of this stranger who has come up to your door and is not very trusting of what he has to say.

Instead, a savvy salesperson will work to get you comfortable, perhaps asking about your day or even picking up on your body's cues about how you are feeling. If you are feeling harassed, he might sympathize with you. If you are in a festive mood, he might enhance that feeling by being equally expressive, hence building a feeling of camaraderie between the two of you.

Then, he will move onto asking questions and making the meeting about you and fulfilling your needs. Many salespeople's mistakes are talking about themselves rather than allowing their clients to talk about their needs and wants. Always make it about the person you are trying to persuade. Asking questions and listening to the target makes them think that you care about their needs and wants; you respect their beliefs and, thus, have their best interest at heart. It creates conditions where this person is more likely to actively listen to what you have to say and be persuaded.

Even when the conditions are prime for stating your point, remain subtle. There is a notion in marketing that people are less likely to buy when they know they are being sold. The same applies to the art of persuasion. Suppose a person knows that you are actively trying to change their point of view. In that case, if that is plainly stated, the person will likely put up mental guards to prevent them from being persuaded even if the material being imparted is helpful to them. A person is more likely to be persuaded if their guards are down. Therefore, you need to be low key about how you impart your persuasion. That is not mean that there are not instances where being blatant with persuasion does not work, but most often, the subtle route yields faster and better results. Subtle methods of persuasion include storytelling, drawing comparisons, and recognizing the integrity of the target.

It is also essential that you learn and understand to agree with your target even when you disagree with their view. You will never see you agree with anyone every time, and that applies to the target of your persuasion as well. While you must agree with your target as often as possible to indicate that you value their opinion, it is also okay to disagree at times. It would be best if you disagreed since you are trying to convince the target to take on a different perspective. The key is to do so diplomatically and respectfully. Keep your posture and body language open and engaging. An agreeable attitude must be maintained even when you are disagreeing.

Chapter 21. Methods of Persuasion and Tricks Used By Mass Media And Advertising

Usage of Force

The manipulator may decide to use some degree of force to successfully persuade the victim to think in some specific way. It is, however, dependent on the situation at that particular moment. It is seen to be deployed in instances where both the manipulator's ideas and the victim do not seem to match up. The type of conversation they are having don't seem to bear fruit, or where the subject appears to be irritated or frustrated with the turn the conversation has taken. It may be classified as a scare tactic by most since it gives the victim minimal time to think logically of the events that seem to be transpiring instead of when the victim is in a normal state of mind.

A manipulator is usually inclined to use force as a method of persuasion, generally at that particular instance, when they may have hit a wall on their journey of persuasion. They may also do this if the manipulator feels as though he is losing control of the grasp he had on the victim or when the victim presents them with solid evidence of the manipulator contradicting them.

Asking Leading Questions

Another method that a dark manipulator skillfully uses is to ask leading questions. It could be considered one of the strongest verbal techniques because they ask the victims questions to obtain a specific set of responses. For example, a dark persuader may ask their target, "How bad do you think these people are?" This issue already means that the individuals at issue are certainly bad to a certain extent. Dark persuaders ask these leading questions such skillfully that they instantly feel the victim is whipped up to leave the vessel and only go back to the questioning line where the victim appears to be in a relaxed position. Dark manipulators also use their real intentions to mask dark persuasion. To be easily exposed to dark persuasion, the dark manipulator hides his true intentions from the outset. Otherwise, he will fail. Skilled persuaders may mask their real intentions in several ways, depending on the individual victim and circumstance.

Create a Need

If it is executed professionally, the victim will be eating out of the persuader's palm in no time. It means that the manipulator will need to tap into their victims' fundamental needs, such as their need for self-actualization. In most cases, this technique will work well for the manipulator because the victim will need these things. For example, food is usually something that we as humans need to survive, and a prolonged lack will cause a big problem

Utilizing Illustrative and Words

The choice of words one chooses to use comes a long way in the success of using persuasion. There are many ways in which you can phrase sentences when talking about one thing. Saying the right words in the right way will make all the difference when attempting to use persuasion.

Tricks Used by Mass Media and Advertising

The media uses two main methods to persuade the masses. The first is through the use of images, and secondly, the use of sounds.

Media Persuasion by the Use of Images

Our sighs and visual processing areas of the brain are very powerful. Just think about it for a minute. Have you ever thought of a person without ending up picturing how they look? It is because of this that makes imagery and visual manipulation a preferred method by the media. Companies will often include split-second images of their product or individuals inserted into an advertisement that seems quite innocent by face value. It is usually a form of subliminal persuasion.

Media Persuasion by the Use of Sound

Sound is yet another trick that is used by the media in the persuasion of unsuspected victims. Some people usually underestimate the powers that exist within the sound. But how will you answer this? How many times have you listen or heard a song somewhere only to have it loop through your mind continuously? Songs usually influence us even though we are not aware of it despite knowing we are listening. It is what the media tends to exploit in their quest for persuasion of the masses. An example of this is seen at McDonald's. The melody "I love it" is often repeated in a manner that persuades the victims to purchase their meals continually.

Chapter 22. The Benefits of Learning About Persuasion

Your power of position will be one of the easiest ways to have persuasion. People with more real or perceived power will have more influence. However, people with power tend to talk more than others, interrupt conversations, and force the conversation to go in specific directions, thus damaging the power of their position. A person who controls their power of persuasion by engaging in meaningful dialogue can be even more influential.

Emotional control is critical. Letting your emotions run your conversation can be detrimental to your influence, but allowing emotion to pepper your argument or persuasion can be powerful. Think about how best to show your passion for your perspective or way of thinking and use it wisely. Sometimes, a well-placed expletive or watery eye can showcase how deeply you feel about what you are speaking about. Sobbing or turning red while cursing is the opposite. No matter how knowing you are on a topic, being too emotional can degrade your authority quickly.

Passion links well with expertise. When a person is knowledgeable and well prepared and passionate, they are an almost unstoppable persuasion force. It is especially helpful if you are not in a position of power in the conversation. It is a terrible truth that experts can be ignored if they cannot communicate their knowledge well, and people with little experience can be followed because they can sway a crowd with a stirring oration.

The final pillar of persuasion in communication includes controlling the connection. It is not the most powerful pillar, but it is essential. It is not just through conversation and verbal information but over your body language and understanding how others present themselves.

When you are dedicated to communicating with people, you need to be aware of these pillars of persuasion and control almost any situation with the correct words or actions. The following are here to guide you in understanding how different conversational tactics can provide you with the ultimate influence in any scenario.

Persuasion is a strong and valuable skill that not everyone has, but everyone should have. It comes in handy throughout your life in virtually any aspect of your existence, from sweet-talking your way into free movie tickets to convincing your boss you deserve a raise. By learning about persuasion will provide you with the following benefits:

In Your Personal Life

Your Relationship with Your Spouse

They say a good marriage or romantic relationship is all about compromise, but if you've ever been in a relationship, you know that's not always possible. You have to pick one side or the other, and why wouldn't it be your side? Far from being unfair or manipulative, having the ability to convince your significant other can improve your relationship because you have fewer fights about your disagreements and lack of compromise.

Your Relationship with Your Friends

We all have that one friend who always makes terrible life choices, and no one can get through to them and steer them towards the right path except you, that is. If you have influence and persuasion skills, don't keep them for yourself. Use them for good, not evil. Repeat these lines:

- "No, maybe you shouldn't marry that guy you just met."

- "Yes, limiting your day drinking is a wonderful idea!"

- "Please get that weird rash checked at the doctor."

- "Stop stealing from your workplace; you're going to get in trouble."

In Your Professional Life

Get Paid What You Deserve

Negotiating falls under persuasion, so really, absolutely everyone should have this skill. No matter if you're haggling at the market or talking a higher salary, you need to have the ability to convince your 'opponent' that you deserve this, and you should have it.

It's mostly applicable in the workplace, where—let's be real—no boss will ever willingly part with their money and hand it over to you. It's your job to convince them to do it. You've earned it, you deserve it, and it's rightfully yours. You have to ask for it, but you have to know-how, and persuasive skills help with that.

Earn the Trust and Respect of Your Boss

But of course, your only interaction with your boss isn't the yearly salary tug-of-war. If you're ever going to attain your career dreams and climb the corporate ladder, you need to have an excellent relationship with your boss, which means winning their respect and their trust.

You can accomplish that by becoming their go-to person. Offer your bright ideas, come up with solutions to problems the company is facing, persuade them to implement your suggestions, and that they're the contribution the company needs right now. In time, you will reap the rewards when your boss comes to consult with your first.

Be a Good Leader to Your Colleagues

To be effective in any leadership position—whether you're a manager, a team leader, etc. you need the power to convince people to:

- Do what you tell them

- Take you seriously

Your persuasive abilities will prove invaluable to a position like this if you want people to respect you, your work, and your ideas. It should be obvious for everyone that your way is the right way, and there will be minimal dissent if you have the necessary influence over them.

In Everyday Life

Persuasion is of unbelievable and utmost importance in our world today. Almost every human interaction involves an attempt to persuade or influence others to the speaker's way of thinking.

It is true, regardless of professions, age, sex, philosophical beliefs, or religion. If you can persuade other people, then you have a power that you can use to make your life better. Think about every person in your entire life who had influenced you to do your best and become successful.

Persuasive people can improve lives, avoid wars, and keep adolescents free from drugs or alcohol. However, some persuasive people can also destroy lives, start wars, and convince kids to try drugs or alcohol. That means persuasion is a powerful ability you can use for positive or negative things, depending on your motives. On the contrary, it would be best to use this power to attain self-improvement and overall growth for the entire community.

Get Out of Paying Tickets

Legally, a ticket is a mandatory consequence of breaking the law in some way, by speeding, failing to wear your seatbelt, talking on your cell while driving, etc. Practically, however, a ticket can be a negotiation, as long as you have the necessary skills.

Get into Coveted Clubs or Restaurants

How many times have you stood in line for hours to get into a popular club or restaurant, only to be turned away at the door by an unfriendly bouncer or snotty hostess? Well, let's see if you need to have a reservation. If you're persuasive enough, you can influence any menial gatekeeper and convince them to just let you through without needing to jump through fiery hoops or grease the well-meaning palms of anyone. Talk about some sweet perks!

Get Important Information

Do you feel like you're always being left out of the loop when it comes to important info among your family or group of friends? You don't have to guess what the drama is if you can convince someone to tell you, even if they promised they wouldn't.

If you can talk the talk well enough, you can convince anyone to tell you anything. Gossip from your friend preferred client sales dates from sales attendants, where they keep the extra free peanuts from the flight attendant, you get the idea. Sweet talk yourself into perks and valuable info.

Chapter 23. Dark Persuasion

The diversion between normal persuasion and dark persuasion is that dark persuasion does not always justify moral justification. While a normal persuader may try to persuade someone for that person's good, a dark persuader does so with motivations that aren't always good for the other person. They try to get a full grasp of the understanding of the person they wish to persuade, and they take pains to do so because they know what the biggest motivation is.

While persuasion always has moral implications, a dark persuader does not concern themselves with these implications. They are aware of them but choose to place their eyes on their objective(s) instead.

Persuasion is a psychological phenomenon in the everyday life of a human being. It is either that you are the one trying to persuade someone else or you are being persuaded. What makes the difference between dark and normal is the motivation behind it. In mass media, politics, advertising, and legal decisions, persuasion comes into play all the time. The outcome of practicing it in these fields is determined by ways of persuasion, which will influence the subject of persuasion.

There are some obvious and crucial differences between persuasion and other types of mind control, such as brainwashing and hypnosis. While these two requirements that the subject should be isolated to change their minds and identity, persuasion does not also require isolation.

To get to the goal, manipulation is used on one person. Although persuasion can also be done on a single subject to change their minds, there's a possibility of using it on a large scale to change a whole group's minds or even an entire society.

For this reason, persuasion is a more effective mind control technique and perhaps more dangerous because it can change the minds of many people at the same time instead of the mind of just one person at a time.

Several people make the mistake of thinking they have immunity to the effects of persuasion because they believe that they will always see every sales pitch that comes their way. They believe they will always be able to use logic to grasp what is going on and then find a logical conclusion.

Thanks to the fact that people are not always going to fall for everything they hear, this may be true if they use logic. It is also possible to avoid persuasion because the argument does not augur well with the person's beliefs, no matter the argument's strength.

Nevertheless, some people know how to use persuasive messages to encourage people to patronize the latest gadgets or products in the market. This act of persuasion is very subtle, so the subject will not always identify it, so it will be quite challenging for them to always form an opinion about the information they will get.

Every time persuasion is mentioned, one likely thinks of it in a bad light. They automatically think of a conman or salesman trying to change their perspective and eventually push them until this change is achieved.

While dark persuasion is prominent in sales and conning practices, there are also ways that persuasion can be used for good, like in diplomatic relations between international bodies or in public service campaigns. The contrast only lies in the way the process of persuasion is brought to play.

Dark Persuasion Techniques

When a person is willing to change their subject's mind by persuading them to do something contrary to their initial state of mind, the persuader will have some well laid out techniques to help them achieve their goals.

Each day that passes, the target is going to face different types of persuasion. For food makers, their goal will be to get their target to try out their new recipes or have them stick to the old ones, while studios will flash their latest blockbuster movies on the faces of their targets.

Whatever the case may be or whatever product they are selling, their main aim is to make more sales, and that is why they are trying to persuade you. They really couldn't care less about how this will impact you, and this is the reason why they must be very careful and skilled in the art of subtle persuasion to ensure that they do not tip you off or get you agitated. Since there are also many other brands trying to persuade you, they must find a unique way to impress their views on you.

Due to the influence of persuasion on a wide range of people, the techniques used in it have been studied for many years, dating back to ancient times. It is because influence is a very useful tool in the hands of a wide range of people.

Starting from the early 20th century, the formal study of these techniques began to grow. Remember that the goal of trying to persuade people is to push a persuasive argument on an audience and have them convinced. They will then internalize this message and adopt it as their new attitude or even way of life. For this point, there is a great need to discover the most successful persuasion techniques. Three dark persuasion techniques have proven to be of great value over the years.

Create a Need

It is one of the most fruitful ways of changing their perspective or way of life. The person trying to persuade a target will either create a need or capitalize on a need that the subject already has. If this is done properly, it has the potential of appealing a great deal to the target.

It means that to be successful, the persuader must appeal to the needs that are of more importance to the target. It may be their need to fulfill their dreams or boosting their self-esteem. It may also be their want for love, shelter, or food.

This method will always work out well because there is no way the subject will not need it. Since there is no way the target isn't going to have dreams and aspirations, the persuader will only have to find ways to make the victim understand how they can easily help them achieve those dreams.

The persuader may also tell their target that the target will realize their dreams if they make specific alterations to their beliefs or perspective. Doing this, according to the persuader, will give the target a higher chance of achieving success.

Appealing to Social Needs

The other technique that the persuader can use is identifying the target's social needs. While this may not yield as many results and the target's primary needs will, it is still an essential tool in the persuader's hands.

Some people are naturally drawn to crowds and desire to be wanted. They always want to have specific items, not because they need them, but because it comes with certain prestige that makes them feel like they belong to a higher class.

The notion of appealing to the target's social needs is obtainable through many TV commercials where viewers are encouraged to buy a product not to be "left behind." When they can identify and appeal to the target's social needs, the result is they can reach a new area of the target's interest.

Making Use of Loaded Words and Images

When someone is persuading someone else, they must be careful with their choice of words as words can make all the difference. While there are many ways to say a thing, one way of saying it may be more potent than the other.

When it has to do with persuasion, one of the essential things knows how to say the right thing at the right time. Words are always essential tools in communication and knowing the right call-to-action words.

Dark persuasion is one of the most powerful dark psychology concepts, but sadly it is always overlooked and underestimated. It may be because, unlike the other methods of mind control, persuasion leaves the target with a choice. In the other mind control methods, the target is forced into submission. Sometimes, this is done by putting them in isolation not to have any say in the outcome.

When it comes to persuasion, the chips are laid bare (although with an ulterior motive in dark persuasion) so that the target is left to make the decision that they think will suit them best.

Chapter 24. Covert Persuasion

Covert persuasion typically addresses the exact prediction of human behavior in any given context. Numerous attempts have been made in history to categorize people to understand them better and anticipate their behavior. A brief overview of this initiative shows various of the most famous names in psychology, consumer behavior, philosophy (NLP), and business from the periods of Aristotle, Freud, B.F. Skinner, Jung, Carl Rogers, Abraham Maslow, and William James, to the more modern brains of psychology, industry, and marketing, came up with some brilliant ways of understanding our collective thought and decision making to persuade us and influence and direct our behavior.

The Hermann Brain Superiority Predictor, the Myers Briggs Type Indicator, and the Language and Behavioral Profile are some examples of attempts to categorize us all. Of course, there are the endless personality tests that try to determine if you are well suited to a sales career. Moreover, there is the Enneagram of individuality and, obviously, the traditional 4-quadrant explanation of us as a Relator, Socializer, Thinker, or Director.

There is a famous theory that all of our actions stem from our need to avoid grief and attain pleasure. But it's not as easy as that. There's also the whole area of language analysis where it's assumed the words you're using will dictate your feelings. The labels (words) you put on your experiences determine your emotions.

Examples of Great People Manifesting Effectiveness of Covert Persuasion

Everything you have or will ever get, become, do, or learn, you'll get with and through others. Life is but persuasion! The world is the perfect context for persuasion and convincing. Marketers and advertisers are making virtually endless attempts to understand every one of us accurately. Every year they will spend hundreds of millions of dollars trying to catch our attention, convince us to buy their product or service, sample their offer, vote for their candidate, and donate to their cause. In reality, if you live in the US, each year, you alone are the recipient of more than $3,200 of marketing and advertising messages. That's a lot of money that's invested in convincing people.

Persuasion techniques help you understand and apply these to achieve your goals in the real world. Starting with the self-talk inside your mind that is important for the trust required to manipulate others, all the way to the final action of communicating straight to the one you want to convince, your target, are all here.

Through mastering the powers of persuasion, you will find it easy to get more of what you want and when you want. If you are in sales, you will now have tools at your disposal, which will double or even triple your profits and commissions if you consciously and regularly put the ideas and techniques to use every day in your work life. It sounds insane, but you're not going to be in the first 1,000 to tell us this was what happened. If you're in business, you have to convince colleagues, managers, and superiors to go along with your proposals. Here you will find plenty of methods that you can use instantly to persuade others to think your way covertly.

Persuasion strategies also include phrases that are more convincing when it comes to your personal and business life. Combining these terms with powerful stories will help you convince more people, more often.

The strategies and techniques would encourage you to have more of what you want more often by subtly or covertly persuading the other person to think your way. It doesn't take any more time to achieve it; however, you get everything you want, and you don't have to compromise or give up anything.

The persuasion methods often consist of powerful hidden powers like emotions and the influence of well-structured, well-thought-out, result-based questions.

Persuasion starts in the mind. Many words are written about how the human brain works, and many different opinions and hypotheses on how we think precisely. Yet, one thing is sure. To convince someone else to believe your way, you have to sync your mind with theirs. Effective persuasion begins and ends when a "mind meld" of real meaning, emotion, and comprehension is present. So how do we create this mind meld? How do we become more adept at persuading other people to think our way? The answer lies in knowing what motivates the other person and pushes him. Equipped with that experience, you can organize your thoughts and demands so that other individuals with little or no questions can easily and quickly embrace them. They will see you as much as they do and feel compelled to satisfy your requests.

Persuasion bypasses the vital human mind component without the message recipient being aware of the process. It is a question of getting through both resistance and response. It is achieved when one person sends a message, and it is received from the recipient without any critical thinking or questioning.

Persuasion is sometimes about controlling and handling the "state." What is the state of mind of that other person? For example, in the selling atmosphere, the consumer does not have to buy the product or service; in fact, purchasing is not an indication that there has been Covert Persuasion. An individual without money could easily be convinced and put in a purchase state, whereas he did not have the money.

Chapter 25. Ethical Persuasion

With persuasion and manipulation so closely related and only differentiated in a few key ways, you may be wondering how to keep your persuasion ethical. You may even be wondering why anyone would want to persuade, even ethically. There is a simple reason for this: Persuading others can often be quite beneficial to the other person, especially when you do so to better the other. Think of the best leader you may have ever encountered in your life. Perhaps it was a teacher that just had a way about him that always swayed people to behave. His very presence was enough to keep even the most troublesome students in line, even though those students rarely wanted actually to be in class. He could genuinely keep people involved in class and appeal to everyone, keeping even the students who would largely avoid learning in school engaged. He was able to do this through the persuasion of his own. Does this make the teacher a bad person? Not at all—he knew how best to deliver his messages to his targets, and in doing so, he was able to persuade those around him to pay attention.

Ethical persuasion can be used in a wide range of situations; it can be used with your children to keep them behaving well. It can be used at work to defuse stressful situations. It can be used to come to some agreement with a spouse or friend. There are endless possibilities for ethical persuasion if you are willing to give it a chance.

Remaining Ethical

While it may seem challenging to juggle ethics when attempting to persuade someone else of something, there is a helpful anagram to help you: TARES. It stands for truthfulness, authenticity, respect, equity, and social responsibility. When you keep this in mind while attempting to persuade those around you, you will be better able to keep your behavior in check. Remember, persuasion, in the right context, can be beneficial to everyone involved. It does not have to be avoided simply because it falls within the same category of social influences as manipulation. If done correctly, persuasion is a powerful tool that will enable you to continue to act ethically while still persuading someone else to do what you see is right.

Truthfulness

When you test your persuasion and intent, start first with analyzing the truthfulness of what you are saying. You want to remain truthful and honest when attempting to persuade those around you for a good reason—you want the other person to be informed. When staying ethical, you should recognize the other person as their person with their own free will that deserves respect, just as you would want for yourself. You would not want someone else infringing upon your own free will, and as such, you should make it a point not to infringe on the free will of others either.

When testing for truthfulness, ask yourself if what you have said is true. Beyond that, though, you must ask yourself if you have omitted any information you felt would negatively influence the person or keep the person away from acting in the way you would prefer him or her to do so. You must make sure that you are truthful in your communication as well as in your lack of communication—make sure you leave no pertinent information out, regardless of whether the other person has asked about it or not. You want to make sure that the other person is as informed as possible because you want the other person to willingly agree to do what you ask without coercion and manipulation.

Authenticity

The other test for ethical persuasion is determining the authenticity of what is being presented. At a glance, this may seem similar to verifying truthfulness, but it goes a little further. In truthfulness, the important part was making sure that everything was accurate and reported wholly and truthfully. With authenticity, you are checking the integrity of the message you are trying to convey. You must ask yourself whether you are doing what you are doing with good intentions. It means that you are not stereotyping, generalizing, or using fear to scare the person into an agreement with you.

Ultimately, you must make sure that the message you are conveying is done for good reasons. An easy and straightforward way to test for this is to ask if you would buy into it if you were presented with just the information on its own. For example, if you are trying to persuade someone to buy a car and you were in that person's situation, such as buying a family car that will fit three car seats, would you take the message you are presenting as honest, authentic, and trustworthy? If you feel as though you would agree with the reasoning being provided, the message is likely authentic. If you think that you may have a problem with the information presented, you should probably reevaluate the situation and your behavior and words. To make sure you are lining your persuasion up with ethics.

Respect

Then, you want to evaluate to make sure you are acting and persuading with respect. Are you recognizing the individual needs of the person you are attempting to persuade? Is what you are saying something that you would be comfortable announcing to other people as well, or would you be embarrassed or ashamed to be trying to persuade a perfect stranger of the message you are delivering? For example, if you aim to persuade someone to buy a minivan, are you appealing to some gender stereotype, or are you genuinely offering up the benefits a van has to offer entirely neutrally, such as talking about how spacious the seats are and how nice it is to have doors that slide open instead of swinging open when trying to keep track of kids.

Suppose you feel that your message hinges upon something stereotypical in any way or are not tailored to the individual. In that case, you are attempting to target with your persuasion, and you should probably look into ways to change the message. Just ensure that what you are attempting to persuade the other person is not offensive, nor is it done offensively. For example, you should not say that the other person must not be educated because they are from a specific minority with a lower rate of higher education. Because of that, they likely want this one specific car that many lower-educated minorities ask for. That would not be appropriate in this situation—it does not respect the individual as a person and is not respectful in general. Avoid the stereotypes and seek to get to know and understand the individual you are helping to ensure that the information you present is as relevant, respectful, and persuasive as possible.

Equity

The fourth step in analyzing your persuasion, then, is equity. When you are attempting to ensure that your message is equitable, you seek to ensure that both you and the other person are on an even playing field. It is incredibly essential that you are not looking to lead by coercion or by playing upon the other person's ignorance. You should seek to make sure that you are offering up as much information as possible to ensure that they feel that an informed decision is possible when trying to persuade the other person.

Often, when people attempt to persuade others, they play off of a lack of information. When someone is misinformed, it is much easier to take advantage of that misinformation. For example, if someone came in for medical treatment and asked for something far more expensive and far more than the person needed, it would be unethical for the doctor to accept that without ever talking about less invasive options appropriate for treatment. You want to do the same and precisely with your persuasion. Back to the example of the car salesperson, if you have someone coming in to trade in his car because he has hit 100,000 miles and the person has always heard that after 100,000 miles, the car is no longer reliable and needs to be replaced. As a salesperson, you may have thought it would be the perfect opportunity to get in an extra sale. Still, as the conversation continues, you learn that the person is not in a good place to get a new car but felt that he had to do so merely because of the mileage, even though everything was working correctly. It would be unethical not to point out the information you know would keep the person from buying the car because not pointing that out would only take advantage of his lack of information on the topic. That is not equitable—the other person deserves an even playing field when making decisions, even if giving that information can cause the person to decide against what you are attempting to persuade him to do in the first place.

Social Responsibility

Finally, the last method to check for ethical persuasion is social responsibility. It is when you stop to see if your persuasion is beneficial advice as a whole. If it is not, how can you change how you are persuading to ensure that you are doing so in a way that protects those who may be at a disadvantage? Remember, the point of persuasion is to convince people to do things on their own—it is not intended to be harmful to other people, nor should it cause others distress.

Suppose your persuasion is generally a good thing and will not have negative implications to the world at large, for example. In that case, you are not persuading someone to think of something in a racially biased manner, and it has passed through all of the other steps, then your persuasion method is likely to sound, and you are free to move forward with it. If it failed anywhere along the way, you would likely want to make sure that you are working to make your persuasion methods more ethical. Remember, ethics are respectful. They treat people with basic human decency, something that everyone deserves.

Chapter 26. Difference Between Persuasion and Negotiation

What Is Negotiation?

Negotiation is a way of resolving differences. It is a mechanism through which consensus or agreement is achieved while disagreements and conflicts are avoided. In any conflict, people understandably try to accomplish the best result (or perhaps an entity they represent) for their status. However, the foundations for a successful outcome are the core values of fairness, mutual benefit, and relationship maintenance.

In many situations, specific negotiation types are being used in international affairs, law, administration, industrial disputes, or intra-regional relations. But in a variety of activities, overall negotiation skills could be managed to learn and applied. Negotiation experience can help solve the conflicts between you and anyone.

Negotiation Phases

A formal negotiation strategy can be beneficial in securing a favorable outcome. For instance, in a job situation, it may be appropriate to schedule a conference where all the parties concerned will interact. The negotiation process contains the following phases:

Preparedness

A decision must be made before discussions. About when and where to talk about the issue and who will be involved. It is also beneficial to establish a limited period to avoid more conflicts. This phase consists of making sure all the relevant facts are known to explain your position. In the above example, the knowledge of your organization's "rules" for which assistance is given is included when aid is not deemed appropriate and the reasons for such refusals. The rules you can adhere to in preparing talks may be in the organization. While addressing the dispute, planning can help prevent future disagreements and unintentionally waste time during the session.

Talk of the Matter

Individuals or representatives of each side put the case as they choose, i.e., their awareness of the situation, forward during this stage. In this step, key skills involve interviewing, listening, and explanation. It is sometimes helpful to note all points rose during the debate stage if further clarification is necessary. Listening is essential, as it is simple to make the error that you talk too much and listen too little when there is conflict. Each hand should have the same chance of presenting its case.

Objectives Clarity

The aims, interests, and views of the dispute's two fronts must be clarified from the discussion. Such considerations should be identified as objectives. Through this explanation, absolute mutual respect can often be found or created. Clarification is an integral part of the negotiation phase. Unless it is overlooked, difficulties and challenges to obtaining a positive outcome can occur.

Discuss the Win-Win Results

In this phase, a win-win situation is focused on where the two parties feel their views are considered. This phase concentrates on what is called a win-win output. Generally, the best result is a win-win outcome. It may not always be feasible, but this should be the final goal through mediation. Various strategies and sacrifices suggestions need to be considered here. Commitments are often positive choices, often more beneficial than holding the initial positions for all concerned.

Agreement

Accord can be established after attention has been extended to recognizing the opinions and desires of both parties. To reach an acceptable outcome, everyone concerned must remain open-minded. Any contract must be made clear so that the decisions have been taken on both sides. The intervention plan must be followed to carry out the determination under the agreement.

Non-Agreement

If the negotiation process breaks down, and no agreement is reached, another meeting is expected. It prohibits both sides from engulfing themselves in warm debates or disputes that not only bother wasting time but can also affect future interactions. The negotiation phases should always be repeated at the upcoming meeting. Some new ideas or desires must be addressed, and the condition revisited. It could also be useful to look at alternatives and to mediate in another individual.

Informal Discussions

Sometimes, more unofficially, it is necessary to negotiate. In those cases, it might be difficult or essential to take the above steps officially if there is a disagreement. However, in various casual settings, it can be beneficial to remember the main points in the stage of formal negotiations.

The following three components are essential and will likely affect the outcome of negotiations in any talks:

Attitudes

The attitudes to the system itself, for instance, attitudes towards problems and individuals involved with the individual case or attitudes aligned with social acknowledgment requirements, have strongly influenced all conversation. Know always that: mediation is not a place for personal successes to be accomplished. The need to bargain with the government can be resentful. Through bargaining, characteristics may affect the actions of a human, such as that of individuals.

Awareness

The more awareness you have of the issues concerned, the greater your involvement in the negotiation process. Well-preparedness is essential, in other words.

Gain as much knowledge about your assignments as possible about the issues. Therefore, it is essential to understand how things are resolved because mediation can require different approaches in various situations.

Interpersonal Competencies

Strong interpersonal skills are important to successful talks, informal settings, and non-formal or less formal or one-to-one meetings. Such competencies include:

- Successful verbal contact

- Hearing

- Project study

- Solving question

- I am deciding

- Stability

- Tackling difficult circumstances

Are Negotiation and Persuasion the Same?

Negotiation is defined as two, or even more, people interact to reach an agreement on one or more issues and talk with another person to agree.

Persuasion can be described as the act or method of manipulating or moving to a new opinion, place, or course of action–through argument or intercession. It's the key to all discussions to transfer somebody to a new post or action path. Throughout immobilization negotiations, two parties try to find a compromise. It is mainly the case. While anyone may try to negotiate, an efficient and persuasive negotiator typically works more successfully.

Bringing up persuasion as a negotiation strategy means looking at the various types of conviction values related to property transactions; there are six different opportunities for self-interest, individuality, comparison, swap, sameness, and logical sense in property negotiations.

In the other perfect world, everybody would agree with you, and you would still be correct. About 99% of the time is not like that. What are you doing? Frequently people use manipulation to manipulate their stance on the other side. Persuasion is perfect if it succeeds because it does not cost you much but often does not succeed, so that you may have to bargain. So, what the distinction between persuasion and bargaining is.

It is best to switch to a dictionary to describe persuasion. The meaning 'to persuade' of Merriam-Webster is 'to compel (somebody) to do something by questioning, debating, and giving reasons.'

A brilliant short book called "Eristic Dialectic, the Art of Being Wrong" has been published by Arthur Schopenhauer and is still one of the day's popular rhetoric. Its 38 stratagems educate you about using logical errors, false proposals, generalization, and other handy instruments. There are some essential differences in both processes: the point of persuasion is to say, and trade is a negotiation. Strategies of persuasion are to explain, to promote, to manipulate, to inspire, to argue, to advise, and to contest.

On the other hand, negotiation implies that concerns, desires, shortcomings, motivations, and goals can be considered so that a better understanding can be made available from both sides. There is not strictly exclusive convincing and mediation either.

Both could be close to their results or goal. All strategies are very successful, and citizens are often persuaded that they prefer their reasoning and beliefs above compromise. The other party's reasoning and views tend to us not to be particularly interested. The individual may find it difficult to change his position, but we still choose it as persuading is which we've developed with since childhood and used again. Negotiation is challenging because we must be attentive to the other party's views, values, and reasoning and consider ways of dealing with them.

If we speak about compromise, there is some uncertainty about whether we say mediation or coercion. Negotiations, in their very essence, warrant a rapprochement between the two sides to reach a compromise. Convincing or manipulating, though, is the process of making the other party do what they want.

The Art of Convincing Is Often Termed Negotiation

Good negotiation leverage you will learn when and how to use effective skills to be a good negotiator. It is probably happening at times when you seem unable to agree on negotiations. In these cases, it is also necessary to understand how and when to persuade efficiently.

Use of Queries to Help Persuade Others to Compromise

Comments are high as they speak to the other arm. Yet reacting to what is being said is the real art of interrogation. It doesn't mean that you hang on each word. "The detection, selection, and interpretation of keywords that turn information into intelligence" is the definition of Mullender's listening. His conceptual model is 'information you use for your benefit.'

In sales situations, implied and explicit requirements are the keywords that a client of our SPIN Selling Skills model would listen to. An effective sales representative can turn that information in the form of profit statements into intelligence.

The profit statement requires that sellers dive into issues or perceived concerns, precisely the same as that recommended by Mullender, to "steer anxiety" in circumstances of recovery. You will define the specific desires (what the other side wants to do about this) and render helpful suggestions only by finding the real source of the pain. Unsurprisingly, in these cases, Mullender points to SPIN as a "stunningly clever" template.

Ultimately, while talks can be seen as a separate part of a process and a different ability to sell/persuade, a successful leader must still be willing in a negotiating scenario to execute suitable persuasive techniques. They recommend that negotiators develop strong selling strategies and negotiation skills to help them produce win-win outcomes. It is why they support

What Should You Select?

Seek first to convince and see whether it fits for you. Though, we were all on the other hand of someone who told us constantly that we don't approve. It cannot be very pleasant. Although persuading and bargaining, know when you hit an impasse.

The persuasion of sound is always stronger than the power of language. When you have the point of no-return, substitute the tone to be more convincing or switch your bargaining dialogue—you are much more likely to get a response. The persuasion of sound is always better than the persuasion of words.

Chapter 27. Deception

When someone is trying to deceive another person, the intentions are usually going to be pretty bad. It is a useful tool for being a dark manipulator, but you have to remember that most people will not be happy if they find out it is being used against them.

Perceiving Deception

Suppose the subject is enthused about maintaining a strategic distance from deception in their life to keep up a key decent way from the mind games that go with it. In that case, it is as frequently as conceivable a sharp plan to understand how to recognize when deception is going on. Reliably, it is difficult for the subject to find that deception is going on, except for if the master goofs and lies are clear or noticeable, or they repudiate something that the subject undeniably knows to be genuine. While it might be difficult for the chairman to cheat the subject for an important stretch, it will, by and large, happen in typical ordinary nearness between people who know one another. Recognizing when deception happens is regularly hazardous, considering the path that there few pointers that are completely solid to tell when deception occurs.

Techniques Used in Deception

Deception is a type of expression that utilizes lies and omissions to persuade the victim to fit into the world that the agent wants. A form of interaction or communication has to be involved. Deception can manifest itself in different types, according to the situation where it is applied. It is challenging to tell when someone is trying to deceive others. Luckily, though, there are a few components that, when identified, point to the likelihood of deception being involved. After many years of studying deception, psychologists have developed three classifications of deception: camouflage, simulation, and disguise. Out of the three classifications of deception, we can identify the common techniques used in deception. Let us first define the classifications.

Camouflage

Camouflage is the first classification of deception. The deceiver works to conceal the truth of their intentions in a way that the subject cannot decode. Just like the typical camouflage deployed by animals and plants to hide from predators or to approach prey without being detected, deceivers make use of methods that are hard to detect without extra observation.

Simulation

The second classification of deception is simulation. Simulation is the act of imitating to be something. In deception, simulation is defined as exposing the victim to false information as a tool of misleading them. There are three types of simulation described below.

Fabrication

Fabrication means altering reality. The deceiver can use a real thing and change it to work in their favor. For example, they can add or reduce details to a story to make it better or worse to convince the subject. A real-life example is when a suspect in court over stealing tells the judge that they stole food because they were almost starving, yet they intended to sell their loot for financial gain.

Mimicry

The second type of simulation is known as mimicry. Mimicry is defined as the art of imitating to ridicule or confuse a situation. In deception, mimicry happens when the deceiver pretends to be something or someone that they are not. A deceiver might steal an idea from someone, and instead of citing the owner; they use it as their own. An example of mimicry is when an author uses a famous writer's name to fool readers to purchase their book.

Distraction

The final type of simulation is called distraction. Distraction is the act of cunningly forcing the victim to shift their attention from reality and focus on falsehood. To divert the subject, a deceiver can use a form of bait, which might appear to be more convincing or beneficial than the truth.

Disguise

The third classification of deception is a disguise. Disguise is defined as the act of faking a different appearance to conceal one's identity. When it is being deployed, the deceiver puts up the impression of being somebody or something different from what they are. Practically, disguise means the agent keeps something from the victim, as their intentions, what they do for a living, etc.

Lies

A lie refers to the agent's act in making up and feeding the victim information that is not true. When presenting a lie, the deceiver makes it appear as a fact, thereby making the subject absorb it as the truth. Lies are the most common techniques used in deception since they divert the victim from verifiable facts and make them easy targets of manipulation.

Concealment

Concealment is the act of preventing something from being recognized. In deception, it is mostly deployed by the use of half-truths. While giving information, the deceiver intentionally omits some essential parts to keep some truth from the receiver. While the deceiver will not have lied to the victim directly, they will have ensured that the most important information has been kept from them.

Creating Illusions

Deceivers are experts at creating convincing illusions. Once they have acquired the subject's attention, they demonstrate imaginary pictures that sway them into partnering with them. They come up with illusions that appear to be realistic and workable in every way. The first step of creating the illusions is to explain their "ideas" to the target's mind. After that, they pull back a little to wait and see if the subject will develop an interest in the illusions.

Equivocations

Waffling is the application of ambiguous language to hide the truth. Ambiguous language can be indirect or contradictory. The equivocations' objective is to confuse the victim, so they are not aware of what is happening. If a deceiver is asked a question, he avoids giving definite answers and provides general responses. They can also be used by the deceiver to escape blame if they are found out. If they are suspected, they give many explanations about whose aim is to confuse the accuser.

Understatements

An understatement is a situation that has been minimized but can cause more effects than what has been portrayed. The deceiver delivers a statement to their victim while making it appear like a small deal than what it is. However, the statement can influence the victim more than they have been made to believe.

Exaggeration

Exaggeration is the opposite of an understatement. It is whereby a situation is overstretched or overstated to alter it. The deceiver might not be lying directly to the victim, but they turn a situation into a far bigger deal than it is. Exaggerations can be used to convince the victim in a situation where they would not be, had they been given the genuine version of the situation.

Seduction

Seduction is typical on social media, where a person can write an attractive bio about themselves and top it up with carefully processed photos or videos to catch others' attention. The problem is that both the bio and the media provided by such people might be false and only intended to lure followers or lovers.

Rationalization

Rationalization is the deployment of weak or far-fetched arguments with the intent of convincing someone that something is more pleasant than it appears. In the context of deception, the agent comes up with clear ideas to convince the victim to do something difficult to accept or is unpleasant under normal circumstances.

Playing the Servant

Another method used to deceive people is playing the volunteer or servant role. In this case, the deceiver hides their agenda by making their victims believe that they are doing something for a noble cause. The subjects are less likely to suspect that someone is up to some mischief, who claims to be doing something to assist others. Therefore, they end up trusting them and concurrently lowering their defense mechanisms. Once the deceivers have their way, they unravel their evil plans.

Diversion

Diversion is the action of changing the natural or acceptable course of something. In deception, diversion is a tricky endeavor that aims at destroying a subject. Mind controllers are aware of the human traits which direct their responses, behaviors, and personalities, such as self-esteem and discipline.

Playing the Victim

Deception takes a lot of consideration for emotions. A deceiver uses playing victims to appear weaker or hurt, whereas they are the ones in control. The idea is to make others believe that they are victims of circumstances to evoke sympathy, compassion, and pity from the people they look forward to deceiving. Once a victim shows some form of concern for the deceiver, they cooperate with them and become easy to deceive.

Chapter 28. The Dark Triad

Often, abusers fall within this category—the dark triad. The dreaded three personality types combine to create a human storm capable of destroying lives so utterly that the individuals have little hope of reassembling them without intensive professional assistance. These personality types are dark—they do not care about people and encompass everything wrong, and everything toxic about humanity. They are often monstering within human skin, staring out into the world, and looking to wreak as much havoc as they can as quickly as possible. These three traits are Machiavellianism, narcissism, and psychopathy. They are dangerous enough on their own, but when you find an individual who harnesses them all, be forewarned—you are better off leaving while you still can and escaping all of the nonsense altogether as quickly as possible.

Machiavellianism

If you had to simplify Machiavellianism into the shortest possible phrase— "The ends justify the means." Though never directly stated by Niccolò Machiavelli, an Italian politician and philosopher from the 1500s, this phrase came from the text he wrote in The Prince in 1513. He informed the prince that was being instructed within the document to present himself in one way, honest and benevolent, even though he was ready to behave as harshly as necessary because everyone can see a person. But very few people will ever actually get close enough to realize the truth. The message is essentially summed up by saying that the ends justify the means, meaning that it was acceptable to lie because it made the prince more well-liked. A well-liked leader is far more likely to be a successful leader that can maintain power.

Drawing from that principle, Machiavellian people are adept at appearing how those around them wish to see them. They will say whatever those around them want to hear because they know that it is unlikely that those around them will ever know the truth, and telling them what they want to hear makes them happier and gets the Machiavellian person what he or she wants. Then, getting the desired result, the end justifies the means of lying, even though lying is typically considered morally wrong and reprehensible.

This personality type is quite insidious—you never know whether you see what you are getting. The Machiavellian individual is deceitful and a master at deceiving people around him or her. They will only tell the truth if it is beneficial to them or is the most desired result, which it usually is not. They assume that it is more important to seem desirable and make good connections than developing proper relationships. Still, when you see people as nothing more than a means to an end, you are not likely to ever want to develop a relationship with others. When people are nothing but means they have been dehumanized, it turned into nothing but tools to be utilized to get what you want in any way possible simply because you want that result. Ultimately, despite the immorality of the behavior, you will do whatever it is that you must get the result you wish to only because it will get you what you want, and that is all you care about at the end of the day.

These people should never be trusted—they always have an ulterior motive, no matter how truthful they may seem in the moment. There is always something motivating them to behave in specific ways; whether it is innocent or not is up for debate. You are better off avoiding and not trusting this person whenever possible.

Narcissism

The other one is the narcissist—those with narcissism have a narcissistic personality disorder. It is characterized when an individual present with a grandiose sense of self, meaning he is quite egotistical and believes that he is far superior to a pervasive lack of empathy and an excessive need for admiration and attention. The narcissist thrives off of getting his or her sense of self-justified through actions such as praise or admiration—they only see themselves as worthwhile if others around see them as worthwhile first. They want to be recognized as worthy and will do whatever it takes to get that.

It means that narcissists are often willing to lie about who they are or what they like. They have no true sense of self beyond someone that desperately seeks the approval and admiration of others, no matter what the cost, and is willing to do whatever it takes to get it, even if that means lying about who they are.

The narcissist typically creates an alter ego of sorts, a persona that he presents to the world that is everything he wishes he was—charismatic, powerful, influential, and well-liked. He then utilizes several dark psychology manipulation techniques to keep people under the spell he seeks to create. He creates a sense of self and then always plays mind games and manipulates those around him. Only those who get close to the narcissist to be trapped in his web of lies beyond hope of getting out ever see his true self. The malicious individual lies beneath the persona, lurking for the first possible chance to lash out at those around him.

After snaring a victim within his trap, he will systematically manipulate the other person, conditioning them into doing whatever the narcissist desires. Over time, he can mold his victim into the perfect source of constant admiration, something referred to as his narcissistic supply. He will then always utilize manipulation and mind control techniques to keep his new toy under his thumb for as long as possible, attempting to break down his victim by any means necessary systematically.

Psychopathy

Psychopaths suffer from their personality disorders, in which they are often characterized through a series of persistent antisocial actions. They almost always lack any real sense of empathy—the innate human ability to connect emotionally with others at any meaningful level. This lack of empathy makes them incredibly dangerous. Without empathy, which is a built-in red flag system that lets us understand when something is wrong with those around us, particularly in regards to our behaviors to others, the psychopath has no real fail-safe to his or her behaviors—he will continue to push and push, even with the most aggressive behaviors, simply because he does not feel any need to stop. For those who do feel empathy, the pain they, themselves, feel as they harm someone else is usually enough to make them stop. The pain and guilt become overwhelming, and they stop before making it worse. The psychopath, however, does not feel that.

Beyond the lack of empathy and, therefore, remorse, psychopaths typically exhibit disinhibited behaviors—in simpler words, they are impulsive. A thought will pop into their mind with some random impulse, such as stealing a purse from someone or deciding to hurt another person, and they are far more likely to act upon it simply because they like to act upon their impulses.

Psychopaths are frequently also bold—they do not fear anything they are approached with. Consequences are not intimidating. People are not intimidating. Even dying or being harmed is not intimidating to the psychopath. The psychopath is incredibly tolerant of danger and is frequently noticed to have high confidence and assertiveness. Even though he is not likely to want to do anything meaningful with that confidence—he sees no point in engaging in social conventions.

The Dark Triad

With those three personality types now described in an easy-to-understand manner, you may now be wondering what happens when the three are combined. The results are an aggressive, toxic individual who does not care to act in a normal manner. They are fantastic at exploitation, lacking the empathy necessary to impede such negative, harmful behavior, and having the right amount of lack of impulse control to encourage it. They manipulate, they hurt, they steal, and they lie. They are callous, meaning they do not care about others' feelings and revel in seeing people hurt, angry, or sad. Research has shown that people with the dark triad personality type all enjoyed seeing people with negative expressions on their faces.

Ultimately, those possessing the dark triad are not forces to be reckoned with—they will do anything that will hurt you if you wrong them, and they do not care enough about social conventions to be held back from seriously harming you.

Chapter 29. How To Analyze People

It is the knowledge of the character by the features of the face and hand. It is about moving from an empirical art to an observation science. The character is not independent of the physical constitution. The state of our body conditions it. On the other hand, the body is influenced by the emotions of the soul.

Life is due to a double movement: a dilation movement and a conservation movement, which analyzes any human being's personality.

The Dilation-Expansion

Its adaptability characterizes it to the environment, an externalization of intuitive and affective tendencies, sociability, cheerful humor, need to be in groups, intelligence adapted to the useful and directed to practical realizations.

The Conservation-Seclusion

Oppositely manifests itself, with an elective adaptation to a privileged environment. Since withdrawal is a defense process, it acts only in a medium that does not suit you.

While the expansive individual is a friend of the whole world, disperses his activity in all directions, reacts impulsively, is determined, and has a sensory intelligence of immediate contact, the withdrawn has only friends of choice. If he does not have them, he prefers loneliness, concentrates, and is only active in some directions. It is not resolved unless he has reflected, does not trust his sensory impressions, and is more idealistic, replacing reality with abstractions, distrusting his senses, and reason.

The Expansive Individual

It is characterized by having a thick structure, colored and warm skin, wide round face, largemouth, snub nose, large eyes, and a smiling expression, with ease and abundance of exchanges.

The Retracted Individual

It is thin in nature, short limbs, dry and cold skin, and pale dye. The face is elongated, narrow, and bony. It is economical, selective in the exchanges, smallmouth, narrow and bony nose, sunken eyes, hermetic face, and little communicative.

The Expansive-Retracted

It is an intermediate of the recent two; the face is rectangular, large eyes slightly sunken. It opens or closes, depending on the situation.

Physiological Tricks to Analyzing People

In valuing people we have just met, we are often victims of our psychological mechanisms. It can lead to misunderstandings and preconceptions that eventually affect our ability to socialize. The best way to counteract these mistakes is to know how to identify them, so here are the common mistakes we make when valuing others.

Confuse Personality and Situations

When we observe someone's specific behavior, we immediately think that they act according to their personality. Instead, when we think about our behavior, we usually value it based on the situation in which we find ourselves.

For example, we know that we are distant when we are worried about something. However, if a person you just met acts in this way, you may directly assume that he is a jerk. To avoid falling into this trap, we should always consider the so-called situational conditions when valuing other people.

Confirmation Bias

Once we have a specific idea about someone, we usually see everything they do through the filter of these preconceptions. For example, if you consider a co-worker to be selfish, you look at the behaviors that confirm it, but not those who deny it.

Although our first impressions are usually quite reliable, they are not infallible, so it is essential to consider our judgments as we continue to relate to that person. The best way to prevent confirmation bias is to seek evidence that challenges your initial assumptions actively. Psychology calls this process "positive DE confirmation of expectations."

The Wavy Effect

The wavy effect is a cognitive bias whereby we make a generalization wrong from a person's single characteristic. The variable that most causes this effect is physical attractiveness; that is, we tend to value those who seem attractive to us more positively. Similarly, we also tend to value better those who resemble us.

An effective way to understand how it works is to identify when it occurs in critical situations. For example, when you hire someone for a job or when you are in a situation that involves many new people. If we pay attention, we will see that, in both cases, we tend to gravitate towards those people with whom we share certain features, whether physical or cultural background.

Let Us Influence the Past

A bad experience with a postal officer can lead us to assess all civil servants negatively. In the same way, knowing a person who reminds us of someone from our past can influence our judgment about that new person. For example, if the most undesirable person in your class at the school was named Alberto, you will have more difficulty positively assessing a person with that name.

One way to avoid this negative influence is to pay attention to our reactions' proportionality and identify when we approach a situation with a negative or defensive attitude.

The Supposed Similarity Bias

Usually, we tend to assume that others think like us and have our same preferences. But obviously, this is a mistake. If you want to skip this type of cognitive prejudice is to create a habit of warning people about diversity in people's preferences and expectations. That is, allow people to let you know that their comfort zone is different from yours.

Secrets of How to Analyze a Person

You surely wanted to be able to read the minds of other people more than once. With the aid of their formed instincts, some are spared, but if you are not so wise, you have only one way out: learn to decode the body's language.

It's no longer a secret that we get 55% of the information with the aid of non-verbal communication. Face expressions, emotions, and actions of the body will strip anyone's disguise and reveal their true thoughts and feelings.

Closing Your Eyes

If a person closes his eyes, talking to you, you must know that he is trying to hide or protect himself from the outside world. That doesn't mean I'm scared of you. Alternatively, the other way around, He wants to take you out of his dream area. You may already have bored it. Open and bam your head! You're done.

Protecting the Mouth by Hand

It's a vivid example from childhood that we all come. Remember, when you didn't want to say anything, you covered your mouth with the palm of your hand. It's the same person. Many fingertips, fist, or palm allow us to express the words. Sometimes with a feigned cough, we mask it.

Biting the Rim of Your Glasses

Does your buddy intentionally bite his glasses rings? Try to encourage and support him. He must surely be concerned about something, and he wants to feel safe at his subconscious level, as in childhood with the mother's breast. By the way, the same applies to a pencil, pad, finger, cigarette, or even chewing gum in hand.

Stroking the Chin

The person is trying to decide this way. Your attention can be focused downwards, sideways, to the left, or any other side at the same time. He doesn't know what he sees at that exact moment because he's immersed in his feelings.

Crossed Arms

One of the most repeated movements. It is not shocking that many people feel very comfortable with this posture, as this gesture helps separate themselves from others. When we're not happy with something, we use it several times. The crossed arms are a clear sign of your interlocutor's negative attitude.

Self-Exposure

This posture is more accessible, right? When a woman wants to like a friend, by revealing her best sides, she starts to reveal herself. She straightens and bends her thighs to show her breasts. The folded arms below are a clear signal of the interlocutor's attention.

Leaning Forward

Normally, he leans forward when a person feels concerned for their interlocutor and needs to contact him or her. The feet that remain in the same place at the same time, but the body moves unconsciously.

Leaning Back

If the individual leans against his seat's back, he clarifies that the conversation is boring. In your interlocutor's company, you can feel uncomfortable.

Handshake "Glove"

It indicates you can trust him if your interlocutor embraces you with both paws.

Squeeze with Palm Up

The palm-up displays sensitivity, protecting the interlocutor's face, but only if achieved at once. If the hands were already holding for a particular moment, and then somebody placed the hand palm up, it may signify a desire to show who is in charge.

Squeeze with a Touch

The person can touch the forearm, elbow, or back of the person he greets with a single hand. This personal space invasion shows the need for contact. And the smaller the body becomes, the more important it is.

Straightening the Bond

It depends on the situation here. If it's a man who does it in a woman's presence, he may very much like it. But this gesture can also mean the person is not feeling comfortable. You may have been lying or just wanting to leave.

Collecting Non-Existent Hair

The gesture of repression is thus called. We use it most of the time to express their overt dissatisfaction. We don't express their opinion freely, in other words, but we certainly disagree with what's going on around them.

Feet on the Table

This expression can mean many things: bad manners, arrogance, the desire to show off as a great boss, or health concern. Nonetheless, psychologists tend to believe that it would be safer to use it at home or in your relatives' company, even if you are very confident in this role.

Riding the Chair

A chair is not a saddle, and the back is not a shield, although it seems to be in some respects. It was also designed for other uses. This way of sitting around is troubling so many people, so we feel a lot of hostility from the "hung" individual at the intuitive level. Powerful men usually use this position.

Eye Contact

The eyes are the soul's mirror as well as a natural interactive device. There we can read all the interlocutor's feelings and emotions. Lovers look at each other's heads, expecting unintentionally to see how they get larger. And this shows a lot as, relative to their normal state, the pupils will increase in size up to four times. By the way, if the person gets mad, their eyes become like accounts because of the pupils' full reduction.

Chapter 30. Speed Reading to Understand People

If you are ready to read other people, then this is the guide for you. Ultimately, being able to read other people is highly essential. If you want to understand what is going on in someone else's mind, you need to tell what is going on with their bodies first. The truth is, people are quite easy to learn to read if you know what you are doing. All you have to do is make sure that you are looking at specific clusters.

Ultimately, we all communicate with people in different ways. We have both verbal and non-verbal signals that we give off at all times. However, the bulk of our communication is non-verbal. We have plenty of body language that we use in different ways to understand what is going on with other people. We look at proximity to each other and general demeanor to figure out what is going on inside one person's mind to get more information from them. When you do this, you learn to recognize how you can interpret what they are about to do, if they are going to do anything at all.

Within this guide, we will take a look at what it will take for you to begin understanding other people at a glance. You will learn how to understand the basic expressions, attraction, closed behavior, assertiveness, and dominance. All of these are important in their ways, serving essential roles that you can utilize. All you have to do is make sure that you know what to look for!

Reading Expressions

Ultimately, we have seven primary expressions—these are known as our universal expressions because you can spot them pretty much in any culture. Every one of us knows what a smile is, and you can recognize it immediately. That is because a smile is an expression that is considered universal. Let's look at the six universal emotions now so that you can better see what to expect with them.

Happiness

Happiness is easy to understand. When you see someone that's happy, you can recognize it by the smile primarily. However, the most obvious sign of happiness is the crinkle in the eyes—this is how you know that the smile and happiness are legitimate.

Sadness

When it comes to sadness, you can identify it by the fact that the entire face melts. You can see that the eyebrows go down. The corners of the mouth do as well, and the inner corners of the brows go up. There may or may not be crying involved as well.

Anger

Anger is defined by three primary characteristics, aside from the demeanor that goes with it. Usually, someone who is angry will have their brows lowered while pressing their lips together firmly. Alternatively, the mouth may be open, bearing teeth and squared.

Fear

Fear is usually shown as brows up high on the face, but still flat, with the eyes widened. The mouth usually opens widely as well.

Surprise

The surprise is similar to fear in people, but the marked difference is that the jaw lowers alongside the mouth's opening, and the eyes are usually opened wider, showing whites on both sides. The brows are also arched instead of just raised.

Disgust

Disgust is noticed primarily by taking a look at how the face comes together. The upper lip goes up, rising slightly. The nose bridge usually wrinkles as well, and the cheeks pinch in and up to try to protect the eyes.

Reading Attraction

When a person is attracted to someone else, they show undeniable body language as well. In particular, you can expect to see all sorts of specific actions. The body does not usually lie, and because of that, you can look directly at the behaviors that someone is doing to figure out if they are attracted to you or not. In particular, you want to look for the following behaviors:

Sustained Eye Contact

You will see that the other person will maintain eye contact more when attracted to you. Additionally, they will usually look away and then glance right back to see if you're still watching them.

Smiling

There is a reason we assume smiling is flirting—it happens often. The flirty, attracted smile usually lasts longer and includes flirty eye contact, and fleeting, but regular.

Self-grooming

Men and women both do this—they brush their hair with their hands, adjust their clothes, and otherwise tamper with their appearance when they are flirting or talking to someone they find attractive. If they do this regularly, they may be attracted to you.

Looking Nervous

Being nervous is a very normal thing when attracted to someone else, and this usually shows itself through fiddling with something repeatedly.

Leaning in

Typically, people will lean toward things that they are attracted to, and people are no exception to that rule. You will also notice that the feet will point at the person that the individual is attracted to.

Licking the lips

This is a common one, but it is subtle and easy to miss. However, you can notice it if you pay close attention. Usually, it is noticeable by a quick part of the lips and a small suck or lick.

Reading Assertiveness

Assertiveness is calm, confident, and in control. Effectively, if someone is assertive, they behave as if they are in control—they take charge, are comfortable with themselves, and won't go out of their way to overstep on other people. They sit back and allow things to play out without letting anyone else dominate them. The most common signs of assertiveness include:

Smooth Body Movements

When you are assertive over something, you don't have jerky movements. They are smooth and in control without much of a problem, even when energized or emotional. The voice sounds smooth as well, and they slowly and steadily look about.

Balanced

The assertive individual is usually upright, relaxed, but also well balanced and comfortable.

Open Body Language

Usually, these people will show that they are open to engagement without threatening or provocative. They do not block off their bodies at all and show open hands as well.

Eye Contact Regularly

Eye contact is usually steady and maintained comfortably without much of a problem.

Smiling

There are plenty of polite smiles and listening well with this body language as well. Usually, you can expect the other person to be quite comfortable, and they will smile efficiently and appropriately.

Firm

While they are firm, they usually have a solid stance without much of a problem. They are not confrontational and typically show that they are willing to listen, but they are also firm. They do not escalate anything and tend to avoid aggression in any form.

Reading Domination

Domination is a little more than assertiveness. Usually, with assertiveness, you see someone that is showing that they are confident without being threatening. However, with dominance, you can expect to see a much more threatening demeanor. A dominating body is going to show signs such as:

Facial Aggressiveness

You will be able to see the aggression in the face—usually in the form of frowning and sneering or even snarling.

Starring

The aggressive individual will usually stare at someone they don't like or may also squint or attempt to avoid looking at someone entirely.

Widebody Stance

They will usually stand out with their shoulders widened and may even hold their arms wide open as well. They may also stand with their hands placed firmly on their hips in a crotch display.

You may notice sudden movements that the aggressor is very rough with his movements, moving about suddenly and even erratically sometimes. It is a good sign that they are not in a perfect spot and may do something else aggressive.

Large Gestures

You may notice that as the individual moves, he will signal with aggressive, almost too big or wide movements that get close to you without ever getting close enough to touch you.

Reading Closed Behavior

Finally, let's go over closed behavior before we continue. Closed behavior shows that the individual is not interested in engaging with the other party at all. When you see closed behavior, you know that the individual will not want to engage with you; you will see that they want to be left alone. You can expect to see symptoms or signs of this sort of behavior, such as:

Crossed Arms

This is perhaps the most telltale sign. When someone feels closed off, they will almost always cross their arms and keep their hands near their bodies. When they speak during this time, they will keep a monotone voice. Think as your sign that you create a barrier between yourself and the other party with your arms. You want to be alone, so you close yourself off entirely.

Crossed Legs

You can also cross off legs as well—when you do this, you see that the knees are across from each other when sitting down, or they can cross the ankles as well. It creates an even more closed off image that shows that you are defensive and unwilling to listen or change your viewpoint on something.

Looking Away

It is also prevalent to see that the closed-off person wants nothing to do with those around them. They don't want to look at the person that is engaging with them.

Leaning Away

You may also see that the closed-off person wants nothing to do with getting close to the individual engaging with them either.

Instead, they will pull away and lean back, trying to put as much distance between them as possible.

Feet Turned Away

Look to the feet when you want to know how engaged someone else is. If you see that the other person is standing away, feet pointing away from you, they are closed off and don't want to engage in the conversation at all.

Chapter 31. Advanced Tips and Tricks to Control People

So you're playing the seduction game and leading someone to get intimidated by you? Again, manipulation is a powerful weapon in your arsenal that can be used negatively or positively to achieve your objectives with the person, even though it may have largely negative connotations. There are plenty of psychological tricks that can be used to get close to a person or lead them to be intimate with you.

Exercise due caution and diligence when it comes to using these techniques because your dignity and reputation are at stake here. Playing with other people's emotions always to have your way will make you come across as distrustful, deceptive, and selfish.

Flattery

Flattery is a brilliant way to break the ice with someone you've just met or lead someone you know for ages to do what you want. Ensure that you disguise flattery (however fake it is) in the garb of genuine and specific compliments.

For example, instead of telling someone how lovely they look in a particular piece of clothing, say something like, "I love how the color of your eyes is beautifully complemented by what you are wearing." It sounds more genuine and invariably draws the person to you.

There is a secret strategy when it comes to resorting to flattery. Identify an area where the person is slightly insecure and needs reassurance. Use specific compliments related to that area to win over the person. For instance, if someone has issues related to speaking confidently in public, tell them that they have a wonderful voice texture or always use the right words while talking. It directly squashes their concerns and insecurities and makes them feel nice about an area they aren't too sure about.

Make Them Indebted to You

It is another slightly insidious strategy that can be used to seduce a person or get them to do what you want. It is a universal strategy that is effective across cultures, classes, and genders. You make the subject feel indebted to you by doing them a series of favors. In their mind, they become obliged to you even though they didn't ask for it.

You create a misbalanced equation where you are the giver, and they are the receiver. To make the equation more balanced, they know they have to pay you back in some form. Take advantage of this titled balance and get them to do what you want by straightforwardly asking them when the time comes. There are high chances the person has already mentally conditioned himself or herself to pay you back. Evil as it sounds, the tactic is used by several people who will fund others' lifestyles to make them feel indebted to the manipulator. The subtext is, "I own you because I pay for everything you use." It may start with small things that the subject voluntarily opts for, which then becomes impossible to get out of.

Use Shame or Guilt

There's no denying that the manipulation seduction game can get sneaky and complicated with blurred right and wrong lines.

However, the manipulator widely uses another technique to charm people into going out or sleeping with them. It comprises inducing feelings of guilt or shame on the subject.

If the manipulator's requests are continuously turned down, he or she will make the subject feel guilty or shameful about refusing them. For example, "You know how lonely I am, living all alone away from my family. I've had a very rough and lonely childhood where no one ever loved or cared for me. You are also adding to my feelings of being lonely and uncared for with your cold and disinterested attitude. I know the world is against me, and no one wants me."

Manipulators know how to induce feelings of guilt by pushing the right emotional buttons. You will make more sweeping statements (no one loves me, the world is against me, or I've had a rough childhood) rather than state-specific instances. Manipulators cleverly study what makes the other person feel guilty and target those areas to get what they want.

Another disturbing yet highly successful seduction manipulation technique is to make the other person feel shameful about their past actions repeatedly. Though it may help you get what you want in the short run, it will certainly not set the basis for a healthy, rewarding, and meaningful relationship in the future.

Steer the Conversation

Seducers who've mastered the art of manipulation will almost always hold the remote control of a conversation to lead their subject into doing what they want. For example, if you want to sweet talk with a date, spouse, crush, or friend who is nagging you about something, you steer the course of the conversation by changing the topic to a more favorable one.

"Hey, I just saw a gorgeous blue, low-cut outfit that would look flattering on you at Mary Ann's boutique the other day" or "I saw the most jaw-droppingly beautiful house at Lakeview Lane on my way to work the other day, what do you think about living there together?" It takes the conversation from a rather unpleasant tone into a more welcoming and inviting tone that sets the pace for wooing someone or triggering feelings of intimacy in them.

False Logic

Teens and adolescents mostly use this one, but there's no denying that plenty of adults resort to it too. The logical fallacy or false logic creation technique comprises creating a seemingly false argument and making it sound that it is indeed true. When you tell someone that if a particular thing is true, they will not do something that you deem undesirable.

For example, "if you love me, you will get married to me immediately" or "if you trust me, you won't hesitate to go to bed with me" You are challenging them to prove their feelings and emotions by getting them to do what you want them to.

Make it Appear Normal

So what you as a manipulator are doing here is making the subject feel like what you've asked for or what you want them to do is normal. To do this, you stealthily use numbers, statistics, and research findings for your advantage. You make someone feel like they think differently, while what you are asking for is normal. This way, they are led into believing that something is wrong with their thinking.

For example, "statistics reveal that 75% of people end up sleeping with each other right after the first date." You establish that it's a norm and that most people would do it, and they are crazy or abnormal if they think otherwise.

Silent Treatment

Seduction experts using manipulation know how to use the silent treatment all too well. It works like magic when you're getting someone to obey your wishes. When you remain silent, it impacts the other person by making them feel like they have done something wrong or hurtful.

They become even more eager to make up for it when they realize that you are hurt, angry, or upset with their actions.

The Mirror Effect

As someone who uses the mirror effect manipulation technique for seducing the subject, you attempt to establish a level of trust and emotional comfort by convincing the other person that you are exactly like them. The manipulator pretends to have the same background, values, interests, personality traits as the subject. You may also share fake stories, secrets, or confessions to build a sense of trust, familiarity, and emotional proximity with the other person. You let them know what they want to hear emotionally, and they return the favor with what you do to them, often sexual.

It is the basis of most seduction-manipulation techniques. Manipulate someone's emotions to lead them to think and feel in a particular way, and then get them to bed with you.

Create a Compelling Want

Seduction is all about creating a compelling desire and then presenting yourself as the source for fulfilling it. It is pretty much what every advertiser, salesperson, and internet marketer use.

They create a specific thing in their prospective clients' lives and then present their products or services as the only solution.

Build a strong need for what you have to offer. Make them feel like they need you to fulfill their physical and emotional objectives. Do not be afraid to show them how you can help them or what you can offer them. Strut your strengths and tease until they are convinced that you've got what they need!

Maintain a little distance from the subject to show them what they desire is slightly out of their reach. They will be yearning for you more when they realize that you have everything they want and are yet out of their reach. It makes them strive for your attention even harder!

Chapter 32. The Most Powerful Mind-Power Tool

Humans spend countless hours seeking new ways to work just about anything. Through endless hours of research, they pour over books and journals looking for the message that will tell them the secret to harnessing mind power. Many never realize that the most powerful mind power tool is already on board and just aching to be used. It is the human brain, the mind itself.

Every time a person practices a new habit or thinks a new thought, they make a new pathway in the brain. Every time the habit is used, or the idea is thought, the nerve pathway becomes even stronger. The human brain is wired at birth to be an efficient machine, and it is ready, from birth, to make an ever-increasing amount of nerve pathways and strengthen the pathways used the most.

Sometimes thoughts and habits need to be changed for the improvement of the person. When people decide that they would like to change their lives, there will be a period of adjustment. It is true whether the change is mental, emotional, or physical. During this period of adjustment, there will be some level of discomfort. When a habit or a thought is already formed, it has made its path in the brain. When a stimulus is seen or heard, the message travels along the preset nerve pathway to the brain's spot that controls that thought or habit. To change a thought or a habit, the nerve path must be changed. Until the nerve path is changed, the old nerve path will remain in the brain. The brain's discomfort is trying to access the old pathway, and the new pathway simultaneously automatically. It is painful for the brain to do.

It is easy to become frustrated when the brain goes back to its old thought and habit patterns. Never fall into the habit of placing blame on a lack of willpower. Willpower has nothing to do with it. It is a challenging thing to override preset pathways in the brain. The brain is a very powerful tool. When will power fail, and mistakes happen, always remember to use kindness and compassion to deal with the failure? The brain is very efficient at doing what it does. The only way to change the brain's pathways is to keep working on new pathways that will eventually obliterate the old, undesirable ones.

The brain needs a clear understanding that changes are about to occur, and new pathways are about to be laid down. Remind the brain that new habits and new thoughts will be replacing the old ones. Blaming failure on a lack of willpower is a self-defeating statement. The process of making new nerve paths in the brain takes hard work and time. It will help to keep reminding oneself of the impending change. By doing this over and over, it makes the process no longer about possible character flaws. The focus is now put on the habit of thought that is being built.

Is it possible to build new nerve pathways in the brain? Yes, it is possible, and it can be done. If more proof is needed, compare the adult brain to the baby's brain. Every current habit and thought a person has the direct result of practicing them repeatedly until they created a brain pathway. New pathways can be created. The baby's brain has no idea of anything. It has no thoughts or habits. Every nerve path currently in the brain was practiced until it became a part of the brain. Think of the baby. The baby lies around day after day and does baby things. Then one day, the baby notices the shiny rattle that mommy is waving in front of its little face. The baby wants the rattle. As the baby is waving its tiny arms around, the mommy puts the rattle close enough so the baby can touch it with its wavering hand. After a few of these sessions, the baby gets the idea that it can touch the rattle if the arm is in the air. A nerve pathway is beginning to grow. So the baby decides to lift its arm to reach for the rattle actively. The baby will be unsuccessful because the arms will wave wildly and will not connect with the rattle. One day, the baby will grab the rattle, and the nerve pathway is then complete.

While this may seem like a straightforward example, it is precisely how nerve pathways are created in the brain. Every action, thought, or habit has its nerve pathway. All pathways must be created. No one was born knowing to sit in front of the television and mindlessly eat dip with chips. No one was born lamenting the excess pounds they carry in strange places. No one was born hating their body; all behaviors are learned, good and bad. And the bad ones can be replaced with good ones.

So if the ability to program negative thoughts into the brain exists, then the ability to disrupt those negative thoughts with positive thoughts also exists. The brain can be reprogrammed. It is a powerful tool, and its main function is to turn thoughts into reality. The brain is always working, so why not use the brain's power to benefit rather than harm? Just because a particular habit or thought has been around forever, it does not mean it needs to stay. Use the brain's power to choose new habits and thoughts to focus on and replace the brain's old, negative thought pathways.

The new thought needs to be believable; the new habit needs to be doable. It does not look really good to try to stick to a habit that is impossible to accomplish or to try to believe an unbelievable thought. After years of seeing an obese body's reality, it would be nearly impossible to suddenly believe that the mirror image is that of a skinny person. But the brain will likely accept something that mentions learning to take care of the body or learning to accept the body to correct its flaws. The brain will turn a belief into reality. Believing a positive thought will lead to a different result than the ending where only negative thoughts are present.

Be prepared to repeat and repeat some more. The primary key to being able to make a new habit stay is repeating it constantly. The more a new, desirable habit is practiced, the more the brain begins to accept it. The nerve path becomes stronger every day. With constant practice, this new nerve path will become the path the brain will prefer to use, and the old one will cease to exist.

In any case, be sure to allow enough time to create a change effectively. Accept the starting point and continuously visualize the ending point. Accept that the path to the goal of a new habit or thought will not be easy or perfect. The path will rarely travel in a straight line. Sometimes people fall entirely off the path, and that is okay too. Do not get sidetracked by the idea that this journey will be comfortable and carefree because it will not be. Just keep thinking of the new nerve pathway created by the new thought or habit, and it will eventually become a reality.

Most of the pathways in the brain are stored in the subconscious mind. It is the part of the mind that is always working without always being thought of. Think of learned skills like tying shoes, zipping a coat, and pouring milk into a glass. These were all learned behavior whose nerve pathways are firmly set in the subconscious part of the mind. This part of the brain is the bank of data for all life functions.

The communication between the conscious mind and the unconscious mind works in both directions. Whenever a person has a memory, and emotion, or an idea, it is rooted in the subconscious mind and translated to the conscious mind through mind power. The subconscious has the power to control just about anything a human regularly does.

For example, during meditation, steady, deep breathing is usually practiced. The control of the breath is brought from the subconscious mind and given to the conscious mind to control the breathing. Once a pattern of deep, steady breathing is begun by the conscious mind, the subconscious mind takes over and keeps the set rhythm going until it is told to stop. It is done by a conscious end to deep breathing. The subconscious mind also processes the great wealth of information received daily and only passes along to the conscious mind those necessary for the brain to remember.

When sending thoughts from the conscious mind to the subconscious mind, the brain will only send those thoughts attached to great emotion. The only thoughts that remain in the subconscious are those that are kept there with strong emotions. Unfortunately, the brain does not know the difference between positive emotions and negative emotions. Any strong emotion will work. Both negative emotions and positive emotions can be quite strong. Also, unfortunately, negative emotions tend to be stronger than positive emotions.

Step one in learning to use the subconscious part of the mind's power will be to eliminate any thoughts that come with negative emotions. Also, negative mental comments will need to cease. Fears will usually come true, precisely because they are drowning in negative emotion. Negative ideas need to be eliminated because they can be very harmful roadblocks on the road to harnessing brainpower.

One best practice to use to get rid of negative thoughts is to counter them with positive thoughts. It will take time and practice, but it is a very powerful and useful technique. Whenever a negative thought pops in the conscious mind, immediately counter it with a positive thought dripping with strong emotion. The actual truth will come out somewhere in between the two thoughts.

Another way to counter negative emotions is to delete them, just like using a remote control. When a negative thought comes into the conscious mind, imagine destroying it. Imagine writing that thought on paper and burning it. Imagine pointing a remote control at the thought and pressing a huge delete button. Whatever form used to imagine deleting the thought, the important thing is to get rid of it before taking hold in the subconscious mind.

Find something energizing and use it to reach a goal. Those things that are found to be energizing bring boundless energy to positive thoughts. It is often necessary to invent motivation to learn to create new habits and thoughts, at least in the beginning. But with a bit of practice and a lot of positive thought, new positive habits will soon be burned into the subconscious mind, and the old negative thoughts and habits will fade away.

Chapter 33. NLP Conclusion

You learned all about NLP, persuasion, and other subjects connected to these two. Remember all of the body languages you were taught—out of everything, that maybe one of the best skills to foster and develop. You learned of several different ways people can control, influence, and persuade other people to do what they want or need. You learned all about how people prefer to interact with others and genuinely and naturally develop the persuasion and influence that so many people desire. You were also taught how to develop several social skills that are of the utmost importance if you wish to be successful.

Ultimately, the information should guide your behaviors. Let this allow you to go through your life, be informed, and aware of how your behaviors influence others. Focus on those around you with their body language and see how easily your behaviors can sway them. Learn from negotiation skills to ensure that you can get what you want while still giving back to others. Remember how to keep your interactions with those around you ethical, even if you understand how to take over and manipulate them into obedience to do whatever it is you are seeking.

Neuro-linguistic Programming practitioners and trainers have put forward exemplary approaches and techniques to persuade, which can be used in various environments. Studies state that these techniques develop personal performances and help the individual maintain good intrapersonal and interpersonal relationships.

To persuade someone entails a process of altering and rebuilding their opinions, beliefs, values, and behaviors towards an outcome. Humans are programmed to find it extremely difficult to move out of their comfort zone, no matter their comfort zone. For some individuals, even if their comfort is unhealthy, they wouldn't mind staying in it because, well, it's comfortable.

Persuasion is just not about forcing an individual to behave how we want them to behave; it is about allowing them to come out of their comfort zone to achieve a higher comfort zone after the discomfort of the change subsides. Simply put, an individual who regularly smokes will keep smoking because it is his comfort zone. To persuade or convince him will be a pretty challenging task because quitting is uncomfortable for the person. During the non-smoking period, this person might go through considerable discomfort. Still, afterward, he will experience a higher comfort zone due to the absence of his unhealthy behavior.

For persuasion to be successful, the person tries to persuade the individual to figure out what is essential to the individual. The persuader should identify factors that can eventually give the individual a higher level of comfort. For a person who finds staying at home and shunning social life comforting, the persuader should discover a factor that can allow them to move outside the box. By helping them realize that although going out can be, they will have a higher sense of comfort once they achieve their goals. This process needs a skilled persuader to assure the client that the behavior change will make them feel more comfortable.

Advantages of NLP

These NLP techniques can increase the level of influence that you exert on others. Companies that engage in marketing and sales depend entirely on persuading their clients or clients to buy their products; the strategies presented in NLP guide these sellers and dealers to increase the chance of influencing their clients in making decisions. NLP also increases the person's performance; NLP helps you modify and replace your negative behaviors with more positive ones. These strategies also help you to improve your leadership style. Being humble and non-judgmental allows you to have a better communication style, even outside the persuasion process.

Essentials for Persuasion

Empathy

This is an essential quality that a persuader requires. You should not only be thinking about yourself, but you also should try to put yourself in the other person's shoes and think about how they might be feeling. Empathy also helps deter you from being judgmental.

Listening Skills

Only a good listener will persuade another person; a person who is always ready for an argument will never be a good listener. If you want to be a good and positive persuader, you need to listen to what the other individual says and pay attention to their body language.

Indirect and Clever Commands

People tend to be more responsive to suggestions than questions. For example, instead of using the words "Would you like to go to the concert?" You can say "Come, let's go to the concert"; this motivates a more positive response from the individual.

Restrict the Choices That You Provide

Try not to allow the individual to say "No." Taking the same example, instead of asking, "Will you be able to stay long at the concert?" ask them, "Would you like to stay here for three hours or four?" The latter question makes it hard for the individual to say a "No."

Allow the Person to Visualize

Successful persuaders always help the client, or the individual visualize to convince them. An example would be, "this concert will make us scream the lyrics of our favorite songs."

Always Make It Simple as Possible

Trying to convince the other person by bragging will only be a failure; keep it as simple as possible and remember you should never put their views down.

You can use the information you were provided for good. You can use it to better your relationships, your career, and your social life. If you understand how people interact with others, you can ensure that you are interacting positively. You can make every interaction with other people positive and fulfilling for everyone involved. Above all, you can naturally develop the skills you need to create and earn your leadership skills. People will naturally seek to follow you if you build your NLP and persuasion techniques. People will listen to you better if you have advanced social skills. You can use it to your advantage to ensure that you and those around you are happy with life. Use your enlightenment and knowledge for good, and go out there, armed with the knowledge you need to persuade others, both for your benefit and theirs.

So, what are you still waiting for? It is time to embrace this guide so that you'll allow the light inside you to radiate without fear of hurting others of being all that you are meant to be. This guide will help you overcome manipulation so that you can shine brighter!

Chapter 34. Covert Manipulation

Numerous people in the world do not realize that mind control has become a dangerous aspect used by different people to control others and resources. Mind control is used in different aspects of life, and the list below might surprise you by the extent to which it has expanded in modern-day life. When we think of mind control, some of us assume that it is a direct way of getting into the brain and influencing the very mechanism in which we think. However, mind control is much greater than that, and its effects are putting control of the world in a few elite hands.

It is necessary to consider how agencies, companies, and even individuals practice mind control, as it is an important aspect of NLP manipulation. Mind control is basic to begin with, but it can also be complex in practice because different people use different aspects of technology to control those around them. The following list is but a taste of the different approaches to mind control in the world.

Mind Control with NLP for Love and Relationships

We will learn what truly good and fulfilling relationships are based on and built upon. We will explore techniques that can strengthen relationships and those that can help us establish healthy relationships. Many factors play a role in good relationships. We will discuss the importance of our mental health and readiness before entering into any partnership or relationship, and possible outcomes associated with having and not having these factors.

We all want and need certain things. There are basic needs for all of us, and one of the most crucial ways we can have our basic emotional needs met is with healthy relationships. We all want to be loved, desired and needed. We all long for compassion and understanding. All of these can be acquired in good and healthy partnerships. Likewise, a bad relationship can be devastating. Most of us carry around baggage, such as negative emotions, fear, and anxiety from previous unhealthy relationships. This can place barriers between us and others when we find ourselves in new relationships. True fulfillment usually can only be found in the emotional qualities of our relationships.

Every good relationship begins with a clear and comfortable frame and state of mind. The maturity of both parties is a factor, as well as timing. Your goals and wants need to be compatible with the person you want as a partner. Your values and beliefs need to match. These ideas and characteristics are tangible and very important in the overall health of any relationship. If you find yourself in a great relationship, the benefits are numerous. You will gain confidence and a feeling of self-worth that can't be matched. Just as important, you must also remember to transmit this to your partner. You should always treat your partner exactly the way you want to be treated. In doing this, and having this knowledge, you can know what it is that your partner wants. You just need to see what it is that your partner is doing and take it from there.

Before we can be the kind of partner we should, we must first be good within ourselves. If you enter into a relationship, while you have self-doubt or internal difficulties, you are entering a partnership that is doomed from the start. A perfect couple consists of two people who can function well as individuals but function as a partner just as well, if not better. This is the first step in entering any relationship. You must be good with yourself. This is a must and shouldn't ever be compromised. The second important point that needs to be addressed is establishing what, or who, it is that you desire. This is your personal decision based on your personality, desires, ideologies, and belief system. It does not matter what others believe you need or what you think you should have. What matters is what you want.

The next part of entering into a good relationship is timing. This isn't just important to you, but it's also important with your partner. Are you looking for "Mr. Right" or "Mr. Right Now?" Are there things going on currently in your life that may prohibit your success in the relationship? Are these things not only able to hinder you, but are they able to hinder your partner as well? Timing is important and crucial to the longevity of the relationship. If you are a point in your life where other priorities take precedence with you, you should wait until those priorities shift. You can become capable of making your partner the priority that he or she deserves.

Once you have decided what you want, have concluded that now is the time for you to enter into a relationship, and have covered all of your predetermining factors. Now you can begin to open up to the possibilities of finding the right person. Here is when rapport becomes important. What is rapport? It's your similarities and likeness with someone with whom you are interested in entering a relationship. It's also the establishment of trust with that person. With rapport, many individual factors can be used for determining compatibility. Some of these are personality types, values, beliefs, culture, political ideologies, interests, religious beliefs, etc. Of course, physical characteristics, such as gender and body types, need to be considered. However, some characteristics can't be over accentuated because it will mimic the other and cause a loss of rapport.

The rapport established in the beginning, the reasons for your attraction to your partner, and his or her attraction to you must be kept at the forefront of each partner's mind throughout the relationship. It all too common for people to enter into relationships with guns blazing, meaning being the perfect partner, only to begin to relax and change once the relationship has been established. One partner, or both, will use all available techniques to get the other to enter into a relationship. Once they are in that relationship, the other partner believes they can initially tone down what they were doing. This is one of the most common reasons for relationships ending. Keep in mind; the reasons for someone falling for you are the same reasons that will make them want to stay with you. If you remove the reasons for their attraction, they have no reasons to stay with you. Often, we see children born of relationships used as new reasons, but this does not work. This leads the partnership to morph into what can be seen as a business relationship. There will be no real emotional connection in the relationship and, even though that couple may remain together, they will lack the comforts and fulfillment of needs they desire.

Now you have identified what you want, making sure the timing is right, and have met that special someone. Now, what do you do? You need to make sure that your partner feels the same about you. There are several ways in which a person can see that they are loved by the other. These ways should be identified at the relationships beginning. A few methods are by what the other person buys and place him, or she takes you. There are also things such as how they touch you, the looks they give, or what they say. Identification of these is important as they can gauge the continuance of love throughout the relationship.

The best way to determine how you can best assure your partner that you love him or her is by doing what they tend to do for you. For instance, most likely, if your partner puts her arm around you at times to assure you of her love and affection, you can bet that if you do the same, she will believe that you do love and appreciate her. We don't tend to do things to or for others, especially those whom we care about the most, that we wouldn't want to be done to us. Although this is commons sense, it's also a great method to gauge or determine how your significant other feels about you. As the relationship progresses, this will come naturally and will take much less conscious effort. Just be sure not to allow these things to stop because the relationship is no longer new.

NLP has devised a few strategies to determine areas in relationships. Areas such as attraction, love, and desire are all strategized with NLP techniques. First, you must know your partner. This means that you should know what those subtle gestures and tones of voice your partner will display depending on how they feel. Know what your partner fears and what he or she wants. You will pick up ideas as to how to carry these things out simply by learning your partner. Be sure never to use this knowledge for manipulation. There isn't a positive outcome in relationships where manipulation takes place.

One technique you can use to ensure that your partner is in love with you and wants you is to remove yourself from his or her presence temporarily. This does not mean that you can tell your wife that you are going to the store for a lottery ticket to not return for a week. However, in short time frames, absence can signal want or lack thereof. Just like the cliché, absence makes the heart grow fonder; this is built on the same premise. When using these kinds of tactics, please never overuse them. Here is some advice. If you are an insecure person needing constant approval and reassurance that you are loved, you should take care of that issue before entering into a serious relationship.

If not, you are not going to be a good partner. If your shortcoming does not end the relationship, it could lead it to become a codependent partnership or, at the very least, a very unhealthy relationship. Again, you must first make sure that you are a good candidate for entering into a relationship before taking that other step.

With relationships, you are not simply selling yourself to another, and then the job is over. It's a continuing process forever. Never relax and believe that you have your partner, and he or she isn't going anywhere, no matter what you may or may not do.

Many divorcees have made this mistake countless times. You should always be selling yourself, your worth, compassion, and desire for your partner.

Chapter 35. What is Manipulation?

When coming from a psychological point of reference, manipulation is mostly about perception. How we perceive things or actions determines our laws, social formalities, and even our lives.

The manipulator changes these norms with tactics. The determination of the positive or negative connotation of these actions remains subjective. Psychological manipulation is often considered devious. With the subject of dark psychology, we can take into account that the manipulation practiced is often exploitative at the expense of others.

So, what is the manipulation of the dark?

Sources tell us that it is concealment—hiding in the shadows knowing when to strike. It is also a false front, hiding true intentions. When we are talking about this level of deception, we are talking about hiding aggression. When we take, there is a certain level of aggressive behavior that happens. A small part of manipulation is hiding that aggressive behavior so that the victim sees only good nature.

This is accomplished in various ways and means, one being knowledge. When we allow another to know us, we display vulnerability along with strengths. The knowledge of these personality traits can give the manipulator the ability to maneuver around without any alarms going off.

The effectiveness of manipulating those strengths and vulnerabilities arrives when the dark practitioner knows what is vulnerable and what inspires pride.

A reoccurring ideology that drives us to war takes into consideration that war is more negative than positive. We want to avoid it. The manipulation process sees pride in all of us and plays to that pride. It is our strength. However, when used to drive an army to slaughter others, the intention of our pride has been manipulated to enforce the agendas of others.

There is ruthlessness when we talk about psychological manipulation. When dealing with someone other than the pure psychopath who feels little to nothing, ruthlessness can be measured. Often soft ruthless behavior can sneak up on its prey and snag it before it knows what is happening. This harm of the prey becomes less than even a momentary qualm in the mind of the manipulator.

Often the practitioners of dark psychology use aggression and fear to drive us. The less dark side still falls into the category of knowing what weakness is, and that weakness leaves the individual open to control.

How the manipulator uses that control determines the severity of manipulation. There are positive versions of manipulating others, such as convincing someone that they are not doing well and need help. However, we are looking at the darker side of this. The manipulator uses their control skills to get what they want—and the cost does not apply.

There are many ways to move another into a place of being controlled. From the positive to the negative, psychological manipulators utilize all tactics.

When positive reinforcement is used, the charm is displayed. A forced smile or laughter can trigger laughter in all of us. As when we were infants, we copy what we see. When we see tears, we want them to stop. When we see a smile, we find ourselves smiling as well.

Using positive reinforcement, the manipulator can shower money, charm, and gifts to get us to feel something. The usage of these things allows control of us on an instinctual level. We follow those who tell us what we want to hear.

Psychological manipulation can also implement negative reinforcement. This is a form of deflection—a substitution of one thing for another.

Often, we have things we need or have to do, and we do not really want to do them. The psychological manipulation of negative reinforcement uses that power of negativity to lure the subject from their original need, pushing them toward something they want to be done instead. The long game, a slow play of putting tasks into another's life and then controlling those tasks, so that the manipulator can get what they want, is an extremely effective and subdued tactic.

Sometimes only partial reinforcement is required to gain control. We are talking about elevating the fear or doubt regarding the tasks needed to be done. The partial is the long play. It knows that in the end, the victim will lose. It knows that by planting small seeds now, victory will eventually happen. It knows that we all have our weaknesses and that by planting even a small seed, we can take someone to that weakness. An individual trying to work toward something they already were shaky on or had doubts about, will listen to the lie and flow with that idea, and use it to their own destruction.

The partial manipulator only needs to put the thought in mind, knowing the weakness is already there and utilizing it will take their prey to a destructive end.

Psychological manipulators flat, outright punish. From an actual physical lashing to the victim's passive-aggressive playing, punishment is very effective when one wants to control another.

We skulk, cry, yell, nag, and go completely silent. This is the blackmail of the manipulator. It inspires guilt in us. That "wanting to be the better person" rises to the front, and we do what the manipulator wants.

When the manipulator sets free the crocodile tears, we have no idea if they are real or not. The degree of crying is not up to us to determine. Only the manipulator knows if the tears are legitimate or not.

In this case, the trap is often sprung from the victim's side. They walk up to the hurt individual to help, only to find that the manipulator is just lying in wait to strike.

One extreme version of manipulation is violence.

Violence triggers something inside us. We often do anything to avoid it. The manipulator knows that violence strategically applied can make us go into a state of avoidance. There incites the control. Physical violence can have mental scarring. The manipulator causes the scarring. It places violence in tactical places to get the result they want.

Some would say this is the darkest of the dark.

Taken to the individual, this can mentally damage them for a long period of time, if not permanently. Placed on a world stage, it can lead all the way up to the physical conflict of genocide.

The manipulation process in dark psychology is normally not a single move. It is a complex series of moves, often with the outcome only known by the manipulator. The motivations of manipulators are as convoluted as human nature.

Mostly it is about gain. Manipulators of the dark want to gain something. When we speak about gain, we are talking about power and influence, control and manipulation over others. The trophy is up to the individual. This can be everything as to gaining affections, to money, and even to life itself.

It is about gaining for their own personal reasons and gratifications. The taking of others and making the power and control their own. Selfishness to the extreme. The mind of the dark practitioner sees the ultimate win as gain over others.

They have power. Superiority is the power over another, and taking of someone else's power makes them feel superior. This is a huge driving force behind the manipulator. Often, in the case of immature individuals driving manipulations toward superiority, any is pushed aside for just the feeling of being superior.

In relationships, it is about control. The manipulation of power can put one in control. Although we have looked at the role of the vampire and power, and we know who really has control.

This feeling of control can be overwhelming to the mental state of the dark. Almost drug-like, it is a feeling of emotion that is most logical. Control is one of the easiest manipulation tactics to achieve with only logic to guide. It drives not only the victim but the manipulator as well.

Psychological manipulation can also be about self-esteem. The self of the manipulator is always in question. This is one of the reasons they manipulate, to define themselves. How easily they are able to manipulate another can tell the dark that they are better than others. That weakness and strength can be measured in the tactical playing field of the hustle.

This defines who they are. Can they manipulate? Yes? They are stronger. No? They are weaker. It is a measuring device for self-esteem.

However, we are not saying it is the only device for measurement. Self-esteem can be measured by far less damaging means.

The mind gets bored, and what do we do when we get bored? We seek entertainment. How do we achieve entertainment? We manipulate.

We all do it.

Let us assume we are bored, and we want to remove or alleviate that boredom with something else. Do we just sit back and wait for something new to happen?

No. We actively search for something to replace boredom. Manipulation can take place on many different levels, as well as the severity of which they are applied, from picking up a crayon and coloring to taking a mental absence to massacre everyone around you.

The dark psychological manipulator is bored most of the time more than most. The psychological manipulator will often use manipulation to determine their own validity of feelings and emotions.

What this boils down to is that manipulation applied in relations with others helps the manipulator to regulate reactions to validate or not validate their own emotions. The manipulator measures the self and their self-esteem by how others handle their personal self-questioning.

This happens when the practitioner does not have a grasp on what emotions are. They look at their own emotions as invalid and manipulate the situation in such a way as to validate them.

We are stuck with ourselves, and we cannot get away. Psychological manipulators validate or invalidate themselves by the tactical controlling of others. It is an interesting way of viewing life, although there is one form of manipulation that we all idolize—the con. One common form of manipulation is convincing of another to make their money yours.

This is a hidden agenda of the criminal. This form of mental manipulation preys mostly on the elderly and the rich. However, we all can fall to this form of manipulation. What we choose to spend on and what we do not is our response to a form of psychological manipulation.

Something happens when the buck is passed over. We go from manipulation into action. Something drives us. It is within us, and it is outside forces that drive. What causes this drive and the drive itself is called persuasion.

Chapter 36. Examples of Manipulation?

It is worth noting that manipulative people don't always come out of nowhere. Often we find individuals with this behavior in the workplace, at school, and in the family. The characteristics presented above are shaped according to the mode of friendliness. Here's how to deal with manipulative people in these environments:

At Work

In a professional environment, the manipulator is the employee always ready to help, but remember, it's compulsive help. He stays at the heels of colleagues, reinforcing how much he loves helping colleagues who have difficulties in their tasks. The manipulator on the desktop can stay up and even take a break in the office, all for the "pleasure of helping others." The targets of "goodwill" are charmed with such dedication.

The manipulator is seen as the company's legal person, employee, and fellow stick to for all work. However, this establishes a relationship of dependence. Whoever is the target of "goodwill" is being placed on the web. The one who receives the "help" loses his autonomy since he cannot act without asking for the manipulator's opinion. Consequently, he loses confidence and does everything not to lose this "friendship." When the victim begins to perceive himself as such and tries to escape, the manipulator reverses the roles and convinces his prey that he is bad. The prey, in turn, accepts such a condition and follows the will of his tormentor.

How to Get Rid of the Manipulator at Work?

Be firm and kindly dispense unsolicited favors. When the manipulator takes the day off to flatter you, return the compliments, but make it clear that you are just doing your duty, and anyone else would do the same. The manipulator will be amazed at your steadiness.

In School

At school, the manipulator is the perfect colleague. The manipulator targets unpopular students who are constantly ridiculed.

The manipulator praises the high notes. You are sure that the "new friend" is the best student. When his grades are low, he places the teacher's blame because the teacher certainly did it to harm him. He does not hesitate to defend injustice. There is no bad time that prevents you from helping with the activities, and the manipulator makes a point of doing the work with you. The target of such unknowing friendship reveals what time he leaves home, what time it takes to drive there, reveals possible enmities with other students, tells of his fears and anguish. The manipulator reveals nothing about his life.

When the victim realizes that something is strange and tries to disengage, the manipulator feels extremely offended. He places the "friend" as an unjust person, unable to recognize true friendship. The manipulator depreciates the "friend," listing his defects, and claims that he will return to being a solitary person and be ridiculed if the friendship ends. The prey, who already had low self-esteem, is even more vulnerable. Thus, the victim believes the manipulator, apologizes, and no longer measures their efforts to do all the manipulator's will, so afraid of losing the "friendship."

How to Get Rid of the Manipulator in School?

If you feel that you are being cheated again, move away slowly. Speak only as necessary and ask other people's opinions on how to deal with the situation.

In the Family

In the family, the manipulator sticks close to that shy relative and is considered good by everyone. It may be that cousin who always compliments, even when the victim has done something that isn't so great. The manipulator justifies his "object of affection" blockades and believes that his target is wrong. He insists on telling us how much he loves us and is happy to be with such special people.

The manipulator is always ready to go to the mall, help with school activities, go to the doctor's office, and do some repairs. However, when the target begins to be bothered by the excessive clinginess and flattery, the manipulator turns the tables and lowers his victim. The manipulator underscores his lack of social skills and how he is seen as lonely, poor, and a failure unable to have friends. The sentences that the victim says will continue to be seen as unimportant. The already emotionally unstable target agrees with everything, apologizes, and resumes "friendship," doing everything according to his tormentor's will, afraid of not being able to count on such a valuable person.

How to Get Rid of the Manipulator in the Family?

Family ties make things harder, but we must put an end to this vicious circle. Ask the opinion of people outside the family spectrum. Even if it is not possible to cut the manipulator out of the conversation, talk only when necessary.

Differences Between Male and Female Manipulators

The behavior between men and women is different in several respects. On the question of manipulation, there are also singularities.

Men

Male manipulators have the following characteristics:

- Shy: the manipulator observes the behavior of everyone around him. He transmits fragility and submission to convince himself that he is a needy person.

- Handsome: manipulators are always friendly, extroverted, and know how to live life. They show extremely worried and attentive with their "friends," but they make a point of showing who is in charge. The victims do not feel the courage to disagree with such a nice man, but when he goes to a boring event, he does not bother to disguise his boredom.

- Altruist: he gives many gifts, does numerous favors, always intending to receive something in return. When it is not "reattributed," it gives people a sense of guilt.

- Seductive: vain and attractive. He looks into others' eyes, asks embarrassing questions, and loves to make a mystery of himself.

- Worship: has excessive admiration for diplomas, pompous professional curricula, and social projection. He subtly shows contempt for those who do not have the same knowledge. He loves to embarrass people, monopolizes conversations, and gets annoyed when someone interrupts his speech.

Women

Manipulative women behave in the following ways:

- In front of everyone, they are true porcelain dolls. However, when the target moves away, she's stupid with people. When the victim returns, she will be candid with him/her.

- Use beauty as a weapon to get what she wants. It seems absurd to someone not to praise it.

- She uses a sensual tone of voice and promises a thousand wonders to those who satisfy her requests; she wants the target to guess her wishes and surprise her with trips, restaurants, and luxury gifts. She becomes angry if her requests are not answered.

- Her emotions can be radical. When you are right, she wants to prove that it's better that you are wrong. When she is wrong, she does not admit it and insists until someone believes in her.

- They cry too much. If the victim wants to go out with other people, she cries because she was "betrayed." If she is asked how the car got scratched, she cries because she was accused of being a bad driver. She is "fragile" to the point of not carrying a suitcase or not being able to open the car door.

Manipulative people enter our lives because they see that we are going through a moment of vulnerability. We feed these people by providing intimate information. However, if we allow them to enter our lives, it is up to us to remove them from the scene. The task is difficult, but these tips can be useful:

Do not feel guilty for not satisfying the wishes of the manipulator. Often they are irrational and seem like things a child who wants attention at any cost may request. Ask probing questions; question what will change if you attend to the manipulator's wishes. Ask yourself how your feelings were before and how they are now. Learn not to speak to those who do not do you good; this means you must avoid saying yes to the manipulator.

If none of this works out, move away. If it is not possible to physically get the person out of your life, move away emotionally, and speak only about the basics. Remember that manipulative people are "toxic people," non-evolved beings who want to suck energy and steal others' autonomy. No one deserves to live in the shadow of others. No one deserves to live, having to consult someone at every step. Emotional independence is the key to a happy existence.

Chapter 37. Introduction on Deception

What is Deception?

How can deception be defined? Deception, alongside subterfuge, mystification, feign, deceit, and beguilement, is an art employed by an agent to spread beliefs in the subject, which are untrue, or truths coated with lies. Deception involves numerous things, for example, dissimulation, sleight of mind, suppression, cover-up, propaganda, etc. The agents win the subjects' favor; they trust him and are unsuspecting of his propensity to be dubious. He can control the subject's mind having won their confidence and trust. The subjects have no doubts about the agent's words. The subjects trust the agent completely and possibly plan their affairs based on the agent's statements.

The deception practiced by the agent can have serious consequential effects if discovered by the subjects. How? The subjects will not be disposed to hearing his words; neither will they accept them anymore; no wonder the agent must be skilled at the deception technique. He must create an escape route to cover up if things boomerang and still retain the trust his subjects have in him.

Deception breaks the laws that govern relationships, and it has been known to affect negatively the hopes that come with relationships. Deception does occur now and then, resulting in feelings of doubt and disloyalty among the two people in the relationship. Nearly everyone desires to have an honest discussion with their partner. However, if they find out that their partner has been dishonest, they, in turn, need to find out how to make use of confusion and distraction to get the reliable and honest information that they require. On the other hand, the trust would be lost in the relationship, making it hard to restore the relationship to its former glory.

The individual on the receiving end of both dishonesty and betrayal would always wonder about the things their partner was telling them, thinking about whether the story was true or false. As a result of this new doubt, most relationships will be brought to an end once the agent realizes their partner's dishonesty.

Types of Deception

Deception is a type of communication-based on omissions and falsehood to convince the world's subject that best fits the agent. There is a need for communication to occur. There will likewise be various kinds of deception. As per the Interpersonal Deception Theory, there are five different sorts of deception. A few of these have been revealed in other types of mind control, showing some similarities.

The five major types of deception include:

1. Lies: this occurs when the agent manufactures information or provides information that is not similar to the truth. They will give this information to the unsuspecting individual as the truth, and the individual will then see this lie to be fact indeed. However, this can be unsafe as the person being given this false information would have no idea about the falsehood. Most likely, if the subject understood that they were being given information that was not true, they would not be on talking terms with the agent, and no deception would have occurred.

2. Equivocations: this is the point at which the agent will make statements that are differing, unclear, or not direct, such that the subject becomes confused and does not understand what is going on. Also, it can help the agent to preserve their reputation, saving face if the subject returns to blame them for the falsehood.

3. Concealments: it is the most frequently used form of deception. It refers to when the agent leaves out information related to or critical to the situation on purpose or displays any such behavior that would cover up information important to the subject for that exact situation. The agent won't have lied straightforwardly to the subject. However, they will ensure that the vital information required never gets to the subject.

4. Exaggeration: occurs when the agent emphasizes too much on a fact or stretch the truth just a little to twist the story to suit them. Although the agent may not directly be lying to the subject, they will manipulate the situation such that it appears as though it is a bigger deal than it is, or they may twist the truth to make the subject do whatever they need them to do.

5. Understatements: this is the inverse of the exaggeration tool in the sense that the agent will present part of the fact as less important, telling the subject that an event is less of a deal, than it is when it really could be what decides whether the subject gets the opportunity to graduate or gets a huge promotion. As such, the agent will return to the subject, saying they had no idea how huge a deal their omission was. They get to keep their reputation, leaving the subject to look petty if they protest.

The above are only some of the forms of deception that there are. The agent of deception will use any means available to reach their final goal, the same as what happens in other types of mind control. However, these methods mentioned are not limiting, as the agent would use any means to get to their goal.

The agent of deception (who will be good at what he does) can be dangerous since the subject will not know the truth or lie.

Reasons for Deception

It has been confirmed by researchers that there are three major reasons for deceptions found in intimate relationships. These motives focused on the partner, on self-image, and focused on a relationship.

In the case of the partner-focused motives, the agent will use deception to keep their partner from harm. They could also use falsehood to save their partner's relationship with an outsider, thereby protecting the subject from worry or keeping the subject's confidence intact. This reason for the deception is often seen to be of benefit to the relationship and socially respectful.

In comparison with some of the other reasons for deception, this one is not as bad. If the agent finds out something terrible that the subject's closest friend said about them, the agent might remain quiet about it. Although this is a type of deception, it not only saves the subject's friendship but also keeps the subject from feeling terrible for themselves. This is the type of deception that is often found in most relationships and also, if found out, might not cause a lot of damage. To protect their partner, a larger percentage of couples would use this form of deception to protect their partner.

The self-focused motive for deception is not thought to be as noble as the partner-focused motive for deception, and as such, is not as acceptable as the other methods. Rather than stressing over the subject and how they are doing, the agent is going to simply consider how they are doing and about their very own self-image. Here, the agent uses deception to protect the agent from criticism, shame, or anger. Using this form of deception in a relationship is typically seen as a serious issue and offense than in partner-focused deception. This is because the agent chooses to act in a self-centered manner instead of protecting their relationship or partner.

Lastly, in the relationship-focused motive of deception, the agent uses deception to prevent any harm coming to the relationship, basically staying away from deception, relational disturbance, and quarrel. This type of deception will either help or harm the relationship, depending on the circumstances. This form of deception could be harmful because it makes things rather complex. For instance, if you do not reveal just how you feel about dinner to prevent a quarrel, this might just help the relationship. If you keep to yourself that you took part in an extra-marital relationship, the situation is only going to become more complex.

No matter the motive of deception in the relationship, deception is not advised. The agent is holding back details that may be vital to the subject; when the subject discovers it, distrust in the agent will set in, and they are left to ponder what other details the agent is keeping from them. However, the subject would not be too worried about the reason behind the deception. They will simply be vexed that they have not been told some things, causing a split in the relationship. Usually, it is best to stick with truthfulness in the relationship and not encircle yourself with individuals who don't put deception into practice in your social circle.

Detecting Deception

An individual interested in preventing deception from avoiding the mind games that come with it should learn how to detect deception when it occurs. It is not usually easy to know when deception is going on, as there are no pointers to rely on, except the agent makes a mistake and either tells an obvious lie or says something that the subject knows to be false. While it might be difficult for the agent to mislead the subject for a long time, it will usually happen regularly between individuals who know one another.

Deception can place a heavyweight on the agent's cognitive thinking because they will need to find a way to remember all their conversations with the subject on the situation. Hence, the story stays believable and dependable. Any mistake will bring the subject to the realization they are being deceived. The stress involved in keeping the story believable is much, and as such, the agent is very much likely to spill out details that will give the subject a clue that they are being deceived either through nonverbal or verbal signs.

Researchers believe that detecting deception is a process that is cognitive, fluid, and complicated and will regularly differ based on the message that is being passed across. As indicated by the Interpersonal Deception Theory, deception is an iterative and dynamic process of influence between the agent, who attempts to manipulate the information and how they need it with the goal that it varies from the truth, and the subject, who will at that point try to know if the message is true or false. The agent's activities will be concerning the actions that the subject makes after they get the information. Through this trade, the agent will uncover the nonverbal and verbal information that will signal the subject into the deceit. Eventually, the subject might have the capacity to tell that the agent has been lying to them.

Chapter 38. Techniques Used in Manipulation: Explication of Different Techniques

So far, I have briefly talked about a few manipulation techniques through personality traits and signs. However, it is important to be thorough about the techniques because there are dozens of techniques that manipulators use. Sometimes, they make up their techniques to gain control as they go through their job or relationship.

Foot in the Door Technique

The foot in the door technique is probably one of the most well-known forms of manipulation. Of course, the salespeople took the phrase a bit more literally than manipulators. While salespeople would place their foot in front of the door so the homeowner couldn't close it on them, manipulators take more of a mental and emotional stance towards this technique.

The first step manipulators use by asking for a small favor or "breaking the ice" through a small conversation. This helps the manipulators build a rapport with their target. For example, if they are trying to find a significant other, they will find a way to become compatible with their target. They will then ask the person questions about what they like and mention they enjoy the same things.

This technique is often how people get to know each other in a social setting. For example, have you ever been sitting at a club or coffee shop when someone came up to you and started small talk? They might have stated it was a busy night or a nice day. You might have agreed in some way, whether verbally or through your actions. Giving a reaction is letting the person keep their foot in the door. While you are probably just trying to be polite, they see it as a step into your life, depending on their motive.

Negative Reinforcement

Master manipulators will often use negative reinforcement to get you to stop doing something they don't like. This could be anything from going back to college or getting a job. Typically, they don't like anything that gives them a loss of control and threatens their environment.

When you start to do something they don't like, they will do something you don't like. This is the first step of negative reinforcement. They will continue to use negative reinforcement and other tactics to try to get you to stop doing what they don't like. Once they have manipulated you to stop, they will then stop.

Negative reinforcement works when the manipulator starts to do something you don't like because you won't do what they want you to do. To get the manipulator to stop doing what you don't like, you have to do what they request of you, even if you don't like it.

The main reason negative reinforcement is used is that it is more likely that you will do what they ask of you in the future without hesitation. This is especially true for manipulators who use any type of abuse to get you to stop doing something or to listen to them.

The Emotional Triangle

The emotional triangle is similar to a love triangle; however, it is used against you. The manipulator will use it to get you to do what they want. They will create a triangle with themselves, you, and a third person who is not directly involved in your relationship.

The manipulator will not hide the fact that they are interested in the third person, even if they aren't in truth. They will flirt with the person in front of you and even show affection toward the person. Sometimes they will use certain affections that you like, whether rubbing the person's back or hugging them.

While it might be obvious they like the other person. They will deny any type of affection in a confrontation. They will blame you, telling you that it is your insecurities and low self-esteem, which is making you believe this.

The emotional triangle's main goal is you become insecure about your relationship, which means you will work harder to make your significant other happy. You will do what they ask, even if you don't want to or feel uncomfortable taking on the assignment.

Establishing Similarities

The foot in the door technique can often lead manipulators into another technique where they establish similarities. For example, the manipulator might learn through observation or a friend who you like a certain coffee shop. Therefore, they will decide to run into you at the coffee shop, where they discuss how much you both enjoy the location and the coffee.

Manipulators will also mirror your actions. They will notice if you are putting your elbows on the table and do the same thing. They will notice your hand gestures and how often you smile. They will then mirror these actions as well. This is a psychological tactic that reaches into your subconscious mind. It makes you feel like you can trust the person because you feel more connected, even if you don't realize they mirror your actions and behaviors.

Fear-Relief Technique

Fear is a strong emotion and can often cause us to react in extreme ways. People are typically uncomfortable with fear, which means they will want to find a way to ease their fears. Because of this, manipulators commonly use the fear-relief technique as it allows them to gain the trust of their target by using emotion.

This technique is heavily used by manipulative people who create a fear in you to give you relief, which makes you more likely to listen to their requests time. You wait a couple of hours, and when they still don't return, you call their cell phone. They don't pick up. Another hour, you try calling them again but receive their voicemail. At this point, you start to become anxious about the situation. You have left dozens of text messages, and they don't answer their phone. You start to worry that something has happened to them. A couple of hours, they send you a text that says they are on their way home, and everything is fine.

When you confront your significant other as they walk in the door about what they were doing, they respond that you left, so they could too. They then tell you that as long as you do something like that to them, they can do it too.

Manipulators Will Put You on the Defense

Manipulators like to reach into your emotions because they are powerful. When you react with your emotions, you stop thinking, make irrational decisions, and have trouble remaining calm. This is how a manipulator wants you to react because conversations where you are calm and think rationally, are not in their favor.

Therefore, manipulators use a tactic where they will put you on the defense. This means that you will feel like you need to explain yourself. You have to defend how you feel, who you are, and what you believe. This is one of the strongest signs of manipulation, but people often don't notice it because it becomes common.

It is significant to understand that just because you find you are explaining something you believe to your significant other doesn't mean you are in a manipulative relationship. There are many times in a relationship that you might find yourself explaining why you support a cause your significant other doesn't or why you find something is fun when your partner doesn't. In a healthy relationship, you will find yourself explaining your beliefs and thoughts when your significant other wants to understand you to support you. You will also ask your loved ones to explain themselves so that you can treat them in the same way. In a manipulative relationship, your significant other will always put you on the defense, no matter what your action was. The only time you might not find yourself on the defense is if they approve of your behavior.

The Gaslighting Technique

Gaslighting is phrasing the manipulator will repeatedly use to make you believe a situation you remember is wrong. Some of the most common phrases include "You can't be serious," "I never said that," "You don't remember it correctly," "Are you crazy?" and "You imagine it." While you might feel that you are right, the manipulator will continue to stand by what they say, believe, or even give you their version of the situation. They might mix gaslighting with other tactics for you to start questioning yourself.

They will continue to break you down through gaslighting or simply find a way to end the conversation.

Gaslighting is a very dangerous tactic because it is used to distort your reality. If used enough, you might start to feel that you are crazy or imagine all these situations. This will mentally and emotionally break you down even further, which will allow the manipulator to gain the upper hand as you start to distrust your thoughts, emotions, and abilities. You start to distrust your reality, making you believe that you do not see what you see, and you do not hear what you hear.

Traumatic One Trial Learning Technique

Manipulators are good at putting on an act. One technique that manipulators use to get you to listen to them better to keep you under control is traumatic one-trial learning.

When a manipulator uses this technique, they will become angry when they feel you have done something wrong. For example, if you come home later than you said you would, your significant other might yell, make you feel ashamed, or become verbally abusive. They will act in a way they know will make you fear their anger, so you are less likely to do something like that again.

Chapter 39. How To Defend Yourself From Manipulation Techniques

To avoid falling victim to manipulators, you have to build your defenses to prepare for any manipulative strategies they may try to use. The best way to build your defenses is by taking steps to improve your self-esteem and your willpower. However, as a point of caution, you should be very careful about building your defenses because you don't want to create restrictions that will keep you from living a fulfilled life.

For example, as you try to guard against manipulation, you can't act out of fear. You can't hide from the world just to avoid scenarios where someone might want to take advantage of you. Recall that the world is full of persons with dark personality traits who may harbor malicious intentions, so acting out of fear won't protect you from anyone. It will just make you more of a target. As you build your defenses, make sure that you start on the premise that you are willing to confront manipulators head-on, and you will never run away or recoil. If you act out of fear, you lose by default.

Acceptance

Acceptance is about assenting to the reality of a given situation. It's about recognizing that a certain condition or process is what it is, even if high levels of discomfort and negativity characterize it. It's about consciously submitting that something cannot be changed and that its reality is not subject to interpretation. It's about making peace with the situation that you are in. Acceptance is the opposite of denial. Denial can be a coping mechanism, one that can keep us from being overwhelmed by the reality of a given situation. However, denial does us more harm than good because unless we can accept something, we can't change it. We will be stuck looking for alternative interpretations and explanations for our prevailing circumstances.

Without acceptance, the door remains wide open for malicious people to exploit us. Take the example of a patient who is told that he/she is terminally ill. After seeking the opinions of several medical professionals and getting the same diagnosis, the patient is still left with the choice of either accepting or denying the situation. The one who accepts it will make peace and try to make the best of what little time he has. The one who stays in denial will become susceptible to tricksters who may offer "alternative cures," and he may end up losing all his savings paying such people so that in the end, he leaves his family with nothing. That is an extreme example, but it perfectly illustrates why acceptance is important in avoiding manipulation, even if the reality may seem too painful to accept.

The most crucial form of acceptance is self-acceptance. It refers to the state of being satisfied with yourself, the way you currently are. Self-acceptance is a kind of covenant that you make to validate, support, and appreciate who you are instead of constantly criticizing yourself and wishing you were someone else. Most people have trouble accepting themselves as they are. We are all in a constant strive for self-improvement. We want to be more successful, be wealthier, be more attractive, or be perceived more positively by others. Even the most accomplished among us have issues with self-acceptance.

In many ways, the desire to be a better version of yourself can be seen as a positive thing; it can help you study harder in school, work harder to earn a promotion at work or exercise more to get in shape. However, there is always room for improvement, so no matter how high you ascend, the dissatisfaction will always be there. It will make you vulnerable to manipulation by people who want to take advantage of your desires.

To defend against manipulation, you have to accept your reality, and you have to accept yourself. People tend to think that if they accept themselves, they won't try to improve—that couldn't be further from the truth. Accepting yourself means owning up to your flaws, and that gives you control over your life. With self-acceptance, attempts at self-improvement would come from within, so when you decide to change, you will.

Increase Awareness

Increasing your awareness means having a higher level of alertness when it comes to an understanding of what's going on in your environment. It means paying close attention to your surroundings and to the way people behave around you. The higher your level of awareness, the better you will be in adapting to your surroundings and understanding the motivations of the people you interact with.

When you become more aware, you will be able to catch on quickly when people try to manipulate you. Numerous of us tend to be preoccupied with our thoughts that we hardly ever notice the cues of the people we interact with. We tend to live life on autopilot, so when other people try to seize control over our lives, we only notice it when it's too late. If you increase your awareness, you will be equipped with the skills necessary to identify all the red flags, and you will be able to stop most manipulators in their tracks before they can do any real harm.

The first step towards increasing your awareness is to learn about the tendencies of manipulative people. Reading this puts you ahead of the curve; you now know enough to be able to spot people with ill motives, but you should understand that the worst kinds of manipulators are very good at concealing their motives, so you have to keep working on increasing your awareness.

To be truly aware of manipulative people, you have to approach all interactions with skepticism levels. We are not telling you to turn into a paranoid person who doesn't let anyone in; we are just saying that you should take a deeper look at each person you interact with. Try to study their body language and their words and see if they are trying to hide something.

Apart from increasing your awareness, you have to increase your self-awareness as well. Many people confuse those two things, but they entirely different concepts. Self-awareness is about understanding yourself. It's about having a clear concept of your personality. You have to examine yourself and figure out your strengths and weaknesses, values and motivations, and what kind of thoughts and emotions you are likely to have in specific situations. Self-awareness helps you understand both who you are and how other people perceive you.

Self-awareness works as a defense against manipulation because when you know who you truly are, it becomes more difficult for someone to alter your thoughts and perceptions. If you have strong and well-articulated values, it becomes harder for a manipulator to get you to abandon those values. People who like self-awareness are more likely to be gaslighted or subjected to other forms of mind control.

If you end up in a relationship with a manipulative person, self-awareness can help you keep your identity. Manipulators will try to tell you what to think and how to behave. Still, if you are self-aware, you will experience cognitive dissonance, and your brain will push back against any attempts at manipulation.

Detach with Love

Detaching with love is a defense against manipulation that is most commonly used by people who have loved ones who suffer from substance abuse problems. Even though it was conceptualized to help people deal with addicts, you can also work when dealing with manipulators.

Detaching with love is about showing love and compassion for others without taking responsibility for their actions. If the addict doesn't come home, you don't waste your time looking for them in the seedy parts of the city, you stay at home, and you do the things that benefit you and make you happy.

The point of detaching with love is to stop trying to control other people's lives, even if you are doing it for their good. The idea is that you accept that people are different from you and have their own free will.

Detaching from love can defend you from manipulation in many ways. Some manipulators want to exploit you by making you responsible for them. We have mentioned several times that some malicious people will take the submissive position in a relationship because they want your world to revolve around them. They want you to give them all your attention; that is how they control you. When you detach with love, you will learn to stop fixing everyone's problems. So, when the manipulator tries to play the victim to gain your sympathy, you will keep doing whatever is in your best interest, and you will tell him or her to take accountability for his or her actions.

Some manipulators may take up self-destructive habits because they want to dominate you by making you clean up after them. When they do this, you can detach with love by letting them follow the paths they have taken, no matter where they lead them. If they are causing you harm, you can get away from them, but leave your door open. If they find the right path in the future and regain control over their own lives, you can let them in again. You have to make it very clear that you will let them direct their own lives through your words and actions, and you won't take any responsibility for them.

Detaching with love is about accepting others for who they are and respecting them enough to let them be in charge of changing their own lives. When you feel responsible for someone, and he makes a choice that harms you both, you will frequently react with fear, anger, or anxiety. To detach with love, you have to learn to let go of those negative emotions.

Manipulators count on the fact that you will react in a predictable way to their machinations, but when you detach with love, you learn to calm yourself down and think about your role in the other person's life before you take any sort of action. This will keep you from falling into the traps that manipulators will set for you. Detaching with love builds your self-esteem because it allows you to put your own needs ahead of those trying to manipulate you.

Chapter 40. Qualities of a Manipulative Person

If you have ever heard the term "master manipulator," you might have an idea of a few manipulator personality traits. Most manipulators, especially people who are using it for their benefit, share similar characteristics. One factor to note is that there are easily noticeable traits and traits manipulators will hide well.

Manipulators Will Pressure You

A manipulator will pressure you into deciding before you are ready. They might start by doing this subtly at first and then increase their efforts. Their goal is to get you to cave as this will give them what they want.

Manipulators Are Experts at the Silent Treatment

If there is one main way to make a manipulator mad, it is not to give in. When a manipulator starts to feel threatened by your emotional and mental strength, they will resort to isolating you. For example, they might refuse to allow you to answer a question or completely ignore you.

Manipulators use this tactic to remain powerful. They want to make sure they assert their dominance.

Manipulators Will Bully You

Manipulators will do whatever they can to remain powerful, including bullying behavior. They will do whatever they can to shake your confidence as they want to make sure you don't feel emotionally and mentally stronger than them.

They will take part in this behavior anywhere; however, they often become more of a bully in public. This is because it allows them to embarrass you to the point you won't want to socialize with many people.

Manipulators Will Never Admit Their Faults

Manipulators will find someone else to blame, such as their parents, significant other, friends, and even children. They will also make up excuses when someone notices their weaknesses. For example, they might say that they didn't know certain information because someone never told them.

Manipulators Will Test Your Boundaries

No matter how strongly you discuss your boundaries with a manipulator, they will still test them. While they will act like they are sorry initially, telling you that they didn't realize this was a boundary, they don't feel this way. Testing your boundaries is a great way for a manipulator to learn what you will and will not put up with. They want to learn your breaking points to know what they can and cannot do right away. This doesn't mean that they won't cross your breaking points. They will just wait to do this until they have you within their webs.

Manipulators Don't Validate Your Feelings

Manipulators don't care about you as a person. They care about using you to get what they want. Therefore, they aren't going to spend time trying to make you feel better, ask you what is wrong, how your day went, or validate your feelings.

As humans, we need to have our emotions validated to work through them and maintain a healthy mindset. By not validating your emotions, manipulators can keep stronger control over you because you will start to lose your confidence, self-esteem, and self-image. You will become so overwhelmed with emotions; most of them negative, you will become depressed and stop caring about yourself. You might also stop talking to your friends and family. In general, you lose your interest in life.

This gives a manipulator the upper hand because you are more likely to do what they say. You will act how they want you to act. Even if you don't feel it is right, they will start to get you to believe that they are the only ones who care about you. Of course, this will further isolate you from anyone else you know and used to hang out with.

Manipulators Are Compulsive Liars

Manipulators are also known as compulsive liars. This is because they often distort facts to make them seem better than you or the best out of everyone. For a manipulator, it doesn't matter if the facts prove them wrong. They do not believe the facts.

However, their lying goes beyond facts. They will also use half-truths or withhold important information from you. This will allow them to maintain their leverage over you. For example, if you are working on a project with a manipulator, they will try to get information from their supervisor or project manager when you are not there. They will then inform you of what they were told but leave out a lot of information. They can then use this left-out information against you. They could lower your confidence in the project because you don't know everything your partner knows, or they could embarrass you in front of other people.

At this point in life, you have probably known about manipulative people. That is their mantra, many manipulative people have been practicing this art for a very long time, and as they say, practice makes perfect. Many people do not just immediately become manipulative. It can happen over time, generally, after the first time they have successfully gotten what they want, and they realize they can do it repeatedly. That is why it can be so difficult to tell when you are being manipulated because manipulators are not amateurs, so if you think you are being manipulated, remember it is not your fault. You have part of something that is much nuanced and complex, often making you feel as though you have done something wrong when that is not the case.

It would be so much easier if manipulative people signed on their backs, saying that they were indeed manipulators, but it's not that easy. They are usually very charming. One way to get you hooked is when true manipulation starts. They also adapt quickly to different situations very quickly, making it even more difficult to spot them. Unfortunately, this is all part of their game, making it even more complicated because they do change on a dime, and keeping you on your toes is what they are good at. Fortunately, they do typically stick to a certain script, if you will, that combines certain words and phrases, so that is one of the best and easiest ways to find out who in your life are the manipulators.

Traits of Manipulators

Playing the Victim

Many manipulators learn to play the victim, making it seem like they need help when they don't. They often do this by making you feel like you have caused a problem when this is not true. In reality, they are the ones that caused the issue, whatever it may be, and blame you because they do not want to take responsibility. This can be as simple as getting an apology from you or something bigger such as monetary gain. When you owed them nothing, to begin with, but they twisted it around so well, you feel as though you did do something wrong.

Hot and Cold

Manipulators can often be nice one minute and standoffish the next. This is hard to deal with because you don't know which person you will get when you see or talk to them. This is one of the easiest ways to prey on your fears and insecurities and keep you guessing. This is not a healthy friendship or relationship because the person being manipulated is constantly on their toes and worried about how they will treat them, always wondering if something they did to provoke this behavior. It might sound juvenile, but this can be very powerful in lowering someone's self-esteem, especially over a long time.

Aggressive

Many manipulators can take it passed being standoffish and can resort to being extremely aggressive or even vicious. They might not be physical, but they can wear another person down by using personal verbal attacks. All of this is done because that is how badly they want to get what they want. Often, they will not let up or stop until the other person is so worn down that they simply give in just to get the abuse to stop.

Lack of Insight

Many manipulative people lack insight when it comes to how to interact with others healthily. Instead, they truly believe that the only way to deal with situations is their way, and everyone else is wrong because their desires or needs are not being met. So, the scenarios and solutions they create will only benefit them at the expense of everyone else around them. This means that every friendship, relationship, and situation is about them, and everything else does not matter.

No Questions

Manipulative people do not question their behavior. They think they know what is right because it benefits them, which is the end of it. An average person knows how to read a situation and might understand, given certain circumstances, that their beliefs or opinion is wrong and can adjust it appropriately. A manipulative person does not do this. They just don't ask questions or wonder if the problem is them.

Lack of Boundaries

Part of being manipulative is putting their desire above everything else; part of this is not respecting other people's boundaries. They will crowd someone's spiritual, physical, emotional, and psychological space with absolutely no concern to them. This is often how they achieve their goals in the first place, by crossing these boundaries and exploiting the insecurities of others. A great way to think of this is to imagine them like a parasite, something that works in the natural world, but it is unacceptable for humans. Feeding off of someone else at their expense is weakening, demeaning, and exhausting.

Avoids Responsibility

One of the biggest traits of a manipulator is the inability to accept responsibility; everything is always someone else's fault. This does not mean that they do not know what responsibility is; on the contrary, they know what it is enough to blame someone else, just never themselves. Generally, they want you to take responsibility for their happiness, leaving you with no time or resources to get your own.

Preying on Sensibilities

Manipulators know that not everyone makes a great target, so they search out a certain type of person. They look for sensitive and conscientious people because they know this will increase their chances of trapping them into some sort of relationship. Finding the type of person who is kind, caring, feeling, and, most of all, the type of person who enjoys helping others is the perfect prey for them.

In the beginning, a manipulator will often cater to kindness and caring, usually praising the person for what a good person they are. Still, over time this will switch to praising them for what they can do for the manipulator. Again, this is not an overnight change, but one that takes time and is one reason it is so successful.

Disharmony

One common trait of a manipulator is to create disharmony amongst friend groups. They commonly talk negatively about everyone behind others' backs and enjoy stirring the pot. This keeps people uncomfortable, and they can do it in a way that makes them seem more trustworthy.

Chapter 41. Victim of Manipulation

Certain characteristics and behavioral traits make people more vulnerable to manipulation, and people with dark psychology traits know this full well. They tend to seek out victims who have those specific behavioral traits because they are essentially easy targets. Let's discuss 6 of the traits of the favorite victims of manipulators.

Emotional Insecurity and Fragility

Manipulators like to target victims who are emotionally insecure or emotionally fragile. Unfortunately, for these victims, such traits are very easy to identify even in total strangers, so it's easy for experienced manipulators to find them.

Emotionally insecure people tend to be very defensive when attacked or under pressure, making them easy to spot in social situations. Even after just a few interactions, a manipulator can gauge how insecure a person is with a certain degree of accuracy. They'll try to provoke their potential targets subtly and then wait to see how the targets react. If they are overly defensive, manipulators will take it as a sign of insecurity, and they will intensify their manipulative attacks.

Manipulators can also tell if a target is emotionally insecure if he/she redirects accusations or negative comments. They will find a way to put you on the spot, and if you try to throw it back at them or make excuses instead of confronting the situation head-on, the manipulator could conclude that you are insecure and, therefore, an easy target.

People who have social anxiety also tend to have emotional insecurity, and manipulators are aware of it. In social gatherings, they can easily spot individuals who have social anxiety, then target them for manipulation. "Pickup artists" can identify the girls who seem uneasy in social situations by the way they conduct themselves. Social anxiety is difficult to conceal, especially to manipulators who are experienced at preying on emotional vulnerability.

Emotional fragility is different from emotional insecurity. Emotionally insecure people tend to show it all the time, while emotionally fragile people appear to be normal, but they break down emotionally at the slightest provocation. Manipulators like targeting emotionally fragile people because it's very easy to elicit a reaction from them. Once a manipulator finds out that you are emotionally fragile, he will jump at the chance to manipulate you because he knows it would be fairly easy.

Emotional fragility can be temporary, so opportunistic manipulators often target people with these traits. A person may be emotionally stable most of the time. Still, he/she may experience emotional fragility when they are going through a breakup when they are grieving or dealing with an emotionally draining situation. The more sinister manipulators can earn your trust, bid their time, and wait for you to be emotionally fragile. Alternatively, they can use underhanded methods to induce emotional fragility in a person they are targeting.

Sensitive People

Highly sensitive people are those individuals who process information at a deeper level and are more aware of the subtleties in social dynamics. They have lots of positive attributes because they tend to be very considerate of others, and they watch their step to avoid causing people any harm, whether directly or indirectly. Such people tend to dislike any form of violence or cruelty, and they are easily upset by news reports about disastrous occurrences or even depictions of gory scenes in movies. Sensitive people also tend to get emotionally exhausted from taking in other people's feelings. When they walk into a room, they have the immediate ability to detect other people's moods because they are naturally skilled at identifying and interpreting other people's body language cues, facial expressions, and tonal variations.

Manipulators like to target sensitive people because they are easy to manipulate. If you are sensitive to certain things, manipulators can use them against you. They will feign certain emotions to draw sensitive people in so that they can exploit them.

Sensitive people also tend to scare easily. They have a heightened "startle reflex," which means that they are more likely to show clear signs of fear or nervousness in potentially threatening situations. For example, sensitive people are more likely to jump up when someone sneaks up on them, even before determining whether they are in any real danger. If you are a sensitive person, this trait can be very difficult to hide, and malicious individuals will be able to see it from a mile away.

Sensitive people also tend to be withdrawn. They are mostly introverts, and they like to keep to themselves because social stimulation can be emotionally draining for them. Manipulators looking to control others are more likely to target introverted people because that trait makes it easy to isolate potential victims.

Manipulators can also identify sensitive people by listening to how they talk. Sensitive people tend to be very proper; they never use vulgar language, and they tend to be very politically correct because they are trying to avoid offending anyone. They also tend to be polite, and they say please and thank you more often than others. Manipulators go after such people because they know that they are too polite to dismiss them right away; sensitive people will indulge anyone because they don't want to be rude, giving people maliciously away.

Emphatic People

Emphatic people are generally similar to highly sensitive people, except that they are more attuned to others' feelings and the world's energy around them. They tend to internalize other people's suffering to the point that it becomes their own. In fact, for some of them, it can be difficult to distinguish someone's discomfort from their own. Emphatic people make the best partners because they feel everything you feel. However, this makes them particularly easy to manipulate, which is why malicious people like to target them.

Malicious people can feign certain emotions and convey those emotions to emphatic people, who will feel them as though they were real. That opens them up for exploitation. Emphatic people are the favorite targets of psychopathic conmen because they feel so deeply for others. A conman can make up stories about financial difficulties and swindle lots of money from emphatic people.

The problem with being emphatic is that because you have such strong emotions, you easily dismiss your doubts about people because you would much rather offer help to a person who turns out to be a lair than deny help to a person who turns out to be telling the truth.

Emphatic people have a big-hearts, and they tend to be extremely generous, often to their detriment. They are highly charitable, and they feel guilty when others around them suffer, even if it's not their mistake, and they can't do anything about it. Malicious people have a very easy time taking such people on guilt trips. They are the kind of people who would willingly fork over their life savings to help their friends get out of debt, even if it means they would be ruined financially.

Malicious people like to get into relationships with emphatic people because they are easy to take advantage of. Emphatic people try to avoid getting into intimate relationships in the first place because they know that it's easy for them to get engulfed in such relationships and to lose their identities in the process. However, manipulators will doggedly pursue them because they know that they can guilt the emphatic person into doing anything they want once they get it.

Fear of Loneliness

Numerous people are afraid of being alone, but this fear is heightened in a small percentage. This kind of fear can be truly paralyzing for those who experience it, and it can open them up to exploitation by malicious people. For example, many people stay in dysfunctional relationships because they are afraid they will never find somebody else to love them if they break up with an abusive partner. Manipulators can identify this fear in a victim, and they'll often do everything they can to fuel it further to make sure that the person is crippled by it. People who are afraid of being alone can tolerate or even rationalize any kind of abuse.

The fear of being alone can be easy to spot in a potential victim. People with this kind of fear tend to exude some desperation level at the beginning of relationships, and they can sometimes come across as clingy. While ordinary people may think of being clingy as a red flag, manipulative people will see it as an opportunity to exploit somebody. If you are attached to them, they'll use manipulative techniques to make you even more dependent on them. They can withhold love and affection (e.g., by using the silent treatment) to make the victim fear that he/she is about to get dumped so that they act out of desperation and cede more control to the manipulator.

The fear of being alone is, for the most part, a social construct, and it disproportionately affects women more than men. For generations, our society has taught women that their goal in life is to get married and have children, so even the more progressive women who reject this social construct are still plagued by social pressures to adhere to those old standards. That being said, the fact is that men also tend to be afraid of being alone.

People with abandonment issues stemming from childhood tend to experience the fear of loneliness to a higher degree. There are also those people who may not necessarily fear loneliness in general, but they are afraid of being separated from the important people in their lives. For example, many people stay in abusive or dysfunctional relationships because they are afraid of being separated from their children.

Fear of Disappointing Others

We all feel a certain sense of obligation towards the people in our lives, but some are extremely afraid of disappointing others. This kind of fear is similar to the fear of embarrassment and the fear of rejection because it means that the person puts a lot of stock into how others perceive them. The fear of disappointing others can occur naturally. It can be useful in some situations; parents who are afraid of disappointing their families will work harder to provide for them. Children who are afraid of disappointing their parents will study harder at school. In this case, the fear is constructive. However, it becomes unhealthy when directed at the wrong people or when it forces you to compromise your comfort and happiness.

When manipulators find out that you fear disappointing others, they'll try to put you in a place where you sense as you owe them something. They'll do certain favors for you, and then they'll manipulate you into believing that you have a sense of obligation towards them. They will then guilt you into complying with any request whenever they want something from you.

Chapter 42. Strategies for Seduction, a Person with Manipulation

Seduction and sexual conquest are sometimes common features of dark psychology. They will show up so often that we will devote this guide to them and how they work. This is an important topic to discuss because all of us have been or know someone who has been seduced by someone else who used these dark psychological principles.

The human sex drive can be a very powerful urge, and not being able to fulfill it can sometimes lead to unhappiness, worry, and stress in a person's life. On the other side of things, some of the most famous historical figures are known for their frequent and full fulfillment of sexual urges. For example, emperors and kings have often been afforded the finest women as their reward just because of their status.

One very famous example is the powerful seducer King Henry the 8th from England. His women's appetite was so strong that he decided to create a new religion in his country to change his wife and marry any woman he chose. He also exercised utter control over all the wives he had, and many of them were beheaded when they didn't satisfy his needs or help him meet his goals any longer.

This begs the question: is all seduction a form of dark psychological seduction? Of course not! Yes, all seduction is going to involve the perusal of the other person. Those who don't have the skills of dark manipulation will clumsily do this. This is shown in some of the popular romantic comedies that come out, where the clumsy guy keeps making mistakes when they try to pursue the girl.

But a dark seducer will be someone who knows what they want and knows how to get it. They will go after the other person to fulfill their personal needs, and they often don't care how the other person feels about it. They can be charming, and they are not going to be clumsy at all, and they always know the right thing to say and do.

Why Do People Choose Dark Psychological Seduction?

One question that people will have is: why would someone want to choose this path for attraction? Isn't a better idea to go on some dates and court someone in an honest manner?

A dark seducer doesn't want to get into a relationship, at least not into the boring stuff with it. They want to just get certain things out of the area of romance. They don't care about the other person because they know they can use dark psychology techniques to find another partner if this one goes south. This allows them to approach life, and the relationship, with a non-needy and carefree mindset. If the seducer does decide to settle down with someone, they will be able to do it without feeling like they rushed or settled into the first relationship to get what they want.

So, how is a dark seducer have so much success and influence within the world of dating? They understand the dark psychology principles and have the right skills to execute these principles.

One of the key advantages that dark psychology users will have over their rivals, especially in dating, is that they understand the human mind, almost like a secret weapon. While others may feel like the human mind is impossible to understand, the dark seducer can read it like a book and get the information they want.

Someone who works on the principles behind dark psychology in the dating world may find that it will change their dating experiences compared to their past efforts. They will have a feeling of confidence and control, rather than feeling doubtful, needy, and insecure.

Sure, it may seem kind of mean. The dark seducer can jump from one partner to another, using each one in the manner that matters most to the seducer. Some people are harmed in this process, especially those looking for more of a long-term relationship or looking for more out of it.

But a dark seducer is only interested in what matters to them and nothing else. They can read the mind of their victim and be the exact person that the victim wants. However, they only do this to get their foot in the door and get what they want. As soon as the victim isn't meeting the seducer's needs, then the seducer will move on.

Where Does Dark Seduction Begin?

Now that we have an idea of dark seduction basics, it is time to move into how this seduction can work. Most dark seducers are going to have a guiding approach that is going to motivate their efforts. They will also have tactics that are going to come from their philosophy. Let's look at some of the different philosophies that a dark seducer may choose to use.

One approach is the deployment of a process that is rigid and structured. These seducers feel that they have mapped out how the sequence of attraction should be in great detail, and they may have a process that seems like it is from a flowchart. They want their seduction process to be replicable and predictable. These systems work for the dark seducer and work for others who understand these systems and learn how to implement them correctly.

These seducers are going to use a series of stages in their process. They will try to get the target to go through a range of emotions. This range is designed by the seducer to fit their own needs. They will move them through emotions such as interest, attraction, and then excitement. These seducers will see the whole process as a series of checkpoints that they need to pass through to help them reach their goals.

This method's strength is that it gives the dark seducer a feeling of certainty because they know the exact steps to take each time. They won't have any surprises that come up during the seduction, and it kind of becomes routine and habitual for the seducer. The biggest problem with this is that it doesn't consider that sometimes people will be unpredictable and won't go along with the structured emotional program that the seducer planned out.

Another option is the natural approach. This approach will involve the dark seducer cultivating a natural emotional state internal to the seducer and then expressing them freely to the one they are working to seduce. An example of this is when a person who uses this, is likely to spend some time trying to understand their own emotions and then try to perfect these. They are then going to express these to others. The philosophy behind this one is that "I can't make others feel good until I can feel good."

You can also work with hypnotic and Neuro-Linguistic Programming (NLP) seduction. NLP is a combination of neurological processes, language, and behavior. This is kind of a subset of dark seduction. Unlike the structured seduction that we talked about before or even the natural version, NLP and hypnotic seduction involve triggering specific emotional states in the victim and then linking these back to the seducer.

Let's look at an example of this. The NLP approach to seduction involves allowing people to explore their own intense positive emotions. The seducer may even try to get more of those emotions out. Then, they will work to anchor these to the seducer. That way, when the victim sees the seducer, they will naturally feel intense physical pleasure, even though they may not know why that happens.

Hypnotic seduction is another option to work with, but it can be difficult to work with regularly. This is because a few things will make someone suspicious about a seducer than the odd techniques that come with NLP. The other seduction types seem somewhat normal to the victim, but hypnotic seduction doesn't seem this way. However, some will respond to it.

Dark seduction can allow the seducer the ability to get exactly what they want out of the relationship. Those who are not looking to take advantage of others, but who are open about what they are doing and just use the techniques to give them more confidence and avoid a boring relationship can sometimes use it. However, there are plenty of dark seducers who use it as a way to use the other person, with no care about how it is going to affect the other person at all. Either way, it is still important to be on the lookout for this kind of behavior to not get into a bad relationship for you or isn't what you are looking for from the other person.

Chapter 43. Covert Emotional Manipulation: Introduction

Covert emotional manipulation is an exceptional phenomenon that can happen to anybody, even you. Behind the intensity of your mindfulness alertness is where emotional manipulation operates and restrains you emotionally, while as a victim, you know nothing about what is happening.

A skillful emotional manipulator will do to you to influence you to place into their hands all your sensitive safety and senses of self-worth. Manipulators will continually and methodically break off your self-esteem and identity until there is little left the instant you make such a severe miscalculation.

Psychopaths and manipulators manipulate much in the same way as "pick-up artists" and narcissists. As for psychopaths, they have a perception that they are in charge and look down at others as their game to suit their hunting needs. Psychopaths have no compassion, no remorse or guilt, no conscience, and no ability to love. Achieving anything they want, including money, sex, or influence and taking control and power, is a game of manipulators. Not only that, but psychopaths also destroy their victims psychologically, emotionally, physically, and spiritually in the course of their actions. They use all tactics to realize their wishes. They will get going to the next conquest after they have won the game, filled with contempt for you and getting bored.

Covert manipulators cannot have a genuine connection even though they are so smart. They have a strategy from the beginning. Apart from that, they are proficient at reading your mind. Gaining knowledge of your strengths, weaknesses, dreams, fears, and desires is so easy for them. With an armory of valuable manipulation schemes that they have chosen carefully and personalized only for you, it is not for them to hesitate to use all these against you. They yearn for control and power and will always persist to control you, even if it results in harming you.

At a point when you think your life has got the blessing of a tender bond through the magical excitement that has made a comfortable and delightful appearance, it might be that something quite sinister and different is behind it. To conceal their exact strategy and personalities is one of the skills of manipulators. The main goal of these psychopaths is to fool you into trusting that they love and ready to do anything for you so you can confide in them in the course of a frenzied process of passionate illusion. They craft this stage of deep attachment to pin you and make you susceptible to the abuse and manipulation that will ensue.

After a while, demeaning will replace loving. From then on, degrading will follow, and manipulators will confuse, exploit, and diminish your self-worth, self-esteem, and self-respect. To keep you eager to do anything to save the relationship and to let you hold yourself responsible for not cherishing a great relationship and vouching to save the affair no matter what, manipulators will make a pleasant appearance as loving individuals that hook you.

To show your devotion to the relationship, you will be eager to acknowledge sheer morsels. You won't have any thought of talking about your emotions, fears, and needs, which is not the psychopath's concern and consider unacceptable weaknesses. When things go wrong, you will shift the blame on yourself, analyzing every mood and every word, becoming quite confused about what is happening, and recalling the conversations. Your life or job will suffer and your dealings with other people and your mental and physical health.

Your manipulator will try to have you with them, waiting for the time you become a hopeless disaster. At that point, they will let you know with seething contempt and disdain how they are bored with you and don't want you anymore. They will then leave you a sensitive mess who wonders just what happened to your life, speculating your perfect affair crumbled into the gulf of hell from heaven-on-earth.

Struggling with feelings of acute emotional grief and confusion comes to all preys of this deceptive and underhanded manipulation. Many of them also experience rage, obsessive thoughts, insomnia, misplaced self-esteem, panic, anxiety, inability to trust, poor health, fear, use of drugs or alcohol, and absence of support. Sometimes, extreme and irrational behavior can happen, including withdrawal and isolation from family, friends, and society. Suicidal actions or thoughts are part of what most victims face.

The question is, do these manipulators truthfully want love in the first place? Maybe they never have any desire for love. In a situation such as this, the purpose is that of victimization. The manipulator would have had their target plans when they discovered that you are open to their advances.

On the other hand, the occasion might end up badly even if the manipulator has a real attraction for you. Because it is the incentive scheme of the brain, things and people stimulate and excite these people. In fact, for those with features of psychopathy, the system works quite well. Indeed, studies have found that far from that of an average individual, manipulators' reward system is more sensitive. Consequently, it is with the intensity that they establish a relationship.

A Deeper Look at Manipulation Tactics

Covert manipulative individuals make use of tactics to accomplish two things simultaneously:

- Conceal their intention

- Invite you to fear, doubt, and concede

Tactics that are generally the most effective in manipulating other people, especially neurotics, are a few tactics covert manipulative people use more frequently. The key to personal empowerment is to know how to deal with these manipulation methods when you recognize them.

With just about any behavior imaginable to accomplish their aims, it is amazing how capable the more skilled manipulators can be. Armed with these tactics, manipulators will thoroughly evaluate how they will manipulate their target character when the manipulators know their victim inside out and are familiar with their target's fears, sensitivities, conscientiousness level, core beliefs, and so much more. Moreover, in a covert war of dominance, manipulators will have a considerable prospect making way for them to use that person's traits, especially their most collectively attractive characteristics, against them.

It will be appropriate for us to focus our attention on the more conventional approaches they employ and give in-depth details on why the tactics are so efficient. It is not realistic to talk about different feasible behaviors covert manipulators can use to influence another person. Having a good understanding of the fundamentals of manipulation works will reinforce your insight into the various potential tactics manipulators might apply and give you superior conscious control of the nature of upsetting encounters with all manipulators.

There is a rationalization tactic, which we may call "justifying", or "excuse-making." Originated from the Freudian notion, the word rationalization indicates that, on occasion, against the fear they might have suffered by engaging in dealings that damage their principles, people defend themselves unaware. They will assuage any qualms of conscience when they find reasons that appear to make their achievement more benign, appropriate, understandable, and acceptable. However, the assumption for this situation implies that the person has a highly sensitive conscience, and this type of rationalization is a mostly unconscious process and strictly internal.

Manipulators know what they are doing when they make explanations for their actions in some situations. When this set of people is looking to validate themselves, they certainly have obvious intention in mind. They use this approach when they know that they plan to do something or have done something most people would regard as wrong. However, manipulators stay determined to do it even when they know it is wrong and how their actions negatively represent them. They have permission to do it, such as the aggressive characters' situation or the case of more self-absorbed individuals, or they may clash against the accepted rules.

Most essential to identify is that at the time, manipulators are justifying their actions; they are neither unconsciously fending off any anxiety nor defending. Instead, they are actively at war against a set of standard manipulators who know society wants them to accept. More importantly, they are also attempting to get your support. Unlike open defiance, undercover manipulators prefer this type of tactic because it not only helps to mask their manipulative goals and various revealing parts of their personality, but at the same time helps them to preserve a more positive social image by making someone else identify with the supposed rationality of their actions or have a similar perception to their own. When the person accepts their premise with this strategy, the door of wielding the mutual domination and contest of image is opening gradually.

It is not that manipulators don't understand that their actions are wrong or that most people would see them as evil; instead, they hate your negative appraisal of their personality and perhaps end any relationship with them. More importantly, they should not engage in such behavior again because covert manipulative people don't want to incorporate and allow. Even when they still apply the tactic, they oppose a standard and hold up the inculcating that standard into their social ethics. It is the visible signal that they can engage in a similar activity in any related situation.

Now, let us talk about denial, another tactic. Denial is a word that had its origin from the psychology of Freudian. Freud invented it as an unconscious and primitive resistance against intolerable emotional pain. With other tactics such as pretending that they are innocent, manipulators often will use denial. This situation is when someone you have confronted acts as if they know nothing of what you are saying or they pretend in a vain way that they did nothing of which to be guilty or ashamed. They will often use faking gullibility and denial with such apparent confidence and intensity that you start to be curious about your sanity and perception. That moment, you start out knowing that you have caught them on the action, and one way or another, using this tactic, you begin to wonder if you are making any sense at all. This tactic is quite an efficient one-two manipulation blow!

However, the main missiles in the arsenal of any manipulator are the strategy of guilt-tripping and shaming. The fact behind this analysis is that precision defines the high degree of neurotics and cannot stand thinking that their actions are shameful or wrong. As a result, making them believe that what they have done should make them feel ashamed or guilty is the perfect way to control them. Conscientious individuals sometimes attempt to shame or guilt on their prey, hoping that it will somehow induce their behavior.

Covert is when an attempt is made to communicate with the subject's unconscious mind without knowing that they will be put through hypnosis. It comprises a string of techniques such as conversational hypnosis or NLP (neuro-linguistic programming), body language, and other powerful communication and interaction strategies.

Chapter 44. Covert Manipulation in a Love Relationship

The love-bombing is hard to ignore. They will make you feel like you are the most important person in the world to them, and you will be showered with loving gestures such as poems, love letters, gifts, or just merely the fact that they always have time for you.

The first few times they overreact to something, you might be able to justify it in your mind. There is a simple stage in a relationship where a kiss and a few sappy words can fix any argument.

A narcissist cannot have a productive argument. When people in a healthy and loving relationship disagree, their goal is to learn how to communicate better and find out where the miscommunication happened this time. When it is narcissistic abuse, they want to demean and shame you.

It is one that is void of name-calling and hurling accusations at one another. An argument is also not the time to bring up past grievances. This is sometimes referred to as the "kitchen sink" method. This is a very unhealthy way of arguing, but one that is often used by narcissists. They mean to make you feel like a wrong person.

They will not hear you out if you come to them with a concern about how they treat you. They will say something like, "do you think you're perfect?" This focuses the attention away from what they have done that is hurtful to you. For example, you might tell them you don't want them to call you names. Their response is, "You're not always a ray of sunshine around me either." In this situation, they did not hear you out at all. They shut down what you were trying to say to them.

A narcissist's first impulse will always be to self-protect. They are not interested in listening to your point of view, nor do they want to reach a compromise. They want to make sure they do not have any tarnishes on their character. That is because if they are not flawless, they are worthless. That is their thought process. This is most likely because, during childhood, they were only given praise when they succeeded.

The covert narcissist will be honest with you about what their grievances are in a relationship. Instead, they will go to other people. There will often be a cheating situation that arises, but they will rally many people against their partner. They often aim to taint their mutual friends' idea of them.

Venting to a confidant such as a best friend or family member is alright and something you will need to do at times. Speaking ill of your partner is not. When you come to a confidant with a legitimate issue, you still want to preserve the relationship's integrity. This is because you are talking to someone outside of the situation and will not share what you say with other people.

While communicating with your partner is essential, you sometimes need to express that would only harm the other person. It is okay to have things to say that you don't want your partner to hear. Where it becomes morally grey is when a person consistently goes to people outside of the relationship with the intent of bashing their significant other.

There is a difference between venting and bashing. While harsh words may be said when a person is venting, they still value the other person. As humans, we will get frustrated with one another, especially if we have an intimate relationship, which will inevitably come with miscommunications and disagreements.

This is an example of venting: "It hurts my feelings when they talk on the phone at the dinner table. It makes me feel like they would rather spend their free time talking to other people besides me." On the other hand, this is bashing "They're impossible to live with. They're always on the phone, ignoring me. I always try so hard, and they never give anything in return."

In the first example, the person is expressing frustrations but not talking about the person negatively or aiming to damage their reputation. In the second example, the language is inflammatory, and it hints toward a deep resentment towards the other person.

"You always" and "you never" are terms narcissists use in arguments.

Narcissists are infamous for their jealousy. They call every interaction you have with everyone in your life, particularly towards the gender you prefer, into question. You can never reassure them enough that you are not going to leave them for someone else. Acting jealous is designed to isolate you. Everything and everyone in your life makes them feel threatened.

Jealousy is not cute. It does not mean your partner is so in love with you that it hurts them to see you talking to someone else. It might sound very romantic when they word it like that, and it might make you feel loved, but what it means is that they want ownership of you.

It is crucial to remember to keep your priorities straight when you begin college. They are trying to put pressure on you to prove to them that you are faithful to them, which will mean your attention is divided while trying to navigate through the complex environment that is college.

A jealous person will call often and want to have long conversations. You cannot do this and study at the same time. Anyone who makes you feel like you need to choose between them and pursuing your education and the things that will further your career is not suitable for your life. They might tell you that you never loved them in the first place if you choose your education, but they did not put you first if they made you feel like you need to limit yourself to keep them.

This leads to another thing a narcissist does in a relationship. They give ultimatums. They will say, "okay, fine, you either stop going to that class or we're breaking up. It's your choice!" This may sound extreme, but that is how unreasonable the demands of a narcissist will become. They will say it's your choice, but it is a threat.

Covert narcissists harbor resentments indefinitely. They might say the conflict is over, and they have moved past it, but if you do something to cause them narcissistic injury, you will hear about it again in perpetuity. This is where a double standard in the relationship begins. They can say and do extremely rude and hurtful things to you, and they will expect you to forgive them after giving you a half-hearted non-apology.

If you are in a relationship with a narcissist, you will often be compared unfavorably to other people. You will be told that you are much more difficult to get along with than these people. This is because, at their core, a narcissist has a very juvenile mentality. They want what is most beneficial to them at the moment. They also do not understand why everyone else seems to be so much easier to get along with than their partner.

They do not live with these other people who seem so shiny. They only see them when they are at their best, and when they spend time with them, it is the good times: for example, it is a neighborhood get-together, and everyone is dressed their best. Drinks are being poured, and food is on the grill. Everyone is laughing and talking, and when the party is over, everyone leaves. All the cleanup is left to the people who hosted the party. We see every side of our spouses or significant others. We only see a certain depth of our acquaintances. You will have much fewer and less intense conversations with those you don't see as often.

They look at people they only see once in a while and then compare them to the person they live with and therefore see every day in every state, even the least glamorous ones. They might be married and even have children with this person. Marriage is difficult even when the relationship is healthy, especially when children come into the equation. Now, not only are you trying to navigate through life between just the two of you, but now you are both responsible for the life, growth, and well-being of other people.

When you share responsibilities this great with someone, you are not always at your best with each other. When you have financial troubles or one of the children begins to act up, tempers will be short, and arguments will be more often. When you compare two relationships, one complex where you share marriage and children, and another relationship where you only see each other when both are well. Your partner will come out, not seeming as good as the other person. Narcissists also do not think about what habits they have that might be unappealing to their partner. They do not consider the idea that they might not be easy to live with themselves.

A narcissist does not consider these factors when they discard one romantic partner to start a relationship with another person.

While they are unfaithful to their partner, they are also rude to them. This makes their partner feel completely unmotivated to try to be attractive or be intimate with them. They talk to this person like a dog and fantasize about how much better life would be cheating. They think about how much more fun they have with this person. They believe their partner is no fun, and the person they see in secret is so much more exciting than them.

Chapter 45. How the Mind Works When It Is Manipulated?

When it comes to working with dark manipulation, there will be many different methods and techniques that we can use to get what you want. Remember, we are talking about some forms of manipulation that will help us get what we want but may harm the other person in the process. This means that they may not be seen as the best options to work with, and you may feel a bit uncomfortable with them if you have not worked in dark manipulation, or even with dark persuasion, in the past.

However, working with these techniques will help you to get the results that you want. They will ensure that the other person you are using as your target will be likely to do the actions or say what you would like them to, even though it may not be in their best interests. With that said, let's take a look at some of the different dark manipulation tactics that you can use to get someone else to do what you want.

Using Isolation to Get What You Want

The first technique that can be used in mind control includes isolation. Humans are very social creatures. They like to spend some time talking with others, spending time out in public, having close friends and family, and spending time in more social situations. When we take this social aspect away from many individuals, it changes how they look at life.

Complete physical isolation can be the most powerful. This is when the subject is taken away from all contact with others, including email, social media, phone calls, and physical contact. This is something that has been seen in cults and with other groups. They will often take the person far away from others, and then the only human contact that the person can have is with the captors.

This total physical isolation can be really hard to do, and it is usually only done in really intense situations. If you are just trying to use manipulation, you usually don't want to go through and completely isolate the target. However, it is common for a manipulator to try to attempt their target mentally as much as possible.

There are many methods that the manipulator can use to get what they want with the help of manipulation. They could include some seminars that last a week and isolate them from what they usually do. They could be many criticisms of the person's family and close friends so that the target feels bad and stops seeing them. It could be jealousy that keeps the target at home and limits the influence that anyone outside the manipulator has on the person.

Once the manipulator can control the information that goes to the target, they can share information, withhold information, and do anything that they would like to continue influencing the target as much as they would like. The target will become reliant on the manipulator, and this is how the manipulator can work and get what they want from the target. There are no outside influences to tell the target that something is wrong or watch out, ensuring the target even more.

Criticism

The option to work with when it comes to manipulation is the idea of using criticism. This one is sometimes used with isolated or on its own, and it works well because it makes the target feel like they are always doing something that is wrong and that they cannot meet the high standards of the manipulator. The criticism can always show up on various topics and could include how they look, who they hang out with, their clothes, their beliefs, and anything that the manipulator thinks will work for this.

When a manipulator decides to use this tactic, they will be good at hiding it behind one of their compliments to the other person. Alternatively, they will say something nice and add this little jab at the end of it. This allows them to say all the mean things they want, and then they can say that the target misheard or misunderstood them and that they hadn't meant any harm by it. This puts the target in a bad spot because they know the manipulator is mean to them, but they are the ones who look paranoid and bad in this situation.

The criticism that the manipulator is going to use is often going to be small. They don't want to start out using really big criticisms that are obvious because the target doesn't want to be criticized. If the manipulator starts with something big, the target is going to fight back and walk away. However, when it starts small with some little comments along the way, it starts to plant a bit of self-doubt, something that the target will notice, but they often are not going to fight back against.

They will start with something that may seem like a compliment or like that will sound like they are helpful, but they are trying to be hurtful in the process in reality. They may say something like, "I didn't know that you liked the color blue. I think you should go with something else." This one will have the hidden meaning inside it that you don't look good in what you are wearing, and your clothes don't look that well.

Or maybe you bring in your favorite outfit to a meeting to make yourself feel better. You are excited and feel good about how you look and feel in the outfit, but then they are going to say something about how they liked you in some other outfit better. It isn't necessarily mean, but it is said in a manner and at a time that it ends up hurting your feelings in the process.

As time goes on, the type of criticism that is going to be used against the target is going to get worse. Moreover, the criticism will become quite a bit more obvious and add in a bit more self-doubt here. This will make it so that the target starts to rely on the manipulator a bit more. This is since the target will feel like they have so many flaws that are hard to ignore and that the only person who can like them and maybe even loves them through these flaws will be the manipulator. The fact that the manipulator is still around is a good sign that they care, which causes the target to be more willing to do what the manipulator asks.

The manipulator will find that they can use this criticism more of us against them if it works better. They could even choose to move their criticism against the outside world to claim they are superior.

When this happens, the manipulator will claim to their target that they are super lucky that the manipulator is even associating with them. The manipulator will ensure that they are important so that the target is more likely to stick around and do what they want. This alone is meant to be enough if it is done in the right manner so that the target feels lucky just because the manipulator is going to spend time with them.

Alienating the Target to Get What They Want

No one wants to be alienated. They want to feel like they are a part of the group. They want to feel accepted, as they belong, and more. This is never more apparent than when we see a newcomer. When someone is new to town, or to school, to work, or somewhere else, you will notice that they are trying to figure out how to join the group and get them to accept them. They are worried that they will be alienated, and to avoid this, they will do everything to get others to like them and go along with them, which is where the manipulator can come in and get what they want.

Newcomers who start to join a new manipulative group are usually going to receive a very warm welcome. And they will form many new friendships that seem to be much deeper and have a lot more commitment and meaning behind them compared to anything that they were able to experience in the past.

There are several reasons for this one. First, this gets the target to feel welcome and more indebted to the group and the manipulator. They are thankful that they have these deep connections, and it is usually easier to get a friend to go along with something that a stranger, so it works to the benefit of the manipulator. Add in that the target is scared to be alienated, then they are going to do what they can to keep the relationships going strong.

Simply because we do not want to be taken away from the crowd and don't want others to have anything to do with us, we will do what the manipulator wants us to. The fact that humans are very social creatures and like to be included in some kind of group all of the time, it is likely that we are going to give in to these urges to do what the manipulator wants, even if we don't feel like it is the best thing for us.

Using Social Proof as a Form of Peer Pressure

We like it when we can be a part of the group. Sometimes we center this around wanting to fit in, and we will follow the rules and do what we can to make sure that we are liked and part of the group. Even when we are more introverted and don't want to be in the group all of the time, we still want to find a group of people we can be around and fit in.

Chapter 46. Hypnosis

Hypnosis is a state of mind that individual's fall into where they are no longer in control of their actions. This is often done in therapeutic circumstances to help individuals find the peace they need within themselves to confront their deepest and darkest traumas. Hypnosis also offers a means to persuade and influence others.

Hypnosis and mind control may seem like the same thing since they involve exerting control over someone else. However, there are glaring contrasts between the two. To recognize the distinctions, you must become more acquainted with what they depend on.

Hypnosis is an artificially induced condition in which the individual reacts to inquiries or prompts from the hypnotist. The procedure can be used on an individual or a gathering of people for a specific reason. At the point when this is utilized for therapeutic purposes, the process is known as hypnotherapy. In any case, when it is being used as a type of diversion for a crowd of people, it tends to be alluded to as organized hypnosis.

Then again, personality control is the way toward utilizing a few traps in getting the ideal response you need from others. You can use the secret to get aggregate or fractional command over what is happening in someone else's psyche.

When it is utilized amid reflection, it can enable you to center around your examination subject.

You can deal with your feelings and contemplations when you participate in this sort of reflection. As a rule, incredible people who accomplished extraordinary life achievements could have excellent command over their psyches through daily reflection.

Having seen the essential meanings of hypnosis and mind control, it is obvious to pinpoint their disparities. The real contrast you'll see between these two is that hypnosis must be utilized on others. It is doubtful that there is any method by which you can hypnotize yourself. A subliminal specialist is necessary to induce hypnosis.

Then again, personality control reflection can be utilized on oneself just as on others. You can, without much of a stretch, take part in this sort of contemplation anytime. All you need is to find a tranquil spot, take a seat, and afterward think. You can influence others to concur with you on specific focuses using mind control traps.

Once more, another distinction is seen in the manner in which hypnosis is connected with mind control. In case you are having an issue of fear, smoking, or appetite, a trance specialist can enable you to opt-out if the hypnosis was done with the correct mindset at heart.

Sometimes, the hypnosis specialist may utilize a few methods in reflection to get individuals to be comfortable with capturing the reaction they need at a specific point in time. It is highly unlikely you can utilize mind control traps to spellbind somebody. It is intended for strategic purposes.

Hypnosis and mind control have clear contrasts. A few components utilized in one may likewise be used in the other, but they are not the same. Everything relies upon how you are ready to draw in the essential standards included.

Hypnosis includes two principal components: acceptance and proposals. Trancelike acceptance is the major proposal conveyed amid the hypnosis; however, it should comprise a matter of discussion.

Proposals are commonly communicated as suggestions that inspire automatic reactions from the members, who don't trust they have much control over the circumstance. A few people are likewise more susceptible than others, and specialists have discovered that they are more likely to have a decreased feeling of authority while under hypnosis.

Susceptibility to hypnosis has been characterized as the capacity to encounter proposed modifications in physiology, sensations, feelings, musings, or conduct. Neuroimaging procedures have demonstrated that these individuals show higher activity levels in the prefrontal cortex, the foremost cingulate cortex, and the mind's parietal systems amid various hypnosis periods.

These are regions of the mind associated with a scope of complex capacities, including memory and observation, feelings, and assignment learning. Be that as it may, the particular cerebrum components associated with hypnosis are as yet hazy. However, researchers are starting to sort out the neurocognitive profile of this procedure.

How would you know whether somebody has been hypnotized? Various changes indicate that the subject is in a hypnotic trance. NLP calls these profound daze markers, and they are a set of highly detailed observations one can make of the subject. Recognizing such markers requires practice and focus. Not all of these markers need to be present to establish that a subject is under hypnosis.

Hypnotic Strategies

The first step in putting someone in a hypnotic state is opening the individual's mind to suggestion. The hypnosis specialist uses a vast range of techniques and, depending on the specialist's skill and the susceptibility of the subject. The outcome may vary.

Hypnosis by relaxation is one of the most common methods of hypnosis. Have you ever heard a hypnosis specialist ask an individual to make him or herself as comfortable as possible? By doing this, the person being hypnotized falls into a relaxing state where the mind tends to shut down on immediate surroundings.

Here are some basic techniques for unwinding:

- Relax your body and mind

- Settle down

- Count in receding order in your mind

- Control what your body and mind is thinking and doing

- Feel your muscles give in to relaxation

- Tone down your voice to a whisper

The handshake strategy for hypnotism involves a hypnosis expert shaking an individual's hand. However, where you might think this is a usual way for the public to greet or welcome each other, hypnosis specialists use this for another advantage.

Instead of just shaking your hand, they will grab, twist your wrist, or pull you forward towards them, so you become unstable. When you are unstable in that split second, the perfect opportunity arises for a hypnosis specialist to control your mind.

Eye prompts can also be important in hypnosis. Talking to someone, it is only natural for one's eyes to wander to surroundings or perhaps a glimpse of something in the distance. A hypnosis specialist will take note of this and, within a short period, learn what prompts you to move your eyes left, right, up, or down. With that, they gain access to the way you think, feel, and respond to certain things surrounding you.

Another approach for the hypnosis of others includes mesmerizing proposals that aren't always obvious suggestions. This kind of suggestion is proposed by the hypnotizer and involves something they wish the subject to do. These proposals also come after the customer has already fallen into more of a stupor.

This is when they are the most open to impact. Rather than telling the hypnotized to do something, the command is masked in a mystifying suggestion. If you want someone to sit down, you don't say, "Sit down," you might say, "You should take a minute to relax in the chair over there."

One method you can do to help improve your hypnotic tactics is to record yourself doing hypnosis and listen to it. If you can fully hypnotize yourself, you can be assured you will have the skills to do this to others. Start by listening to other hypnosis recordings and determine which methods have managed to work best on you.

After this, you can write your original script. Remember, never hypnotize someone who doesn't consent to it. Hypnosis helps the other person find a state of relaxation while also helping to persuade them to do something healthy or beneficial.

Like NLP, all of these methods take practice to master. Don't be discouraged because you cannot hypnotize someone else the first time you try fully. Take note of each hypnosis session that you have, as well. What about it worked once that didn't work as well the next time?

Remember not to use information gained from another in a hypnotic state against them either. Sometimes, they might fall into such a stupor that they become in a dreamlike state. They might say something they don't fully mean, much like a person on pain medication after getting their wisdom teeth removed might.

In contrast to manipulation, these skills are intended to be used for good purposes, as well. You might find it becomes easy to hypnotize others once you have practiced, but your motivation shouldn't be primarily for your gain. There are benefits that both you and the entranced can gain from your hard-earned skill. However, you choose to use these powerful methods, along with the NLP tips, you can be helpful and empowering to both you and the person you can influence.

Understand that when you agree to hypnotize someone else, you are also given a certain responsibility. They are trusting you with a vulnerable headspace that they probably would not entrust to just anyone. Once you attempt to persuade someone, you agree to accept any negative outcomes due to your influence.

The healthy, positive influence will take time to build, and that is true even when you are using these hypnotic techniques. To have long-lasting persuasion that will benefit all parties is a great privilege, and it is up to you to find a positive way to utilize this power.

Chapter 47. Office Politics or Sociopathic Tricks? – The Workplace Manipulators

The workplace is a fertile ground for the manipulation of various types to occur. Many people will find they encounter at least several of the following types of workplace manipulators throughout their careers. It can be tough to know how to draw the line between normal workplace politics, gossip and banter, and actual manipulation. Classifying some of the main types of manipulators within the world of work can help potential targets stay away from the wrong type of colleague before finding their world turned upside down and their professional life damaged beyond repair.

The Blackmailer

The Blackmailer is a type of workplace manipulator that can have a serious impact not only on their victims' careers but also on their mental wellbeing and overall sanity. The basic method of the blackmailer is to appear friendly and highly trustworthy at first. This is usually achieved by finding a newcomer to the workplace or someone who does not fit in with others particularly well.

Once an appropriate target has been identified, the blackmailer will invest a serious amount of time and effort to win over their target and deceptively earn their trust. This is often done by taking a new member of staff under their wing and offering to mentor them and make their new life at the company as easy as possible.

The blackmailer will often form friendships with their intended target that occurs outside of work and inside work. This is essential for the blackmailer's manipulation to be effective. It must involve the target seeing the blackmailer more as a trusted friend than simply as a colleague.

Over time, the blackmailer will begin to elicit sensitive information from their target subtly. This could involve controversial opinions about the other people that the two work with or even sensitive details of the victim's personal life, such as their sexual orientation or political views. The blackmailer will keep going until they feel they have accumulated sufficient information to use against their victim.

Once the blackmailer has some powerful information to hold against their target, such as a covert phone recording of them saying something disparaging, or a photograph of the target behaving controversially in some way, the blackmailer will begin to hold it against them. They may make threats such as planning to reveal sensitive information to others within the workplace or even the target's loved ones and family.

The blackmailer will often demand increasing money or favors from the victim to keep their secrets safe. The victim lives in a continuous state of fear as they do not know when and if they will have their secrets revealed. This has a destructive effect on the victim's mental health and can lead to breakdowns and major anxiety levels.

The False Ally

The false ally is a type of workplace manipulator who is skilled at hiding their true intentions. They will seem to be a keen ally of their target. They are likely to suggest that they go to big places in the workplace and support each other's climb up the career ladder.

The false ally will often begin by making an over the top show of helping out their intended target. This is designed to ensure that the target sees them as trustworthy figures and feels a debt of gratitude towards the false ally. Once the false ally feels they have earned the trust and respect of their target, they will begin to exert subtle levels of control over them.

Some typical plays in the playbook of the false ally include coercing a victim into acting in the ally's self-interest and not of the victim. This will usually take place under the guise of doing 'what's best for both of us' when it will be anything but. This type of manipulation is especially effective if the victim is naive and idealistic. The false ally can tap into the victim's desires and ambitions to gain their compliance in carrying out the false ally's bidding.

The endgame of the false ally is typically to see their career advance while their targets either stalls or are damaged irreparably. This often takes the form of the false ally gaining some form of recognition, like a promotion, at the target's expense, but due to the efforts and choices the target has been coerced into. Often, the victim has no knowledge that they have been played like a puppet until it is too late, and the false ally has already benefited.

The Abuser of Power

It is a well-known fact that power has the potential to corrupt human beings. The office is one of the most common arenas for such behavior to occur. The abuse of power can take many different forms, but they all involve someone unfairly wielding a position of hierarchical authority over another person.

Some common examples of power abuses include those in supervisory or management positions asking for inappropriate or over the top levels of support and compliance from those they have power over. This can take less serious forms, such as getting workers to put in hours that they are not paid for, or take more serious forms such as pressuring female employees into sexual liaisons to promise promotions and job security.

It is important to distinguish between someone who legitimately exerts power and someone who abuses it. To cross the line into the realms of covert emotional manipulation, it must fulfill the following criteria for the wielding of power to cross the line. Firstly, the manipulator must have authority over their targets, such as their manager or some other formal authority position. Secondly, the manipulator must use their power in a way that is intended to control their victim through the manipulation of their emotions. Abusers of power can draw on their victims' feelings of job insecurity or doubt about their future.

Abusers of power are particularly dangerous types of manipulators as they have very little chance of being caught. This is owed to the point that it can be difficult for someone to blame their boss or superior for their actions. Unless clear evidence exists, which is very rare to happen, it is likely to come down to the victim's word in contradiction of the manipulator's word. Sadly, this is rarely sufficient evidence for a company to take any action against the person who has abused the power they hold.

The Sexual Predator

Sexual predators can take the form of almost any other type of workplace manipulator and exist on their own. Simply put, a sexual predator seeks to act in an inappropriate sexual way towards someone they work with. This can range in severity.

At one end of the scale, workplace sexual predators may simply make another member of staff feel uncomfortable. This can be through looks, gestures, or inappropriate physical contact. Despite this being the mildest type of sexually predatory behavior that can occur, it is still unbelievably serious and should be avoided at all costs.

Sadly, many workplace sexual predators take things a lot further than merely making a victim feel uncomfortable. Many sexual predators will coerce their victims into carrying out a sexual nature that they feel pressured or forced into doing. To ensure that their victim stays quiet about what has occurred, the predator will often gather some kind of compromising evidence, such as photographs. The predator threatens to expose the victim's colleagues and family if they cause any predator problems.

Although many workplaces have policies intended to protect against any type of inappropriate sexual behavior in the workplace, they are rarely enough to stop the worst predators from going about their manipulation. This is owed to the fact that skilled predators of this nature can ensure they do not leave any evidence whatsoever. They are also likely to choose victims who have low self-esteem or have some other reason that makes them unlikely to tell others what has taken place.

The Bully

Bullies may seem to be a fairly trivial workplace manipulator, but this is far from the case. Bullying can severely impact someone's happiness and well-being. Is often hard to detect, and even harder to stop. This is owed to the detail that a skilled manipulator engaged in the practice of bullying is likely to mask their actions as friendship or advice underneath the friendly veneer. However, something far more dangerous and sinister is occurring. Bullying can range in severity. On one end of the scale, a bully may seem to be making jokes that just happen to involve the victim. However, this is not what is happening. What seems like a joke is often an attempt to gradually erode the victim's confidence and leave them vulnerable and doubtful. Cognitive dissonance is created in the victim's mind as, on the one hand, they are aware that the comments or actions of the bully are hurting them, but on the other, they do not want to appear overly sensitive or thin-skinned. This often results in the victim begrudgingly accepting the bullying taking place, even if it is hurting them in the long path. For bullying to work, the manipulator chooses their target carefully. They are likely to select someone who lacks self-confidence and is not particularly popular within the workplace. This is owed to the point that the victim will put up with the bullying, as it is often the only form of attention they have received in the workplace up until that point. Bullying can have severe consequences in the long run. It can chip away at the victim's confidence and happiness and, perversely, create a sense of dependency on the manipulator and the attention they provide. The effects can be with a victim for the rest of their life. They may have severe difficulty trusting another again and forming any type of healthy relationship in the future. This is because they will have fallen into the pattern of seeking approval and validation via negative attention.

Chapter 48. Human Behavior and Manipulation

Once you have gotten a decent read on a person, the step to mastering your environment and analyzing your potential in each situation is learning how to manipulate another person's feelings and reactions through subtler cues, both verbal and non-verbal. This will create an environment where your suggestions can thrive.

Don't beat yourself up for thinking outside the box when it comes to analyzing and influencing people. While some people might call it manipulation, you can simply tell them that you are extremely persuasive. What's more, there is nothing to say that the person you are influencing wasn't waiting for an excuse to move forward in the direction you suggested anyway. It is your creativity in constructing a good plan or formula that turns resistance into compliance.

Besides emotion, successful manipulation is all about the imbalance of power. There may be times when getting what you want from another person means using the home-court advantage, which means keeping the person in an environment where you have primary control. This includes your home, car, office, or even your side of town. This makes it harder for your target to do things such as dodge a conversation or even decide that they think they might hurt your feelings.

While it may seem surprising, letting people dominate the conversation is a good thing when you want to have the upper hand with them. You can establish their underlying weaknesses and strengths by listening to their stories and throwing in limited questions from time to time, which will also ingratiate you to them further. It makes you look as though you are supremely interested in what they have to say. However, you don't want the conversation to be one-sided, which means you want to tell them enough about your situation to make them feel comfortable, while at the same time hiding any information that weakens your point of view or that can be contorted to mean something else. Don't be afraid to lie to protect any weaknesses in your argument.

If someone is pushing you for more than they need, you can use a humble tone and explain that there are things about your no one would understand or that you aren't interesting enough to warrant talking about. This will make them curious, and it will also make them a little nurturing, which is where you can snag them. This is known as flipping the script, and it can be a very effective technique when used selectively.

Suppose you have to speak about facts and statistics. Ramble about as many as you can to be a bit overwhelming. At this time, you need to show interest in their part but establish that if you are to go along with whatever they are suggesting, you will have your own rules. Depending on the state you are currently in, this may be enough for them to "decide" to complete the task in question or give in to your suggestion because it is easier than going along with your stipulations.

Another way to manipulate a person is to change the modulation of your voice. If you are trying to intimidate a person, you will want to be loud. If you are seeking sympathy, lose the loud tone for a depressed, defeated tone instead. Most people are inclined to help a person who is feeling down. Now that you have their sympathy, ask for something. Suggest what you want in a way that seems impossible to achieve. Wait for their response, which should be some variation of, "I want to help you." Some people will want to offer up advice as a way to soothe you. To avoid losing control of the situation, you will need to consider their advice and find that their logic is faulty to ensure things remain under your control.

Manipulation Tools for Specific Situations

A key to pulling off any form of manipulation is to see what drives the person you are dealing with. For example, is it a religion? If so, you would need to focus on their devotion and find a creative way to get your point across using their religion. It is a good way to reinforce their opinion of themselves, most likely that they are godly and intelligent. As long as you focus on their utopian visions and aspirations, you will find this technique to be very effective.

Another tool that is useful from time to time is sarcasm. It allows you to express your discontent with someone while maintaining a doorway out as if you were just joking. However, be cautious, as sarcasm can be insulting and hurtful if misused. After you have been given a chance to vent, turn it around to the sarcastic "what if." This allows the person to hear your opinion, and it comes across like you are just defeated. Now they can save you. When they offer their help, humbly tell them it is not their responsibility, but that you need their support. It is helpful to add, "What would I do without you?"

You must keep in mind that you are being manipulated every day. The news, media, and those in power all deploy tactics to keep your attention or threaten your security for non-compliance. You are bombarded with images and stories that tug at your heart, anger your soul, and move you either into action or into seclusion. Just seeing how easily you can have the same effect on a person will allow you to recognize when it is being done to you. Awareness is life-changing. At this moment, you realize you have tried conventional methods of persuasion, being genuine and truly caring. Formerly, you got nothing in return, but you will from now on.

Be Creative

You will need to focus on your creativity for these manipulative tactics. Your goal is to transform someone's reality and alter their beliefs. Every situation is different, which means you will need to be creative and think on your feet. You must observe the cues a person is giving you. You must observe their reactions to you and others, as these can be very telling. Sometimes, just watching your target interact with others can give you more insight into how to manipulate them.

For example, if you see how a coworker reacted to a customer, you can use that to make them feel justified by adding your opinion to explain how they reacted. They will repeat the excuse you provided them. This can be used against them. If you are trying to get them to do something for you, just point out how they overreacted to that customer, which should shame them into following your suggestion. They should act in the way you suggest to minimize their past actions.

Sometimes all you have to do is create an image. Think of a spin on something that would suggest the person you are dealing with is a victim. Encourage them to see how others have been unappreciative and lazy compared to them. Suggest a course of action and reap the benefits.

If you are dying to know what someone feels about a situation, for example, in politics or religion, make up a story that you read on the internet that is sure to rile them up. Sit back, watch their reaction, and start agreeing with them. Be sure to add your perspective to draw them out of the shocking story into your plan. You might just be harvesting information to keep a profile on someone who is a threat to your vision of success. Building your profile, you will be able to understand their weakness in most situations.

Take Your Time

You can be sure to pay special attention to their strengths and find ways to undermine them. Don't proceed it so far as to where others observing can figure out what your intentions are, and instead always take the high road in public so that at the end of the day, most people will only ever see the public face you decide to show them.

Keep in mind that everyone just wants to be happy, which means they seek to understand and support people around them. They think it is rare for someone to take an interest in them without wanting something in return. This is where patience becomes your ally. You cannot act like someone has to be available at a moment's notice. Anyone can figure out that you have selfish motives if you display this impatient tendency. It might be killing you to lie in wait for the perfect opportunity, but it would kill you more to be seen as a fake. So, wait. Even encourage them to ask others about the situation. Once you have proven that you are only worried about them or want to see them succeed, then you can wiggle into their mind with subtle manipulation.

While playing on the heartstrings of another, you weaken their response. You cannot simply ignore that they might say no to your request or idea. You have to come across as genuine in trying to help or care about them. Find a way to make their "no" seem unreasonable without saying it directly. You will have to point out that if someone else acted as they did, they would see it as being stubborn or pig-headed with their closed mind. Let them know that the brain has a chemical response to doing something new and brave. Tell them that the brain lights up like a Christmas tree when changes are occurring.

The bottom line is that there is potential for manipulation. It is a creative process. It takes a little planning and observing, but if mastered, it can change your life. You will feel powerful every day. You will start to see every rejection as a canvas. It is your starting point. A word for word or gesture-by-gesture guarantee that you are in control.

Self-preservation is an important aspect of manipulation. You do not want to be perceived as a manipulator. You want to be known as the neutral person who sees all sides but uses logic to decide why your decision is more valid. Maintain a solid reputation for being thoughtful, and people will seek your opinion often. This is an advantage from the start. In a new group of people, you can find a way to agree with everyone and make a statement that you were always taught to show respect and think of all sides before making a decision.

Chapter 49. Psychological Manipulation

Covert psychological manipulation is essential to the art of dark psychology. Many of the methods utilized with dark psychology will utilize this type of emotional manipulation, whether in part or entirely. As you learn a bit more about the world of dark psychology and its various symptoms, you will soon begin to see the signs of CPM. This is why it is so crucial to comprehend what CPM is precisely so that you can watch out for it in your daily life.

Covert psychological manipulation, or CPM, will attempt by a single person to attempt and influence the feelings and ideas of the other person in a manner that is considered deceptive and undiscovered by the one who is being manipulated. Being able to break down each of the words in CPM is very important to help you understand this subject's structures. Covert refers to the way that a manipulator can conceal their intentions. They wish to have the ability to hide the true nature of all their actions. Remember that not all types of influence and psychological manipulation will be classified as hidden. The victims of the concealed type, though, will usually not realize they are being controlled and will not have the ability to comprehend the way the manipulation is performed. Sometimes, they are not even able to look and determine the motivation of their manipulator.

This is why CPM is such a stealth bomber in the world of dark psychology. Its point is to prevent detection and defense up until it is far too late for the victim. The psychological side of the manipulator is going to be the specific focus of that manipulator. Other kinds of manipulation might include things like the other person's self-discipline, beliefs, and habits. Numerous manipulators will concentrate on this area of impact as they know that the other person's feelings are essential to the other elements of their character. Being able to manipulate the feelings of the other individual is essential. If a person has emotional control over the other individual, they will have complete control over them. The last piece of CPM is manipulation. It is typically thought that manipulation and impact are the same things. This is not true, though. Manipulation refers to the surprise and underhand process of influence outside the awareness of the one who is being controlled.

The objective behind this compared to someone who has the intent to influence can be a huge difference. They will enter into this with an influencer with the idea of "I wish to assist you in deciding that benefits you." With the manipulator, they have the thoughts of "I want to control you to supply advantage to myself secretly." As you can see, both of these are quite a bit different, so comprehending the objective behind any offered behavior is going to be a big part of choosing whether the scenario is hidden psychological manipulation or not.

Manipulative Circumstances

There are four primary situations in which CPM can take place. These consist of the household, romantic, individual, and professional parts of your life. Among the most typical kinds of CPM is romantic, and it can sometimes be the deadliest. There are some less obvious kinds of CPM that you can discover anywhere, and because they are less typical, they can often be the most unsafe. A good example of CPM is a managing romantic partner. If a woman remains in a relationship and her partner is trying to control her, she will be revolted by what is going on as soon as she figures it out. She might wish to discover a way to leave the circumstance. Thus, many times the controlling partner is going to exercise their impact as covertly as possible. They don't desire their partner to understand they are being managed, or the victim leaves, and there is nobody delegated control. If the manipulator achieves success, their spouse or sweetheart will continue to be a psychological manipulation victim. They might have difficulty recognizing that it is going on. This permits the manipulator to keep the control that they want with no danger of being found and losing the other person for good.

This can likewise occur with a buddy who would use CPM to get the outcomes they want when they have a relationship with another individual. In this group, one of the common types of manipulators will be covertly induced feelings of obligation, compassion, and guilt in a pal. The friend is being controlled in this way without understanding that they are being influenced. They may understand that they are acting differently to that buddy; however, they won't have the ability to explain why and how. You will discover that the expert part of your life can be another place for hidden emotional manipulators. Many people have worked for an employer or another person who had authority, who seems to set off some unidentified sensations of duty, worry, and regret in them.

Individuals who are manipulated in this manner might never identify why these feelings exist or where they come from, and in the world of CPM, the family can be the most troublesome. A proficient manipulator can discover a victim, even within their household, and the amount of influence they exercise can be dangerous. This is because the manipulator and the victim will have a very deep connection together. After all, they are related. When blood relations are included, the amount of influence and control can increase a fair bit. These family circumstances are so matched to utilizing CPM because most people currently feel a social responsibility to help their own family. They are willing to go a little more to guarantee the requirements of their family are addressed. Because of this predisposition, covert psychological manipulative practices will give you a malleable victim.

The (Bad) Love Giver

This consists of the severe, unforeseen, and robust expression of positive feelings towards a victim. It may, in the beginning, seem counterintuitive. Why do they behave so intensively positive at first if that individual is attempting to damage them? Since it matches its functions—that's why! This produces a deep sense of self-confidence, affection, and appreciation from a specific victim to their manipulator, and this is the principle behind love providing. Based on the manipulator's analysis, the degree to which enjoy providing is utilized, and the people on whom it is pre-owned forms the basis. A lonely, helpless victim who seeks help and consolation is most likely to be more love-bombed by the manipulator because the manipulator will know the victim will be more responsive to it. The more the victim is grounded, the less effort the manipulator will have to put into positivity. The meaning of the love giving technique offers two essential lessons on Emotional Manipulation. Firstly, the covert nature of Emotional Manipulation is well shown. Envision is trying to comprehend that love giving is an unfortunate thing. "Well, this guy was very sweet to me, and he made me feel very good." The red flags or warning signs of abuse are unlikely to be raised by such a declaration. This is a textbook example of how something can be provided as something favorable but has a negative result. The second general lesson pertinent to Emotional Manipulation that can be learned from love offering is how emotional manipulation is formed to suit every unique circumstance. Experienced manipulators have discreetly tested and learned from lots of encounters in their history. In any given scenario, you understand the strength and timing of each Emotional Manipulation strategy.

What is Empathy

Empathy is the capability to put yourself in another person's shoes and consider their emotions and sensations. An empath is an individual who can interact with others on several levels to experience their emotional wellness with precision. How empaths have this capacity has yet to be comprehended to many individuals, but numerous believe it is innate and transmitted through our DNA. As for how it runs, everything in deep space resonates with electrical energy; empaths are believed to can perceiving the shifts in the electrical energy around them. Empaths are usually considered compassionate, loving, sensitive to other individuals' feelings, and sympathetic. Would you be astonished to learn there's a dark side to being an empath? The essence of compassion itself makes sure that lots of are helped and supported by an empath. It likewise means empaths can see the world a lot more than we do, and as such, issues can happen in various areas of their lives. The dark side of empaths is that their sensations can't be managed. You might believe they are well versed in emotions, but the truth is they are in a constant fight to keep them under control. Sometimes, it can bring them down to depression since they so strongly feel others' feelings, specifically others' grief. They discover it difficult to separate their feelings and others and find other empaths to reveal their sensations. Empaths can accommodate a large amount of information from their sensitivity to electrical energy when managing negative energy resulting in fatigue. This can puzzle and exhaust them badly while attempting to understand everything. They are particularly prone to negative energy, as it greatly upsets them. They will easily end up being tired when all they can feel is negative energy. They are used by the less scrupulous amongst us because empaths are compassionate individuals who always believe in people's good nature. Empaths are generous and kind; they will attract only those who take and never return.

An empath can quickly fall under deep anxiety when they discover they have been conned. Because empathy tends to give to others instead of getting, it is most likely that they overlook their wellness, including their bodies and minds. This is the dark side all frequently since it's all too easy to forget how to appreciate them because of the pressure of what they feel. They keep back a little piece of their heart just if they're wounded in the future.

They can't permit themselves to fall deeply in love because they are terrified of all that love. After all, it could be a lot for them to manage.

Empaths are selfless people who are day-to-day bombarded with sensory info, so they typically feel like they carry a heavy load.

Chapter 50. Turning the Tables

Whether you're the victim or the one who is doing the manipulating, there's one thing that's for certain. Manipulation is abusive, and no one, especially not the victim, deserves to be subjected to that kind of treatment. Since most manipulators are unlikely to see the error of their ways or want to become a better person, it is up to the victim to do what they can to keep themselves as safe as possible. Cutting all ties with the manipulator will not always be immediate or easy; some relationships take time before you can sever the bonds and walk away for good. In the meantime, what do you need to do to protect yourself from being taken advantage of in that way? Perhaps turn the tables and deflect the manipulator's techniques can onto them.

Manipulation is an emotional and mental game of cat and mouse, but just because you may be the mouse in the scenario, it doesn't mean you're completely at their mercy. The savvy mouse with a few useful strategies up their sleeve can flip things around and take the power dynamic away from the manipulator. Just when the manipulator thinks they have you within their grasp, turn the tables on them and let them know you're not going to tolerate whatever it is they're trying to do to you. It's time to gain payback on the manipulator and let them know you're not as easily fooled as they might think.

Shut down the manipulator's attempts by standing up for your fundamental rights. Among the fundamental human rights that we are all entitled to include the right to be respected, the right to say no without having to feel guilty about it, the right to express your opinions and your feelings, and the right to protect yourself when you feel you might be threatened emotionally, physically or mentally among other things. These basic rights are what you need to remember when fighting back against manipulation because we so often tend to forget when we let others pressure us and play on our emotions to get their way. We forget that we have a right to protect our hearts, minds, and bodies from the people who would trample all over us if given a chance. Make these rights part of the boundaries that you set in your dealings with others, and strengthen your defenses against the manipulator using the following techniques:

Say No, Thank You - Do not feel guilty if you have to say no to the manipulator. They're trying to take advantage of you, and you are well within your rights to say no to them. They do not have any rights to pressure you into deciding or taking action with something you're not comfortable with, and when you firmly say no, remember that you don't owe them an explanation. You can make your own decisions, your own choices, and if you choose to say no, go right ahead. Some manipulators will still attempt to push the boundaries and try to persist despite you telling them no, and you're going to have to be firm and stand your ground. Make it politely but firmly clear that you're not going to change your mind, and you would appreciate it if they could respect your decision. Say no, thank you, and end the conversation there and then.

Saying No to Buy Time - If you have ever been pressured into deciding on the spot without having enough time to think things over, you'll be familiar with that uncomfortable, dissatisfied sensation that often follows when you're not quite sure what you agreed to or whether you've made the right choice. This is the manipulator's favorite tactic to force you into complying with their schedule, and they'll hold you to your agreement. Try to back out of it, and they'll immediately lash out at you, painting you as the "bad guy" because you're backing out on your word. The most effective tactic to stem off this unwanted pressure is to say no to buy yourself some time repeatedly. Tell them firmly that you need time to think things over, and you don't appreciate being put on the spot like that. If they try to make you feel guilty by pretending to be upset or angered at your resistance, let them know you're sorry they feel that way, but you are still sticking to your answer, and you need time to think things over. When they try to bully or intimidate you, once again firmly but politely tell them that you don't appreciate being intimidated into making a decision. They need to respect your need to take some time. At the first sign that you might be onto what they're trying to do, the manipulator would usually retreat.

Avoid Them - The most straightforward way to stop manipulators is to avoid them in the first place. Of course, this is often easier said than done since sometimes these manipulators exist within your own immediate family. Since they're family, it can be hard to sever all ties with them completely, so the best thing you can do is avoid them. Do everything that you can to stay away from them where possible. During those few moments where they're unavoidable, such as family gatherings, for example, minimize your contact with them by surrounding yourself and keeping busy with the other non-toxic family members. They might not be entirely avoidable (unless you were to leave the company for a better job), so the best thing you can do is once again minimize the contact you have with them. Communicate through emails to avoid interacting with them directly, and when you do need to, try to get another colleague to come along with you as a witness of sorts. This leaves the manipulator with little chance of twisting their story or denying what they said.

Fire Back at Them with Questions - If there is one thing that manipulators avoid, it is having others discover what they're really up to. The minute you start firing back at them with probing questions each time they try to force you into meeting an unreasonable demand, flip it around back on them and probe them with questions they'll be reluctant to answer. Since their requests or statements will be unreasonable most of the time, it is an opportunity for you to let them know that you're fully aware of what they're trying to do. Put them on the spot by asking questions that include whether they believe this request is fair or reasonable and how this arrangement will benefit the two of you mutually. These questions will make them uncomfortable, and they won't answer them without revealing themselves. When they're dismissive of your questions, be firmer and keep pressing the issue, making it clear you expect them to answer. An effective way to get them to back off and stop putting so much pressure on you.

There's so much to remember and be mindful of in your dealings with the manipulator. However, there is one reminder that you shouldn't forget, and that is never to blame yourself or feel guilty that you were a victim. Making you feel that way is exactly what they want, but don't let them get inside your head. They're deceptive and conniving, willing to do many things that most people would not, and anyone could have easily become a victim just as much as you were. Just because they picked on you, it doesn't mean that there is anything wrong with you. We all have our strengths and weaknesses; it's part of the dynamic that makes us human. Blaming yourself is playing right into their hands, and if you are beating yourself up over it, don't do it.

Effectively Dealing with the Silent Treatment

Here's something you need to know about manipulators who use the silent treatment. They're emotionally stunted people who resort to this childish approach over choosing to have a mature conversation to resolve any kind of problem. They may look like adults, but their behavior reflects a childish, underlying personality beneath it. They're so used to getting what they want that they kick up a fuss when things don't go their way. Pretty much like what a child would do. Besides ignoring them and refusing to play their game (meaning groveling and begging for their forgiveness the way that they are hoping you would), here's what you can do to stomp on the manipulator's attempts at trying to abuse you with the silent treatment emotionally:

Point Out Their Behavior - They're not going to be used to people calling them out on their bad behavior, since most of the time, the general reaction that tends to follow the silent treatment is the victim continuously trying to reach out to them, asking them what's wrong and what they can do to make things better. Manipulators want to feel in control, and very rarely are they going to encounter someone who pushes back by saying, "I know what you're trying to do, and it's not going to work with me." Whenever they revert to the silent treatment to get you to submit, do the exact opposite. Let them know that you're not going to tolerate being emotionally abused with the silent treatment this way, and when they're ready to have a proper conversation about it, they can come and talk to you. If they choose to keep sulking and ignoring you, let them be, it is not your responsibility to try and fix a situation caused by their bad behavior. Eventually, which is often when they need you, they'll come around, and that's when you move onto the point below.

Discuss Their Behavior - Once they're done throwing their little temper tantrum and start behaving like an adult again, have a discussion with them about what happened. They'll do everything that they can to avoid the subject, but be persistent and let them know that you're not going just to sweep this under the rug. Talk to them about how abusive you through their behavior was (this will put them on the alert, worried about being discovered again), and how you see this affecting your relationship with them. They will try to turn things around and make it out to be your fault that they behaved this way because you were the one who angered them or upset them in the first place. When they do, shut them down and say while you do feel sorry that they felt that way, it was still no way to treat you when they could have chosen other ways of dealing with the issue. Make it clear that regardless of how they felt, silent treatment abuse was never the right approach to take. The manipulator will wake up when they realize that their maneuvers do not as easily fool you as they initially believed.

Don't Resort to Tit for Tat - Dealing with manipulators can be unbelievably frustrating. On several occasions, you may be tempted to give them a taste of their own medicine, use the same approach they are taking with you, and treat them the same way.

Chapter 51. Stages of a Relationship with a Covert Narcissist

A relationship with a narcissist doesn't have the natural flow and is characterized by stages absent in healthy relationships. The natural balance of giving and take is disrupted. Relationships with such individuals start with infatuation and idealization, only to end devaluation, rejection, and complete discard of narcissist's partner. In psychological and therapeutic practice, there are three main stages of a relationship with a narcissist: the idealization phase, devaluation, and discarding.

Idealization

During the idealization stage, the narcissist earns their target's trust by showing them affection, appreciation, praise, and adoration. They lift the other person, cheer for them, offer unlimited support, a shoulder to cry on, act as a friend in need, and a perfect lover who just knows how to make things right. This is called love bombing, and during this phase, narcissists aim to recreate the ideal relationship and earn the trust and loyalty of their targets.

Covert narcissists have a fluid identity that allows them to transform like a chameleon and adapt to any person they are to gain their respect and trust. They are perceptive, analytical and will investigate the target carefully to create the perfect scenario that gives them the green light to the phase of a relationship we will soon talk in the text. It is in a narcissist's interest to be liked, and so they create the persona that is likable as the only thing they care for is admiration. This first stage is about their target's identity to get the admiration they believe they deserve. The behavior almost resembles a teenager who desperately wants to fit in with a group of popular people, just to be popular and liked themselves. Emotional detachment and infertility allow them to reflect on the person they are with, quickly attaching their needs and wants to the other person—they are giving because they know it will be appreciated and make them likable. Needing acceptance and admiration from you, a narcissist will do anything to get it and go about it so smoothly that you will hardly notice they are mirroring who you are. In other words, they will do it covertly.

The love bombing is based on acts and words of adoration that are excessive and "too good to be true." The survivors of narcissistic abuse often say that the relationship with covert was like heaven in the beginning. "It was perfect." "It felt like a fairy tale." "Our relationship was ideal." "I thought I finally found someone who gets me." "They made me feel special." "They seemed like the person I have been waiting for all my life." "I thought I have finally found my soulmate." "We were the best couple." "We had so much in common." "Back then, I felt so lucky I found them." They identify how to target your weaknesses and use them to manipulate you, at this stage by earning your trust by building you up in those areas you feel insecure about. When love bombing, they will realize you and the relationship, make you feel very special and worthy of love, only to make you feel opposite at the two stages of the relationship.

It is very common for survivors of narcissistic abuse to say that they were very impressed by their covert having the same interests, lifestyle, and hobbies. A narcissist does detailed research on their targets and will spend time learning about and absorbing their interests, tastes, likes, and dislikes. While there is a natural incarnation, people have to be open to learning about interest people they like to have. In the light of a narcissistic personality disorder, this is not a result of curiosity, but a lack of identity and the desire to be so desperately liked and worshiped. Many love bomb others by taking care of their needs, giving them gifts, compliments, praise, taking them places, or being overly helpful even when there is no real help needed. This behavior has a certain level of pushiness, but because it seems genuine, the person who is being love-bombed perceives the narcissist as the nice person who just wants to love and care for them. Many of their former partners say they felt unexplainably uncomfortable for receiving so much attention and needing to return the affection or favors but couldn't recognize it as a red flag back then.

Ultimately, in the love-bombing stage of a relationship, the narcissist treats the other person as they were the same. Although it is never a conscious process in their mind, the people they are targeting are seen as an extension of themselves. In the beginning, this person is the extension of their praise-needy, self-important, "ideal" side of the personality, a boost to their ego that shows how valuable they are. The other person is a "replica" of himself or herself. They are a replica of that person, their interests, thoughts, and feelings. This process is called mirroring or projecting the aspects of self to the other person. However, it is a two-way street. At this first stage, a narcissist's target will feel very special, beautiful, respected for their talents, important or praiseworthy—which is exactly what narcissists think about themselves.

Everything they do, they need to be returned and in double or triple doses. If they do a lot of helpful things for you in the beginning stages of a relationship, rest assured they will require you to do little or big favors for them and make you feel guilty when you are not able to put a pause on your life and deliver what they need when they need it. The idealization phase is a base a narcissist builds to create a safe zone where they can be admired while gradually revealing their true selves as the relationship progresses. The paradox of this disorder is that the narcissist knows that connecting with other people is open, empathetic, and interested in the other person. Therefore, they use it to create an environment where they can be who they are—the empathetic, closed-off person who doesn't care about the other. The final goal is to make the target comfortable enough to refocus the relationship towards themselves gradually.

This stage, just like the other two, is as present in work and family environment as much as it in love relationships and friendships. For instance, covert narcissists are often praised and respected members of society, many of which are very involved with charity work or are in important positions. They care about their status and what others think of them, so naturally; many will opt for careers that allow them to be in the spotlight in one way or another. Covert colleagues and bosses will be the first ones to hop in to help you with tasks, help you get things done, and even take on your part of the job on themselves. This, however, lasts only during the first stage, when you get to know them. They appear agreeable, kind, generous, charismatic and everyone seems to love them. Remember, no matter what place they take in your life, there are always three stages of a relationship with the present. Don't be surprised that once the appreciation bombing phase is over, you get criticized, unappreciated for things you were once praised for, or if they take the credit for your ideas or give it to someone else. They want your full trust and give you praise and help whenever you need and don't need it, only to twist the reality and diminish your ambition, work drive, and health.

Devaluation

At this stage, little things they adored about you suddenly become flaws and something you are ashamed of. Once the relationship is established, and the covert has created a haven by gaining your loyalty and trust, they gradually start expressing their dissatisfaction with the relationship and you. Because they have first carefully analyzed your weaknesses and built you up, they will start using your fears and insecurities against you. Although never or rarely openly, they slowly diminish their target's self-confidence by planting the seeds of self-doubt, fear, and even self-hate in them. This happens periodically. It is hard to pinpoint and even harder to understand because it is done subtly and entwined with sporadic acts of love and kindness, especially at the beginning of this stage.

The trouble here is that a covert narcissist devalues their partners subtly and appears completely innocent in the process. Most often than not, this devaluation manifests in little things they don't do for you rather the things they say directly and openly, especially at the beginning of this stage. Because it is a covert narcissist we are talking about, this phase can revolve simply around them not acknowledging your needs, wants, and desires, showing less and less interest in your life and you as a person. They will not shout, be cruel in obvious ways, yell or say mean things. Instead, they will damage your self-esteem in little, subtle ways, turning to more serious manipulation techniques. Devaluation can go from little things like not replying to text messages, not calling when agreed upon, or prioritizing other people or things to give silent treatments, criticizing, nitpicking, or blaming others. The reason for devolution is to make them feel better about themselves because that is the level of emotional maturity the narcissist operates on.

This can manifest as falling from the number one worker to the average one, comparing or praising other employees who put in even less effort than you do. At the beginning of his career at the company, Richard was his boss's favorite employee, always prized for his ambition, problem-solving skills, and efficiency. It was his dream job, so he tried his best to put all his enthusiasm into it. However, as time went on, he could hear his boss complaining about the little mistakes he made in the prospects, the tidiness of his office, or his time-management. These were nothing new, but unlike before, where such tiny mistakes weren't recognized as major, which they are not, were now seen as Richard's lack of professionalism and capability to meet required criteria. He did extra hours and took on more responsibilities than he should prove his dedication, only for his boss to blame it on him for not finishing even more.

Chapter 52. Covert Emotional Manipulation Methods

In a manipulation method that is entirely based upon triggering emotions, it should come as no surprise that at the end of the day, there are nearly endless ways that you can go about manipulating the emotions of others. We will take a look at five different methods that can be used to toy with other people's emotions, allowing you to understand that you will need to use them in any way that may work best for you. We will be going over the use of fear, obligation, and guilt to keep people under your thumb with emotional blackmail. We will look at how you can play the victim, invalidate your target, gaslight, and use a love bombing method and devaluing. These will create emotions within the other person you can use to get exactly what you want or need to see.

Emotional Blackmail

Emotional blackmail is a common way that people can be controlled. When you do this, you are using the threat of either fear, obligation, or guilt to try to get everyone around you in line. Essentially, you will be relying on the fact that fear, obligation, and guilt are all incredible motivators. They can be used to trigger that motivation to make the negative emotions end through, making it a point to trigger them by failing to do what you wanted in the first place. Each of these works in their ways, but at the end of the day, they require you to have some sort of leverage over the other person that can directly be used to control them. That leverage will be what you use to trigger one of these responses.

Fear

When you are using fear, you need to have a credible way to make the other person feel afraid. You may use the fear of losing you. For example, you can threaten to break up with someone. You may use the fear of some sort of punishment or abuse. You may use the fear of just about anything to get someone moving and in line.

Obligation

This is most commonly used in relationships or amongst families. When you attempt to use an obligation to try to get someone working toward what you want them to do, you somehow make what you want them to do an obligation or responsibility of theirs, so they feel like they have no choice but to do so. Frequently, you see this in relationships in ways such as saying, "But you owe me after everything that I did for you!" This is meant to make the other person feel like they do have no choice in the matter—if they do not live up to your expectations, they are left feeling guilty and, therefore, responsible for what has happened or are left feeling like it is otherwise all their fault. Still, either way, it is a struggle for them.

Guilt

Finally, when you use guilt as a weapon, you are frequently telling the other person that it is their fault that things did not work out. You may say that you are now in a very tight or bad spot because of their inaction in doing something, or you may try to make it the other person's fault when something goes wrong. For example, if you need money for something, you could guilt the other person into paying for it by letting them know how badly you need it, but you cannot afford it. You may have been able to afford it just fine—but you will never let the other person know that. You may also try to put down the guilt in other contexts as well—perhaps you remind the other person that they are responsible for their children's safety, so they owe it to their children to buy the most expensive car they are approved for, even if it is going to be pushing their budget a bit more than they are comfortable doing. The guilt they would feel at not buying that car with more safety features is enough to push them toward making it a point to buy the other car instead, despite not wanting to initially.

Playing the Victim

Another common way to emotionally manipulate other people is to play the victim role. When you switch yourself into the victim role, you are essentially making it a point to make the other person feel guilty for whatever they have done. For example, you may be in a situation in which you have messed up somehow. Maybe you forgot to pay a bill, and your partner is now angry about the addition of a fee that would otherwise not have to be paid due to the bill being late at this point. You know that you are at fault, but do you want to take the fall and the blame? Most people would prefer to avoid that blame altogether, so what you have to do is figure out how to redirect somehow. You need to be no longer seen as the perpetrator or the one at fault, but rather to be seen as the victim of some sort of unfortunate circumstance.

When you can shift the attention in that way, you can then take back control. You can no longer be the one at fault, but rather the one who was victimized instead. Perhaps you do this by pointing out how you had tried to pay the bill and that you thought the bill was paid, so it must be a banking error. Maybe you bring up how, on the day that it was due to be paid, something extreme happened that prevented you from paying for said bill. Maybe you even try to reverse the situation to make your partner the one at fault instead.

When you reverse the situation, your partner is the one at fault. This is known as DARVO—Deny, attack, and reverse victim and offender. When you follow these steps, you can make sure that you remain the one that is pitied or seen as the victim in the situation, which then allows you to defend yourself.

Deny: you start by denying the claim somehow. You say that you did not forget what had happened, or you say that you did not avoid paying the bill for some reason. You are going to refute whatever claim has been thrown at you. You could very easily substitute not paying a bill for claims of abuse, for example, or any other fault, whether you have done it or not. Denying it is the first step in the process.

Attack: now, you need to shift the burden onto the other person. You may say that your partner was the one that was responsible for those bills, or you claim that your partner was the one that was abusive or toxic toward you instead. The task here is to put your partner or whoever you are talking to on the defensive—you want them to suddenly feel like they have to refute your claim instead of asserting their own, which allows you to remain shielded.

Reverse victim and offender: finally, in this last stage, you are sort of rewriting the narrative—you are making it clear that you did not cause the problem, but rather, you are the one that is now having to pay more in fees due to the other person's incompetency or whatever else you are blaming. At this point, you want to assert that the other person is the offender and that you are the victim in this particular situation. If you played your cards right, the other person would be so busy trying to prove that they are not, in fact, the ones at fault that they will not realize what you have done.

Invalidation

Another common method to mess with the emotions of someone else is to use invalidation. When you are doing this, you make the other person feel like they are at fault for some reason. You are making them feel like they cannot trust themselves, and then you are preying on that doubt. One such form of this will be gaslighting, which we will be looking at shortly.

When you are using invalidation, you are essentially always saying things to use plausible deniability when they do try to blame you or call you out for the way you are treating them or acting. For example, imagine that you hear someone trying to manipulate say that they have just done something good eventually. Perhaps they are happy about the job that they just got hired for. If you want to make them feel invalidated, you would then shrug it off and mention how you did something better. If they try to tell you that you are hurtful, you can deny this and say that you were just sharing your successes.

You can also invalidate people by constantly pointing out why they are wrong, how they are wrong, and why they should change up what they say or why they are saying it. You can also make snide jokes and sarcastic comments. When they say something about what you have said hurting their feelings, you can then deny it all together—you simply tell them that they are too sensitive and not to be so willing to be hurt over something that was not meant to be taken that way in the first place. When you do this, reminding the other person that you did not do anything that was intended to be hurtful, you make them feel wrong and invalidated. They are stuck, feeling like they cannot defend themselves without looking petty or too sensitive.

Gaslighting

Gaslighting is a very specific form of invalidation. When you are using gaslighting, you are intentionally trying to make the other person doubt their perceptions around them. They may tell you that you did something, and you deny it, saying they are wrong. They may eventually believe the narrative that you are trying to push, and they made a mistake somewhere along the line, and that they are entirely wrong.

Usually, you start small—you correct them about where things came from or where you found something. This does not have to be significant—it just has to plant the seed that they are mistaken regularly. Slowly, you will up the stakes—you will start to remind them that they were wrong about when they did something or if something happened in the first place. Over time, you will eventually plant the idea that they cannot get what is going on around them right. They will stop questioning you when you suggest something and instead look at how they are always wrong. They will not trust themselves, which means that you would be able to lie to their faces about something that just happened practically, and they would take your narrative over their own.

Chapter 53. Knowing Yourself

The key to being able to avoid manipulation is to know yourself. You will not be able to know yourself unless you experience failure in the world. Most people experience enough failure when they become adults to know how they deal with it and learn how to keep going. If you don't know yourself, you will repeatedly use people who don't care a lick about you. They are just more focused on their own goals. When you know yourself, you can know other people better. You will be able to tap into that voice that tells you this is not worth it, that you are being manipulated. If you know yourself, you are less vulnerable to deceit and lies.

This is because people are very self-repressed, and they don't learn about themselves. By not learning about yourself, you are opening yourself up to the worst of interactions and relationships. Relationships are shallower when you are like this. They lack depth and concentration. When you know yourself, you can analyze what is happening to you and other people. When you know yourself, you can protect yourself.

Analyzing people involves keeping knowledge of how we see the world and how we move to observe others. This is why knowing yourself is so important. It takes a lot of effort to understand how other people see you globally, cueing you into their behavior. One way to start this is to look at the Enneagram of personality and see what line up mostly with you. This can tell you about the drives you have in your personality that you might not even realize. When you are trying to find out what type of personality you are, you are engaging in a self-reflexive behavior that will have you become a better person. It will help you to know yourself, and your intuition will be increased as a part of this.

Another way to know oneself is to participate in the art of watching or listening to art. A movie can tell us the story of a world. It is a way by which we understand the world. Every time you speak, you tell a story, either in words or as you say them. This can help you realize your strengths and weaknesses.

When you are reading a great novel, you become immersed in that book, and you get to share a little bit of the writers' world in your imagination. The writer and reader create a continuum, wherein the writer's consciousness is being followed directly by another person. They say that literature is the art that most people can escape their world and get into another person's consciousness. You start to learn the characters, and you start to predict what they are in to do. Characters in the story can be compared to people you know in real life, and the book can give your ideas of how to behave and change the world through your actions. As you get into the story, you are experiencing a ride that is the most positive way of expressing ourselves. This is art. Art is a mysterious way that we participate in the world. Art has the power to incite wars and peace. It is a way to disturb people deeply, and you can keep them happy and calm. Art (we are talking here about the art with a big A, as to mean every category of art, from dance to film to sculpture) is a way that we are in the world that lets us start a feedback loop with the world, and it becomes a source of communication with the world and with others. This is a way that we can find solace and express ourselves to the world.

Art is also a way that we immortalize ourselves. Each human is subject to the lifespan that they are given on this planet, and when you realize when your life is going to end eventually, you start to realize that the world will move on without you. This means that you might be forgotten, at least according to our primal fear. So, we try to do things to counteract this. The most primal and animal way is to have children because then you'll live on in the world through the people who you have created to carry out their own goals and happiness in the world.

Having children is a simple way that people leave a legacy, and it is the ultimate creative act in the world. All other forms of art are underneath this one. That is because art comes from consciousness. That is why humans are not art. We are conscious, we have the power of gods, and when we create another person, we use our power as gods. We are also using the power of gods when we create art, but it is slightly lesser.

Art is a way that you can analyze yourself to deeper levels. Remember the Rorschach test, a way of analyzing people where we look at blobs of ink of paper and say whatever comes to mind first? Well, all art is sort of like that, as a creator and as a viewer. As a creator, when you are creating art, you are creating the ink blob. Sometimes it is very clear what the artist is talking about. When you look at a Norman Rockwell painting, you understand the scene that he has created because he is putting you right there in a scenario that you can recognize and understand. The artist often puts you in a place where you can't understand because you aren't meant to. This kind of art can help us explore what it feels like for other people to experience tarts o fat world's tarts. Abstract art is not about telling you things but rather gets you to think. Many people say that literature is how you can most experience another persons' consciousness, out of all of the art forms. Think about the best book you ever read. You were so into it that you couldn't put it down, and when you read it, you were nowhere else except in the world created by the writer. You were a citizen in his world, and there was nothing to do except to be there in the story and experience whatever was going on.

When you do this, you are experiencing a human mode called flow. Flow is when you are just in the moment, when you are only experiencing something that you are doing, like meditating, playing the piano, running, driving, or something else. It is a state of focus and a state of creativity.

To know yourself, you have to be able to experience the extremes of life. You must have been able to understand the anger and express it. You must know when you feel angry and understand what that feels like to you. You must be able to experience joy at the highest level, for this is an extreme human feat. You must be able to take deep pain and failure and also accept the beauty in life. You must immerse yourself in the book and then pay some bills that you have lying around, which is just menial work that you have to do. You have to deal with all sorts of things that are big and small, and none is less important. It might seem that the small stuff is less important, and in many ways, it is, but the details are something that you can be vigilant with, and they are ways for you to let yourself experience each part of life.

The number-one way to do this concretely every day and learn about you is journaling. You can journal every day but never write the same thing twice. Journaling doesn't have to be your homework. It can be fun, it can be creative, and it can be a way to release yourself from the shackles of what binds you.

When you write about yourself, you are looking at yourself through the lens of another person, or at least not through your own. By writing about yourself, you are also able to tell your story. Let's talk about both of these aspects of writing.

When you write about yourself, you get to look at yourself through your own eyes, but more objectively. Or at least, that's the hope. When you open up the journal and start writing about yourself, and it is all negative stuff, you should tell yourself that you have a problem there. When you are writing about yourself, try to be as subjective as possible. When you find that you cannot do this, it might mean that you are too much up in your head.

You see, we start to develop ideas and concepts about ourselves that may or may not be true. Even if they are true, they might not be so good to dwell on. Many people have problems with intrusive thoughts or automatic negative thoughts. If you are one of these people, just take your writing and see if you notice these thoughts in writing, and see if you can stop yourself and try to write out thoughts that are kinder and more accurate. By talking about ourselves more objectively, we can get more in touch with ourselves regarding our real desires, goals, and ways of living. When we are in our heads, we don't get a really good idea of our perceptions vs the world's perceptions around us. When we are all up in our heads about how we are, the world seems like a movie that we are starring in. When we write about our lives, you are writing a movie. An objective perspective will let you talk about yourself as a friend rather than yourself. You can start to think of this guy or girl as a person who is closer to the world than to your own experience, and when you do that, you reduce the number of feelings and thoughts that might get mixed up with the perspective. When you take out the emotions and thoughts and just go with the facts, you'll find that you can be fairer and more realistic about yourself.

Some people will find that they have self-esteem issues that they need to deal with. Others will be more on the side of narcissism, and they will need to learn about how to reduce their selfishness and start to think more about others. Telling a story is another big part of writing that is so beneficial to us. Writing a story can give you some narrative that will let you be expressive and real about your life. Telling the story tells you how you feel about yourself. You can see yourself as a character in a play or movie. What is the character like? Is he or she an antagonist or protagonist? What are the character's values, their role in life, and their role in the story?

Chapter 54. Psychological Tricks to Examine Human Beings

You must have heard it a lot of times already that communication is the key to everything—be it your relationships or your business deals. Everything is carefully balanced on how you choose to communicate with people, but it's easier said than done. It can be really hard to handle people the right way, but certain psychological tricks can come in handy. They help you examine the people around you to understand their motives, and they will also make your overall life much easier.

By now, you must have already understood that humans are not at all easy to understand, and they are quite complex. However, there are certain patterns in behavior that can be studied to make conclusions. If you think that examining someone can only be done through psychoanalysis and not otherwise, you are wrong because it can also be done through other tricks, which are relatively easier. Even if a person raises an eyebrow or stands in a particular manner, there is meaning to it, and this meaning, when deciphered, will help you understand that person.

I know what you must be wondering. It is just like any other skill you learn. Understanding and examining a human being is not any different. With time, as you keep practicing, you will notice that you have developed an inner intuition that will always guide you in the right direction. Whether you want to understand how you should approach your boss or in what way you should speak to please your client, all of those tactics can be mastered through some simple psychological tricks. Do you know who the top performers in a company are? They are not the ones who are the smartest in the room. They are the ones with the best people skills and know-how to communicate.

You simply need to practice every day to tune in and understand what every person is thinking or how they are as a person. If you want your relationship-building skills to improve, there are different ways to make educated guesses about people from now on.

Let us look at some of these tips and tricks, and I hope you can apply them to the person you meet.

Look Into Their Eyes

I have to say that looking into someone's eyes is the first and foremost trick that everyone should learn. Eyes are the doorway to the mind, and they convey much more than we can imagine. You will often come in situations where you do not particularly prefer the answer you got, and when that happens, you do not understand why things happened the way they did. You might have expected a different answer, and now that the opposite happened, you can't seem to figure out why. Sounds familiar? Well, then you are in luck here because looking into that person's eyes can get you the answer you are looking for. The first reaction that most people have in such a situation is that they ask the question again, but that is most likely to get you the same answer once again. You should look deep into that person's eyes and try to understand what you see. When you do that, the person is automatically going to feel as if they are cornered. In short, they will feel a bit of stress, and this stress itself will bring you a lot of answers. Most of the time, in such situations, the person tries to elaborate on why they said what they said.

Apart from the situation, I just explained, looking into someone's eyes will help you take a peek into their mind. If someone is trying to dismiss what you are saying or is not liking the conversation, you can make it out if you truly look into their eyes.

Now, let us go into some of the details. One of the first things you should keep in mind is to watch for any changes in the pupil's size. I am going to give you an example from a study that was published in the year 1965. It was conducted to show the difference in the pupil's size in response to the people (Eckhart H. Hess, 1965). The psychologists had produced semi-nude pictures belonging to both sexes to female and male participants. There was an increase in the size of the female participants' size when they saw men's pictures. Similarly, there was an increase in the size of the male participants' size when they saw women's pictures.

Subsequent studies were done by the same psychologists to find more information. Homosexual participants were included, and the same result was obtained. Their pupils increased in size when they saw pictures of men in semi-nude condition. Simultaneously, when pictures where mothers were coddling babies, were shown to women, their pupils dilated. So, do you see where this experiment is heading? It is not the only arousal depicted by pupils' dilation, but it also shows whether the information shown is interesting and relatable.

Now, let us move on to something much more complex—when you become an expert at reading the eyes, you can also determine whether a person is telling the truth or lying by simply looking at their eyes. In the year 2009, another study was conducted in which one group of participants did not steal, and the other had stolen $20 (Andrea K. Webb, 2009). Whether the participant had stolen the money or not, every one of them was asked to say the same thing that they had not stolen anything. The detection of a thief was possible when pupil dilation was examined for denying the theft. When the pupil dilation of both groups was compared, it was noticed that the ones who were lying witnessed an increase in pupil size, which was 1 mm more than those who did not commit the theft.

Another thing about the eyes that you should keep in mind is that when people close their eyes in the middle of a conversation, it is usually because there is some feeling that they are trying hard to bury inside themselves. It can also be that they are trying to hide from the chaos of the outside world. However, what you should remember is that closing the eyes does not necessarily mean that the person is afraid of you. It is quite the opposite. They might be finding you annoying, or something about the conversation is irritating them, which is why they want to shut you out. It makes them feel that even when you are in front of them, closing their eyes means that they can shut you out momentarily and not have to see you.

Find the Hot Buttons

If you want to understand someone and their motives, you have to find out more about their hot buttons. It starts with recognizing the hot buttons first. Hot buttons are people's pain points, and they help you understand what they are thinking. The best way to recognize these points is to ask the right questions, and for that, the first step is to build a rapport and a good bond with the person. In short, you have to be a good listener first and a small mouth.

Whenever you want to know more about a person, the trick is to ask questions that give the person room to answer away. These are called open-ended questions. Asking questions whose obvious answers are yes or no is not going to help you here. Questions that require the person to speak about them, their challenges, and their strengths are what you need. Another way to approach this situation is to talk to the person and share stories from your own life where you have done something helpful for other people. Most of the time, you will find people telling you that they have been facing something similar in their life, and this conversation will help you a lot. For starters, it will help you to understand what this person truly needs.

One of the first mistakes that people make is that they think not everyone has triggered, but you are wrong here—everyone has them. The only difference is that some people are good at hiding their triggers. If it is of any help, I am going to give you examples of some of the most common hot buttons that people have:

Fear

I am mentioning fear at the beginning of this list because it is the most powerful hot button. Two of the most common situations, when fear shows itself as a hot button in a person, are avoiding pain or trying to seek pleasure. However, you also have to keep in mind that fear does not act in the same way for everyone. What you fear in life might not be the same for someone else and vice-versa. Fear depends on the experiences that people have in their lives. If you notice this hot button in the person, you have to use it to your benefit. Give them a solution that removes their fear, and this option should eliminate all doubts.

Anger

Anger is something we all experience in our daily lives, and to be honest, quite frequently. However, what is important here is that you have to notice how someone is reacting to this emotion and how it affects their ability to form decisions. If there are any choices that you are looking to change, then you have to keep an eye on how anger is influencing those choices in the person. But if you want to use this hot button for your benefits, the first thing that you should do is try and understand it.

Greed

We make the mistake of thinking that only some people are capable of greed. But no, greed is present in some form in all of us. The degree of greed in a person varies, and yet, it is still there. Greed is mostly about a fear that you won't get anything out of a situation and that you will be left lonely. This gives rise to the thought that no one can take things from you when you have everything. This makes people go to great lengths just because they are looking for approval and acceptance.

Chapter 55. Basic Body Language Signals

Now that you are aware of the "what" and the "why" of body language, let's get into the "how." How can we start to pick up on people's body language? What different secrets are waiting to be discovered within the way that somebody holds their body? It's not easy to know exactly what somebody is trying to tell us, but the more we focus and study these aspects, the easier it will be to get what people are trying to say.

Closed-Off Body Language

Everybody has their reason for wanting to get to know what different body language signals mean. Suppose you are an individual who plans to have closer relationships with people and more successful business interactions. In that case, we must understand what closed-off body language looks like.

Often, when we might be interacting with somebody, the other person could feel a little anxious or reserved because they don't want to share certain parts of their life. While they might continue to talk to you, you could start to pick up how they might be closed off from you so that you can better understand whether or not they want to be in this active conversation or if they're trying to be a little bit more avoidant.

With the use of an arm cross, you can also notice that they might be crossing their legs in the same instance. Because we are primates and animals in general, we focus on self-preservation.

This means that we will often protect ourselves and our bodies no matter what we might be feeling at any certain moment.

What you also have to understand is that there are certain times when we might simply be cold. It's not in a metaphorical sense. We can merely experience times where the temperature is low, and we want to warm ourselves up.

There is another important area we can look at when deciding whether somebody is being closed off or if they are just the type of person who is a little bit more reserved. You can take notice of the tension in their mouths.

Those who are closed off and who do not want to be open with you will have stiff shoulders and flexed muscles. If somebody is cold, they might have little self-soothing habits they're doing, such as touching their arms a little bit or even rubbing their hands together.

When somebody is a little bit more open, then they'll keep their arms to the side and their chest exposed to you. This is because they are not afraid of what you might do to them. When somebody feels comfortable and confident within a situation, they won't exhibit the easily identifiable closed-off body language signals.

Remember, the reason that someone might close themselves off is not necessarily because they are afraid of the other person. Still, rather they could do this is because sometimes they just want to hide or have some other generalized anxiety within that moment and simply do not wish to allow the other person to see what we are doing.

If you want to make somebody with closed-off body language a little more open, you can begin to mirror their behavior. This means that you can mimic how they're closed off and holding their bodies in one instance, and then as they become more comfortable with, you switch into a little bit more of an open body language.

Preening and Repeating

One thing that many humans and other animals frequently do is they will go through an act of preening. Preening is when we are subconsciously cleaning and preparing ourselves for other people. Acts of preening include fixing up somebody's hair. Maybe they are playing with their hair by pulling stray hairs out or smoothing it down as they sit there and talk to you. They might run their fingers through their hair, move it to the side, throw it up in a ponytail, or do anything else that will indicate that they are fixing their hair from a state of what it was to state where it's a little bit cleaner and more presentable. This could also be seen through how we might pick ourselves while we are talking to other people. Some people pick at mini scabs on their faces. They might also be picking at their chapped lips or fidgeting with their hands and picking at the cuticles around their fingernails.

Perhaps they are going through short periods of scratching as well. Scratching isn't always a preening way and can sometimes display that the person is itchy or nervous. Sometimes we scratch ourselves when we're nervous because it feels as though we might be doing some active preening on a smaller scale.

Scratching yourself is a way to heal, but it's something that feels good and alleviates some of the pain or tension we might be feeling from different discomforts in our body.

Think of how dogs need to wear cones after surgery or go through another experience where they might have a wound or sore. Though it might not itch all the time, they might still try to scratch it as often as possible. The dog doesn't realize that this can make things worse; they do it because it's a natural feeling we have inside ourselves to alleviate some of the wound's discomfort.

This feeling gets twisted around in our brains, and we'll do the same kind of action when we're feeling nervous or anxious. It's a form of preening in some instances, but it could also simply indicate that the person is feeling uncomfortable or uneasy. Preening is also seen in how we might pamper ourselves or prep our looks using different products or makeup. Many individuals often associate trimming with women trying to be a little more romantic or flirtatious. The thing that we have to remember about preening is that it doesn't mean that another woman is attracted to you and trying to get your attention. She could only be feeling insecure and want to make herself feel better.

Preening in front of other people can also indicate that there is some form of competition. For example, suppose a woman chose to go into the women's restroom where it's a little bit busier and freshen up her makeup in front of other people. In that case, some might take this as a subconscious signal that she's letting others know that she is the top competition. She's fixing herself up and making sure that those around her know just how beautiful or powerful she might be. Preening is also seen in how we can sometimes clean up the area around us or rub imaginary lint off our bodies when talking to other people.

We go through some acts of preening because we want to feel more confident with our appearance, or we might be showing our worth through our attraction from other people.

If somebody is presenting in front of you, then it could be a sign of insecurity. It could also be a sign that they are making themselves more desirable for you.

Understanding the context of the situation will help you determine the intention of their preening. We also have to consider the repetition movements that somebody is using in their body language. Specific individuals might do the same kind of move over and over again. That could be somebody trying to persuade you, and they want to reiterate a point so that you are more likely to be convinced by the things they're sharing.

This can also be seen in how people are preening if somebody is constantly trimming while in front of you, it could be a sign that they are simply anxious. For example, you might have a friend who's always picking and touching her hair. Maybe she is a little bit more insecure. She might put a high weight on her hair because she identifies herself with these looks.

It's vital to notice repetition in how people use their body language to understand their intention better.

Mirroring Body and Speech

Mirroring body language is something that we have already touched on; however, let's take a more in-depth look into why we reflect and how we can use it to help other people connect with us further. Mirroring is the act of mimicking somebody else's body language. It's as if you are a mirror, and you pick up how they're moving and doing that yourself.

Mirroring happens from the moment we're born. We start to mimic the emotions and facial expressions of the people who raise us because we learn how to feel. For example, if you walked up to any baby between six months and 12 months old and started smiling at them, there's an excellent chance they're going to smile back. They have no idea why they're smiling, but they're going to do it because somebody else is showing them this act.

Mirroring is very normal. If you notice somebody mirroring you, that's not necessarily a sign that they're trying to control you. However, mirroring can be used as a tactic to get closer to somebody. Mirroring can be a way to connect with somebody and let them know that they are in a safe and comfortable space

Mirroring frequently happens subconsciously as a way to connect with other people. It helps remind us that we are not alone and that we are similar to others. In a world where we can sometimes feel like an outcast, we must focus on looking for ways to connect with others. Mirroring can also be very influential. If you are in a situation where you want to help somebody get into a different state, you can start by mirroring them.

For example, let's say that you're talking to a friend and they are having an awful day. They're feeling down about themselves; nothing seems to be going right; they're upset, and they're on the verge of tears. As a good friend, you want to help cheer them up; you want to better mood. So, you would start by mirroring the position that they're in at that moment. They might be hunched over with their arms around their legs, looking down and feeling sad. You don't want to do the same position because that's too obvious; however, you can hunch over as well. Let your arms hang or rest on the top of your knees and maybe tilt your head to the side as you talk to them.

You're letting them know that their feelings are valid and that they aren't alone. You're there to support them, and you're going to help work through these emotions with them. After you mirror their body language and pick up on this, you can change their body language after a few moments and sit like this and let them spill their feelings; maybe you sit up straight.

Chapter 56. Strengthen or Change the Views of Others

If you say anything that is consonant with my views, I, of course, agree with you. The fact is that it is easier to argue an already established opinion than to acquire a new one. Besides, every time you formulate a belief to yourself, it is a little more firmly fixed in your brain. If you tell others about it, it becomes almost impossible for the brain to restructure.

Therefore, wanting to influence a person, try to find out exactly his convictions. If your neighbor thinks that you bake the most delicious cakes in the city and you would like to support this opinion in every way, try to make her conviction even stronger: ask her to tell others about your cakes, preferably to the widest possible range of people. Moreover, even better if she puts out a photo of pastries with praise on Instagram for all her friends. Publishing our views is the most powerful way to convince ourselves that we think so. It does not matter that the judgment was initially not very well thought out —if we wrote it down and shared it with others, it would take a lot of effort to take our words back. Therefore, the keyboard or pen and the public who can read are your best helpers when you need to strengthen someone's rather weak beliefs: for example, that you are the best or that communism is great. (Believe it or not, but this was used by Chinese military leaders during the Korean War, forcing American prisoners of war to write and then read aloud that they renounced capitalism and became true radical socialists. It led to a change of political views: many soldiers returned to the US as Communists. However, the Chinese army overlooked the fact that similar beliefs were used in the United States, so soon, the former prisoners had turned back to capitalism.)

If in this way, you manage to strengthen the person in his views, he will defend them. Even if they try to convince him otherwise, he will persist—just to not look like an idiot, spreading unsubstantiated opinions.

And what if you need not back up the conviction but form it? If the neighbor does not like your cakes, it is necessary to prepare the ground for her to change her mind. Then make sure she doesn't do any of the above. Let him keep his opinion with him and not tell anyone about him. Do not ask what she thinks of her cakes—because then she will be even more convinced that she is right. The less chance she has of expressing her views, the more chances you have to change them. Act as Chinese commanders (although this appeal does not apply to other situations): bring to her the opinion you need—and in full compliance with covert reception, show that there are quite a few people who think the same way.

The neighbor will then be easier to abandon their former weakly expressed opinions and join the "wise" majority's point of view.

Influencing Opinion, Distracting Attention

I suspect that everyone who has an adoring sports partner in life often uses this feature for their good. They know that when a match is broadcast over the radio, the partner loses the ability to hear something else. This phenomenon has deeper roots than adherence to the colors of the local football club. Here we discuss the redistribution of brain resources, which cannot support several active states' functions.

For example, suppose you want to convince your partner that it is very different from his opinion. In that case, it is very useful to distract him from other impressions while you present him with your argument.

It is much easier to incline to your opinion a person who is watching TV while you are talking to him—even if the sound is muted. After all, the interlocutor's brain must process information coming from you and visual information (a football match). So, he can no longer allocate sufficient resources for the search for weighty counter-arguments. Similarly, it is much easier to convince you to buy many things on Amazon.com if you, while wandering around the site, simultaneously talk on the phone.

This conclusion is confirmed time after time. A diffuse consciousness (that is, a brain that performs several operations at once) is easier to manipulate and subject it to changes than when it is focused on one thing.

Dispelling the attention is not difficult. If you make a presentation in your company, you put a model next to you; you will notice that you can get any nonsense out of your audience. You can do the same as in the example with the TV—wait until the one you want to convince of your rightness is distracted by something, and at that moment strike.

However, such distracting techniques are not always convenient to apply in practice. If a distracting object is too noticeable, for example, if only models are wearing swimming trunks from a swimsuit, you risk that the rest will not be up to you. As a result, you will not receive any objections or approval. Meanwhile, there are subtler ways to dispel attention than just turning on the TV or simultaneously talking on the phone. Strictly speaking, it is enough to use random words. When we hear something different than we expected to hear, the brain seems to be dramatically slowing down at full speed and thinks "Stop, what else is that?"

Consider an example. If we discuss the price with you, then there are certain rules by which this discussion is based. Among other things, it usually sounds like the word "crowns." If you suddenly declare that the thing you want to sell is nine thousand cents (instead of ninety dollars, as I expected to hear), my thought will turn off for a moment from the well-groomed road. At this second, you will have the opportunity to turn my desire to buy something in the right direction—for example, saying: "It's fabulously cheap!" Confirmed by experiment: several researchers, selling Christmas cards, almost doubled sales when they started calling prices cents instead of dollars.

Pay attention: it is not enough just to knock the client's thoughts off the beaten path; thus, you only create a "window" in which you can influence the brain. For the reception to work, you must embed your message into the interlocutor's mind about how good or cheap a certain product is or how this person needs it. Researchers went up sales only when they began to pronounce the phrase "This is very cheap!" indicating their postcards' price in the cent. (When they called the price in dollars, nothing happened, no matter how much they claimed that the postcards were cheap.) The man who sold mini-muffins managed to increase sales, distracting customers with the unusual word "half-muffins," followed by the phrase that formed the conviction "They are amazingly delicious!"

Regardless of whether you use a sophisticated version, uttering unusual words, or are discussing plans for a vacation with might and main, with a person immersed in Dark Souls 2, dispersing attention, in any case, is a great way to make others more pliable.

It remains only to tell them what opinion they should hold.

Form "Others" About Them

You may not believe me, but your idea of yourself is largely based on what others say about you. The most famous experiment on this topic was conducted in one of the schools, where pupils of one class were told that their intelligence level was higher than of other children. Delighted with this news, the children immediately began to show much better results in the controls.

For example, this means that you can change your cousin's identity by treating her as if she has already become what you want her to be. With this technique's help, you can influence those around you, so that they correspond to your ideas and act as you need. Perhaps you want to convince someone to vote for your party. Join your church community. Get undressed already on the first date. Or just support your proposal at a workshop on Monday. Think about what type of personality is required to perform such an action. Then, make it clear to the one you have chosen to target that he is the carrier of precisely such value orientations.

It may seem difficult at first glance, and people will resist—they probably have some idea of what they are. However, nothing is easier. For example, a colleague suggests taking a test on personality traits, and then, showing him mysterious figures that are difficult to interpret, explain that he is conservative and prefers well-tested solutions (and therefore should be captivated by your offer). Or—that he is a man of an adventurous warehouse and has nothing against a certain amount of risk (if you need such a turn). Just forget to speak convincingly, leaving no reason to doubt your words.

However, in reality, there is no need to go so far and carry out pseudo-diagnostics. It is enough to talk about what your partner is doing in everyday life and describe his actions, taking into account the value orientations currently beneficial. "Oh, you chose a new sort of ice cream? So it seems to you to always try new things." "You can make an adventure out of everything." "It is very typical for you always to take risks." If a colleague hears several times that his actions indicate a propensity to take risks, he will begin to perceive himself as an adventurous person. He will then easily decide to press the big red button when you ask him about it (or what other actions you have to incline him).

If you need to encourage belonging to a different type of personality, emphasize its inherent qualities. Do you want a colleague to feel like a person with developed empathy? In this case, you ask "You took me coffee too? You, like anybody, always think of others." Alternatively, do you need strategic thinking? Then you will say, "An excellent thought is to drink something cold when it is so hot outside. It is noticeable that you are used to planning everything." When a colleague does something that does not fit the type of personality that you want to encourage, you will, of course, just keep silent.

You do not need much effort to make the desired changes. Secret advice for dating in a bar: First, make a woman interested in you feel like an adventurer—ask her to tell you about the various difficult situations she has been in, and then ask her to show you how much she likes to take risks. Between us, it is much faster and cheaper than to treat her to drinks at the bar.

Chapter 57. The Art of Persuasion

Persuasion, as an art, should be subtle and unnoticed. Less forceful than manipulation, more palatable than coercion, persuasion carries the assumption that those persuaded act out of their own 'fully informed' will and usually in a way that works towards the embitterment of all involved. This is not necessarily the case. However, framing an idea in an altruistic way of thinking is a good place to start. The following methods of persuasion are focused on being passive in our persuasion. We wait for the right time, consider their feelings, values, and standpoints. These tactics complement and support each other to create a practically impossible strategy to see through. So, they cannot be directly argued against or attacked with violating socially agreed-upon rules of conduct.

Using an honorable cause is a great way to get someone's attention. Still, an honorable cause alone is rarely enough to convert others to your way of thinking. To truly convert them, we must shift their focus away from the cause to their self-interest. Linking a great cause to the self-interest of listeners is an overwhelmingly powerful motivator. Once the listener begins to think about what they may get out of modifying their opinions or reassessing their loyalties, the cage door is closed.

As a rule, anyone can be persuaded of anything providing the timing, approach, and context are correct, but there are limitations such as time constraints. Before any attempt at persuasion, analyze the context of the situation as a whole and devise an acceptable approach based around the current underlying mood or general atmosphere, otherwise known as the emotional 'flow' of the situation. Do not go against the flow of the situation. Instead, use the emotional flow to your advantage. Frame your ideas as exciting when people are optimistic and as safe and pre-emptive in times of reflection. Going with the flow in this way allows you to siphon the already existing emotions in the room directly into your initiative. This method is ultimately more effective than simply trying to change the conversation topic to serve your purpose.

Timing is another pivotal factor when persuading others. The time of day greatly affects the expected desires of any particular person. For example, if we try to corner someone at work at 4 pm on a Friday, all they can think about is likely leaving work for the weekend, and so a large part of their brain will have already left the building. This could work to our advantage or against it depending on the goal. The timing of an approach extends beyond hours and days to weeks, months, and years. The longer we can plan, the greater our overall chances of success.

Identify those who are 'on the fence' or easy to influence and concentrate your efforts on these individuals in the same way politicians focus on 'swing' voters.

Most people are their own worst enemy, give them enough rope, and they will only be too happy to tie the noose. Ask questions that get people talking, and they will quickly voice opinions and values that can then be mirrored back at them in the present or used at a date to obtain their consent. Being cordial will cause people to open up to you. They will provide the information needed to devise an approach that speaks directly to their personally held beliefs and values. At that point, they will be powerless to refuse you or refute your way of thinking.

Do's and Don'ts of Arguments

We should be able to avoid most conflicts through clever maneuvering and planning. Still, there will be times when unpredictable people and events catch us off guard and are forced to either publicly or privately defend our position. By not instigating such situations, we automatically begin in a position of power from which we can choose exactly how to respond and set the tone for the rest of the interaction. If someone is attempting to start an argument or become abusive, it is likely caused by uncontrolled emotions, which implies that they have not planned. There are many ways to use this to your convenience, from passively listening (to obtain ammo) to deliberate provocation (to cause someone to lose their temper). From simple distraction to appealing to values, all have their benefits. However, some methods, such as baiting someone into a temper tantrum, will not win over your opponent and should only be used when attempting to influence the audience and as a last resort. The tips include actions and behaviors that should be avoided due to blatant nature and their futility, and the detrimental effect on influence and persuasion.

Do's

Keep Cool

It's easy to become caught up in a passionate moment or feel frustrated when faced with an argumentative and unreasonable individual. However, even a momentary lapse in composure can set us back massively, and it also gives those with an eye an opening to exploit. We do not need to restrain ourselves to the point that we are far removed; a little emotion helps keep the thought process flowing. It is a matter of balance; we must place ourselves somewhere between stoicism and enthusiasm without emotionally engaging any other individual or their point of opinion. Do not resist others' arguments, seek to augment them to your purpose by playing the long game, always be aware of the end goal, and remember that losing your temper is a sign of powerlessness.

Use Slick One-Liners Whenever Possible

Cleverly placed, hard-hitting one-liners can completely throw a person's chain of thought. A smart cliché or witty observation can completely demotivate an opponent for a few seconds, enough time for you to take control of the interaction. These seemingly spontaneous and intelligent interjections need not always make clear sense but sound reasonably sincere. You do not want to be seen as a heckler needlessly interrupting the flow of an otherwise relevant conversation. Here are a few of my favorite examples:

- Don't you think this will come back to bite us?
- Right or wrong, it's still beside the point.
- But what does that mean in the real world?
- What exactly are the parameters?
- You seem defensive.
- You're comparing oranges and apples.
- What research did you do?
- Use tactical contradiction.

When discussing matters in front of an audience, it is possible to convert those who are still undecided by dissecting and contradicting your opponent's proposal's specific points. By contradicting them, we have an opportunity to discredit their entire initiative. Even the 'airtight' points can be undermined through the association with premises that can be proved faulty or, even better, foolish. Don't be afraid of a little humor bordering on the theatrical. The audience will enjoy it; however, take care not to get carried away and become disruptive to proceedings.

Make an Appeal

From time to time, you will find yourself in a situation where you have exhausted your logic, expertise, and powers of persuasion. When this happens, it is no doubt since we missed a step along the way, leaving the listener/audience room for critical thinking. It is almost impossible to reverse engineer the interaction and start over immediately and mush in the same way that it is easier to win a new chess game than to recover one after a few poorly considered moves. In these cases, we can appeal to higher values, which will buy us valuable thinking time and also strengthen our position, so that we can then reapproach the issues from a slightly different angle by following up with some questions like:

- "Don't you think that this would make things safer for everyone involved?"

- "Shouldn't we be working together on this?"

- "Yes, but what kind of world do we want to leave for our children?"

- Practice pinpoint listening skills

People get emotional when they speak, and because of this, they make slip-ups, huge ones. Many people are terrified of speaking in front of others, and those who are not afraid of public oration are often overly confident in either themselves or their message. By intently listening to someone, we will at once be aware of their emotions. We can choose to 'pump' these emotions with questions directed to either excite or annoy. At this point, by pretending that you will concede a good point if only they see your point of view, they are likely to openly agree with you. The instant they do, undermine or contradict their point or objective. This simple 'bait and switch' technique will leave the opposition annoyed and confused, allowing you to take control and move on to other issues in the assumption that you have won this time. The people present will assume the same, and when the opposition sense this, they will internally admit defeat rather than go against the group consensus.

Play Devils' Advocate

By playing the part of the Devil's advocate, we can infuriate our opponent, prodding them until they lose their composure and the debate. Playing Devil's advocate consists of gently arguing against and questioning an idea relentlessly, even if we secretly agree with the point being made. It is a tactic that can also be used on your ideas. Question yourself in the way that you believe an incessantly annoying skeptic would and bolster the foundation of your position, and find better ways to protect and strengthen it. Doing so builds resistance to the negative comments, needless questioning, and others' behavior, which so often drains many of us of our creative juices and sometimes even confidence. When playing Devil's advocate to annoy an opponent, do so with a hint of ridicule and ask questions that severely stretch the premise of your opponent's position until the distortion causes it to appear absurd.

Don'ts

Indulge Distractions

Skeptics, disbelievers, and dissenters will often try to distract you with phoney and half-hearted arguments, and the truly argumentative may even attempt to push extreme examples of your ideas to distort them so that they seem ridicules or even reckless in the hopes of either redirecting your argument or causing you to lose your composure. Avoiding such distractions is not always easy, especially those that carry an emotional edge, but by being firm and focused, you can avoid deviations like digressions and subject changes. Resist the urge to dismiss or stifle others. Allowing others to opine is essential in so many ways. Thank them for their valued input, and Segway through some connection or other back to your original point, ideally using the interjection to strengthen your own ideas.

Make Personal Attacks

Lowering yourself and making personal attacks won't win advocates or arguments. You won't convert a person you've just offended, and anyone else present, will automatically assume that your ideas, as well as your integrity, lack substance.

Chapter 58. Influence Without Manipulation

Of course, not all social influence has to be manipulative either. There are several different ways that you can engage in influencing other people without ever having to step into the realm of manipulation if you would prefer to avoid it. These methods are largely more ethical and are meant to be beneficial to the other person, so you are not only taking advantage of another person for your benefit.

Influence can be particularly useful in situations that are not suitable for manipulation or when manipulation would likely violate any contracts or job descriptions you have now. Overall, you can think of many of the persuasive methods that will be here as the ethical, work-appropriate techniques that can be used without losing a license to practice medicine, sell a product, or practice law.

Principles of Persuasion

The principles of persuasion refer to a set of six different techniques that people find inherently persuasive. Using these persuasion principles, you can convince people to do things legitimately and honestly simply by appealing to one of six different principles. Of course, using any of these is not a guarantee for success, but rather it ups your chances of naturally convincing the other person to do whatever it is you are requesting of them. The six principles of persuasion are reciprocity, likability, authority, social proof, scarcity, consistency, and commitment.

Reciprocity

Reciprocity refers to the idea that people naturally want to return favors after they have had one done for them. Think of the feeling of obligation you may get when someone gives you a birthday present—you feel the need to return the favor when the other person's birthday rolls around. This is for a specific reason: you are convinced through reciprocity. This sort of nature's failsafe to the selfless behavior that humans have developed throughout evolution. With reciprocity, humans feel the need to return the favor whenever anyone helps them in any way.

Good, strong leaders recognize reciprocity as an inherent way the human mind works, and they will frequently bank on it—this is why you will see people ask, "What can I do for you?" when you come in somewhere. They are making it clear that they are interested in helping you, and hopefully, in return, you will help them as well. Good, emotionally intelligent leaders will almost always ask what they can do to help someone else before they ever ask the favor they had in mind. You can do this as well—offer to do something for someone. They will think that you are doing so out of the goodness of your heart. You may be, at least in part, but you will still have an ulterior motive. You can then ask the other person for a favor when you need it. For example, if you need to have your shift changed for a concert you want to attend in two months, you may volunteer the following time one of your coworker's mentions needing time off and needing a shift covered to get it approved. Your coworker then will probably offer to do something if he can repay you, at which point you can mention that you need your shift covered for the concert you want to go to, and your coworker agrees to do so. Now, you are left satisfied because your shift is covered, and you were not required to use manipulation to make it happen.

Likability

Likability refers to the fact that people naturally are more inclined to be persuaded when they like the person doing the persuading. After all, would you rather do a favor for your spouse, who you presumably love, or that coworker that you cannot stand? The answer is almost definitely that you would rather do something for your spouse, and the biggest reason for that is because you like your spouse.

Studies have shown that people are more likely to reach agreements in negotiations when all members take a moment to introduce themselves with some small tidbit of information about themselves that makes them more relatable. The biggest reason for this is because they become relatable, and when you relate to someone, you are more likely to want to come up with a compromise with them because you are more likely to feel empathetic toward them.

Luckily, there are three surefire ways to establish yourself as likable, even if your interaction with someone is relatively short. You will only need to take a few moments to do three simple things. You must first make yourself relatable, such as offering a small detail about yourself into the conversation naturally. Following, you should offer some sort of honest compliment to the other person. Lastly, you need to establish yourself as willing to cooperate to reach the same goal, effectively creating a team mentality. These three things can be the difference between landing that sale at work or failing to close.

Authority

People most often are willing to respect authority. They are usually willing to listen to someone who has established himself as an authority. For that reason, those viewed as authority figures are typically seen as more persuasive than those who are not. After all, you are more likely to listen to your dentist about how to save that tooth than the random cashier at the grocery store. This is due to your inherent bias that the dentist is more knowledgeable about dentistry than the cashier, and you are likely right. However, it is possible (and highly unlikely) that your cashier did go to school for dentistry.

When you want to make yourself an authority, you want to clarify that you know what you are talking about. You can do so by displaying your diplomas and other licenses you may have acquired during your career in your office. You can display awards that show just how good at your job you are. You could try including your credentials on your name placard on your desk or nametag. You could even have a secretary whose job is to sing your praises when answering the phone or greeting prospective clients. Suppose all of that is impractical with your job. In that case, there are other methods you can utilize as well—you can drop hints toward your experience in whatever topic you are discussing in a way that is natural with the client, such as mentioning that when you studied business back in graduate school, you learned certain concepts relevant to the conversation you are having. Simply dropping your experience in conversation makes it clearer that you do have some sort of experience, and therefore, your judgment should be trusted.

Social Proof

Social proof refers to the fact that people are largely more influenced by their peers than simply being told what to do for no real reason. This is essentially utilizing peer pressure to control someone else or recognizing that peer pressure principles are relevant to social interactions. For example, people are more likely to go along with their peers' behaviors than when they feel out of their element.

This can be used in manipulation and persuasion—you can hint that other people in a similar position made a choice similar to whatever you want the other person to do. For example, suppose you want to sell a mother of three children a car. In that case, you may point out that many of the parents that you sell to in the same boat as the mother repeatedly buy a minivan or SUV for the extra space for supplies for sports and extracurricular activities or even just to make up for the fact that children grow and may even outgrow a smaller car, feeling completely cramped if they do not have a third row to spread back toward. The mother may feel pressured as you mention this and be a bit more inclined to defer to what other people are doing simply because she was unsure anyway, and if other people are doing it, it likely works well.

Scarcity

The principle of scarcity is little more than supply and demand—people think that scarce things are more valuable simply because they are not as easily attained. With that in mind, you can make something seem more desirable or valuable simply by creating an artificial scarcity of the item. Companies do this frequently—you will see companies with business models that surround selling seasonal or limited time only items, and they draw out massive amounts of attention simply because everyone wants to get their hands on that new limited edition item, or they have been dying for that seasonal drink for months now. They are thrilled that it is finally available again.

When you want to use scarcity to control someone else, you can do so simply by making yourself scarce. Particularly in relationships, you see this utilized in one partner threatening to break up with the other, making it clear that their presence and commitment to the relationship is not guaranteed. If the other person cannot figure out what they are doing, then the person creating the request is willing to walk away altogether.

Consistency and Commitment

The last of the principles of persuasion is consistency and commitment. This refers to the fact that humans naturally value consistency. The easiest way to get that consistency is through commitments meant to motivate the individual to go through with what was committed to becoming consistent simply. For example, someone who has committed to doing something for you will likely follow through because with commitment comes obligation, and failing at obligations begets guilt, which most people want to avoid. If you want someone to do something, you must first start with a small commitment. It does not have to be particularly significant—even asking to borrow a pen would start this process. When that first commitment has been made, the individual is already in the mindset to continue saying yes, enabling you to continue asking for whatever you need. You can then attempt to get the other person to do something else, and you are somewhat more likely to get them to agree if you have already asked them to do something that they agreed to do.

Ethos, Pathos, Logos

Alongside the principles of persuasion, there is also the theory of ethos, pathos, and logos—three Greek words refer to appeals to different aspects of life to convince other people. When using these, you are essentially creating arguments in which you convince or compel someone to agree to do something because your argument is simply too compelling to deny.

Ethos

Ethos means ethics—it refers to appeals to ethical or moral duties. When you make an argument rooted in ethos, you are arguing for ethics. You are making it a point to spell out exactly why it is important to do things a certain way to avoid violating any inherent values of right vs wrong.

Chapter 59. Escape or Die

You may not die in the sense that your life will end, although that is a very real possibility. However, your freedom is sure to die. Your happiness will die. Your sanity will die. You will suffer a fate that is worse than death. If you were dead, you would be at peace. You would not have to suffer the endless misery that comes with being stuck in a manipulative situation. Instead, your body lives, but your spirit does not. You are trapped in an invisible prison, forced to suffer each day without the promise of ever getting free.

Of course, literal death is a tragic but very real possibility as well. At least three women each day are killed in the USA due to being in an abusive relationship. Countless more choose to end their own lives as it is the only escape from their torment that their broken mind allows them to see.

It doesn't have to come to this. There are several ways that you can retake your freedom and live the life of happiness that you deserve. Is escaping easy? No. Is it worth it? Absolutely. Your choice is none other than that of freedom or a slow, miserable, spiritual, and emotional death.

A strong word of caution must be emphasized before we begin to share how to escape a manipulative situation. Manipulative people are dangerous and devious. They will often stop at nothing to regain control of a situation. For such people, their victim escaping their clutches represents the ultimate loss of control. Many manipulators will stop at absolutely nothing to restore things to the way they want. If they find out that this is not possible, they may resort to acts of violence, stalking, and other forms of extremely dangerous criminal behavior.

That is not to say that these people cannot be escaped from—quite the opposite. Thousands of people each year find the courage and strength to take their life back. By following the advice of this, you will be able to experience the joy of your escape without running the risks that come with escaping in the wrong way.

Before the Escape

The exact nature of your escape from a manipulative person, and situation, depends heavily upon the type of manipulator you find yourself with and the details of the situation. However, every escape has in common is the need to plan very carefully before carrying it out. A well-planned escape makes all the difference between success and failure. Also, more importantly, planning makes the difference between danger and safety. So let's discover how to plan properly.

The first thing to realize when planning an escape is that very few people must know about it beforehand. People have a way of being unable to keep secrets or giving away the wrong information to the wrong person. Even if you tell people and they have your best intentions in mind, they may accidentally let the wrong thing slip at the wrong time.

There is also another key reason for telling as few people as possible about what you have planned. Many manipulators do not respect personal boundaries in any way whatsoever. They may go through your phone, your email, and your social media regularly without you having any idea. If they discover what you are planning, then you are placing yourself in a position of immense physical danger.

Even if you think that your manipulator is not going through your phone or your social media and that you have covered your tracks by deleting messages, there is no way that you can be sure. Did you know that software exists, which can be discretely installed on a PC or phone and allows someone to spy on you in real-time? As you are typing, each button you press could be being transmitted directly to your manipulator. There is no way you would know this is happening, and therefore there is no clear way to protect against it.

That is not to say that you should not tell anyone what you are planning. Rather, it is important to tell one trusted person only. This could be a best friend or a member of your family. You must trust this person with your life, as this is effectively what is at stake. You need to know this person will not let anything slip, even accidentally. The reason for telling them is that they can first support you through the process in any way you need, and secondly so that if anything goes wrong, they can inform the police what has happened and who is responsible.

Choosing the right person to let know what you are up to is only the first stage of the planning process. It is also absolutely vital to choose a physical place you can escape to and spend some time in the aftermath of your escape. This, ideally, will be somewhere out of town, preferably as far away as possible. This is because the manipulator is likely to look everywhere they can think of in the aftermath of you escaping the situation. The place you choose should be far away geographically and somewhere that the manipulator will not be able to figure out easily.

Preparing financially for life without a manipulator is another key aspect of planning. This can be very difficult as some types of manipulators are incredibly controlling when it comes to finances. Ideally, you will have one to two months' expenses saved up and be able to access them in a way that will not arouse suspicion. If this is not possible, your one trusted friend or family member should

be asked to help you out. You will be able to repay them after you have got clear of the situation. This is just a temporary measure. If you are in a situation where you live with your manipulator and want to move out, planning to take the things you need with you is important, but difficult. Anything that is replaceable should be left behind. Only essential things like valuable jewelry, identity documents, and other similar things should be taken. Ideally, you should only take as many things as you can fit into one bag. This makes the practical side of the escape much easier.

In the period leading up to your escape, you should put together a duffel bag or similar sized bag of new purchases from outside of the home. For example, you should pack some underwear, clothes, toiletries, and other similar items. They should not be taken from the home as their absence would likely arouse suspicion. Instead, they should all be new purchases. When you have carefully put together your bag, it is vital to find a safe place to store it. Some good ideas for such places include with your one trusted person or at some kind of rental locker space, such as a gym locker.

The above steps are the essentials you need to consider when planning your escape from a manipulative situation. There may be other steps you need to consider in light of your particular scenario, or some of the above ideas may not apply if you are sure to follow the advice, though. You are putting yourself in a position of preparedness and safety ahead of your escape.

Now that you have made practical preparations for your escape, it's time to plan the escape itself.

The preceding of this gave you all of the information you need to make some preparations ahead of your escape. While essential, it is not enough. Equally, if not more important, is to plan the actual escape. This includes the escape's nature, the escape's timing, and what you will do if something goes wrong. Having a clear plan in mind for the period after the escape is also essential. After the escape, this is often the most difficult time as the manipulator will know what has happened and look for revenge.

The first key step in this process is understanding exactly what an escape means to you. Every situation is different, and not all of them require a dramatic escape, which involves hiding out in some remote location. We will now look at some of the more appropriate escape methods depending on the type of manipulative situation you are trying to get away from. Suppose you are with one of the more serious types of relationship manipulators.

Suppose you are with one of the more serious types of relationship manipulators, such as someone who is violent, or gaslighting, or denying reality. In that case, it is vital to put physical distance between yourself and your manipulator. This is because these types of manipulators are the ones who will cross the line into violence and even murder if they are provoked. This is the most serious type of manipulative situation you can find yourself in, so make sure to leave nothing to chance when attempting to escape it. Some types of relationship manipulators are less dangerous, but you still should err on the side of caution. For example, suppose the person you are with manipulates you through lying and minimizing. In that case, you may not need to plan such a dramatic and comprehensive escape from this type of scenario. It may be enough to break up with such a person from a distance and make sure they know you will go to the police if they attempt to remain in contact with you.

Other types of situations require a different approach. If you are stuck in a manipulative workplace situation, you may find that changing jobs is the only way you can get out. It may be tempting to quit in the heat of the moment, but this is the wrong way to go about it. It is vital to have another job, known as a parachute job, lined up before you quit. Otherwise, you will face serious financial trouble after quitting the manipulative situation. Schedule interviews for days off from the office and consider using vacation time for all your new job interviews into two weeks. This can allow the job search process to be less stressful for you.

Conclusion

A healthy life with a narcissist is impossible. They do not know how to communicate with others in a way that is not manipulative. This is likely because as a child, they could not get their needs met by asking for them and had to go about it in an underhanded way, and as an adult, they continue this behavior. They will likely use these stories of childhood tragedies as a way of playing on your sympathy and getting you not to leave them. You can feel compassion for what they endured as a child, but you owe it to yourself not to tolerate abuse from who they have become as an adult.

It cannot be stressed enough how important it is that a survivor does not contact the narcissist. This means they cannot share phone calls, messages, or visit this person. It will only be detrimental to their mental health and put them right back into the position they worked so hard to get out of. They need to keep themselves out of the risk of breaking no contact.

This means their time needs to be filled with something else, so they won't have time to think about and contact the person they are trying to distance themselves from. This is the time to make new friends and reconnect with old ones. Taking up a new hobby or a class will take up your time and introduce you to new people.

Everyone who dealt with a covert narcissist knows the pain, toxicity, and hardships such an individual brings. As a result of being exposed to narcissistic abuse for a prolonged period, victims, future survivors face many challenges. They are faced with a great task: to leave it all behind and heal from what has transpired due to that relationship. Healing from abuse is never easy as it leaves deep marks on one's personality and diminishes their wellbeing. Covert narcissism is a set of destructive behavioral patterns that harm everyone involved with a person who harbors these behaviors. Unfortunately, because it is a personality disorder that is very much conceived, there are no proven ways to foresee you are dealing with one unless you've experienced being abused by a narcissist in your past.

Hard to diagnose, covert narcissists, because they are so well-liked and accepted in society represent a real threat to everyone they are involved with, as their destructive patterns, manipulation techniques, and controlling behavior can be extremely damaging to one's mental, physical, and emotional body. Being part of the Cluster B spectrum, covert narcissism represents a real danger to one's sense of self, self-worth, and mental health in general. It is threatening, disturbing, which is why a healing process for those who suffered from narcissistic abuse is a lengthy process that is never light and easy.

One of the most important things to do to heal from narcissistic abuse is to create and strengthen interpersonal relationships with others. You need to be focused on something outside of the relationship between you and a toxic person. If a bond does not replace the bond you break with them with someone else, it will be effortless to break no contact.

Realizing what led you to the place you are now is the first step to getting to a different one. Many times those who get into prolonged relationships with a narcissist, were raised by one. In reality, they were most likely raised by two. One parent was the overt narcissist who victimized the child with their rage, while the other parent allowed their child to be mistreated.

You have every right to be angry with a parent who mistreated you. However, you also need to permit yourself to be angry with the parent who kept that parent in the house and refused to leave them. This is a natural feeling, and you cannot feel guilty about it. Even if there were extenuating circumstances, the parent who allowed you to be exposed to narcissistic abuse throughout your upbringing did not do right by you. You probably also had to be a therapist for them. They needed to vent to you so that they could go on another day.

They will talk of the burden they bore for you, but there was also a burden you bore. Often, the child carries the heaviest weight throughout the entire family in a dysfunctional situation. There were probably times this parent turned the narcissistic parent's anger away from you and onto them, but there were also most likely times when they couldn't handle it anymore, and so it was "your turn" to deal with it. That act was abuse from them. A family is not supposed to be a dynamic to where there is a parent who flies into rages, and the child has to take the brunt of it on days when the other parent has had all they can stand.

A child who grew up with a parent who was prone to angry outbursts might internalize that behavior. Not realizing their parent's behavior came from within, they will think they were responsible for it. This theory will be confirmed by the fact that sometimes making themselves as small as possible, groveling, and going along with whatever the parent wanted would give them a reprieve. When this child grows into an adult, they will think they are responsible for other people's anger. They will feel a sense of guilt when another person gets angry and insults them. They will think, had they not done something wrong. They wouldn't be getting treated like this.

When a person has had long-term dealings with a narcissist, they come out of it with wounds that will take time and work to heal. There is an argument that a form of PTSD forms after suffering this type of abuse. Anxiety management is something you will need to learn while recovering from narcissistic abuse. Studies have shown that people are breaking away from a relationship with a narcissist exhibit symptom reminiscent of post-traumatic stress disorder.

They are hyper-vigilant because they never knew what would set off the narcissistic rage. People who are recovering from narcissistic abuse invariably have high levels of anxiety. They are traumatized by the way they have been treated. This is why it is essential to seek ongoing treatment for a little while after breaking free from psychological abuse.

While there is anxiety, there is also a feeling of numbness. This is another aspect of trauma. You cannot handle the sheer amount of stress you are under from the house's amount of tension. To feel all of it would be overwhelming to feel, so you choose not to feel it and then go into survival mode. Your mind is on getting through the situations that are thrown at you throughout the day.

There is a sad reality that people who were raised by a narcissist has to face. They have to watch out for narcissistic tics, also called fleas. These terms are used to refer to the tendencies they learned from their narcissistic caregiver. It is a way they further damage the children under their care. It is not enough to put them through the wringer that is narcissistic abuse. They also, whether it is conscious or not, try to teach their children narcissism. It can become a legacy if the child does not monitor their behavior as an adult. Humans respond to their environment and learn from the examples set for them by their caregivers.

Before you start to panic, be reassured, a tic does not mean you have become a narcissist. It means you have learned certain behaviors from those who raised you, as we all do. You are not a bad person because you were told lies as a child.

Think about it this way. A person raised by people who held prejudices against a specific religious or ethnic group would have been taught incorrect lessons about an entire population of people.

Their family went through a lot of trouble to program this person into thinking similarly to them. When you are a small child, you think your own family is a representation of all families. However, when you get out into the world, you will start to notice there are beliefs your family held that are not shared by other people. In the case of a person raised by a prejudiced family, they would have to learn some harsh truths about how they were raised.

They would discover that the belief they had always been taught to have was frowned upon by society and morally incorrect. It would be a complicated process for them to shed this thought process and take on a healthier one because our minds do not have switches that can be turned back and forth at our convenience. The person would go through a most likely lifelong journey of monitoring their biases and recognize when the old thought patterns were trying to creep their way back in.

Now let's apply this lesson to a person who had picked up a narcissistic tic from a parent. Melissa's mother was a covert narcissist. She had a very manipulative way of navigating through her relationships with others and yet would portray herself as a victim. As covert narcissists tend to do, she would seek out the company of overt narcissists. She would choose the same type of man to start a relationship with over and over again and be just as devastated every time these men let her down in the same ways as the ones did.

It is difficult to make connections in a situation when you are going through it personally. Melissa did not realize the similarities between her behaviors and that of her mother. When she thought about her, she felt a deep-seated resentment because she gave her a difficult childhood. When she started cognitive behavioral therapy, she began to realize her relationship patterns went the same way as her mother did—abrupt and ending chaotically. Her therapist reminds her that a child sees what is presented to them as normal.

They think the example their parents set for them is representative of how it is supposed to be and what everyone else does. She comes to realize she doesn't know what a healthy relationship looks like. She decides to take a break from dating until she learns how to choose better partners, be a better partner herself, and navigate through relationships in a more productive way. She realized she had developed thought patterns that were wrong due to her raising and is now working towards transforming these beliefs into healthier ones. That is the goal of cognitive-behavioral therapy.